T0315235

Integrating
ERP, CRM,
Supply Chain
Management,
and
Smart Materials

OTHER AUERBACH PUBLICATIONS

A Technical Guide to IPSec Virtual Private Networks
James S. Tiller
ISBN: 0-8493-0876-3

Analyzing Business Information Systems
Shouhong Wang
ISBN: 0-8493-9240-3

Application Servers for E-Business
Lisa M. Lindgren
ISBN: 0-8493-0827-5

Broadband Networking
James Trulove, Editor
ISBN: 0-8493-9821-5

Computer Telephony Integration
William Yarberry, Jr.
ISBN: 0-8493-9995-5

Enterprise Operations Management Handbook, 2nd Edition
Steve F. Blanding, Editor
ISBN: 0-8493-9824-X

Enterprise Systems Architectures
Andersen Consulting
ISBN: 0-8493-9836-3

Enterprise Systems Integration
John Wyzalek, Editor
ISBN: 0-8493-9837-1

Healthcare Information Systems
Phillip L. Davidson, Editor
ISBN: 0-8493-9963-7

Information Security Architecture
Jan Killmeyer Tudor
ISBN: 0-8493-9988-2

Information Security Management Handbook, 4th Edition, Volume 2
Harold F. Tipton and Micki Krause, Editors
ISBN: 0-8493-0800-3

IS Management Handbook, 7th Edition
Carol V. Brown, Editor
ISBN: 0-8493-9820-7

Information Technology Control and Audit
Frederick Gallegos, Sandra Allen-Senft, and Daniel P. Manson
ISBN: 0-8493-9994-7

Information Security Risk Analysis
Thomas Peltier
ISBN: 0-8493-0880-1

Integrating ERP, CRM, Supply Chain Management, and Smart Materials
Dimitris N. Chorafas
ISBN: 0-8493-1076-8

Internet Management
Jessica Keyes, Editor
ISBN: 0-8493-9987-4

Multi-Operating System Networking: Living with UNIX, NetWare, and NT
Raj Rajagopal, Editor
ISBN: 0-8493-9831-2

TCP/IP Professional Reference Guide
Gilbert Held
ISBN: 0-8493-0824-0

The Network Manager's Handbook, 3rd Edition
John Lusa, Editor
ISBN: 0-8493-9841-X

Project Management
Paul C. Tinnirello, Editor
ISBN: 0-8493-9998-X

Roadmap to the e-Factory
Alex N. Beavers, Jr.
ISBN: 0-8493-0099-1

Securing E-Business Applications and Communications
Jonathan S. Held
John R. Bowers
ISBN: 0-8493-0963-8

AUERBACH PUBLICATIONS

www.auerbach-publications.com
TO Order: Call: 1-800-272-7737 • Fax: 1-800-374-3401
E-mail: orders@crcpress.com

DIMITRIS N. CHORAFAS

Integrating
ERP, CRM,
Supply Chain
Management,
and
Smart Materials

CRC Press
Taylor & Francis Group
Boca Raton London New York

CRC Press is an imprint of the
Taylor & Francis Group, an **informa** business

AN AUERBACH BOOK

CRC Press
Taylor & Francis Group
6000 Broken Sound Parkway NW, Suite 300
Boca Raton, FL 33487-2742

First issued in hardback 2018

© 2001 by Taylor & Francis Group, LLC
CRC Press is an imprint of Taylor & Francis Group, an Informa business

No claim to original U.S. Government works

ISBN-13: 978-0-8493-1076-8 (pbk)
ISBN-13: 978-1-138-46852-8 (hbk)

Library of Congress Cataloging-in-Publication Data

Chorafas, Dimitris N.
    Integrating ERP, CRM, supply chain management, and smart materials / Dimitris N. Chorafas.
        p.   cm.
    Includes bibliographical references and index.
    ISBN 0-8493-1076-8 (alk. paper)
    1. Business logistics.   2. Customer relations.   I. Title.

HD38.5 .C44 2001
658.5—dc21
                                                                          2001022227

Library of Congress Card Number 2001022227

Visit the Taylor & Francis Web site at
http://www.taylorandfrancis.com

and the CRC Press Web site at
http://www.crcpress.com

Contents

Acknowledgments

The following organizations, through their senior executives and system specialists, participated in the recent research projects that led to the contents of this book and its documentation. (Countries are listed in alphabetical order.)

AUSTRIA

National Bank of Austria
3, Otto Wagner Platz, Postfach 61,
  A-1011 Vienna
Dr. Martin Ohms, Finance Market Analysis
  Department

Association of Austrian Banks
  and Bankers
11, Boersengasse, 1013 Vienna
Dr. Fritz Diwok, Secretary General

Bank Austria
2, Am Hof, 1010 Vienna
Dr. Peter Fischer, Senior General Manager,
  Treasury Division
Peter Gabriel, Deputy General Manager,
  Trading

Creditanstalt
Julius Tandler Platz 3, A-1090 Vienna
Dr. Wolfgang Lichtl, Market Risk Management

Wiener Betriebs- and Baugesellschaft mbH
1, Anschützstrasse, 1153 Vienna
Dr. Josef Fritz, General Manager

FRANCE

Banque de France
39, rue Croix des Petits Champs, 75001 Paris
Pierre Jaillet, Director, Monetary Studies
  and Statistics
Yvan Oronnal, Manager, Monetary Analyses
  and Statistics
G. Tournemire, Analyst, Monetary Studies

Secretariat Général de la Commission
  Bancaire – Banque de France
73, rue de Richelieu, 75002 Paris
Didier Peny, Director, Control of Big Banks
  and International Banks

115, Rue Réaumur, 75049 Paris Cedex 01
F. Visnowsky, Manager of International Affairs,
  Supervisory Policy and Research Division
Benjamin Sahel, Market Risk Control

Ministry of Finance and the Economy,
  Conseil National de la Comptabilité
6, rue Louise Weiss, 75703 Paris Cedex 13
Alain Le Bars, Director International Relations
  and Cooperation

GERMANY

Deutsche Bundesbank
Wilhelm-Epstein Strasse 14, 60431 Frankfurt-am-Main
Hans-Dietrich Peters, Director
Hans Werner Voth, Director

Federal Banking Supervisory Office
71-101 Gardeschützenweg, 12203 Berlin
Hans-Joachim Dohr, Director Dept. 1
Jochen Kayser, Risk Model Examination
Ludger Hanenberg, Internal Controls

European Central Bank
29 Kaiserstrasse, 29th Floor, 60216 Frankfurt-am-Main
Mauro Grande, Director

Deutsches Aktieninstitut
Biebergasse 6 bis 10, 60313 Frankfurt-am-Main
Dr. Rüdiger Von Rosen, President

Commerzbank
Kaiserplatz, 60261 Frankfurt-am-Main
Peter Bürger, Senior Vice President, Strategy and Controlling
Markus Rumpel, Senior Vice President, Credit Risk Management

Deutsche Bank
12, Taunusanlage, 60325 Frankfurt
Professor Manfred Timmermann, Head of Controlling
Hans Voit, Head of Process Management, Controlling Department

Dresdner Bank
1, Jürgen Ponto Platz, 60301 Frankfurt
Dr. Marita Balks, Investment Bank, Risk Control
Dr. Hermann Haaf, Mathematical Models for Risk Control
Claas Carsten Kohl, Financial Engineer

GMD First – Research Institute for Computer Architecture, Software Technology and Graphics
5, Rudower Chaussee, D-1199 Berlin
Prof. Dr. Ing. Wolfgang K. Giloi, General Manager

HUNGARY

Hungarian Banking and Capital Market Supervision
Csalogany u. 9-11, H-1027 Budapest
Dr. Janos Kun, Head, Department of Regulation and Analyses
Dr. Erika Vörös, Senior Economist, Department of Regulation and Analyses
Dr. Géza Nyiry, Head, Section of Information Audit

Hungarian Academy of Sciences
Nador U. 7, 1051 Budapest
Prof.Dr. Tibor Vamos, Chairman, Computer and Automation Research Institute

ICELAND

The National Bank of Iceland Ltd.
Laugavegur 77, 155 Reykjavik
Gunnar T. Andersen, Managing Director, International Banking & Treasury

ITALY

Banca d'Italia
91, via Nazionale, 00184 Rome
Eugene Gaiotti, Research Department, Monetary and Financial Division
Ing. Dario Focarelli, Research Department

Istituto Bancario San Paolo di Torino
27, via G. Camozzi, 24121 Bergamo
Dr. Paolo Chiulenti, Director of Budgeting
Roberto Costa, Director of Private Banking
Pino Ravelli, Director, Bergamo Region

LUXEMBOURG

Banque Générale de Luxembourg
27, avenue Monterey, L-2951 Luxembourg
Prof. Dr. Yves Wagner, Director of Asset and Risk Management
Hans Jörg Paris, International Risk Manager

Clearstream
3-5 Place Winston Churchill, L-2964 Luxembourg
André Lussi, President and CEO

POLAND

Securities and Exchange Commission
1, Pl Powstancow Warszawy, 00-950 Warsaw
Beata Stelmach, Secretary of the Commission

SWEDEN

Skandinaviska Enskilda Banken
Box 16067, 10322 Stockholm
Bernt Gyllenswärd, Head of Group Audit

Irdem AB
19, Flintlasvagen, S-19154 Sollentuna
Gian Medri, Former Director of Research
at Nordbanken

SWITZERLAND

Swiss National Bank
15, Börsenstrasse, Zurich
Dr. Werner Hermann, Head of International
Monetary Relations
Dr. Christian Walter, Representative
to the Basle Committee
Robert Fluri, Assistant Director, Statistics
Section

Federal Banking Commission
Marktgasse 37, 3001 Bern
Dr. Susanne Brandenberger, Risk Management
Renate Lischer, Representative to Risk
Management
Subgroup, Basle Committee

Bank for International Settlements
2, Centralplatz, 4002 Basle
Mr. Claude Sivy, Head of Internal Audit
Herbie Poenisch, Senior Economist, Monetary
and Economic Department

Bank Leu AG
32, Bahnhofstrasse, Zurich
Dr. Urs Morgenthaler, Member of Management,
Director of Risk Control

Bank J. Vontobel and Vontobel Holding
Tödistrasse 23, CH-8022 Zurich
Heinz Frauchiger, Chief, Internal Audit
Department

Union Bank of Switzerland
Claridenstrasse, 8021 Zurich
Dr. Heinrich Steinmann, Member
of the Executive Board (Retired)

UNITED KINGDOM

Bank of England, and Financial Services Authority
Threadneedle Street, London EC2R 8AH
Richard Britton, Director, Complex Groups
Division, CGD Policy Department

British Bankers Association
*Pinners Hall, 105-108 Old Broad Street,
London EC2N 1EX*
Paul Chisnall, Assistant Director

Accounting Standards Board
*Holborn Hall, 100 Gray's Inn Road, London
WC1X 8AL*
A.V.C. Cook, Technical Director
Sandra Thompson, Project Director

Barclays Bank Plc
54 Lombard Street, London EC3P 3AH
Brandon Davies, Treasurer, Global Corporate
Banking
Alan Brown, Director, Group Risk

Abbey National Treasury Services plc
*Abbey House, 215-229 Baker Street, London
NW1 6XL*
John Hasson, Director of Information
Technology & Treasury Operations

ABN-AMRO Investment Bank N.V.
199 Bishopsgate, London EC2M 3TY
David Woods, Chief Operations Officer, Global
Equity Directorate

Bankgesellschaft Berlin
1 Crown Court, Cheapside, London
Stephen F. Myers, Head of Market Risk

Standard & Poor's
*Garden House, 18, Finsbury Circus, London
EC2M 7BP*
David T. Beers, Managing Director, Sovereign
Ratings

Moody's Investor Services
2, Minster Court, Mincing Lange, London EC3R 7XB
Samuel S. Theodore, Managing Director, European Banks
David Frohriep, Communications Manager, Europe

Fitch IBCA
Eldon House, 2, Eldon Street, London EC2M 7UA
Charles Prescott, Group Managing Director, Banks
David Andrews, Managing Director, Financial Institutions
Travor Pitman, Managing Director, Corporations
Richard Fox, Director, International Public Finance

Merrill Lynch International
Ropemaker Place, London EC2Y 9LY
Erik Banks, Managing Director of Risk Management

The Auditing Practices Board
P.O. Box 433, Moorgate Place, London EC2P 2BJ
Jonathan E.C. Grant, Technical Director
Steve Leonard, Internal Controls Project Manager

International Accounting Standards Committee
166 Fleet Street, London EC4A 2DY
Ms. Liesel Knorr, Technical Director

MeesPierson ICS
Camomile Court, 23 Camomile Street, London EC3A 7PP
Arjan P. Verkerk, Director, Market Risk

Charles Schwab
Crosby Court, 38 Bishopsgate, London EC2N 4AJ
Dan Hattrup, International Investment Specialist

City University Business School
Frobisher Crescent, Barbican Centre, London EC2Y 8BH
Prof. Elias Dinenis, Head, Department of Investment, Risk Management & Insurance
Prof.Dr. John Hagnioannides, Department of Finance

UNITED STATES

Federal Reserve System, Board of Governors
20th and Constitution NW, Washington, D.C. 20551
David L. Robinson, Deputy Director, Chief Federal Reserve Examiner
Alan H. Osterholm, CIA, CISA, Manager, Financial Examinations Section
Paul W. Bettge, Assistant Director, Division of Reserve Bank Operations
Gregory E. Eller, Supervisory Financial Analyst, Banking
Gregory L. Evans, Manager, Financial Accounting
Martha Stallard, Financial Accounting, Reserve Bank Operations

Federal Reserve Bank of Boston
P.O. Box 2076, 600 Atlantic Avenue, Boston, Massachusetts
William McDonough, Executive Vice President
James T. Nolan, Assistant Vice President

Federal Reserve Bank of San Francisco
101 Market Street, San Francisco, California
Nigel R. Ogilvie, CFA, Supervising Financial Analyst, Emerging Issues

Seattle Branch, Federal Reserve Bank of San Francisco
1015 2nd Avenue, Seattle, Washington 98122-3567
Jimmy F. Kamada, Assistant Vice President
Gale P. Ansell, Assistant Vice President, Business Development

Office of the Comptroller of the Currency (OCC)
250 E Street SW, 7th Floor, Washington, D.C. 20024-3208
Bill Morris, National Bank Examiner/Policy Analyst, Core Policy Development Division
Gene Green, Deputy Chief Accountant, Office of the Chief Accountant

Federal Deposit Insurance Corporation (FDIC)
550 17th Street NW, Washington, D.C. 20429-0002
Curtis Wong, Capital Markets, Examination Support
Tanya Smith, Examination Specialist, International Branch
Doris L. Marsh, Examination Specialist, Policy Branch

Office of Thrift Supervision (OTS)
1700 G Street NW, Washington, D.C. 20552
Timothy J. Stier, Chief Accountant

**Securities and Exchange Commission,
Washington, D.C.**
*Office of the Chief Accountant, Securities
and Exchange Commission,
450 Fifth Street NW, Washington, D.C. 20549*
Robert Uhl, Professional Accounting Fellow
Pascal Desroches, Professional Accounting
Fellow
John W. Albert, Associate Chief Accountant
Scott Bayless, Associate Chief Accountant

**Securities and Exchange Commission,
New York**
*7 World Trade Center, 12th Floor, New York,
New York 10048*
Robert A. Sollazzo, Associate Regional Director

**Securities and Exchange Commission,
Boston**
*Boston District Office, 73 Tremont Street,
6th Floor, Boston, Massachusetts 02108-3912*
Edward A. Ryan, Jr., Assistant District
Administrator (Regulations)

International Monetary Fund
700 19th Street NW, Washington, D.C. 20431
Alain Coune, Assistant Director, Office
of Internal Audit and Inspection

Financial Accounting Standards Board
401 Merritt, Norwalk, Connecticut 06856
Halsey G. Bullen, Project Manager
Jeannot Blanchet, Project Manager
Teri L. List, Practice Fellow

Henry Kaufman & Company
*660 Madison Avenue, New York, New York
10021-8405*
Dr. Henry Kaufman

Soros Fund Management
*888 Seventh Avenue, Suite 3300, New York,
New York 10106*
George Soros, Chairman

Carnegie Corporation of New York
*437 Madison Avenue, New York, New York
10022*
Armanda Famiglietti, Associate Corporate
Secretary, Director of Grants Management

Alfred P. Sloan Foundation
*630 Fifth Avenue, Suite 2550, New York,
New York 10111*
Stewart F. Campbell, Financial Vice President
and Secretary

Rockefeller Brothers Fund
*437 Madison Avenue, New York, New York
10022-7001*
Benjamin R. Shute, Jr., Secretary

The Foundation Center
*79 Fifth Avenue, New York, New York
10003-4230*

Citibank
909 Third Avenue, New York, New York 10022
Daniel Schutzer, Vice President, Director
of Advanced Technology

Prudential-Bache Securities
*1 New York Plaza, New York, New York
10004-1901*
Bella Loykhter, Senior Vice President,
Information Technology
Kenneth Musco, First Vice President
and Director, Management Internal Control
Neil S. Lerner, Vice President, Management
Internal Control

Merrill Lynch
*Corporate and Institutional Client Group,
World Financial Center, North Tower,
New York, New York 10281-1316*
John J. Fosina, Director, Planning and Analysis
Paul J. Fitzsimmons, Senior Vice President,
District Trust Manager
David E. Radcliffe, Senior Vice President,
National Manager Philanthropic Consulting

HSBC Republic
*452 Fifth Avenue, Tower 6, New York, New York
10018*
Susan G. Pearce, Senior Vice President
Philip A. Salazar, Executive Director

**International Swaps and Derivatives
Association (ISDA)**
*600 Fifth Avenue, 27th Floor, Rockefeller
Center, New York, New York 10020-2302*
Susan Hinko, Director of Policy

Standard & Poor's
25 Broadway, New York, New York 10004-1064
Clifford Griep, Managing Director

55 Water Street, New York, New York 10041-0003
Mary Peloquin-Dodd, Director, Public Finance Ratings

Moody's Investor Services
99 Church Street, New York, New York 10022
Lea Carty, Director, Corporate

State Street Bank and Trust
225 Franklin Street, Boston, Massachusetts 02105-1992
James J. Barr, Executive Vice President, U.S. Financial Assets Services

MBIA Insurance Corporation
113 King Street, Armonk, New York 10504
John B. Caouette, Vice Chairman

Global Association of Risk Professionals (GARP)
980 Broadway, Suite 242, Thornwood, New York 10594-1139
Lev Borodovski, Executive Director, GARP, and Director of Risk Management, Credit Suisse First Boston (CSFB), New York
Yong Li, Director of Education, GARP, and Vice President, Lehman Brothers, New York
Dr. Frank Leiber, Research Director, and Assistant Director of Computational Finance, Cornell University, Theory Center, New York
Roy Nawal, Director of Risk Forums, GARP

Group of Thirty
1990 M Street NW, Suite 450, Washington, D.C. 20036
John Walsh, Director

Broadcom Corporation
16215 Alton Parkway, P.O. Box 57013, Irvine, California 92619-7013
Dr. Henry Samueli, Co-Chairman of the Board, Chief Technical Officer

Edward Jones
201 Progress Parkway, Maryland Heights, Missouri 63043-3042
Ann Ficken (Mrs.), Director, Internal Audit

Teachers Insurance and Annuity Association/College Retirement Equities Fund (TIAA/CREF)
730 Third Avenue, New York, New York 10017-3206
John W. Sullivan, Senior Institutional Trust Consultant
Charles S. Dvorkin, Vice President and Chief Technology Officer
Harry D. Perrin, Assistant Vice President, Information Technology

Grenzebach Glier & Associates, Inc.
55 West Wacker Drive, Suite 1500, Chicago, Illinois 60601
John J. Glier, President and Chief Executive Officer

Massachusetts Institute of Technology
Building 38, Room 444, 50 Vassar Street, Cambridge, Massachusetts 02139
Ms. Peggy Carney, Administrator, Graduate Office
Michael Coen, Ph.D., Candidate, ARPA Intelligent Environment Project
Department of Electrical Engineering and Computer Science

Henry Samueli School of Engineering and Applied Science
University of California, Los Angeles
Dean A.R. Frank Wazzan, School of Engineering and Applied Science
Prof. Stephen E. Jacobson, Dean of Student Affairs
Dr. Les Lackman, Mechanical and Aerospace Engineering Department
Prof. Richard Muntz, Chair, Computer Science Department
Prof. Dr. Leonard Kleinrock, Telecommunications and Networks
Prof. Chih-Ming Ho, Ph.D., Ben Rich- Lockheed Martin Professor, Mechanical and Aerospace Engineering Department
Dr. Gang Chen, Mechanical and Aerospace Engineering Department
Prof. Harold G. Monbouquette, Ph.D., Chemical Engineering Department
Prof. Jack W. Judy, Electrical Engineering Department
Abeer Alwan, Bioengineering
Prof. Greg Pottie, Electrical Engineering Department
Prof. Lieven Vandenberghe, Electrical Engineering Department

Anderson Graduate School of Management
University of California, Los Angeles
Prof. John Mamer, Former Dean
Prof. Bruce Miller

Roundtable Discussion on Engineering and Management Curriculum (October 2, 2000)
Westwood Village, Los Angeles, California 90024
Dr. Henry Borenstein, Honeywell
Dr. F. Issacci, Honeywell
Dr. Ray Haynes, TRW
Dr. Richard Croxall, TRW
Dr. Steven Bouley, Boeing
Dr. Derek Cheung, Rockwell

University of Maryland
Van Munching Hall, College Park, Maryland 20742-1815
Prof. Howard Frank, Dean,
    The Robert H. Smith School of Business
Prof. Lemma W. Senbert, Chair, Finance
    Department
Prof. Haluk Unal, Associate Professor
    of Finance

Preface

Companies in general appear to enjoy two kinds of strategic advantages. One is transitory: being in the right place, with the right products, at the right time — like riding a wave. The other comes from having first-class management and instituting processes that can mobilize an organization, keeping it ahead of its competition.

The capable use of enterprise resource planning (ERP) and customer relationship management (CRM) software falls under the second type of strategic advantage. So does the introduction and use of new technology such as smart materials, and of new methods such as Six Sigma. Properly used, new technology delivers concrete business advantages, allowing an organization to stay one step ahead of its competitors.

Another strategic process that helps management stay in charge is auditing the company's databases and records — including accounting, financial information, ERP, CRM, and other applications. Auditing helps to ensure that ERP and CRM contribute to problem-solving and permit a company's executives and professionals to see complex interrelationships, rather than ephemeral partnerships and linear supply chains, and appreciate the way the process of change affects the bottom line, in day-to-day operations and in the long term.

This book was born out of an intensive research project, which took place in the United States and Europe from June 1998 to October 2000, on the interrelationship of these strategic issues. It addresses problems and opportunities presented by the integration of ERP and CRM software into supply chains, outlines organizational requirements that should be fulfilled for the effective use of smart materials, and introduces the reader to the need for auditing financial reports and ERP/CRM records.

This project has involved 161 senior executives in 84 different organizations in the United States and Europe. Numerous one-on-one meetings between myself and these senior executives revealed the strong and weak points in the implementation of ERP and CRM. They also allowed me to examine supply chain integration involving ERP, CRM, and Web-based software; gain insight and foresight about what can be expected from smart materials; and develop real-life case studies on auditing enterprisewide resource management systems.

The terms ERP, CRM, and Web-based software need no explaining. The same is true of auditing enterprise-wide resources. By contrast, not every reader may have been exposed to the concept of *smart materials,* which constitutes the theme of Section II. This concept can be explained in two short paragraphs because it has the potential to revolutionize materials handling.

Smart materials is a term developed by the Massachusetts Institute of Techology in a joint project with 60 major industrial enterprises, including Motorola, International Paper, Gillette, Microsoft, and Nokia. The term identifies materials of all sorts, from razor blades and package boxes to assembled products, all embedded with a very-low cost microprocessor that endows each of them with computing and storage capacity.

This makes possible a wide range of applications in inventory management and in expediting of goods, not feasible with dumb materials. Among other important applications is the implementation of a new electronic product code (EPC) developed by the MIT cooperative industry project. This will replace the parochial identification systems — including the UPC — making possible auto-identification of smart materials and providing them with the ability to communicate their code proactively.

I compiled these findings for this book, which was written for the following audiences:

- IT managers and their systems specialists
- ERP, CRM, and Web software implementers
- Finance managers who must approve ERP, CRM, Internet, and smart materials projects
- Managers of logistics and inventory control executives
- Managers of procurement and supply chain specialists
- Project members of new technology implementation teams
- IT specialists involved in ERP and CRM procurement
- Professionals responsible for supply chain design and control
- Technical executives in charge of smart materials projects
- Auditors of information technology budgets and expenditures
- Controllers of ERP, CRM, and supply chain applications
- Managers of product planning of vendor firms
- Marketing and sales managers of vendor companies

Divided into three sections, this book brings the reader through the transition of software products: ERP, CRM, and Web applications into integrative management tools. It also addresses issues companies will encounter as they become global providers of Internet-enabled solutions, and it explains what business opportunities and cost savings can be expected from:

- Restructuring and updating of ERP and CRM software as it integrates supply chain requirements and delivers new killer applications
- Evolving opportunities that will develop from the implementation of smart materials, automatic identification, classification systems, and quality assurance projects
- Auditing the implementation, operation, and maintenance of ERP and CRM software, as well as the corrective action taken on the basis of audit results

The book outlines why the wider application of off-the-shelf programming products, new answers to supply chain requirements, and the advent of smart materials must be examined within the perspective of each company's business challenges. It discusses value differentiation through new technology and suggests that there is a synergy between supply chain management and developing business opportunities. It also underlines top management's accountability for being ahead of the curve in the first decade of this new century.

Internet commerce, online supply chain, and advances in technology available at low cost are making obsolete many things known in the past. People are starting to appreciate that they live in a physical world with objects that are becoming smarter and smarter. These smart materials must also be uniquely identified in order to connect the physical world to the virtual world of data and of management practices.

ERP and CRM programming products, smart materials concepts, organization, classification, and automatic identification work in synergy. However, just as new technology can create great opportunities, it can also create new, and often unforeseen consequences. Thus, in dealing with smart technologies, one must also deal with the law of unwanted consequences and put in place rigorous auditing procedures to handle any unpredicted outcome.

By binding a wealth of interdependent issues between the two covers of a book, this text closes a gap that currently exists in publications about the junction of ERP and CRM applications, proactive inventory management, smart materials, and internal control exercised over systems and procedures. It is precisely at this junction that companies can create proprietary, high value-added solutions.

*   *   *

I am indebted to a long list of knowledgeable people and organizations, for their contribution to the research that has made this book feasible. Also to several experts for constructive criticism during the preparation of the manuscript. The complete list of the cognizant executives and organizations that participated in this research is presented in the Acknowledgments.

Let me take this opportunity to thank John Wyzalek for suggesting this project and Gerry Jaffe for her editing work. To Eva-Maria Binder goes the credit for compiling the research results, typing the text, and making the camera-ready artwork and index.

Dr. Dimitris N. Chorafas
March 25, 2001

ENTERPRISE RESOURCE PLANNING, SUPPLY CHAIN, AND CUSTOMER RELATIONSHIP MANAGEMENT

1

Chapter 1

Concepts, Functionality, and Cost-Effectiveness of Internet-Oriented ERP Systems

Perceptive people in both enterprise management and information technology suggest that in the coming years there is going to be available on a commercial basis a truly integrated software solution. It will combine many of today's discrete-island subsystems and replace others by means of much more efficient programming products than can presently be found off-the-shelf. At the core of this integration lies the Internet-oriented Enterprise Resource Planning (ERP) solution, and its morphing into an intelligent Supply Chain Management, able to handle smart materials.

To better appreciate this evolutionary approach from present-day ERP towards a sophisticated Internet supply chain system, it is advisable to take a quick look into the evolution of ERP software over the last dozen years. A focal point in this bird's eye view will be the functionality supported through the evolutionary development of Enterprise Resource Planning and the new charges imposed by the advent of smart materials, which is the subject of Section II.

Software, particularly those programming products that find significant market demand, evolves over time. During the late 1980s and the decade of the 1990s, Enterprise Resource Planning systems have developed new facilities to meet the requirements of user organizations. This has been a moving target. Down to its fundamentals, since its introduction to the market, ERP software has been seen as an off-the-shelf instrument for improving business processes in accounting, manufacturing, purchasing, and distribution.

One of the challenges has been the successful implementation of ERP. This is not done in the abstract. It involves the analysis of current business processes and the services they provide; their handling through bought software rather than designing an application system from scratch; and internal control activities necessary to keep the system functioning at all times. The target is integration of middle and lower senior management functions, keeping in mind that business processes are complex.

Exhibit 1.1 illustrates the main lines of ERP functionality. Notice in this description that top management support and general accounting chores are not directly addressed. General accounting, however, has been part of an ERP solution, as is the case with SAP's R/2 and R/3. In fact, R/2 started as a general

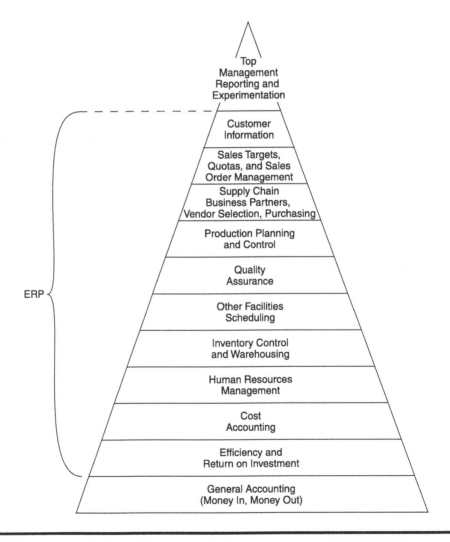

Exhibit 1.1   ERP Solutions Address Some Senior Management and All Middle Management Concerns

accounting package. Therefore, ERP can be historically linked to the development of commodity software for accounting purposes.

1.1 The Evolution from MIS and Logistics to ERP and Beyond

Readers old enough to remember the evolution of information technology in the 1960s and 1970s will recall that at that time there was an effort to integrate discrete applications islands into one processing platform, whose primary goal was to serve management requirements. In the 1960s, this was attempted through database management systems (DBMS). In the 1970s, it was the management information system (MIS) effort that attracted attention, including the following *logistics* operations: analytical accounting, order handling, and inventory control

At the origin of the word *logistics* (noun, singular) is a Greek term meaning something logical, but also a calculator and accountant. *Webster's Dictionary* defines *logistics* as the branch of military science having to do with moving, supplying, and quartering troops. This definition, and its predecessors, are too narrow and need to be extended in two ways:

1. Conceptually, to encompass not only military science and calculation, but also the support of basic entrepreneurial activities addressing all sectors of the economy
2. In depth, to include prognostication, computation, planning, scheduling, controlling, and other vital support activities that increasingly require online, interactive database mining

In this sense, the mission assigned to logistics, and by extension to ERP software, is both tactical and strategic as shown in Exhibit 1.2. Many, if not most, logistics problems are medium range. Although short-range approaches are often targeted, these cannot be sustained in an effective manner without extending them to the medium term — which requires a host of other supporting services.

This need has evidently reflected itself in the way commodity enterprise software evolved during the 1980s. A study of off-the-shelf offerings during that period has revealed that tier-1 organizations required this type of support because they were in the early stages of a process to make themselves more efficient. They needed processes able to reinvigorate their business activities, and these largely related to customer information, market analysis, and human resources management.

During the 1980s, the concepts underpinning MIS were extended beyond integrating discrete islands and providing some form of seamless access to databases. One of the significant developments was expert systems.[1] Another was the attention paid to facilitating one's ability to reach better and faster decisions, as a way to improve management's productivity.

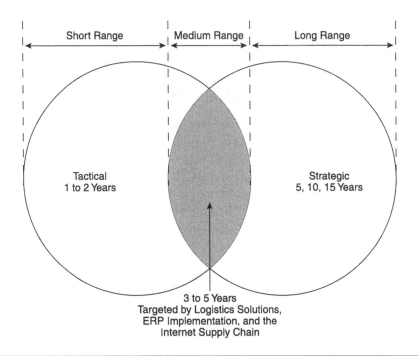

Exhibit 1.2   Strategic and Tactical Goals Overlap in Medium-Range Planning

In my opinion, enterprise resource planning has been the direct aftermath of this drive. To better appreciate the transformation that took place as well as the information requirements posed by this transformation, one should recall that in the 1980s, *mass production,* a concept of the early 20th century, was giving way to *lean production.* This process persisted for nearly 20 years, and its aftermath changed the modern industrial world.

Then a new agent of transformation came along in the 1990s. By the mid- to late 1990s, the Internet spawned a wave of *innovation* that required industry leaders to reinvent both internal and external business partnerships or be overtaken by competitors. By 2001 this wave had hit all sectors of the economy: automobiles, aerospace, materials systems, telecommunications, environmental services, and, of course, technology. This wave of industrial sectors moving to Internet commerce led Goldman Sachs to the growth forecast shown in Exhibit 1.3.

In a way, it is only normal to experience a major evolution in management information requirements,which has been the driving force behind the change from MIS to Internet-oriented ERP solutions. Nearly a quarter century down the line, after the advent of MIS, it should be expected that:

- New integrative software systems are necessary.
- New systems are much more sophisticated than those they replace.
- The software industry will come forward with valid solutions.

Internet-oriented ERP software is increasingly richer in agents,[2] has direct online access to live databases (rather than extracts from operational databases

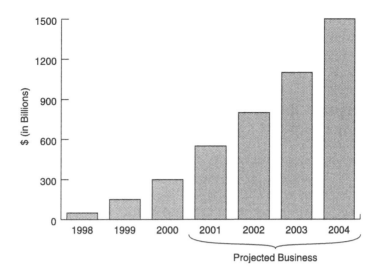

Exhibit 1.3   A Forecast of Global Market Growth in Business-to-Business Commerce, by Goldman Sachs

that were typically used by MIS), and can be severely handicapped by delays in data streams, information element updates, as well as errors and mistakes. There are, as well, other differences:

■ MIS approaches were typically developed in-house, with the vendor providing the extract routine and some advice.
■ ERP software comes off-the-shelf, seamlessly integrates with live databases, and is immediately available for testing and implementation.

This is what we already have. In contrast, Internet-oriented ERP software must offer more than that, but also it demands a great deal of preparation for its implementation to be successful. Among crucial queries demanding factual and documented answers are: What tools do managers need to assess their distant partners? Given the increasingly global business-to-business (B2B) Internet partnerships, how can one's company match — without any delay and in a cost-effective manner — one's business partners' best practices? The answer to some of the queries requires considerable study and experimentation. For example:

■ What costs and what benefits may result if all industries adapt the so-called "Dell direct" model of customized ordering?
■ How will information available on the Internet shape the tactics of small- and medium-size companies?

Answers to these and other critical questions provide a context for the analysis and evaluation of business practices that will characterize the first decade of the 21st century. It is increasingly necessary to exchange ideas on ways to apply multidisciplinary expertise to emerging issues facing industrial sectors worldwide. It is just as important to develop scenarios on how government regulation will, or might, support greater transparency. This will facilitate consumer access to vital information. It will also help verify quality of service in Internet commerce.

1.2 Enterprise Resource Planning Can Be Implemented at Different Levels of Sophistication

The effort that began a dozen years ago with ERP programming products and associated tools providing an off-the-shelf integrative solution has been long overdue. Basically, it was a reaction to the fact that most software produced until then was delivered as monolithic code for one specific application or function. It did not address the very sensible concepts of seamless system integration. This was true whether the programming effort was done in-house or the company bought one of the available packages.

Looking at Exhibit 1.1, one sees that the functions shown in the middle layers evidently existed well before ERP software came into being. The difference is that each was a discrete island, badly connected to the others, which significantly increased system complexity. One of the goals of ERP has been that of reducing this complexity to help better understand the evolution of business processes and their new requirements in software support.

Precisely for this reason, various aspects of business processes must be thoroughly studied, including the daily interaction of organizational units, input-output requirements, communication flows, semantic relationships, and, obviously, the online connection to business partners through the Internet.

User organizations have become increasingly aware of the requirements expressed in the preceding paragraph. This has been a major reason why by the mid- to late 1990s, as Chapter 1.1 explained, a rather widespread consensus had developed showing that integrative techniques are an essential quality for applications development. The primary rule of system integration is that one should be able to make use of software subsystems working together without undue technical difficulties, a reduced systems functionality, inordinate implementation costs, or significant delays in deliverables.

This is the principle, but not all vendors of ERP packages respect this rule. The reason is that their wares have evolved from simple beginnings and therefore lack a master plan. To make matters worse, some ERP packages are comprised of large functional modules, such as logistics, finance, manufacturing, and inventory management, that integrate together rather poorly. In addition, not all vendors are effective in their internal product development operations, even if it is a matter of survival to deliver new functionality faster than their competitors.

The reader should also be aware that while this book is generally favorable to ERP, there does exist a contrary view, and it comes from people with experience in its implementation. Some who participated in my research expressed reservations in connection with the size of benefits a company gets by applying ERP software. They stressed that:

- Vendors do not necessarily provide the functionality users need for the replacement of legacy software.
- Off-the-shelf ERP solutions have become too large to handle efficiently, let alone integrate with old routines.

True enough, some ERP vendors have embarked on exercises to break up their larger application modules into finer components, or even to rebuild their wares for greater adaptability and integrability with the client company's in-house applications and legacy routines. A good solution in reinventing ERP (see also Chapter 6) has been to create service-based architectures enabling more efficient handling from outside core applications. This is particularly important for customer relationship management (CRM), supply chain business transactions, and internal management information requests.

Can commodity software address these needs in an able manner? "ERP and CRM," said a knowledgeable director of IT, "the name changes, but that seems to be the same elusive dream." His thesis is that, over the past three decades, many things called MIS, DSS, expert systems … ERP, CRM, etc., were supposed to solve all our customer problems and streamline business processes.

This did not happen as promised because, to a large extent, from MIS to ERP, one is primarily talking about lines of code and tools. MIS and ERP can help, but they are no substitute for establishing sound management practices, choosing and training first-class people, providing a thorough organizational job, and controlling that processes run properly.

Perceptive people in business and industry who do not believe that software alone can accomplish the job that must be done, also point out that ERP vendors have been rather slow in recognizing the need to facilitate integration of their routines with third-party software and legacy programs, as well as in responding to interactive requirements posed by Internet supply chain solutions and other interactive applications.

In the late 1990s, particularly in connection with the year 2000 (Y2K) problem, the more clear-eyed vendors have been those who sensed ahead of their competitors that the replacement market of legacy software could be lucrative. In response to this, their ERP products targeted the replacement of legacy applications that are ineffectual, cannot be easily maintained, and are cast in monolithic code not built for easy integration.

This led to a handholding with information technology departments that tried to move away from 20-year-old or even 30-year-old code by adopting a flexible software architecture with an incremental evolution of systems, subsystems, functions, and utilities. But other problems remained. For example, ERP software collided with the widely available Web software that is easy to manage, upgrade, and make work with other routines.

- Granularity, scope boundaries, and internal cohesion are important attributes of all Internet software.
- Fine-grained components are simple to exchange and integrate with other code, without undue technical complexities.

Thus far, Web software and ERP have been different paradigms, although ERP vendors move the Internet software way and therefore have developed both interfaces and overlaps. ERP vendors say that because the scope and functionality of their ware is greater than that of Web software, the impact of change is also greater. I do not buy this argument, and if given a choice to use intranets and extranets for certain functions, I will give them preference over more classical networking functions associated with ERP software.

There is also a different way of looking at this process. Whether one is talking about Web software, the more traditional ERP approaches, or the integrating of ERP with Internet-oriented solutions, one is well-advised to accurately describe one's goals and apply modeling methods in an able manner. Modeling makes possible an experimental evaluation of projected solution; therefore, it provides a means for better-documented decisions as to the approach(es) one should use.

User organizations with experience in ERP and in Web software appreciate that there are prerequisites to their successful introduction into existing applications environments. Quite similarly, a properly designed business architecture and properly chosen implementation methodology are most crucial to a successful application. They help in leveraging the effort put into introducing an Internet-oriented ERP system into the user organization. Modeling techniques assist in:

- Experimenting with goals and ways to attain them, prior to settling on them
- Complementing the technical description and increasing its clarity
- Providing benchmarks against which the results of design reviews can be measured

For this reason, not only with ERP but also with any systems solution, it is wise to document system requirements through conceptual modeling. This provides a framework that makes the system logic better understandable to specialists and end users. It also assists in explaining where and how ERP functionality fits into a company's business cycle and in defining the specific benefits one expects to get from its implementation.

1.3   The Cost-Effectiveness of ERP Systems Is Always Relative to the Investments We Make and to the Job We Do

Studies that have focused on the cost-effectiveness of ERP implementation suggest that to make the system work into their applications environment, user organizations spend 200 to 800 percent more than they paid for their off-the-shelf software. There are several reasons for this major add-on cost and these reasons relate to the work being done. The lower end of the cost ratio, at the 200 to 300 percent level, characterizes those companies that do not change the bought ERP code and have more or less homogeneous computer system solutions.

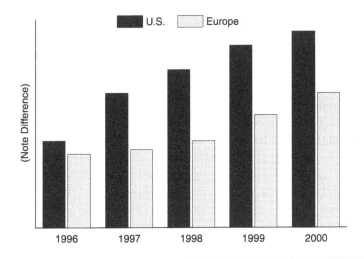

Exhibit 1.4   Major Investment in Technology Underpins the U.S. Economic Boom

The higher end, at the 700 to 800 percent level or beyond, is characteristic of exactly the opposite approach, unwise as this may be. User organizations alter some or most of the ERP code to make it "fit" their environment (definitely a very bad practice), and their computers, databases, and gateways run on quite heterogeneous platforms.

On the one hand, other things being equal, the more a company or a nation spends on technology, the better off it is in terms of productivity and growth. This is well demonstrated through five years of statistics on technological investment in the United States and the European Union, as shown through the histograms in Exhibit 1.4.

In contrast, to get return on investment (ROI), the money should be spent wisely and in the most effective manner. It should not be thrown at the problem, but properly invested to improve the infrastructure, the product, and the service quality; shorten the time to market; and swamp inventory costs. This is what one aims to achieve through an able implementation of ERP and the supply chain one manages on the Internet.

Invested money and costs are not the only issues on which senior management must concentrate its attention. Timetables are another key variable and they are evidently affected, often in a significant way, by management's action. The implementation of a core ERP system can take three months or two years, depending on a number of reasons internal to the user organization. For example, the:

- Effectiveness of project management entrusted with the task of implementing ERP
- Existence of regular, rigorous design reviews and subsequent corrective action
- Internal IT culture of working hard or taking it easy with deliverables

- Attention given by top management to getting results, as well as on return on investment
- Homogeneity or heterogeneity of the computer system environment in existence

Another basic factor impacting costs and timetables is that while ERP systems are not necessarily difficult to install in an average way, they do require significant effort to get the best out of them. This is pretty well-known in the industry, yet many companies delay the definition of goals they want to reach until after the purchase of the ERP package — and then they take a rather leisurely approach to its implementation.

Other things being equal, the better defined the objectives of an ERP applications and the parameters coming into play, the more effective and timely will be the end result. This definition of goals and of method cannot — and should not — be done outside the perspectives of the user organization's business architecture to which reference was made in Chapter 1.2. Yet, very frequently, the concept of a business architecture is missing, or it has fallen way behind times. As a result, many of the 3000 to 7000 different parameters involved in an ERP implementation do not find a home, and when this happens, the net result is many loose ends that do not allow one to get the best out of purchased software.

Nowhere is this reference more applicable than in the evolution toward Internet-oriented ERP applications. This has been a challenge for many companies, big and small, as the first supply chain implementation on the Internet by General Motors documents. In November 1999, the automaker embarked on a project to build an Internet supply chain network. Dubbed TradeXchange, this project was aimed at changing the way GM buys raw materials and finished components that go into its vehicles, and controlling supplier expenditures, which stood at about 50 percent of labor and materials costs per car.

Since its initial steps toward realization, GM judged that this project was very important to the evolution of internal ERP because it transformed the way GM itself and its industry suppliers looked at the impact on Internet purchasing on the control of their internal operations. It also affected the way suppliers bid on requests for goods and services. Like so many other companies, the auto manufacturer found that with the classical supply chain:

- The process of orchestrating bids and other business transactions had become labor intensive, time-consuming, and expensive.
- A method (the old method) relying primarily on telephone calls, faxes, and hard-copy proposals was no longer compatible with today's fast business pace and emphasis on swamping costs.

Add to this the fact that ERP implementation in the early and mid-1990s did not correct these shortcomings. Only by the late 1990s did it become evident that something big had to change to improve return on investment in a significant way. Hence, the TradeXchange of 1999 at GM — which aimed to assist both the auto manufacturer and its suppliers — and subsequently the cooperative solutions we examined in Chapters 2 and 3.

In this particular case, the essential difference between TradeXchange and COVISINT is that with the former, suppliers had to tune their system not only for GM requirements but also for every other auto manufacturer with which they do business. Internally, such tuning per business partner had severe repercussions — ERP and otherwise. Maintaining separate and redundant systems solutions is a major organizational problem as well as a huge financial burden for all suppliers.

Under the old method, prior to the advent of the Internet supply chain, suppliers also shouldered the burden of traveling to the auto manufacturer's headquarters to sell their products and services. With TradeXchange this has been relieved; but in exchange, auto suppliers have to install complex computer systems, sophisticated software, and communications services to access the network and be in the game.

Accumulating experience with the type of problems being discussed points to a pitfall. It demonstrates that the approach many companies chose to solve the maze of challenging issues is to use back-office support to "beef up" ERP applications to Internet standard. Invariably, however, they find out that without the necessary preparatory work, the net result is to transfer the coordination problems to the back end without really cutting the Gordian knot.

1.4 Project Definition for a Successful Internet-Oriented Implementation of ERP

Chapter 1.2 made the point that half-baked approaches, such as pushing the coordination problems to the back-office, would not give satisfactory results in linking ERP to the Internet supply chain, and vice versa. From the beginning, a project must be defined in an accurate and comprehensive manner, both in technical and cost/benefit terms. This requires a dual approach that includes a rich database on costs and schedules and an interactive design management definition process able to:

- Provide firm, properly studied solutions to functional, cost, and scheduling challenges
- Reduce the risk of investing in new facilities and software routines prior to having thought out a valid solution

A surprising number of companies do not abide by the standard described by these two bullets. Therefore, it is not surprising that they have difficulty both in implementing ERP and in taking advantage of the Internet. A recent study in the United States came up with the result that the majority of small businesses do not believe that the Internet helps them a great deal — as Exhibit 1.5 shows through a pie chart. *If* a company does not have the right preparation to get results, *then* it is to be expected that it will be dissatisfied with the outcome of any new technology.

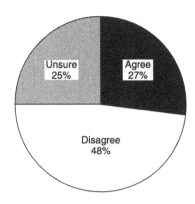

Exhibit 1.5   Small Businesses Do Not Believe the Internet Helps Them

Even large companies fall into the trap of not paying enough attention to the aftermath of the commitments they make, or to the likelihood of a downside. In 1997 the avon.com Web site was launched, selling directly to customers for the first time. This created tension among many of Avon's 500,000 U.S. sales representatives. The Web site's results have been uninspiring.[3]

With regard to personal experience with new systems and advanced solutions, a sound procedure essentially consists of two steps. The first step is a comprehensive analytical activity capable of outlining project objectives, establishing baseline performance parameters, and elaborating tight functionality criteria that must be observed. Then comes the establishment of cost and schedule boundaries within which the project must move.

The definition process suggested here is typically multifunctional. Therefore, it needs to be accomplished by a team of competent experts, including design staff, cost estimators, and schedulers, as well as information technologists. The output of the first system design must be a summary of criteria, objectives, and requirements that represents the convergence of all viewpoints — but also focuses on the likely aftermath and on pitfalls.

The deliverables of this early planning phase should be followed immediately by more detailed conceptual development and the listing of the means necessary to manage change during project implementation. Attention should be paid to the fact that with the ever-reduced product life cycles of software and the accelerating rate of technology migration, any process tends to be in constant evolution. Therefore, the methodology must be kept dynamic at all times.

Experience with dynamic methodologies teaches that one of the significant risk factors is *point in time* selection of the most current process and manufacturing tools required for each product mission. Just as important is keeping open the changes to be made to optimize this selection during the implementation phase of the new facility. For this reason, some companies have instituted a *live change management* through task forces. These involve representatives from project management and facility systems groups meeting at least weekly with the service provider's project manager and lead engineers.

- Costs and schedules are assessed and on-the-spot decisions made as to incorporation of add-on features.
- Such meetings critically evaluate the impact on schedule of all proposed changes, prior to approving them.

The aftermath of good planning and control is that it helps to speed development. Proper implementation requires a framework able to accelerate sequential tasks and avoid delays from poor overlapping practices. Tier-1 companies are eager to use project monitoring tools capable of providing a critical path method.

Analytical tools are necessary to decide on tactical moves by modeling upstream activities. Real-time information must provide accurate appreciation of such activities, as well as downstream sensitivity to changes taking place upstream. Some of the tools available today, such as Critical Path Method (CPM), have been around since the 1960s,[4] but have fallen into disuse because people and companies have short memories.

In a nutshell, here are the fundamentals. To operate along a critical path, one must program the different phases of an integrated solution, aiming to reduce mismatch risk at early stages by identifying key items that must be targeted and by following their progress through the pipeline. Such targeting is necessary to guarantee timeliness, quality of product, and cost-effective implementation. Successful integration requires firm management of internal resources, hence ERP chores, and it must provide the assurance that numerous suppliers will adhere to schedule deadlines.

The multiplicity of Internet-oriented links increases the challenge of the message that the two bullets above have conveyed. Exhibit 1.6 dramatizes an early 1990s experience in moving from one mainframe vendor to a multi-vendor environment, because of a change to client/server. With the Internet

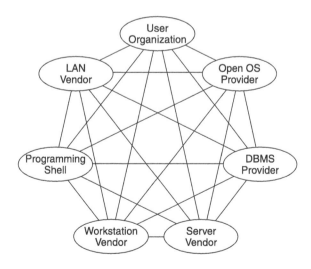

Exhibit 1.6   A Web of Vendor Relations Underpins a Client/Server Solution; Internet Supply Chain Is Much More Complex

supply chain, the ERP implementation is faced with a situation much more complex than the one presented in this exhibit.

Items that potentially jeopardize a streamlined solution must be prioritized in the test sequences to avoid subsequently derailing the schedule. Combining ERP software and CPM modeling helps to create a synergy between production facilities, procurement chores, inventory control, and other systems. It also permits simulation of automated scheduling rules and follow-up methods.

A flexible master schedule must be available, in connection with an Internet-oriented ERP implementation, to assist in identifying, qualifying, installing, and testing all components of an integrated system. This must be done according to prioritization of critical elements that could impede operations or otherwise upset the master schedule, but without losing track of the vendor relationship.

Every ERP implementer must keep in mind the lessons learned since the 1950s from production management. For example, optimizing the scheduling of individual tools alone will not lead to improvements in overall productivity because no machine is isolated. Therefore, the ultimate objective must be a highly effective integrated system that not only runs efficiently but also can achieve uptimes of 99.9 percent or better.

Whether or not they target Internet links with their suppliers to attack the limitations of their legacy systems and processes, companies must use the best available enterprise solutions that, when properly implemented, can play the role of driver of organizational change. In addition to ERP systems and the critical path method, examples of off-the-shelf software include:

- Supply chain management (SCM)
- Customer relationship management (CRM)

A well-done study that capitalizes on Web software, ERP, CPM, SCM, and CRM can provide an integrated environment with seamless access to a global database. The integration of the aforementioned routines should result in a networked operation in the service of management, keeping in mind that the needed systems work is far from trivial.

Attention should also focus on the fact that the explosion in shop-floor scheduling systems and supply-chain management tools makes the task of their effective integration so much more complex. Many vendors offer manufacturing execution systems and enterprise resource planning software as part of the supply-chain revolution, but these routines do not necessarily work together in an efficient way — if they work together at all.

In conclusion, while off-the-shelf software helps to avoid reinventing the wheel and can help in cutting development costs, the user organization should do a lot of homework to ensure that existing programming products run properly and that the new routines it acquires work in synergy, not only with those within its premises but also up and down its supply chain. When this is accomplished, it will allow one to work closely with all one's clients and suppliers and have knowledge of the current status of all of one's products.

Such integration also makes it feasible to identify issues leading to potential conflict and ensure that contingency plans are in place. Without it, major disconnects can surface at any time, in any place, leading to inefficient application of automation technology, inability to optimize production runs, quality problems, scant attention to logistics requirements, and other system limitations.

1.5 How to Ascertain that Integrated Solutions Work Well in Daily Practice

People and companies participating in my research pressed the point that effective solutions to Internet-oriented ERP challenges — from manufacturing to logistics — recast business and industry in a new pattern. They also warned that factual and documented optimization studies need far better information technology than has been classically provided through legacy data processing and mainframes or by means of client/server solutions done primarily for "me-too" reasons.

Crucial along this line of reference is the timeliness, accuracy, and quality of analytical information provided to senior management. Typically, in the vast majority of companies, the so-called electronic data processing (EDP) operations paid only lip service to management information — despite MIS (see Chapter 1.1). This is highly counterproductive as is shown in Exhibit 1.7.

- Top tier companies such as TIAA/CREF dedicate two thirds of their IT budgets to the service of management.
- In contrast, the vast majority of companies spend no more than 5 percent of their IT budget on management information as well as on modeling and experimentation.

Yet, modeling and experimentation are needed for many managerial reasons, including the more efficient movement of products inside and outside

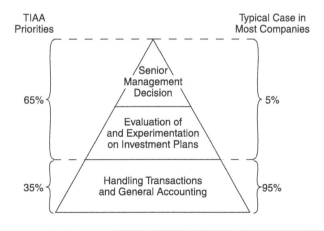

Exhibit 1.7 Largest Part of the IT Budget Allocated to Management Support Through Technology

the firm, as well as the reduction of delays; closing gaps in quality assurance; and optimizing storage and transport expenditures. Decisions regarding efficiency in production and distribution have common elements with asset allocation. A proactive approach to asset allocation leads to the strategy of getting the best out of the customer relationship, using an integrated logistics management system, and organizing to provide on-time, high-quality customer services.

All of these are very relevant to Internet-oriented ERP systems because they impact not only the supply chain of other manufacturers but also wholesale and retail outlets. Many people have heralded "The New Age of Retail," but most companies have been unable or unwilling to capitalize on such opportunities because they fail to fulfill the prerequisites. A new age of retail is indivisible from retail business models enhanced by *everything online,* from POS to databases of business partners.

The Internet may lead to new strategies of competition but one should not forget that many of the elements coming into play were developed before the boom of the Internet — and they are an integral part of a valid solution. This is the proper place to bring to the reader's attention the fact that highly competitive strategies on Internet commerce require board decisions for which all directors, the CEO, and the CFO assume the responsibility — another reference to the need for modeling.

Making money in an online supply chain is no different than making money in a traditional supply chain. What is different with the Web is the strategy and the means. ERP and CRM are two examples of basic software supports, and therefore the means. There are other examples; an Internet merchandiser, for example, needs to do three things to become a retail powerhouse:

1. Attract consumer and business traffic to his side
2. Sell merchandise without giving away the store
3. Convert business-to-business (B2B) browsers to fit the buyers

This may sound simple and obvious, but it is not necessarily so. ERP experts and logistics planners are faced with the task of solving problems that become increasingly complex in a delivery sense. They are charged with the job of quickly developing an optimal course of action for moving supplies in an environment where it is inherently impossible to outguess future consumption patterns and therefore get an exact amount of supplies anywhere at any time. Optimization is not doable without the use of sophisticated technology (see Chapter 1.6).

As an alternative, big manufacturing concerns develop smaller, limited-scope captive companies specializing in reverse auctions. Visteon is an $18 billion captive supplier of Ford Motor Company. Its auctions and reverse auctions on the Internet have achieved a rumored 15 percent cost savings on the $500 million amount of new business it puts up for bid in several auctions. The company's goal is to use electronic bidding to determine market prices, open up the supply base, and gain significant cost savings.

One of the results of this intensive activity in B2B auctions has been that Visteon located new business partners. For example, winners of seven consecutive auctions were new suppliers, not incumbents that had previously been selling their products to Ford. The automaker's new business partners have typically been those able to orient their in-house ERP applications toward Internet commerce.

Specialization through captive companies is one way to beat the rapidly developing overpopulation of processes, products, transactions, and their permutations. This growing complexity is one of the reasons why management must increasingly use analytical models to identify customer patterns, map supply relationships, and analyze distribution networks. Internet commerce adds to these requirements, leading to more explicit needs for high-performance ERP solutions necessary in:

- Anticipating process boundaries at any given time
- Shrinking to a bare minimum the lead-time required to transit from production to distribution
- Elaborating and analyzing a seemingly endless list of interdependent variables

Until new technology served as an enabling agent in logistics planning, the then-prevailing conditions were dramatically over-constrained. Not only were the mainframes of EDP a poor way of handling the concepts and models that mathematicians, logicians, and production management experts were developing, but they were (and continue to be) too slow and too costly; and they never succeeded in doing more than a routine job.

No production planner or logistics expert worth his salt can forget the snafus in trying to balance supply and demand. Industrial history is littered with stories of these snafus. Optimization is a management philosophy that can be successfully applied to *all business processes* or, alternatively, to none of them. In fact, if it is not applied in a rational manner to all processes, it is by definition applied to no problem at all. It is schizophrenic to make exceptions for "this" or "that" case, yet this is what many companies do.

In conclusion, top management must be co-involved in Internet-oriented ERP solutions. The members of the board, the CEO, the CFO, the CIO, and other senior executives should appreciate that the principles behind evaluations of cost-effectiveness are applicable to all engineering, manufacturing, merchandising, and financial operations. Because it is known that supplying all business units with everything required at every instant is impossible if one is unable to reach great detail at high speed, then the job is to:

- *Assess the risk* associated with not meeting each and every one of the ongoing requirements.
- Decide how to achieve the best possible *allocation of resources,* everything considered.

A crucial criterion of success is to respond instantly to changing market conditions and customer demands. Most employees, customers, suppliers, and other business partners are willing and able to collaborate in ways that allow them to be more productive, adapt to change, and make effective decisions. But do we appreciate the amount of attention that must be paid to high technology? Are we indeed ready to assume leadership?

1.6   The Synergy in Managing Information Technology and Procurement

Some companies have introduced into their organization a new job: the Chief Web Officer (CWO). Others, such as General Electric (GE), have given the CIO the responsibility of looking after the synergy of IT and procurement. Either way, job requirements must be met, and these include overseeing information systems and Internet strategies, creating and running the interwoven network of extrastructure, and forging flexible Internet commerce links with business partners.

At GE, the CIO works closely with suppliers to get them seamlessly online and manages all links connected to GE's massive procurement program. This synergy will, in all likelihood, increase in the coming years because technology moves so fast. It will also become better focused because of Six Sigma (see Chapter 12).

The perspectives of synergies continue to expand. As computers and communications become increasingly pervasive in our work, in our daily lives, and in our transportation environment, many instances of convergence are developing in the functionality of products and processes and the accompanying communications infrastructure. For example, cell phones are starting to incorporate the functions of personal digital assistants (PDAs); PDA capability overlaps significantly with desktop and laptop computers; and cable companies that have offered multimedia Internet access are now also offering phone service.

There is no question that IT and Internet solutions are merging. Personal computers function as Web access points, phones, entertainment outlets, and home automation controllers all at the same time. Software is being designed to allow multi-purpose products, while hardware is becoming more and more flexible. Personal devices and communications infrastructure converge to provide new functionality and handle all data, including voice, video, and the Internet.

It is not difficult to see how ERP solutions fit squarely within this perspective, whether their integration into the Internet environment is the responsibility of the CIO or the CWO. But the implementation of ERP also generates a rich knowledge stream that should be preserved for further usage. The appreciation of this fact has led to the institution of knowledge management procedures by leading organizations. A Year 2000 Conference Board survey of 200 executives at 158 large multinational companies found that 80 percent had knowledge management projects in the works, and many had already appointed a chief knowledge officer (CKO) or hired knowledge management consultants.

Knowledge management projects include a corporate memory facility (CMF) into which are registered all decisions as well as their reasons and aftermath; expert systems and agents that improve productivity and replace old approaches to computer programming; and a growing array of tools for knowledge management. Among them are chaos theory,[5] stochastic processes, chi-square analysis, test of hypothesis, and experimental design.[6]

What kind of knowledge does one want to preserve and reuse in connection with ERP and supply chain? Here are a couple of factual answers. Danone, a French milk products company, increased inventory turnover by 30 percent and decreased order lead-time by 57 percent after three weeks of implementing an ERP system. Only 110 days after implementing ERP, IBM was able to reduce the time for checking customer credit and for responding to customer inquiries from 20 minutes to instantaneously. At the same time, pricing data entry dropped from 80 days to 5 minutes.

At Bell Atlantic, information that once took a month to retrieve now takes a few seconds. Using ERP as a catalyst, Borden sharply reduced the number of computer platforms and applications. It also reduced operating systems from four to one. At Nike, supply chain applications resulted in a 40 percent increase in order fill rate and a 27 percent increase in revenues. At Warner Lambert, the order fill rate increased to 99 percent and supply chain costs were sharply reduced.

In another case, the Internet-oriented implementation of ERP grew into a cross-partner supply chain management. This provided multi-company transaction data and planning information, helping to reduce inventory by 25 percent. At the same time, on-time shipments were boosted from 85 to 95 percent, and lead-times were lowered from 80 to 27 days.

What is particularly interesting about these references and accompanying statistics is the knowledge acquired by the people who put in place the applications in reference. It is the job of the CKO to work closely with the CIO and CWO to capture the acquired experience and make it available interactively over a wider reference frame. Online database mining helps significantly in this endeavor.

The fact that knowledge is the most important asset of an organization needs no explaining. As Chapter 1.5 demonstrates, the allocation of assets and their management must be done in real-time because the CEO and his or her assistants have much less time than in the past to assess the viability of a planned course of action. While professionals in this field have long considered how to improve the speed and accuracy of the planning process, the technologies and methods available were not adequate to handle a problem of this size and complexity or they were not to be found at an affordable cost.

This situation has radically changed. We are now in a phase of "plenty" as some very sophisticated processing is entering into administrative science. However, solutions need to be interactive and it can be expected that as experimentation goes on, successful projects will bring to the foreground a number of surprises. The good news is that well-managed companies will see to it that today's surprises will be part of tomorrow's management model.

Notes

1. D.N. Chorafas and Heinrich Steinmann, *Expert Systems in Banking,* Macmillan, London, 1991; D.N. Chorafas, *Expert Systems in Manufacturing,* van Nostrand Reinhold, New York, 1992.
2. D.N. Chorafas, *Agent Technology Handbook,* McGraw-Hill, New York, 1998.
3. *Business Week,* September 18, 2000.
4. On Program Evaluation and Review Technique (PERT) and Critical Path Method, see D.N. Chorafas *Systems and Simulation,* Academic Press, New York, 1965.
5. D.N. Chorafas, *Chaos Theory in the Financial Markets,* Probus, Chicago, 1994.
6. D.N. Chorafas, *Statistical Processes and Reliability Engineering,* D. Van Nostrand Co., Princeton, NJ, 1960.

Chapter 2

Why Killer Applications Can Be Assisted by ERP and CRM Software

Well-managed companies are not interested in "any" implementation of enterprise resource planning systems. Neither do they target a "me-too" type of Internet-enabled solution. They are satisfied only with the best, and they look forward to killer applications (see Chapter 2.1) that can give them significant competitive advantages in a demanding market where the stakeholders have the upper hand.

Being satisfied only with the best is, in my judgment, a very healthy policy. It is also commensurate with the high level of technology investments which, as shown in Exhibit 2.1, zoomed from 15 to 40 percent of all money spent on equipment by business and industry. To appreciate this trend, keep in mind that this change took place in the short span of a quarter century, and technology investments in 1975 were already way ahead of those in 1970, which hovered around 10 percent.

Since 1999, this acceleration in technology investments and improved management methods has led to pioneering projects that have allowed top-tier companies to carry out a growing range of transactions on the Web, from ordering personalized items to doing auctions and reverse auctions. Web sites are built, maintained, and hosted because companies see advantages in handholding online with business partners, all the way to reaching internal information in each other's ERP systems.

- Using the Internet for procurement makes it possible to swamp costs in quite a significant way.
- Among other benefits, this also permits them to devote extra resources to improving their offline services.

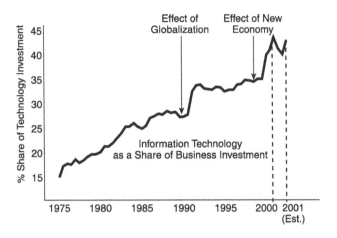

Exhibit 2.1   Three Major Forces Brought Technical Spending from 15 to 40 Percent of All Investments

Here is an example of what the leaders do. Cisco has gained some $450 million annually in cost savings by moving many of its supply chain operations to the Internet, making it feasible for its suppliers to access the company's enterprise resource planning system. This permits Cisco and its suppliers to see product demand and product planning on a real-time basis; it also makes efficiency processes feasible (e.g., dynamic replenishment), enabling both to reduce their respective inventories in a significant way, and to do so without compromising production processes and product availability.

Cisco's customers can configure products and place orders entirely over the Internet. At the root of this application has been technology and methodology. The visible part is improvements in customer service, making it easier for clients to interact with the vendor. The next most important gain is that, presently, 55 percent of orders received by Cisco are shipped without any intervention by any of its employees. The company has enabled itself to scale its operations without having to proportionately increase the number of people required, and has reached the point where it is doing 85 percent of its total business over the Internet, which amounts to $1.66 billion monthly.

This kind of success story obviously has prerequisites beyond the proverbial work hard and pay attention to detail. Reengineering studies are an example of the prerequisites, as will be seen in this chapter, and the results are gratifying. Reinventing a company was a fashionable but premature idea a decade ago, but now it is possible — both because one has the tools and because management finally realizes that this is a "do it or die" situation.

2.1   Killer Applications Create a Great Market for Hardware and Software

The title of this chapter and of the present section has made reference to *killer applications*. These have been the background of dramatic surges in market demand, such as personal computer sales, starting with Apple Computer in the late 1970s. In the same timeframe, word processor software — the first ever successful off-the-shelf package at low cost — put computers into the hands of office workers whose technological fears were overcome because they abhorred typing the same sentence many times over.

Readers old enough to recall the technological breakthroughs of the early 1980s realize that the next killer application was spreadsheets. Commodity software such as VisiCalc came in handy as the Apple I, TRS-80, and other early personal computers began appearing on store shelves. At first, clients were curious about what sort of benefits the spreadsheets might provide. Then they found out that the spreadsheets made it possible to do something completely new with PCs, and their functionality appealed to people from many walks of life: accountants, engineers, and the educated man in the street.

Another killer application, PageMaker, gave the Macintosh a big boost. A golden horde of graphics and publishing routines available at low cost, as commodities, kept Macintosh alive through some dark years. Advancements in graphics helped Apple Computer conquer a good chunk of the market as well as create a population of faithful followers.

With the Internet getting the market's attention, Mosaic and then Netscape started circulating. They appealed to a swarm of personal computer users who understood the benefits of effortless browsing on the Internet. The browsers also turned public attention to the case of working interactively with the World Wide Web. Eventually, this changed the way businesses looked at the Internet and the services that it provides.

Enterprise resource planning (ERP) software cannot be classified in the category of killer applications unless the ERP implementation undertaken by the company using it is really *avant-garde,* such as the Cisco example discussed above. The concept is that the highly competitive environment an enterprise puts in place can be greatly assisted by ERP, particularly if the information that it carries is fully networked.

There are three reasons for this. One is that ERP frees human resources that would otherwise be applied to providing the functionality that can now be bought off-the-shelf. Second, and this is true for any advanced or highly imaginative technological development, the market success of an innovative product is highly dependent on the vendor's continuing ability to deliver. When this is interrupted, the market moves to the next product and experience shows that it is very difficult to re-conquer lost market clout. The third reason is that because the successful implementation of an ERP system requires a significant amount of reorganization, a company that gets itself better prepared, will be in a good position to respond to market requirements such as very short delivery timetables. This is important in creating the environment for killer applications. As Exhibit 2.2 suggests, costs skyrocket and quality drops with a long development and delivery time.

It is vital to have in place and operate an information supply system such as the one supported by ERP because technology advances in a steady manner and new challenges are continuously surfacing. One of these new challenges is linkage to software for open systems telephony. With much of telecom

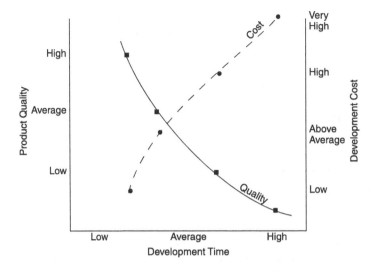

Exhibit 2.2   Costs Are Booming and Quality Drops with Long Development Time

design embracing open-system hardware architectures, new opportunities for product development lie mostly in software. Telecom software has as fundamental need that it must be absolutely reliable.

Contrary to what many textbooks say, achieving high reliability is not just a matter of careful design and testing, although this is important. Telecom software must accommodate the redundancy and failover behavior in the hardware platforms.

A killer software development in communications will permit the handling of hardware upgrades without a hitch. Interestingly, the same is true of information systems support for smart materials applications, the focus of Section II, and also for quality assurance methodologies such as Six Sigma (explained in Chapter 12).

As discussed in Chapters 8 and 9, the physical component of smart materials is coming into place. There are also good ideas available on how to handle it and a number of projects are under way. However, killer applications will come from the software side, and these are still to be invented. Another domain for killer applications is security with Internet commerce, which still leaves much to be desired. ERP finds itself in the middle of this evolution toward a new generation of software that encompasses products, processes, and solutions.

The secret behind killer applications goes well beyond high-tech products and innovative services able to set a market on fire. Without very low-cost solutions, the brightest technological advance and most creative new service offerings will not instantly attract wide public attention. This is a lesson the vendors of ERP software should have learned from their successes and their failures in the marketplace.

One of the characteristics of killer applications, and of the products they promote, is their fast rise in market acceptance. Eventually, as Exhibit 2.3

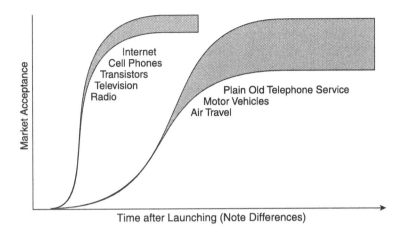

Exhibit 2.3 Product Acceptance and Market Growth for Killer Applications and Other Successful Products

shows, they will reach saturation, and they will do so much faster than other products that do not immediately catch the end-user's eye, mind, and purse.

The key to market success of all killer applications lies not only in their novelty, but also in the fact that they are able to move rapidly through the ripples of the market. Otherwise, by the time people start seeing their advantages, they may be overtaken by other products — unless they all reinvent themselves in a technological and marketing sense. The message these references aim to convey is that high-tech products require meticulous attention not only to detail, but also to market appeal in order to succeed. To stand a chance of becoming a killer application, any programming product requires:

- Engineers who are technical visionaries as well as careful and methodological in their design work, and who are able to see their product through its life cycle
- Efficiency and marketing experts who have a key sense of pricing, packaging, and offering opportunities that the business and consumer markets cannot miss

The interface between engineering wizardry and pricing efficiency is the ability to perceive the evolution of a market changing at almost exponential speed, therefore requiring flexible, quick decision-making on the part of executives responsible for product management. Short of this, it is not possible to provide the type of service that the market will buy, at a price it is willing to pay. This is the role of market visionaries.

The careful reader of technology's history will appreciate that a technical solution that does not incorporate market vision will not work. How companies deal with this challenge influences their fortunes; whether they address the home or business market is immaterial. What is important is the thrust behind the product to turn it into a success story. That is where real-time information assisted by ERP can make its contribution.

2.2   Organizational Studies, Reengineering, and ERP Support

As Chapter 2.1 demonstrated, there have been two major classes of killer applications in off-the-shelf programming. One is commodity software such as a spreadsheet, which was a new invention and received the market's eye almost instantaneously. The other is word packages, constituting a smart evolution of what already existed, albeit in hardware form. My prognostication is that advanced software solutions for smart materials and the Internet supply chain will largely fall into this second class, to which ERP also belongs.

Management that is worth its salt would see to it that it takes technology investment decisions in a way that makes it feasible to capitalize on this second class of advanced applications — much more common than the first. In terms of return on investment, as Exhibit 2.4 suggests, this is equivalent to taking the high road. This is precisely what the winners are doing; they are espousing high technology. In contrast, the losers, and that is the majority of firms, choose the low road because they lack the vision and the guts to manage change.

Like the able use of commodity word processing software, which in the 1970s was required for the reengineering of the office as people knew it, the advent of killer applications in the smart supply chain will call for major restructuring efforts to bear benefits. Therefore, this and the following chapter section focus on what is needed for reengineering and for advanced organizational solutions.

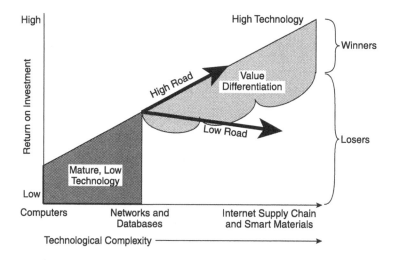

Exhibit 2.4   Only Winners Know How to Reap Results from Spending Money on Technology

Consider first an example from the author's personal experience on the disconnection currently existing between investments and return on investment. When asked by a company to make an audit of its technology status, my bet is that there is more than an 80 percent chance it has allowed both its headquarters and many of its subordinate organizations to maintain separate, functionally duplicative systems that are difficult to integrate; bought software that has been massaged beyond recognition to fit "this" or "that" old procedure; and significant diversity to the support for operational requirements concerning various business components.

Because all this makes up a highly heterogeneous environment that is difficult to maintain, it becomes so much more complex to collect, analyze, and process data at higher organizational levels. In fact, when diverse platforms and incompatible operating systems are being used, collecting vital information for auditing reasons is a nearly impossible task in a short timeframe. Forget about real-time response and intraday virtual balance sheets.

From a bill-of-health perspective, it matters less if the company has in place a properly managed ERP implementation than if its computers and communications supports are streamlined and fairly homogeneous. When this is not the case, the probability is that ERP software is misused, and invariably the technical audit proves that it is so.

Senior management should understand that what matters most is to get its company ready for a quantum leap and to do so with clear objectives in mind. The best way to proceed, in my judgment, is to follow the advice of Jean Monet, an investment banker and father of the European Union, who suggested the pathway depicted in Exhibit 2.5.

- For planning purposes, start at the end with the deliverables and the time at which they should be presented.
- Obviously, the execution path will start at the beginning, observing the milestones the planning phase has established.

The second guess when confronted with heterogeneity, this too being dictated by experience, is that the company's top management is not really in charge of information technology. The old closed-shop practices are still around and do the organization a great disservice because they bend its competitiveness.

It does not really matter if management has asked for a consolidation of data from lower levels. This collection process depends on subordinate organizational units feeding information upstream — a job quite often performed manually despite huge amounts of money spent on IT. Delays and costs aside, there is also a problem of timeliness and accuracy. Under the described conditions, experience teaches that consistency and accuracy of data flows is a practically impossible job. It is simply not possible to maintain and control data flows in a consistent manner — hence the need for reengineering.

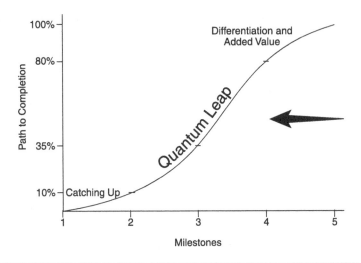

Exhibit 2.5   Working on Goals and Accomplishments: From End Results to the Allocation of Resources

If one only listens to the assertions of IT managers, it would appear that this need to reengineer a major part of the company's technological infrastructure is not urgent; it is not even self-evident. This attitude escapes answering some of the key questions facing companies today — questions to which there are no easy answers:

- What kinds of *new* skills are necessary to capitalize on technology investments?
- How long after a new technology is used should it be substituted?
- How can one avoid the transition period being accompanied by problems that affect the end user's ability to perform his or her daily work?

Valid answers to the first two queries are most urgent if one accounts for the fact that practically every company has, at least in some part of its operations, EDP remains from the 1970s and even from the 1960s, characterized by a crying need for restructuring. But rarely is management willing or able to answer the query: "How long are the technological Middle Ages going to continue?"

Restructuring is, to a large extent, an organizational mission, invariably accompanied by the need for new, more efficient programming products. That is where ERP comes in, because re-equipping in software should not be done by reinventing the wheel but by following the policy described in Exhibit 2.6. This is based, in large part, on packages purchased off-the-shelf that do, however, require skill to be appropriately implemented.

The principle is that of setting the right priorities. Neither the introduction of bought software nor the reengineering effort that should address the technological dark corners solve the salient problems all by themselves. Change is necessary, but such change should not disrupt the current IT support. To the contrary, it should target continuity of the ongoing information services

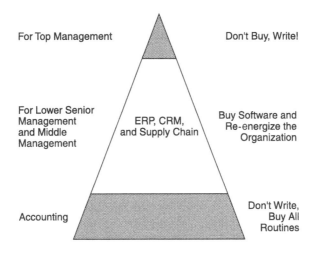

For Top Management   Don't Buy, Write!

For Lower Senior Management and Middle Management   ERP, CRM, and Supply Chain   Buy Software and Re-energize the Organization

Accounting   Don't Write, Buy All Routines

Exhibit 2.6   The Policy to be Followed in Connection with Programming Products

until such time, in the near future, that these are replaced by a system that is state-of-the-art, integrated, functional, seamless, reliable, flexible, and operating at reasonable cost.

The speed of work associated with reengineering complex systems and associated expenditures depends on how this work is organized, the availability of appropriate human capital, the retooling necessary to get results, the ability to utilize relevant solutions previously attained and therefore tested, and other factors along this frame of reference.

Two of the processes that have been successfully tested over the years and are part and parcel of the infrastructural layer to reorganization and reengineering are classification and identification. Both are discussed in detail, along with practical examples, in Chapters 10 and 11. Classification raises the perceptual knowledge of objects into the conceptual knowledge of relationships, sequences, and laws. This knowledge belongs to us by the inherent nature and structure of the mind. However, it can be brought into perspective only through rigorous organizational work.

Classification and identification are so crucial to the successful implementation of ERP and the advent and use of smart materials that Section II provides not only the principles, but also the hands-on experience in how to implement a rational classification solution that is valid throughout the organization, and describes how to associate with it a paralleled identification structure.

For starters, classification has to do with order and also with intellect and with the senses. The philosopher Locke was wrong when he said, "There is nothing in the intellect except what was in the senses." The mathematician Leibnitz was right when he added, "Nothing except the intellect itself." Another philosopher, Emanuel Kant, advised that perceptions wove themselves into ordered thought. If mind were not an active entity hammering out order from chaos, how could the same experience leave one man mediocre while another more tireless person is raised to the light of wisdom?

Classification and identification are valuable intangibles. As discussed in Chapter 2.4, the measurement of benefits derived from a forward leap in intangibles could be instrumental in evaluating the killer applications in the years to come. Some others will concern idea databases and complex concepts embedded in documents.

Historically, computers have processed information while people have handled documents. While computers have been capable of both scanning documents and processing the information in them for many years, legacy systems have been unable to search documents through concepts and content — which is what underpins idea databases.[1]

Quite similarly, with legacy applications, corporate information is kept in many places and in many incompatible forms. While a great wealth of data — even knowledge — is stored on a company's computer system, it is not readily accessible nor easy to find. With legacy software data, retrieval procedures are time-consuming and it becomes expensive to access the database online. This has also led to massive ongoing errors that must be corrected through reengineering. However, unless a thorough classification and identification job is performed, solutions are mostly elusive.

2.3 Policies and Procedures that Can Make Reengineering More Effective

My experience with restructuring, reorganization, and reengineering suggests that information technology and other projects will be so much more effective if one follows a methodology that has proven its worth, and therefore its ability to provide deliverables. In project after project, six basic steps characterize such a methodology:

1. Write down the objective(s).
2. Examine the basic elements to be reengineered.
3. Define if these elements must be high duty or low duty.
4. Put to work a small, well-trained group under an able leader.
5. Apply stringent timetables for deliverables.
6. Perform design reviews with authority to kill the project.

In my opinion, the best way to look at reengineering is as a method of maximizing the results of a thorough information technology reorganization, one that affects all or most platforms, basic software solutions, and applications domains. A crucial issue is restructuring of data components based on their dependency relationships, as established through logical data models. This produces the nearest thing to an optimal order to follow in platform unification, database design and datamining, networking of available resources, system integration, and overall performance.

How simple or how complex can this job be? The answer is largely situational. In the general case, the inventory of physical and logical evidence regarding IT resources is difficult to collect and analyze — but the job is doable. Even if there is documentation on past programming efforts, which is no forgone conclusion, it is often outdated or of poor quality. In addition, people with the required knowledge for reengineering are often not available.

In addition to the difficulties outlined in the preceding paragraph, the existing interfaces between information elements, whose job is transferring data instances, do not represent completely identifiable or shareable data structures. This is a problem of classification. There exist, as well, semantic requirements that must be addressed beyond what was done in the past.

To provide a dependable picture of information elements and data sharing requirements, reengineering must determine much more than how interface information elements are generated and used among different platforms and systems. It must also list all other, non-interface information elements that are synonymous among systems and are therefore sharable; and it should establish if indeed they can talk to one another.

In turn, because the information facilities themselves are sharable, the strategic objectives of reengineering the information system must be identified and prioritized. From an end-user viewpoint, this should be done with respect to each user — man, machine, or software routine. Quite similarly, reengineering objectives and priorities must be synchronized with and agreed to by the end users.

Sometimes, the collaboration promoted by the preceding paragraph involves a major selling job because end users tend to resist changing their habits. Take, as an example, an Internet-enabled ERP solution versus the now-obsolete electronic data interchange (EDI) protocol, which continues to serve a number of companies, particularly in industries such as auto manufacturing and chemicals.

The use of advanced ERP as a communications medium is way ahead of the traditional, expensive, complex, and labor-intensive systems such as mainframe processing and EDI. Both the dinosaurs of IT and EDI were made for large, deep-pocketed companies that kept their scheduling and other data close to their chest, or, alternatively, shared information no matter what the cost.

In contrast, tier-1 companies appreciate that flexible, low-cost ERP solutions are promoted by the fact that software vendors are rolling out products such as demand-planning applications that increase efficiency much better than their predecessors. They permit management to accurately gauge product demand, develop reliable forecasts, and keep rock-bottom inventories.

To a very substantial extent, these results are obtained through information shared with the supply chain. Therefore, the reengineering program must support integrated analysis and design activities required to modernize the programs selected for migration to Internet-enabled ERP. The chosen methodology should implement streamlined functional and data requirements, even if the legacy systems being replaced had overlapping information and esoteric domain characteristics. The target configuration should be:

- A set of homogeneous machines
- An intelligent high-speed network
- Shared distributed databases
- A user-friendly programming environment that is strong in visualization and visibilization

The chosen software must be adaptable to a range of applications by augmenting them with specific functional or performance capabilities, without requiring one to re-start the reengineering job or do a complete redesign. And mentioned in Chapter 2.1, this job should be performed without a hitch while the system is running.

Process descriptions and data models must be developed that are able to represent the company's strategies and tactics in terms of organizational solutions and day-to-day operations, including classification, identification, validation, and linking of defined business functions and rules. This poses coordination problems between the functionality specified by the company and what is really supported by ERP software. To meet the outlined requirements, the reengineering effort must address conceptual and logical dimensions of data models, data transformation procedures prevailing in the system, logical and physical design characteristics including schemata, evolving applications development perspectives, testing plans, and migration plans.

It is only obvious that the able execution of this work requires a systematic framework, including a reengineering database, tools to help in developing normalized logical data models, and a fair amount of restructuring to respond to the new business architecture and its rules. It also calls for metrics able to assist system designers in determining the cost-effectiveness of reengineering jobs (see Chapter 2.4).

It is always important to follow up on cost-effectiveness, even if the need for reengineering is part and parcel of the decision to replace legacy systems in a functional domain through off-the-shelf ERP software. The message conveyed here is that the implementation of new systems and procedures will not be successful unless:

- Unique critical requirements of the legacy system are identified, documented, and addressed by the replacement system.
- The remaining legacy routines in the organization can be readily adapted to open architectures and current technologies — or, alternatively, replaced.

Solutions designated to make use of a migration system capable of serving the entire company must have well-defined functional and technical characteristics. In turn, this calls for enterprise standards that do away with the logical and physical limitations of legacy approaches, are able to serve more end users, and are far from reaching design and operational limits.

Furthermore, any evaluation of cost-effectiveness should pay full attention to the fact that management approval, coordination, negotiation, and buy-in processes for reengineering can be exceptionally complicated and time-consuming.

The justification for reorganization and reengineering lies in the fact that they are critical to the success of the company in a market more competitive than ever. Within this perspective, the contribution ERP software can offer should be judged.

2.4 Challenges Posed by a Multi-Site Supply Chain Implementation

Organizations with multiple sites requiring Internet-oriented ERP support should study ways to implement supply chain solutions so that data and processes of the entire enterprise can be integraed into a unified aggregate. In organizational terms, one of the first issues arising in a multi-site supply chain situation is scope and expected benefit: defining the extent and type of competitive advantages that can be derived. For a major firm, the application of supply chain solutions in only one or two business units provides much more limited benefits than implementation in every business unit. However, the use of one standard software across multiple units poses organizational and reengineering challenges, along the lines discussed in Chapters 2.2 and 2.3, that must be solved.

Precisely because of these reengineering challenges, many companies have chosen in the past to implement different ERP packages at their sites. This provided for a local choice that might better fit the local conditions. On the other hand, implementation of several different off-the-shelf packages has increased the in-house heterogeneity of ERP software and its interface(s) to the distributed database.

In an extranet sense, heterogeneity and problems derived from it are particularly pronounced in collaborative ventures, such as common Internet purchasing activities, where different companies work together to gain economies of scale in terms of procurement. Reengineering across a spectrum of companies — particularly big corporations — is not a job that is doable at current state-of-the-art. What can be done as a start is to establish dependable common metrics. This should be followed by:

- A project capable of identifying key processes relative to strategic goals of the common effort, understanding and evaluating them from stakeholders' viewpoints, as well as identifying quality attributes important to those processes
- A parallel project targeting cost/benefit, also from stakeholders' viewpoints; poor estimates during budgeting typically result in frequent project overruns, wrong perceptions of quality of the projected solution, and friction

In a nutshell, the challenge for these projects is to first identify all the stakeholders and concerns regarding quality of deliverables and costs, and then to integrate their diverse measures and metrics into a common denominator understandable by every business partner. Particular attention should be paid to metrics used by business partners to do dependable measurements, evaluate alternatives, and reach decisions.

On one hand, both software availability and the cost of programming products must be included with all the other costs of the process, and they must be justified on the basis of the business being generated. On the other hand, derived benefits must be measurable, which is no simple task because much of what one needs to measure is intangibles, including web-enabled business planning, speed of product development, quality of workflow management, availability of enterprise information, and quality of customer relationship handling.

ERP is a tool that impacts the benefits side of the equation, the results of which must be evaluated rather steadily. Companies need to determine and measure the critical success factors of the new business processes and models, all the way to supply chain management. The goal should be one of monitoring the operational and financial critical success factors, using common standards.

Whether referring to one company with many sites or to a cooperative Internet-oriented effort among many independent firms, each node in a multi-site ERP or supply chain implementation has a significant impact on the technology solution being sought, and vice versa. A similar statement is obviously true for the chosen business architecture, remote access mechanism, and telecommunications infrastructure.

It is quite evident that distributed implementations pose different challenges than centralized ones in terms of data replication, response time, and systems supports. A distributed architecture should be preferred for reasons of greater reliability, database performance, telecommunications costs, and other factors. Generally, distributed applications make it easier to handle incompatibilities between organizational conditions and standard ERP supports.

A rigorous analytical procedure can play a key role in attaining better performance. Effective analysis requires both a comprehensive understanding of critical organizational processes and a detailed knowledge of the ERP software to be implemented. Crucial to a successful application is the need to merge traditional system development with a process of organizational adaptation that has the ability to close the knowledge gap often characterizing the crevasse between existing IT infrastructure and supported ERP functionality.

The multi-site problem amplifies the fact that decisions made by top management must be specific to the degree to which the implementation of an Internet-oriented ERP solution will change operational autonomy, business coordination, and process integration. All three have an aftermath in the different business units of the enterprise. Organizational conflicts might arise and need to be resolved — if not in advance, then at least in real-enough-time. The same is true of structural changes that might be required to realize the intended benefits.

In many cases, user organizations have the ability to arrange relationships among business units in different ways, but the ways must converge toward the common goal. In so doing, companies and their management should appreciate that the method they choose will impact on configuring and managing multi-site ERP projects. The alternatives are total autonomy for organizational business units, headquarters guidance but not control of local processes, strong head-quarters coordination of ERP applications in business units, and the exercise of timely control over local decisions.

A hybrid between the first and second alternatives is that local business units, and therefore local operations, have access to each other's information, thus permitting a certain level of coordination among equals, but without top-down control. A hybrid between the second and third alternatives is that some decisions are made centrally and communicated to local operations for exe-cution, while others are made locally, according to prevailing requirements, and communicated to the center for information. The fourth alternative char-acterizes a centralized solution.

Which approach is chosen depends primarily on company culture and the way authority is exercised. There is no general, good-for-every-case solution. This obviously complicates multi-site ERP implementation. Planning may also become more involved because good plans are based on a thorough under-standing of the effort one must put in place to reach really significant results as well as on feedback from the execution of these plans.

2.5   Complexity in Information Technology and Its Effects on Enterprise Resource Planning

As the preceding sections brought to the reader's attention, to a very substantial extent, companies run their mission-critical applications across a variety of platforms that are poorly integrated. They have been put together under one or many roots as if they were never intended to communicate with one another. Both the time to introduce ERP software and the risk that these mismatched platforms will not work as a system increase geometrically as the complexity of the communications chores and hardware/software configura-tions increases.

The fact that most computer applications available today grew like wild-fires in the 1954 to 2000 timeframe is not surprising. What is surprising is that far too many companies stick to this mismatch of technology platforms that offers them far too little gain. Sometimes they do so because of inertia. In other cases, they hope that their obsolete and expensive technology will not erode their finances or their competitive edge. They are wrong, of course.

- Nothing alienates customers and internal users more than technology that does not work in user-friendly and effective ways.
- In a period of fast change, there are duties and challenges that cannot be put on the back burner while sticking to the old stuff.

There is no better example of how counterproductive expensive old pro-gramming libraries can become than the huge amount of code maintained by the U.S. Department of Defense (DOD). A 1994 study asserted that (at the time) the DOD had more than 1.4 billion lines of code associated with thousands of heterogeneous, non-combat information systems. These were located at more than 1700 data centers.[2] This enormous inventory featured many functionally duplicative systems, thereby creating two classes of problems:

1. The cost of operating this applications software inventory consumed an enormous portion of total DOD information technology-related spending, which stood at $9 billion annually.
2. Despite such a high level of expenditures, the DOD was often unable to obtain correct information from various existing databases, due to the lack of standardized information elements and data structures across systems.

This situation fits hand in glove with that prevailing in many industrial and financial organizations today, albeit on a smaller scale. Making the same query to each of the disparate, parochial, and heterogeneous payroll systems can result not only in multiple answers, but also in several different, incompatible, and contradictory answers. Consolidating the responses to online queries has proved to be an impossible task for many companies and government agencies as well. In such an environment, even the best ERP software will offer no benefits to its user, and might even add to the confusion. The benefits we project from ERP, the Internet, or any other system are always proportional to the organization and preparatory work being done.

Let's face it; our society is not that successful with the implementation of computer technology. Not long ago, reference was made in an article by Todd Ramsey, IBM's worldwide head of government services, who said that: "About 85 percent of all public-sector IT projects are deemed to be failures."[3] This, of course, does not mean they are total disasters, but they usually take longer to implement, cost more money than planned, and deliver less than what was originally thought.

The same article aptly commented that, by and large, the reasons why big government IT projects get into difficulties are by now understood. The problem often starts with how contracts are awarded. Steve Dempsey, Andersen Consulting's E-government specialist in Britain, says that tender documents often run to 1000 pages and picking a winner can take 18 months.

In a fast-moving technology, both the 1000-page document and the 18-month delay in choosing a contractor can be unmitigated disasters. This and the previous example help explain how awkward are the ways the administration works, and why what is obtained in terms of deliverables is so often substandard. By the time the 1000-page tender is completed, technology has changed enough to make the description rather obsolete. Some 18 months down the line, the wrong "winner" is chosen and is being asked to do exactly what he should not do.

If one thinks this happens only to the bureaucrats of government services, think again. It also takes place in industrial companies and financial institutions.

In my 1999 seminar on "High Technology" in Rome, Italy, one of the participants was the IT director of a large insurance company. Summing up what he said in a few words gives the message that the Middle Ages of EDP are still the "right stuff" today: "What was valid in the 1960s continues to be the best solution." At least that is how they think in his company — and how they act.

These facts are brought to the reader's attention because I have found them in existence — albeit in less acute terms — when ERP commodity software is introduced to a firm. Only the best companies changed things significantly, including their culture; and this because of the Internet's open standards which, when correctly implemented, allow everyone to effectively communicate with everybody else following the same norms.

Another problem to be brought to the reader's attention regarding the efficiency of ERP implementation is a tendency for IT integration firms to over-customize applications, which is synonymous with over-complicating them. This runs contrary to the principle that off-the-shelf programming products should be used straight-out-of-the-box. As case-after-case demonstrates, changes run deep into the structure and functionality of bought software.

The cases of two recent IT auditing projects come to mind with this reference. One was a bank that bought off-the-shelf software to replace some of its aged commercial banking routines. This happened nearly three years before an audit, and the package they bought was still not running because so much massaging was done that the bugs continued to multiply. The self-made customization reduced the bought software's functionality to below that of the old routines and introduced so many weak points that there were continuous interruptions during runtime.

The second example is exactly the same case of irrationality but with ERP software massaged by a manufacturing company. Here, too, there was a programming product massacre, which also negatively affected other applications. With so much scar tissue around, the confidence shown in the prospects for ERP implementation waned, the end users rejected the service, and the entire project was discarded.

Where both the manufacturing company and the bank failed is that they altered the off-the-shelf software rather than reengineering their old systems and procedures. Perhaps the former course looked easier at the start; perhaps they lacked the skill to do a neat job in restructuring; or perhaps (and this is the most likely), by being computer illiterate, top management was taken for a ride.

One is justified in asking, "How can computer user organizations reach that level of confusion?" The answer is that over the years their basic information system has been continuously modified — to a large extent through patches — without the benefit of a master plan. It has been supposedly beefed up, and these were presented as made to meet changing needs and upgrades, including functional requirements, evolving business rules, new data architectures, and requests for management information.

However, the deliverables were not forthcoming and what was available was substandard. Several user organizations have recognized this problem of working without the grand design of a business architecture, but few have taken the necessary steps to correct the situation. As a result, the variety of incompatible computers, operating systems, database management systems, transaction processors, and data structures not only continue to exist, but are also made worse over time. This is the prevailing situation and, as such, it dramatizes the need for reengineering and reorganizing operations prior to planning for killer applications.

Notes

1. D.N. Chorafas and H. Steinmann, *Supercomputers*, McGraw-Hill, New York, 1990.
2. *Communications of the ACM,* 37(5), May 1994.
3. *The Economists,* June 24, 2000.

Chapter 3

ERP Solutions, Supply Chain, and Web-Based Enterprise Management

Web-Based Enterprise Management (WBEM) is a new term identifying an approach to networking that has been adopted by hardware vendors, such as Cisco and Compaq, as well as by software companies such as Microsoft. The goal of WBEM is to build on the success of HyperText Transfer Protocol (HTTP) and its successors as communications tools, and to capitalize on the possibilities opened up by running management applications written as Java or ActiveX components with a HyperText Mark-up Language (HTML) browser and those that followed it.

One way of looking at WBEM is as the extranet counterpart of ERP. The two complement one another, given their particular areas of competence. WBEM is based on a series of standards covering hypermedia management. As such, it is providing a theoretical framework for the management of information within an organization and between entities engaged in transactions.

As a practical example of communications services to be rendered by appropriate software support, Xerox currently utilizes more than 200 servers on the Web and has more than 20,000 employees working with browsers. In other companies, too, statistics on similar functions have grown exponentially over the past couple of years and are expected to continue doing so in the near future.

Companies will pay practically any price for solutions that allow them to hold the high ground in the market, identify advances by competitors, monitor their own activities and those of business partners, assess their strengths and weaknesses, survey global and local trends in their industry, ensure that no one is infringing their rights, and discover new business opportunities. Companies are also eager to finish with the paper jungle that has escaped control by legacy DP applications or that even grew along with huge investments in mainframes.

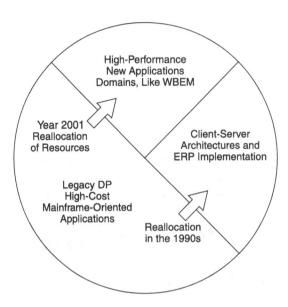

Exhibit 3.1   The Shift in the Allocation of Information Technology Resources Involves ERP

Meeting these goals calls for reallocating information technology resources. For the past ten years, money has gone away from legacy DP and its mainframe-oriented applications toward what was then high-performance domains such as client/servers. Exhibit 3.1 suggests that in the 1990s this reallocation benefited enterprise resource planning. Now, new implementation opportunities like WBEM attract attention. Unless ERP is able to reinvent itself, it risks being on the side of the losers in budgeting and new appropriations.

Which way should this ERP reinventing go? Greater efficiency is always a focal point. A couple of years ago, Visa International estimated it would save two million pieces of paper per day by letting its 19,000 banks into its intranet. The idea is to enable the partner institutions to check their own transactions and get up-to-date details on anything from fraud alerts to marketing campaigns.

Cisco already provided such direct online access by making it possible for business partners to reach its enterprise resource planning system. Extranet-oriented, Web-based enterprise management solutions and intranet/ERP information technologies can work well with one another. They can also enhance WBEM, which currently lacks a very flexible interface and does not have a finished security specification (which is true of many programming products). However, companies that have adopted WBEM say that the software is steadily enriched and even as is, it serves a number of purposes.

3.1   Why Any-to-Any Access to Virtual Information Is So Important to Business Partners

Web designer Tim Berners-Lee once explained how the idea of any-to-any networked access to stored information elements came to him. He felt that the interesting thing about information elements was all the connections between them. By contrast, the then-prevailing method of storing information in computers favored its organization into hierarchical files. This made it difficult to access data, particularly so because it required the intervention of programmers to retrieve it.[1]

To get out of that hierarchical lockbox, Berners-Lee wrote a simple program that would store and retrieve information elements on the basis of their connections to other information elements. He also developed an effective means of accessing it, one that imposed a bare minimum of technical constraints on the user. Out of this was born the World Wide Web (WWW).

The concept behind the Web combines hypertext, which interconnects *information*, with the functional notion behind the Internet, which interconnects *computers*. As in so many other cases, the environment contributed to the invention. CERN had heterogeneous computer platforms but its researchers needed to share information. This made Berners-Lee aware of the importance of a simple, platform-independent means for managing and communicating information.

Berners-Lee's ingenuity is evidenced by the fact that he was able to conceptualize a solution that had escaped thousands of other information scientists faced with a similar environment: handling any-to-any connectivity in a landscape composed of heterogeneous computer platforms and incompatible software, and therefore enabling users to communicate with one another over the system.

This is precisely what we are doing by interconnecting the ERP systems of manufacturing companies and their suppliers. The paradigm of integrating enterprise resource planning into the smart supply chain is no different than the one that led to WWW.

The basic concept, Berners-Lee suggests, is that the solution has to be completely decentralized. That would be the only way the system would scale, so that as more people used it or some failures occurred here or there, it would not get bogged down. The basic notion, then as now, is that there should be no centralized point of control. If there is one, it would rapidly become a bottleneck, severely restricting the growth of integrative ERP applications and seeing to it that the ERP would never scale up to the task that must be performed.

The practical example of a successful application concerning WWW is very appealing because it helps to explain how one should work with an ERP system integrated into the supply chain. A first goal of this any-to-any design must be to shield users from systems complexity by hiding those technical aspects that were constantly in the way of finding the information they needed. The next goal is that of ensuring that information is easy to locate and use for any authorized person or machine.

On the Web, this is the background of the Universal Resource Locator (URL), which gives every page in the database a standard address. Other innovations that have come with the Web include the HyperText Markup Language for page formatting and the HyperText Transfer Protocol (HTTP), which permits handling pages in an efficient, user-friendly manner. Berners-Lee also developed what was at the time a rudimentary browser for searching and editing text.

Integrators of ERP into the smart supply chain can learn a great deal from the interesting features briefly described in the preceding paragraphs because these have helped to create a cross-platform program for sharing documents. Notice, however, that they have not been the last breakthroughs as the Web has seen a golden horde of other contributions. Good solutions tend to grow as a function of time, as Exhibit 3.2 suggests.

If the new applications environment is successful, and one can hope that the integration of ERP into the smart supply chain will match this goal, *then* the way to bet is that the envelope of future requirements will be much greater than the one currently projected. As with the Web, from the start, users should love their new-found freedom in using computers and networks. Only then, in a short time span, can this make the ERP/supply chain integration a place that is:

- Universal in the type of information it can accommodate and in the ability of people to access it
- Intercreatively oriented, allowing personal creativity and collaborative efforts to have a positive impact

The lessons from the history of WWW do not end here. Recall that during the 1990s, many new contributions enhanced the Web. It also became evident that any new system must be multimedia oriented, while in terms of programming languages, new facilities must go well beyond C++, HTML, and HTTP. HTML's successor, Extensible Markup Language (XML) has helped to create a semantic web of interconnected information elements and has made feasible rich associations between elementary database contents.

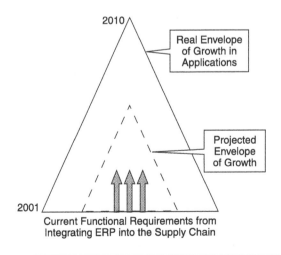

Exhibit 3.2   The Functionality of Any Solution Must Match the Requirements Imposed by the Information Environment

Supported through sophisticated software, advanced facilities should allow users to upload, download, or otherwise access information as easily as exchanging information over the telephone; deal with information that constantly changes; and be able to modify such information when necessary by branching out in a nonlinear way. In ERP/supply chain integration terms, this means that current browsers, from AOL/Netscape Navigator to Microsoft Explorer, must become increasingly more flexible, sophisticated, and functional.

As will be seen in Chapter 3.2, in connection with globalization, the more advanced software that will be coming to the market during the coming years must fulfill a host of novel functional requirements. One such requirement is to make the Internet system operate faster in a way that allows one to measure product performance as well as support yardsticks for productivity. Well-managed companies are continually aiming to:

■ Increase the productivity of their staff
■ Accelerate product development cycles
■ Reduce their time-to-market
■ Improve the market appeal of their products

One of the reasons the Internet has been instrumental in expanding the commercial horizons is that 65 to 70 percent of important functions in everyday trades are still not automated. As Exhibit 3.3 suggests, their efficient handling is not just a matter of using computers, but requires agents, multimedia support, an expanded range of personal services, and specific goals.

Under certain conditions, the Internet can help in this direction. This is seen in the fact that all sorts of manufacturers and vendors extensively use the Net to support their cross-border design effort and accelerate delivery of documentation, including results of models and tests. The Web influences their ability to deliver engineering samples and to provide some level of

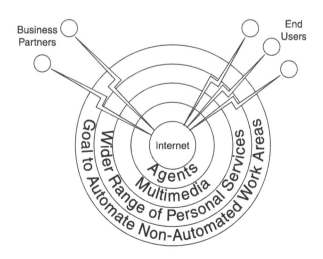

Exhibit 3.3   65 to 70 Percent of Important Commercial Functions Are Still Not Automated

customization without compromising performance, quality, price, or project scheduling.

However, a great deal still remains to be done in avoiding costly duplication of R&D efforts. Cognizant sources estimate that up to a third of all R&D money is wasted on copying an existing technology; and existing patents are not properly exploited on a global scale. Therefore, recent faculty meetings at UCLA have emphasized the importance of teaching engineering students the Critical Path Method (CPM). I, however, would opt for a blend of CPM and ERP.

Equally important are better tools for database mining. It is estimated that 70 to 90 percent of the technical information published in patents is never published elsewhere. Organizations that do not have a regular patent alerting service in place significantly increase the risk of both duplication and infringement. The Internet could help by providing the missing link.

At the marketing end, while customers have the possibility to optimize their costs, the vendor also gains because an auction can be used as a channel to clear out a backlog of unsold products. Better inventory management is promoted by the fact that computer companies selling on the Net never have on hand more than six days' worth of inventory. This is crucial in a business where the value of products is constantly shrinking and technological advancements can make the products obsolete overnight.

Another advantage of the direct, online customer/vendor relationship promoted through ERP information is Internet-assisted personalization of products at the vendor site. Companies that have mastered this process are saying it is rewarding, both in the way it impacts the customer base and in terms of better focused R&D.

Finally, another benefit comes from better balanced production lines and distribution channels. In the past, many layoffs came in response to shortfalls in product demand. By contrast, the planning process of downsizing involves job reductions driven by a desire, and the associated possibility, to operate more efficiently even when demand is strong.

Speaking from personal experience, the best type of downsizing occurs when the board wants to flatten the organizational structure and when managers and other professionals are rewarded for higher efficiency through profit-sharing and stock options. Without the Internet, while downsizing can reduce labor costs per worker, it also tends to reduce sales per worker. By contrast, the ingenious use of supply chain software, the way tier-1 companies are doing, significantly increases sales per worker even in a trimmed-down organization.

3.2   Prerequisites to the Successful Use of Web Software and the Transition to an Intelligent ERP Implementation

Web-based supply chain software is currently sold as a packaged total solution to a range of businesses and is aimed to solve organizational and technical problems. In principle, these include business partner relationships, internal structural functionality, and technical issues relating to timely delivery of IT support services.

This total solution aspect of Web software appeals to many companies as they now go beyond ERP to Internet-based routines in the hope of correcting a relatively mediocre previous technology track record. However, as can be learned from past experience, the delivery of basic supply chain services is not just a matter of another programming product even if Web software is regarded as the new reference for development of a technology infrastructure whose programming routines are largely outsourced.

Company after company with whom the author has discussed this issue underlined that successful conversion of ERP applications to an intelligent supply chain is not just a matter of substituting some of the old routines with Web software. The entire solution must be architectured, as shown in Exhibit 3.4. There are prerequisites to a successful migration from ERP to a combined Web-based enterprise management.

■ When a properly architectured system is not in place, the pitfalls increase by so much, while goals might overlap or even conflict with one another.

One of the most important pitfalls found in my practice is that supply chain software gets implemented without the reengineering and training necessary and without due attention to integrating with ERP. As a result, the applications timetables become long, while at the same time causing a sharp rise in

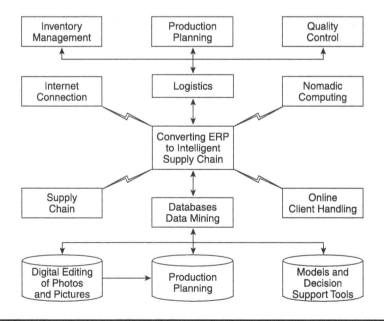

Exhibit 3.4 The Transition from ERP to an Intelligent Supply Chain Must be Carefully Architectured

development and maintenance budgets for the legacy applications that are still retained.

- When no stringent timetables are in place, foot-dragging characterizes all kinds of software development projects and major maintenance/upgrade applications.

New departures in software management depend significantly on training the human resources, both on the IT and end-user sides. Regretfully, it has been the practice since the beginning of the computer age back in the 1950s, that too many senior managers and even chief information officers (CIOs) have not been sufficiently prepared to step up to the business challenges represented by new information technologies, increased competitiveness, and ever-pressing new requirements from customers.

To make matters worse, the board itself has not set a suitable policy that can father a rapid evolution in functionality. Part and parcel of current troubles, wherever they exist, are inflexible policies, inadequate management of change, lack of pay incentives, and wanting career development. Few boards have shown sufficient leadership in properly filling and planning for operational skills gaps; building relationships that help in reorienting business thinking; and motivating to a new level of key responsibilities on how information technology works.

Regardless of whether or not one is talking about Web software, about a renewal in the applications to which ERP routines are put, or about a new generation of in-house programs designed to replace legacy applications that aged long ago, the net result of the lack of high-tech leadership is expressed in long delays, inordinate costs, and suboptimal utilization of new technology.

While both off-the-shelf Internet software and commodity ERP models can be used for a variety of purposes, in every case it is important to ensure that the user organization is able to semantically organize the knowledge about its operations and redefine the mission that computer processing must attain. This is key to the integration of ERP solutions with Web-based enterprise management. A reengineered model should describe processes, their interactions, and their relationships with organizational functions; integrate a large number of concepts expressing functional, organizational, and resource views; and put in place a flexible business architecture in which both web software and ERP routines co-exist.

As Chapter 2 brought to the reader's attention, the migration from the ERP approaches of the 1990s to a sophisticated supply chain for the early part of the twenty-first century and beyond makes reengineering mandatory, and this affects the entire user organization — from design to manufacturing to sales; from customer handling to supplier management; and from accounting to the very roots of the finance function.

The same background reasons outlined in the preceding paragraph see to it that a successful transition from ERP processes — let alone from legacy routines — cannot be achieved without a sound methodology. An orderly approach is even more critical when one contemplates the integration of all enterprise processes in terms of input/output activities, supporting organizations, and resources put at the disposal of this effort.

A sound methodology should provide a procedural background able to explain the handling of business processes by management, including work associated with the various business functions. Essential to this is the capability to handle nonroutine technical problems as they develop in the supply chain. Another prerequisite is what has been called "informed buying," or the ability to develop a dynamic sourcing strategy.

In conclusion, the migration from what is now a classical implementation of ERP to new intelligent supply chain solutions calls for a significant amount of architectural planning, able to create the global technical platform that meets future business needs, not only those current and evident. While a fair amount of technology fixing and troubleshooting is unavoidable, one must concentrate on workable approaches to business needs, leaving less and less of ongoing functions to the fire brigade. For this, one needs a steady supply of know-how, as Chapter 3.3 suggests.

3.3 A Steady Stream of Know-How Is Crucial to a Web-Based Enterprise

The point has been made — beginning in Chapter 1 — that globalization significantly increases investors' clout, and this plays out in several ways. It shifts power toward an entrepreneurial class and reduces the influence of both political fringes. The forces behind the New Economy (see page 256) have become not only family talk topics but also kitchen-table issues, and the same is true for the services provided by the Internet.

At the same time, at the business end of the spectrum, the Internet has destroyed corporate-pricing power, and it continues to do so. The Internet allows customers, suppliers, and other business partners to compare prices from hundreds of sources, not just half a dozen. A net result is that this greater freedom of choice swamps the better-known market inefficiencies.

- Any-to-any interactivity between bid and ask quickly bids down prices toward marginal cost.
- It also makes it particularly easy to copy and distribute digitized products.

Effective approaches to Web-based enterprise management have become so crucial because globalization and networks accelerate the pace of development not just of products, but also of marketing approaches. Changes that previously took place in a decade can now occur in one to two years. Therefore, companies that are successful have a culture that thrives on change, even if change makes most people feel uncomfortable and brings along product obsolescence.

A different way of looking at this issue is that in the Internet-dominated global economy, companies need to create the kind of culture that keeps the best minds engaged. In the 1990s, ERP software made a significant contribution in this direction, but as of now the frame of reference changed. With the New Economy, the inflexible hierarchies, with their civil-service mentality and low reward wages, are crumbling.

- The New Economy favors organizations that empower people and reward the best of them for their deliverables.
- The company of the future calls on talent and intellectual capital wherever it can be found around the globe.

Software that is ahead of the curve is, of course, only a small part of the problem. The transition to a fast-growth, technology-based economy requires serious debate on principles and policies — not only at the corporate level, but also at the national policy level, and including leadership issues.

- How can the spirit of innovation be seeded all over industry?
- What might dampen initiative and discourage investing?
- What is needed in a high-tech recession and its aftermath?
- What kind of antitrust action works when information industries tend toward monopoly?

Even more important are the educational challenges in a society that depends more and more on knowledge. What is the best way to educate the younger generation to participate in the information economy? How can one induce people to respect the privacy and security of their neighbors, or of all other players in the global market? The answer to these queries is a matter not only of *knowledge,* but also of *virtue* — which Socrates has defined as knowledge that cannot be taught.

However, there are both teachers and students of knowledge. A recent conference at MIT focused on how university graduates look after their future. It also brought to the foreground the fact that approximately half the bachelor's and master's students are going into doctoral programs and joining start-ups. This leaves the other 50 percent of graduates available for companies in established industries, and this 50 percent is not at the top of the class.

In short, globalization, rapid economic growth, and the Internet have seen to it that, at least in the Western World, there is a shortage of skilled workers. This explains how and why in knowledge-hungry industries (e.g., software and semiconductors), the ever-increasing need for graduates has resulted in a permanent skills shortage that impacts at two levels:

1. Qualitatively: on the best of available professional experience and technological background

2. Quantitatively: on the supply of specialized engineers, physicists, and mathematicians, which has become increasingly global

These two shortages happen at a time when the market requires permanent adjustments and changes in product design, testing, and the manufacturing processes themselves, and in the implementation of ERP. Moreover, while engineers and science graduates are rather well educated in university disciplines, they still enter some industries (e.g., semiconductors) without the appropriate knowledge of the technicalities underlying microelectronics and nanoelectronics.

As a result of this rapid evolution that takes place over shorter and shorter periods of time, design methodology must change to avoid a widening gap between technological capability, development time, and incurred cost. The need for steady retraining in product innovation and in design methodology is acute. A solution space that has passed the test of the marketplace is shown in Exhibit 3.5.

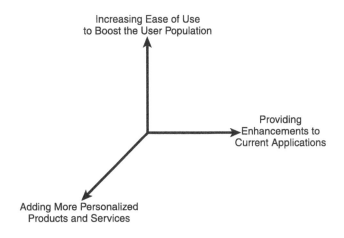

Exhibit 3.5   Future Development of Sophisticated Technology Falls in a Coordinate System Defined by Three Crucial Factors

Future development of sophisticated technology depends not on one factor, but on three: (1) increasing ease of use to further boost the user population (e.g., as Kettering's automatic starter did in the auto industry); (2) providing a steady stream of enhancements to current implementation; and (3) personalizing innovative applications while making them widely available to others.

Whatever has been said thus far can only be achieved through superior know-how and skill at all levels of the organization. This requires changing the culture of the company. Literally every entity must be able to reinvent itself as its customers and their requirements, as well as its suppliers, also change. Keeping one's finger on the pulse of one's customers is both a competitive need and a sign of good management.

- Customer priorities evolve so rapidly because the market is on the move.
- There is synergy in change, and customers pay a premium for partnerships that can keep up at their pace.

The needed dynamic response cannot be provided by big companies with long lines of command and sprawling laboratories. As John Chambers said in a mid-2000 interview: "We realized early on that a world-class engineer with five peers can out-produce 200 regular engineers."[2] That is what the startups do so well in Silicon Valley.

3.4   Web-Based Enterprises Must Always Account for Market Shifts

In the course of the *Business Week* interview to which reference was made in Chapter 3.3,[2] John Chambers phrased it nicely when he said: "Really good players want to be around other really good players… people like to work for good leadership. So creating a culture of leaders that people like is key." This reference to human capital can best be appreciated if one keeps in mind that, at least in developed countries, the workforce is undergoing a major transformation from manufacturing goods to providing services, and these services are increasingly intelligence-oriented and in full evolution in terms of content.

Internet-oriented services are highly sensitive with regard to costs and pricing. As I never get tired of repeating, "because pricing power is so much reduced, companies are well-advised to understand the role of software agents, not only in Internet commerce but in any and every implementation of computers and communications."[3] Agents can be used to evaluate competitive price offerings, monitor and filter important information, analyze business and consumer behavior patterns, and buy and sell on behalf of both consumers and providers of goods and services.

Intelligent software helps to integrate ERP solutions in supply chain and Web-based enterprise management, enhance targeted marketing, ensure continuous and detailed user feedback, both expand and narrow the consumer base as the situation warrants, and create more active trading environments: To gain such advantages, companies must be focused in their selection by tuning choices to their business strategy and the practices they choose to follow and by establishing in advance expected benefits and the pitfalls associated to each business course.

What agents cannot do — because silicon intelligence is still in its early developmental stage — is evaluate the alternatives and choice of tactics referred to in the preceding paragraph. My personal experience through more than 50 years of professional practice suggests that the main reason behind a company's woes is never bad luck; it is bad judgment, particularly a bad choice of the direction of change.

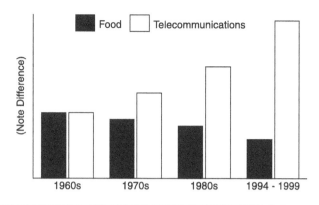

Exhibit 3.6   The Major Change in Spending Habits by the Public in Less than 40 Years (U.S. Statistics)

In the twenty-first century, no company can be guilty of a cavalier disregard of the knowledge-based use of technology and continue to survive. Internet commerce and technology at large have another aftermath of which it is wise to take notice: the changing habits of total consumer spending, from physical food to logical food. This is shown in Exhibit 3.6, which is based on American statistics. Taking the 1960s as the 100-percent level of reference, in the second half of the 1990s:

- Consumer spending on food shrank by nearly 27 percent, currently representing 14.7 percent of the total family budget.
- In contrast, expenditures relating to telecommunications services zoomed. They are up 240 percent compared to the 1960s, albeit still at 1.9 percent of total spending.

This major change in how the American public allocates its priorities and its finances has taken place in less than 40 years and is accompanied by critical issues of which one is well advised to take notice. One of them is the Internet restructuring of purchasing processes, which now involves a much larger number of price comparisons and at the same time is creating more knowledgeable and more active customers.

Another issue is the loss of pricing power by companies, to which reference has been made. This should be seen as a direct benefit of today's pace of technological change. With some advanced technology companies, customers can use an online configurator of wares to choose among a variety of options. In Dell's case, for example, the system makes available choices of memory size, hard-drive capacity, modem type, etc., up to 19 million permutations.

Yet another critical factor is the advent of Internet *portals*, which has made online interactive information and associated transactions so much easier for the end user. Since 1998, Netscape's Netcenter, among other examples, has become one of a handful of powerhouse portals, or full-service Web sites that are shopping malls, online launching pads, and entertainment networks.

All three are rolled into one. After the acquisition of Netscape, between netscape.com, aol.com, and the AOL basic service itself, the AOL audience numbers in the tens of millions. This represents a good daytime-nighttime fit of Internet business. Any talk about merging ERP solutions with Web-based enterprise management must take account of these facts.

Indeed, this is one of the better examples of how and why as industrial companies and financial institutions entered cyberspace through the Net, the World Wide Web gained commercial importance. Corporations have been spending millions of dollars to design Web sites and the demand for site designers is still outstripping supply. In terms of recent statistics, Exhibit 3.7 presents the ten top industry sectors in I-commerce in the United States, and Exhibit 3.8 gives a glimpse of the nine top American I-commerce sites for Christmas 1999–New Year 2000.

Exhibit 3.7   Top Ten Industry Sectors in I-Commerce in the United States

Computer hardware and software	100
Travel	98
Stock broking	78
Collectibles	72
Entertainment (music, video)	24
Books	20
Clothing	18
Flowers and other gifts	17
Department store business	16
Event tickets	14

Note: Taking computer hardware and software as 100 in terms of contracted business.

Exhibit 3.8   Top Nine I-Commerce Sites in the United States during Christmas 1999 – New Year 2000

Amazon.com	100
eBay.com	70
eToys.com	31
Barnesandnoble.com	29
Toysrus.com	26
CDNow.com	24
eGreetings.com	17
Travelocity.com	15
Egghead.com	14

Note: Taking Amazon.com as 100 percent in terms of contracted business.

In connection with the statistics in Exhibit 3.7, note that other top-selling products are electronics, automotive, home and garden items, as well as toys, food, and wine. Because this is a continuous race, the relative positioning of different wares varies as a function of time — but the pattern is characterized by an evolution in relative position rather than a revolution in wares.

European statistics tend to trail those in the United States. As 1999 came to a close, sales of computer hardware and software in Europe were roughly 40 percent of the American level, travel was 38 percent, books were 35 percent, stock brokering was 30 percent, and event tickets were at a mere 5-percent level. On average, I-commerce in Europe stood at about 33 percent of the U.S. level, but its growth was nearly twice that in North America. This suggests that in a few years these numbers might be totally different. Exhibit 3.9 presents the relative strength of Internet commerce in ten different markets.

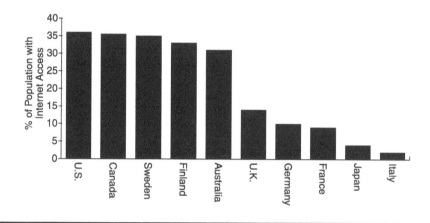

Exhibit 3.9   Internet Connection in North American Homes and Offices Leads that of Continental Europe by a Margin of More than 3 to 1

Something North America and Europe have in common is that as far as Internet commerce goes, the dominant force is in the hands of the same firms. A number of U.S. companies now have a key position in the European market; among them, Amazon.com has European revenues five times that of its closest Continental rival, Bertelsmann's BOL. Yahoo! is Europe's largest portal with nine million users, dwarfing the 5.4 million of No. 2 T-Online; AOL and Lycos have more visitors than European competitors; and eBay, while late to arrive in Europe, is ranked No. 1 in visitors and sales in both Germany and Britain.

In conclusion, in their quest to master online interactive media, designers refocus their vision with emphasis not only on graphics, but on a flood of services. An integral part of these services is information originating in ERP and flowing all the way into the supply chain; hence, the recent emphasis on Web-based enterprise management (WBEM).

In addition to mainstream applications come the value-differentiation approaches. For example, Web animation is becoming a space-time phenomenon — an interactive, participatory virtual-reality experience. Because digital networks are dimensionless with respect to information transfer, connectivity —

not location — is the key. Some experts think that this can lead to digital demographics provided the Internet infrastructure is able to respond to the challenge.

3.5   Prerequisites for a Valid Internet Infrastructure and Associated Cost Factors

Since the mid-1990s, the Internet revolution has represented a major technological shift, but it is no less true that major changes in regime can take decades to have a measurable impact on the economy. Exactly because of their breadth and depth, they require the development of a vast range of complementary supports, both tangible and intangible. These include:

- New investments in physical plant and equipment
- Development and sustenance of different kinds of workforce skills
- Increasingly more sophisticated organizational forms
- A global definition of legal property and legal limits
- New regulatory frameworks reaching every place accessing the Internet

In terms of physical plant and equipment, it is necessary not only to steadily increase the Web server farm, but also to keep links and nodes up and running 24 hours a day, 7 days a week. The network infrastructure must be positioned to quickly detect failures and take action to keep the sites up. The network must quickly handle large increases in server capacity, and all sites should be protected against attacks.

Infrastructural costs are an important test ground. Economies can be obtained, for example, using many smaller servers as opposed to scaling up by adding more processors to one box. I would expect well-managed companies to use incidents such as the December 1999 eBay crash as an example of why it is better to have redundancy of failures built into the system, instead of single points. One must be able to maintain the reliability and performance of the network at all times.

If the network design fails any of the critical technical and functional tests, this results in losing customers and possibly making the national news. Such negative publicity could affect business and stock price. Quality of service, capacity, and reliability matter a great deal. Averages are not at all satisfactory. The peak number of concurrent users may be four times the average number. What effect does increasing the number of concurrent connections have on the solution? Where are the limits influencing design considerations?

Just as rigorous, questions must be asked, and answered, regarding staffing. Staffing Internet commerce shops requires far fewer but more highly skilled employees. As an example, Federal Express has stated that its online customer service system represents savings of thousands of new hires, to the tune of 14 percent of the labor force, but the new hires must be much more qualified than previously.

Organizational requirements have also increased because Internet commerce calls for a substantial infrastructure, much of it outsourced. While those entities providing infrastructural services could well be the main beneficiaries of the growth of online business, they will be able to reap benefits only in proportion to their organizational skills. An analogy may be the Gold Rush of the 1800s, where the real winners were not the miners but the suppliers that sold them food, clothes, pick axes, girls, and booze.

One of the organizational issues connected to the whole Internet commerce enterprise, which has not yet received the attention it deserves, is that of an end-to-end perspective and the context assigned to it. Context is a complex notion with criteria: time, location, the status of "this" device, other devices present, user's explicit profile, user's implicit profile, and user's history of use.

No less important are the new concepts and solutions regarding legal and regulatory issues that should receive full attention by governments, businesses, and consumers — with a look toward future challenges rather than the past. It is silly to spend time fighting yesterday's battles when so many issues have a crying need for a new, more homogeneous global legal framework and for regulations that make sense in the Internet's worldwide landscape.

For example, the antitrust proceedings against Microsoft, by the Department of Justice, took place in the PC market of yesteryear and were loaded with the prevailing conditions of the early to mid-1990s. In contrast, this entire antitrust affair had very little if any relevance to the market dynamics of today and tomorrow.

Microsoft has a 90-percent-plus market share of desktop PCs, and any antitrust penalties handed down two to three years hence will be moot. The February 2001 oral arguments and questioning in the appeal of the Microsoft antitrust trial led many experts to the opinion that the Appeals Court might overturn some or all of the lower court's ruling.

Even before such an event, nobody expected PC makers, application developers, or distributors to suddenly turn away from such an enormous market and installed base of technology simply because of an adverse court ruling. Microsoft's actions in the I-commerce markets and business-to-consumer Internet space would have been much more pertinent to antitrust regulation, anticipating the effects on competition three or five years hence.

One of the main reasons for prudential legislation and regulation is to inspire confidence. As Demosthenes said 24 centuries ago, business is made on confidence. A high degree of confidence by credit institutions, investors, and brick-and-click outfits is necessary to face the huge investments required by the boom in Internet commerce.

In monetary terms, in the 1995 to 2000 timeframe, investments in Internet-related infrastructure were estimated to have reached $80 billion. Who gained the most from such investments? The answer is those firms that were among the first to supply the infrastructure that permits one to exploit the advantages of electronic commerce.

Furthermore, while the costs of setting up and maintaining a Web site are less than for a physical site, and a Web site has the added advantage that it can be accessed around the globe, support services including infrastructure, marketing, and payments/settlements are of no negligible incidence. A successful Web site may involve considerable customer acquisition and advertising costs. Taking Amazon.com, the world's largest online retailer, as an example, the company has never made a profit, and over the years its losses keep mounting, while break-even is elusive (see also Chapter 4.6).

This is causing skeptics to make it the symbol of everything they dislike about the new economy. The pros are evidently disagreeing; they say that the company has a powerful brand and is evolving into a world-class retailer. They also point out that Amazon.com now turns a profit on sales of books and that in the first quarter of 2000 on sales of $400 million in books, music, and video combined, the company roughly broke even on an operating basis — not including financing costs.

Critics answer that for third quarter 2000 (the latest figures available when this text was written), total sales at Amazon.com were $574 million and losses were also a three-digit number, including interest charges on $2.1 billion in loans. What disturbs the more reasonable people among the skeptics about Amazon.com is that as the company increases sales it also increases losses. For example, in 1998, revenues were $610 million and losses were $125 million; in 1999, revenue was $1.6 billion, and losses were $179 million. This is another way of saying that the moment of truth has come and costs are of vital importance in the dot.com world, as companies are required to start showing bottom-line performance. Every cost item matters. No company, whether on the Internet or anywhere else, can run afoul of its stakeholders and hope to survive.

Everything told, the issue for investors is not whether there is risk of failure, which there is, but whether the dot.com's price is low enough to take that risk into account; and also whether future economies will allow to show a profit in the near term, particularly economies from providing customer support online. Cisco, for example, estimated that it saved appoximately 17 percent of total operating costs by moving 70 percent of its support online on the Internet.

However, as will be discussed in Chapter 4, Cisco has benefited greatly by streamlining its internal procedures, employing in the most effective way information synergies, exploiting its enterprise resource planning system in the best possible way, and making its ERP information accessible online to its business partners, clients, and suppliers. No company should expect to make a fortune by falling behind the curve. The Internet is a tough critter.

Notes

1. *The MIT Report*, November 1999, Volume XXVII, Number 9.
2. *Business Week*, August 28, 2000.
3. D.N. Chorafas, *Agent Technology Handbook*, McGraw-Hill, New York, 1998.

Chapter 4

Contributions of ERP and the Vulnerability of the Internet Supply Chain

The Internet's value-added chain covers both the upstream and downstream business through which a product travels — from raw materials to manufacturing and from manufacturing to marketing and after-sales service. At each stage, an intermediary performs functions that add value to products and services, facilitate their flow, and compensate for them through a counterflow of money.

These activities add costs. A contribution of the Internet supply chain is to eliminate paperwork and cut overhead in both directions of this flow. An indiscriminate pricing mechanism, however, has consequences that are not fully appreciated at the present time and, as Exhibit 4.1 illustrates, it might lead to unwanted results. The crisis of liquidity of many dot.coms in the second half of 2000 documents this statement.

What the reader should appreciate is that while Internet commerce helps to reduce the involvement of intermediaries, greater efficiency will not come as a matter of course. Swamping costs require contributions from many parties, and here is where ERP and CRM can be helpful. There is a rather widespread opinion that the Internet should result in the scaling back of two classes of intermediaries: (1) wholesalers and retailers and (2) interfacing service providers.

The Organization for Economic Cooperation and Development (OECD) has estimated that, in the long run, the Internet could result in the disintermediation of 14 percent of U.S. wholesale and 25 percent of U.S. retail sales business. This is not a sure bet. While some traditional intermediaries may disappear, new Internet commerce intermediaries are likely to rise, particularly those addressing an improved allocation of resources as well as new types of trade such as "me-commerce" (see Chapter 4.4).

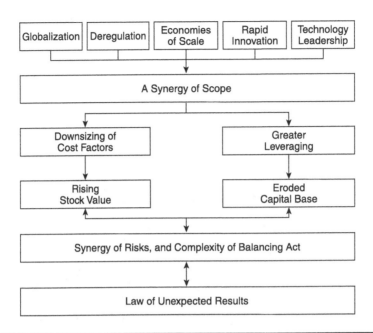

Exhibit 4.1   Drivers Behind an Internet Supply Chain in the New Economy and Intermediate Nodes of Expected and Unexpected Results

Neither is it sure that I-commerce will survive in its current form. In addition to the collapse of many dot.coms (see Chapter 4.5), perceptive people believe that new trends will upset the current pattern of Internet commerce even if sales continue to grow. Dell Computer provides an example of how fast online business can develop. On September 1, 2000, daily sales via the Internet stood at $6 million, up from $2 million a year earlier, accounting for about 15 percent of total sales. Dell's plan for its Internet sales mix is about 50 percent of total revenue by the end of this decade. To capitalize on this cost-efficient channel, Dell is devising new marketing strategies that leave the present ones in the dust.

By and large, these strategies target disintermediation of current brick-and-mortar sales outlets. Dell sees this as a way to continue being several steps ahead of its competition. Although today the company is the leader in Internet PC sales and support, it appreciates that being complacent may well result in falling behind.

Amazon.com is an intermediary that in its first couple of years of operations caught the market's eye by bringing book sales from the Old Economy to the New Economy. Although Amazon continued losing money quarter after quarter, financial analysts felt that this red ink was well spent as a market entry price and to strengthen the company's infrastructure. But by April 2000, this wisdom was questioned and with the severe correction of the NASDAQ in September 2000, Amazon lost more than 40 percent of its capitalization.

Another industry sector that did not fare very well in the Internet supply chain is that of credit institutions. With Videotex in the late 1970s and early 1980s, consumers sent the message that home banking was no killer application. The lesson, however, was not learned by credit institutions and grandiose, very expensive home banking offerings, such as Wingspan.com by Banc One and the Egg by Prudential Insurance in Britain, which have been confronted with a sea of red ink.

4.1 Internet Commerce Must Be Supported by Sophisticated Services

Down to its fundamentals, the term "Internet commerce" refers to trades that actually take place over the Internet, usually through a fairly standard procedure; a buyer visits a seller's Web site and either searches for information or makes a transaction. At present, the largest volume of trade by far is business-to-business (B2B). Compared to B2B, business-to-consumer (B2C) is only part of I-commerce. There are also latent trading possibilities: consumer-to-business (C2B) and consumer-to-consumer (C2C).

Looking for information is, in the general case, a prelude to a transaction that might be done online or at a brick-and-mortar outlet. Some estimates suggest that while only 2.7 percent of new-car sales in America in 1999 took place over the Internet, as many as 40 percent involved the Web at some point. For example, consumers use the Web to compare prices or to look at the latest models. This information or transaction process takes place at the global scale and while it is more pronounced in the United States, it also ties together different markets.

Stock exchanges are a special and most interesting case of the New Economy. According to economists William Goetzmann of Yale and Phillippe Jorion of the University of California, Irvine, only twice in history have markets been tied so tightly.[1] This happened during the gold-standard days of the late 1800s and in the Great Depression. The current 24-hour electronic worldwide stock market is especially powerful for technology, media, telecom — the so-called TMT — pharmaceuticals, and other globally appealing stocks.

Sophisticated services, however, are not being offered in the abstract. They must be focused. This requires prognostication and along with it a whole system of decision-making that goes from perception to feedback, as shown in Exhibit 4.2. The first of the seven basic steps to decisions made by intelligent organisms is perception. In the case of a producer, for example, it is perception

Feedback
Task Execution
Planning
Modeling
Forecasting
Conception
Perception

Exhibit 4.2   From Perception to Response: Seven Successive Layers in Intelligent Organisms

of market need. The cycle of decisions connected to market activities closes with the feedback.

What makes I-commerce so interesting is that it is not only widely accessible, but it also — if not primarily — speeds up the aforementioned cycle of decision steps. This is the sense of *Internet time*. Etymologically, *accessible* is something easy to approach or enter; something obtainable without great difficulty; something open to the influence of something else. But one needs tools that enable accessibility. *Enabling* means to provide an object, process, or entity with the means, knowledge, and authority to do some specific acts that have an aftermath. In this sense, software making accessibility feasible has a system effect.

ERP is part and parcel of the enabling software solution being sought. It integrates into an information process from concept to the end of the life cycle. However, there are requirements as well, such as: developing formal policies and procedures, tying the organization to the online business process, defining new business models and staffing levels with appropriate skills, identifying the new trading pattern for the twenty-first century, and managing customer expectations by setting appropriate customer service levels. CRM software contributes to this process.

Each of the elements the preceding paragraph brought into perspective requires decisions by the board and the CEO that outline appropriate business policies, as well as give factual and documented answers to crucial questions: Do we wish to be the No. 1 or No. 2 player relative to the competition? What are the legal implications of globalization? What kinds of international business partner connections are needed? Other vital queries are technical including:

- Are there ways to avoid costly software reengineering as new markets are being developed?
- How does one build a truly international Web site that appeals to different cultures?
- How does one present information and respond to customers in their own language?
- How does one effectively translate technical documents in a way that is comprehensive and comprehensible?

It is not enough to obtain timely information from an enterprise resource planning system and feed it upstream and downstream to one's business partners through the Internet. Or, to open one's databases to customers and suppliers for online access — although this is quite important. One must also ensure that this data flow is properly interpreted and that it is not misunderstood.

Many companies that launched themselves on the Internet found out the hard way that from initial financial analysis through the planning process and the launch of a new business, product, or service on an international scale, they needed a total picture that was lacking at the start. Post-mortem, they also found out that they had to ensure that this global picture was properly interpreted by all business partners.

- It is not the objective of ERP, CRM, or Web software to provide a comprehensive global picture.
- This can only be assured by a well-focused strategic project, which follows specific decisions by the board and CEO.

Even the best expertise and knowledge of technological innovations does not necessarily give, all by itself, a clear understanding of how to successfully bring products into the global marketplace. Typically, the company that wins in Internet commerce is the company that is better organized, better disciplined, and feistier. Its people have a common culture that is based on ideas that are entrepreneurial — not bureaucratic. Typically, such a company is horizontally organized, innovative, and able to focus on cost reduction in production, distribution, procurement, and inventories.

Distribution costs are most significantly reduced for digital products such as software, financial services, and travel services, which are important Internet commerce segments. Some estimates bring the level of reduction at 50 to 80 percent, but estimates often tend to be optimistic because they overplay the benefits and at the same time omit from the equation some of the cost figures that are difficult to reduce.

True enough, in sectors where buying and selling can be shifted more and more toward online, business costs can be swamped. However, the customers may resist the disconnection of personal relationships. During the Monte Carlo Investment Forum,[2] Michael Bloomberg aptly suggested that automatic telephone answering services such as "… 1, press 2, etc." are counterproductive. Customers want to hear a human voice; otherwise, they take their business elsewhere. Bloomberg's company reverted to a human answering service.

Several hypotheses made about cost reduction are undocumented. Theoretically, savings from Internet commerce for banking services can be significant, provided the institution has the appropriate infrastructure and software support. In recognition of this, several banks are currently using ERP software — even if its original purpose was for the manufacturing industry. I-commerce, however, sees to it that the all-important personal relationship in finance is weeded out. Contrary to what is usually written in literature, not all sectors benefit the same way from economies of I-commerce. If it were not for this uneven benefit, Wingspan.com would have been an outstanding success.

There may be a downside even in connection with handling material goods. For example, shipping expenses can increase the cost of many products purchased online, adding substantially to the final price. And while payment systems are digitized, security reasons see to it that they are confronted with another type of problem — lack of confidence relating to privacy — as well as to the secure execution of a financial transaction (more about this later).

Procurement is an often-used example where a significant cost reduction is being targeted, typically at the 10 to 15 percent level. The costs of procurement are for any practical purpose internal, and therefore information provided by ERP systems can be instrumental in swamping costs. Again, theoretically, Internet commerce makes it possible to apply a rational approach to relatively

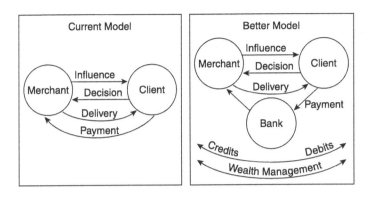

Exhibit 4.3   Two Models for Trading and Paying in Internet Commerce

small purchases, thereby drastically reducing transcription and recording errors, ensuring compliance with organizational policies and norms, and speeding the process of order transmission and execution.

Practically, a great deal depends on how well one is prepared to reap benefits. Within the realm of the ERP reference, a major beneficiary from I-commerce is inventory management.[3] The general tightening of supply chains as B2B Internet commerce becomes more pervasive is likely to have a significant effect on inventory levels and their associated costs. *If* one implements improved demand forecasting and models for replenishment of stocks, *then* this may lead to a reduction in overall inventories to the tune of 20 to 25 percent.

This is the good news. The bad news is that there are unsolved problems in the way. As already mentioned, in my judgment the most crucial element in this class is online payments because security on the Internet is still wanting despite so many pronouncements to the contrary. Exhibit 4.3 shows two payments models: the current model, which is fully online, but not so dependable; and what I consider to be a better model, one that brings into the picture the bank as an intermediary. This trusted party should be contacted through an independent (non-Internet) channel.

4.2   How Tier-1 Companies Use the Internet to Their Advantage

As seen through practical examples in Chapter 2, among companies very active in Internet commerce, Cisco is years ahead of its competitors when it comes to using the Web to link itself to customers and suppliers. For several reasons, not all TMT companies act that way, yet Cisco's statistics are startling. The company sells 80 to 85 percent of its equipment over the Net, and productivity is so high that it produces $650,000 of revenue per employee per year.

By comparison, rival Lucent Technologies sells only 30 percent of its equipment on the Web and brings in just $250,000 per employee per year.

The difference in productivity is 2.6-to-1. Aiming for profitability, not just for growth, Cisco has gained some $450 million annually by moving many of its supply chain operations to the Web. Clients can configure products and place orders entirely on the Internet, and some 55 percent of orders received are shipped without any human intervention.

Most important in the context of this book is that business partners can tie directly into Cisco's enterprise resource planning system. This provides access to valuable information, available in real-time. The reference to retain is that Cisco has been able to solve the technical problems *and* is managerially willing to permit other businesses to link their ERP systems to its own.

This transition from keeping one's own data close to one's chest to open communications can be best appreciated if one looks into the successive steps a company has to cross to reach Cisco's, Dell's, and Intel's level of Web-enabled real-time access to information. The way to bet is that the two pillars on which this transition rests are:

- Top management's decision to permit free exchange of information in the supply chain
- The establishment of a technological infrastructure making it possible to proceed with such a solution

A batch processing environment inhibits any meaningful data exchange. Yet many companies are still using this medieval software and hardware. Neither is the next stage of development, private online networks, a valid infrastructure for data exchange. Exhibit 4.4 suggests that cooperative online systems also fall short of a complete answer. The target should be a broadband Internet that business partners can exploit.

In terms of management decisions, the strategy of Intel provides a good paradigm. Its supply chain extends across the entire product life cycle, from idea generation through development and deployment. Supporting an aggregate of operations along this entire chain involves coordinating information,

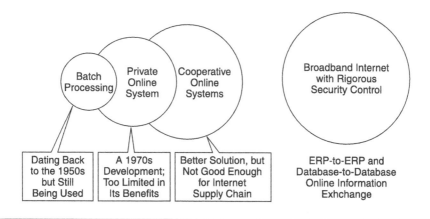

Exhibit 4.4   Advances in Infrastructural Solutions Should Target a Global, Sophisticated Interconnection

incentives, organizational linkages, and information to be obtained from ERP and CRM.

Intel says that capitalizing on the Internet makes it possible to integrate information across its entire supply chain, and does so quite effectively. The adopted solution sees to it that many of the company's business functions are Web-enabled. The top five that I retain from a long list of functions are (1) integrated planning, (2) global procurement, (3) worldwide manufacturing, (4) online marketing, and (5) cross-enterprise logistics.

One of the key benefits that Intel obtains through this strategic solution is consignment visibility. Other companies that are able to handle the complete cycle on the Web say that results have met expectations. From setting a goal of doing $1 billion in business over the Internet per year, Intel was soon doing $1 billion of business over the Internet per month. The new objective is that 100 percent of the company's supply chain will be conducted through the Internet.

Volkswagen is one of the auto manufacturers that has globalized its supply chain operations through the Internet. This made a large difference in procurement. In the mid-1990s, Volkswagen operations were centered in a single hub in Germany. Parts were shipped from this hub to other areas of operations. By 2000, Volkswagen was operating a global network with no unique center. Parts are procured or manufactured in one of 50 production plants around the world, based on capacity. The parts are then sent to wherever they are needed, as supply chain solutions facilitate the flow of materials.

A Web-based approach has permitted the integration of Volkswagen's nine brands. One of the innovations is the notion of demand capacity management, a proactive administration of supply chain designed to anticipate problems rather than react to them. Volkswagen has also created a build-to-order system in which customers can order cars through the Web by specifying the options they want. The delivery lag, however, is three weeks — still way too long compared to Toyota.

As it is to be expected, several companies are faced with resistance to Internet-based methods, or see conflicts regarding the way the new economy and the old operate together. For example, while Volkswagen is ready to sell cars through the Web, giving consumers the opportunity to select the auto and options they want, its dealers are resistant to the Internet sales channel for two reasons: (1) they are not ready to exploit its potential; and (2) they fear they may be disintermediated.

With sales of $38 billion, Procter & Gamble (P&G) operates in 140 countries and has 110,000 employees worldwide. The company's goal for supply chain activities is to increase sales and profits across the entire supply chain. The objective sought by management is to provide all of its business partners with real-time information and enable them to access P&G's own databases. An internal P&G study found that the reason for excess inventory in the supply chain has largely been supply variation, not demand variation. It was not lack of forecasting of customer behavior that was causing the problem, but the lack of timely information on deliveries through the supply chain.

This is the kind of service provided by online access to ERP databases. Inefficiency in real-time information was costing P&G excess inventory and lost sales. When an item was out of stock, the company lost the sale 50 percent of the time. Therefore, it is now using online data streams for point-of-sale (POS) equipment to communicate demand, and has developed a Collaborative Planning, Forecasting, and Replenishment (CPFR) system to interact in real-time with its supply chain partners.

Wal-Mart, a merchandising company, has been ingeniously using the Internet not only for sales, but also for handling product returns. The company currently offers 25,000 different products for sale through its Web site, leveraging the presence of its 2700 stores nationwide to handle one of the more difficult aspects of Internet commerce: products returned by clients.

In apparel, for example, returns average 25 percent due to size and color variations. Handling this amount of returns is expensive. Wal-Mart lets customers return merchandise to any store rather than mailing it to a central warehouse because its information system makes feasible that any product sold anywhere by Wal-Mart shows up on a Master Item List (MIL). Information databased in MIL is transparent, with the result that any store can put any item back on the sales floor, regardless of whether that store typically sells the item or not. The system also knows that the return was from a Web-based sale and does not penalize the accepting store for receiving the returned items.

As these examples help document, there are many aspects of electronic commerce, other than direct sales, that must be handled in an efficient manner if the entire operation is going to be successful. An internal management information system such as ERP is instrumental in providing the needed support, whether one is talking about manufacturing, merchandising, or banking. However, it will not deliver significant results automatically just by being around; 80 percent of the work is organizational and it must be done by skilled professionals.

4.3   Trading in Intangibles Has Different Requirements than Trading in Physical Goods

As is to be expected, much of the Internet business is trading in intangibles, and this contrast has different requirements than trading in tangible, physical goods. In the Old Economy, marketing information, advertising, ordering, payments, and other activities (that today can be easily digitized) were services complementing the physical delivery of goods, and sometimes they were prerequisite to them. But the New Economy involves a great deal of trading in intangibles as target entities. This is true from establishing the initial contact between consumers and merchants to after-sales service through help desks and other means of online client support.

Brands are important in all environments, but even more so when Internet commerce brings along a growing number of disconnects between the customer and the sales agent. As the level of depersonalization in marketing and

Exhibit 4.5   The Value of Branding

Brands	Est. Brand Value in $ Billions[a]
Coca-Cola	$73
Microsoft Windows	$70
IBM	$53
Intel	$39
Nokia	$39
General Electric	$38
Ford	$36
Disney	$34
McDonald's	$28
AT&T	$26

[a] *Forbes*, October 2, 2000. The $ figures have been rounded to two significant digits.

sales increases, branding fills much of the gap created by this lack of human contact. Based on statistics by *Forbes*, Exhibit 4.5 gives a bird's-eye view of the value of branding for ten of the best-known companies, seven of which are technology firms.

It is therefore not surprising that a good part of the cost of the Internet market's infrastructure is for big budgets spent on branding and advertising. This has become particularly important given that both businesses and their consumers are now confronted with a vast array of Web sites from which to choose. Reputation, too, is critical in the choice of business partners; indeed, reputation is targeted by branding.

One can look at reputation and branding from a different angle. Because it permits companies to squeeze personnel costs out of the system, depersonalization is not necessarily all negative. To better appreciate its aftermath, one must think constructively about the changes it brings along, from manufacturing to financial services, administrative chores, order taking and handling, certification of delivery documents, accounting entries, billing, payments, and financial reports.[4] However, one must also account for reputational variables.

Not just branding, but also — if not primarily — the able execution of processes such as quality control and automated customer handholding through interconnected platforms, enhances a firm's reputation. This also requires knowledge about intangibles and their handling, involving database mining, patterning, profiling, ontology for products and services, property descriptions, focused pricing, and customized offers. Other elements are one-to-one marketing, online negotiations, and agent-assisted contracting.[5]

Other necessary services in the environment under discussion, which fit the description of intangibles, include copyright protection, privacy security, authorization, authentication, and digital signatures, as well as legal and administrative issues, taxation, and auditing practices (see Section III). The core of the matter is that:

- These services can be unbundled from the physical goods and sold on their own, providing an income stream.
- Both information and knowledge have a cost and they should be sold at a price, but to do so they must be of high quality.

Every company is well advised to find its own solution space in the context of the reference made by these two bullets. There is as well a general framework and this is shown in Exhibit 4.6. What is needed for effective re-personalization of depersonalized services is express novelty, assured quality, fast time-to-market, marketing thrust, and competitive applications in the company's own focused terms. Data streams from ERP and CRM can be instrumental in supporting these re-personalization factors.

Internet-based intermediaries appreciate that major efficiency gains can be obtained in areas of B2B commerce such as inventory control and procurement, which also involve many intangibles. On the other hand, continuing efficiency gains from commerce on the Web are less certain because the growth of some intermediaries is offsetting the removal of others. Thus far, among the beneficiaries have been the providers of Internet search engines; but these, too, are undergoing a shakedown, as demonstrated by the difficulties faced by Lycos and Yahoo! in the second half of 2000.

The construction industry provides a practical example for which intangibles play critical role in Internet commerce and digitization services. An online business recently developed in the United Kingdom targets something like £30 billion (U.S. $45 billion) worth of products traded in the British construction industry every year — but also brings into perspective alliances and preparatory activities.

To capture this market, Emap, a London-based information services company, developed the *Construction Plus* site on the Internet, and launched it in early 2000. It capitalized on the fact that, as suggested by different research projects in the construction industry, half of U.K. transactions in construction

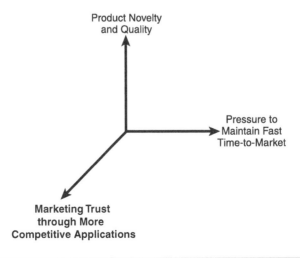

Exhibit 4.6   A Framework Defining the Solution Space for Success in Internet Commerce

material will probably be done online by 2005. Emap plans to offer up to 150,000 products online in conjunction with the brick-and-mortar sales network of Wolseley Centers.

In the background of this Emap-Wolseley alliance lies the fact that since 1999, Wolseley has operated its own Web sites allowing customers to buy and sell online. It plans to keep these Web sites going even after the link with Emap, but the materials distributor expects the Emap deal to send far more online traffic its way. Among the assets Emap uses is that its publications in the United Kingdom include the 130-year-old *Construction News* and the 103-year-old *Architects Journal.* Architects and builders are believed to be natural visitors to Emap's publication Web sites; they can now migrate to I-commerce pages.

With these credentials, which largely rest on intangibles from its publications business, Emap's management is betting on the likelihood that the unglamorous construction trade will become the launchpad for its Internet commerce strategy. This underscores how traditional media companies are using their existing product and channel assets, such as trade magazines, to tap into I-commerce revenue streams.

Armed with this background on the synergy between physical goods and services that are intangibles, one can make a hypothesis about joining something like Emap's digital media with the digital media of Cisco, which are to a significant degree ERP based. In doing so, one sees that the merged media part constitutes a foreground that can serve any physical goods background — its products being knowledge and information.

Not only construction companies and electronic equipment manufacturers, but also project managers, auditors of technical projects, cost accountants, and other professionals can effectively use this digital media background after it is in place. Securum, a Swedish holding company, had an excellent program to manage its real estate assets and audit its construction sites. Deutsche Bank lacked such a program and was taken to the cleaners by Jürgen Schneider, who was granted loans for a finished 20,000 m² (220,000 sq. ft.) marketing mall. After Schneider's demise, this mall was found, too late, to be only 9000 m² (99,000 sq. ft.) and half-ready.

4.4　Mobile Me-Commerce, Wireless Solutions, and Smart Tags

In 1999, global I-commerce was worth a little over $150 billion, with about 80 percent of those transactions between one company and another. Business-to-business Web exchanges mushroomed while the absolute level of consumer I-commerce remained relatively small. On average, its value represents a little over 1 percent of American retail sales, although in some areas its share is much higher, at the level of 5 percent of book sales and 15 percent of retail stockbrokering.

Still, while the retail market on the Internet is small, there is no reason why in terms of speed and capacity, mobile electronic commerce should not take a chunk of Internet commerce. Experts are now projecting that overall, by 2005, 7 percent of all Internet transactions will be done over cellular phones. This is expected to rise to 24 percent by 2010, based in a large part on B2B transactions.

The Gartner Group projects that mobile electronic commerce will eventually account for approximately 40 percent of all online transactions. Other prognosticators suggest that mobile I-commerce will become *me-commerce*, so consumers and smaller businesses are likely to migrate to portable devices. The unraveling of many dot.coms (see Chapter 4.6) may, however, upset such forecasts.

There are two ways of looking at me-commerce: as an abbreviation of mobile electronic commerce; and as Internet commerce intended for *me*. These two notions correlate (see also Chapter 9.5). According to many experts:

- The major parts of the wares offered in me-commerce will be customized.
- The transactions taking place will integrate, to a significant extent, with personal services.

Both bullets reflect the fact that to a significant extent, Internet commerce is, in reality, a proxy for consumer spending. John Chambers, CEO of Cisco Systems, said the Internet revolution will be over in a decade or two when all business entities become Internet companies, completely incorporating the Net in their operations.[6]

As mobile electronic commerce begins the descent from hype to reality, manufacturers, merchandisers, and bankers are not just addressing their classical market functions, but also trying to cover their neighbor's business — at least as far as they are able to capitalize on their current expertise. Because, in all likelihood, for each one of them, current expertise is limited within an expanding me-commerce landscape, there is a flurry of partnership activity and redefinition of roles. This goes all the way to reestablishing which type of organization owns which role.

Current projections on mobile commerce are based on estimates that third-generation phones (3GP) are likely to be well established in Europe and Japan by the end of 2003; in my opinion, this is too optimistic. In contrast, the United States is running some years behind Europe in mobile technology and its telephone market is still fragmented. Rightly or wrongly, some individuals think that the growth potential for 3GP is stupendous. According to Deutsche Bank there are already around 500 million mobile phones in use worldwide, roughly 100 million more than the number of PCs connected to the Internet. It is likely that in the next four years, mobile phone subscribers will top the 1.5 billion mark, around 20 percent more than all households with a television anywhere in the world.

There is, of course, a downside that is not widely discussed, but it is present. To buy the 3GP licenses, telephone companies became hopelessly indebted. They now have to service these debts while the cash flow from such costly licenses will not show up for several years, even in the best case.

If one of the telephone companies, or the banks that financed them, capsizes, this will delay me-commerce from taking off for several years.

If, and only if, everything goes according to plan, me-commerce will be boosted by the fact that the developing intelligent directory software technology makes it possible for consumers to create digital profiles of themselves and their priorities. This will give a boost to CRM programming products, probably bringing them down to the level of portable devices. At the same time, smart tags (electronic tags or e-tags) and automatic identification (auto-ID) solutions will permit inanimate objects to broadcast their availability. This subject is discussed at length in Section II.

As discussed in Chapters 8 and 9, to be successful as a product, e-tags must provide much more than what is offered today through the bar code, which has already simplified input to the computer, but has also left some wide gaps in data entry sequence. Nobody can escape the fact that the more advanced solutions, which capitalize on high technology, need a large amount of imagination; otherwise, e-tags will go the way of smart cards — nowhere in particular.

In their own way, auto-ID, smart tags, mobile phones, and me-commerce correlate. If current forecasts are worth their salt and there is no global financial crisis in the coming years, Europe's mobile phone market is expected to grow by 40 to 50 percent annually over the next three years. A fairly persistent forecast is that by 2005, individual I-commerce services will be primarily delivered by wireless, and the wireless terminal will become the window of choice for *nomadic transactions* (location-independent).

To leave its mark on the highly competitive environment of nomadic transactions, me-commerce must benefit from analytical business processes that help in building a series of supports. Both ERP and CRM can be instrumental in getting such business processes under way and in providing the tools that allow one to:

- Analyze information about customers taken from one or multiple systems operating online
- Understand customer needs, differentiating between customers via market segmentation
- Predict the likelihood of customer churn, loyalty, and profitability through rigorous analysis
- Evaluate channel effectiveness, campaign performance, sales results, and other critical factors

An example of the potential of nomadic transactions and nomadic computing is given by the Japanese wireless market, which is now at the center of attention with the success of i-mode, Docomo's mobile Internet service. Introduced in early 1999, its acceptance by the public has been overwhelming, with over 5 million subscribers having signed up by mid-2000 — that translates to about 10,000 new i-mode subscribers per day.

For starters, i-mode is a packet-based mobile Internet service that allows users to effortlessly hop on the Internet without having to dial up an Internet service provider. It is text based, with limited capabilities to send low-quality still images. The i-mode is a boost to wireless systems, but the latter also have, so to speak, their own lives. Wireless systems are frequently categorized by the range they cover. One of the most popular limited-range applications is in wireless local area networks (LANs). These have all of the functionality of wired LANs, but without the cable connection.

Service companies are experimenting with dramatic price reductions and with the expansion of wireless beyond the workplace into residence, for business-type and purely consumer applications. Furthermore, with low-cost personal area networks (PAN) technologies, such as *Bluetooth*, almost every mobile device could benefit somewhere down the line from high-performance connectivity.

It looks as if there is a range of wireless solutions to almost every application of technology currently available — but there are also constraints. Both business plans and the businesses themselves can fail, with the result that forecasts must be put on the back burner. The market is never really moving according to plan.

4.5   Lessons that New Economy Companies Can Learn from Old Economy Companies

Most likely, the best example of an Old Economy technology company that managed to survive is that of the reborn IBM. What is peculiar about IBM is that it has rarely succeeded because it had the best or most glamorous products. Instead, it became big on the back of strategies having to do with customers, pursuing a strategy of singleness. *Singleness* means being the prime supplier of information technology to targeted accounts, while presenting a single face to the customer. Another facet of singleness is being all things to *some* customers, those who count the most for continued business success.

Contrary to many Internet start-ups, IBM has avoided being a one-hit wonder; but by the end of the 1980s, it could not avoid the frustration of having a disintegrated client base because it stuck too long to mainframes. In the early 1990s, however, IBM reinvented itself by focusing on software and diversifying its hardware line.

This is an interesting example as far as the integration of ERP into the smart supply chain is concerned. Not only is the sought-after effect one of *virtual singleness*, but this effect must also be kept dynamic. ERP should reinvent itself. Being all things, in an information supply sense, to all business partners in the chain is not enough.

- ERP functionality should be reinvented all the time.
- ERP must also be product independent because products die — and so do product-specific information channels.

Valuable lessons can be learned from the software industry of the 1960s, 1970s, and 1980s, and its difficulty in changing direction. As long as the mainframe culture persisted, those firms that produced, marketed, and supported mainframe-based transaction processing systems flourished. One such company marketed a programming product whose major strength was the nightly balancing of all accounts. The procedure required the system manager to examine each night's reports and verify that various totals balanced. This approach worked well until the product became popular with larger clients, and it was found out the hard way that several hours were needed to verify the previous night's processing. This dramatized the limitation of the solution in reference because it led to unacceptable delays, high processing costs, and a number of errors. Eventually, the change toward real-time made this batch-based package an oddity and threw its maker out of the market.

During the 1990s, companies that developed and sold mainframe programming products, such as Computer Associates, BMC Software, and Compuware, were feeling the pinch as their clients moved to Internet-based systems and ERP solutions. As more and more organizations became Web-enabled, through a medium- to longer-term transition process, software producers that could not adapt found it more and more difficult to survive.

This is a lesson that New Economy companies must learn from Old Economy companies. Another lesson is that quite often technological innovation is not the thing that really makes a firm successful. In a number of cases, technology turns out to be less important than sales and distribution methods and sales force quotas. This is shown in the case of IBM versus Univac. In the late 1950s and throughout the 1960s, IBM consistently outsold competitors that had better technology, because it knew how to:

- Motivate its sales force, keeping it on the run
- Put the sales story before the customer
- Install the machines and run them
- Hang on to customers once it had them in its books

Fine-tuning the sales process is something Old Economy companies know how to do very well. Where they have failed is in the management of change. The ability to lead in a practical sense and the management of change correlate. Leadership extends all the way to how good is one's team, because the quality of the team is a crucial determining factor and it has much to do with the ability to attract, retain, and develop able associates.

Growth also plays an important role in management leadership. If a company grows by 40 percent in slightly more than two years, this requires doubling the leadership to stay where one already was. It also calls for steady improvement in communication skills as the diameter of the population that intercommunicates explodes.

Growth both complicates the management of change and makes it more urgent than ever before. Yet, many companies today are burdened with too many middle managers who resist change. For example, they pay only lip service in using the Internet. According to International Data Corporation, 60 percent of American companies have in-house Web sites, but only about 25 percent of companies actually sell anything over the Web.

On June 5, 2000, an article in *Business Week* brought into perspective the means that industry leaders have used to change the business culture of employees. In Japan, when the management team at Sega Enterprises resisted change, Isao Okawa, the president, went against the consensus-charged, lifetime-employment culture by announcing that those who did not espouse change would be fired, thereby risking shame. Resistance vanished overnight.

In the United States, at Enron, Jeffrey Skilling, the president, moved the energy company from bureaucratic thinking to Internet culture by ripping out nearly all of the elevators at headquarters. His goal was to force people to use the stairs, creating more chance encounters, boosting collaboration, and demonstrating that resistance to change is not a one-way street. Even elevators can be decommissioned.

At GE Aircraft Engines, James McNerney, the CEO, converted an old warehouse into an *idea laboratory*. Then McNerney appointed *e-belts*, the equivalent of Six Sigma black belts (see Chapter 12), to lead the process of change. As this and other examples document, companies whose management and employees resist change are attacking completely the wrong target. For them, no Web-based enterprise management will be the salvation, and no ERP or CRM software will be the solution.

4.6 Bad News in I-Commerce: The Collapse of Dot.Coms

At the end of 1999, a good three months before the NASDAQ plunged from 5000 to 3000, a Wall Street analyst predicted that "Internet companies might be our Indonesia." The euphoria with start-ups that were long on red ink and short on profits was in his judgment a passing fancy. It could not last forever and eventually the bubble would burst. All bubbles have this nasty habit.

The facts of business life proved that this prophecy on forthcoming failures of Internet companies was right. According to a survey by Webmergers, in the first seven months of 2000, of 238 dot.com start-ups, 41 collapsed, 29 were sold in fire sales, and 83 withdrew their plans for initial public offerings (IPOs).[7] These companies knew many things, but not how to make money. As Internet stocks investors run for cover, the market for initial public offerings has all but dried up. By mid-2000, many of the once high-flyers of the New Economy had lost one half to two thirds of their capitalization.

This is clearly shown by the price-to-sales ratio of dot.coms. At the top of everybody's examples is Priceline.com, which between the end of March and mid-October 2000 saw its price-to-earnings ratio fall by a factor of 17.5 from 16.0 to 0.9. Amazon.com also lost a large portion of its capitalization, as its price-to-earnings ratio went from 11.6 to 3.5. "We love Amazon as consumers, we don't like it as investors," says James A. Hillary of Marsico's 21st Century Fund.[8]

By providing early cash for new ideas, investors had helped to power one of the most extraordinary flowerings of innovation in history. But when they turned away from funding money-losing start-ups, the then-prevailing market dynamics turned on its head. Take as an example StorageNetworks, which lost $23.9 million on sales of $3.9 million — a trivial amount. This data storage utility has been forced to lower its latest proposed offering price to well below its last-round valuation of $2 billion.

Even Amazon.com, the window display of the New Economy, ran up losses totaling $1.5 billion from its inception in 1994 to July 2000, and its stock fell some 70 percent from its all-time high. In contrast, some brick-and-mortar companies such as Wal-Mart performed well. They even started beating I-commerce companies at their own game, with multiple channels: stores, catalogs, and the Net (see Chapter 4.2).

Internet companies are not foolproof. They are fragile. In late September 2000, the warning by Priceline.com that third-quarter revenues would fall as much as 10 percent short of expectations sent its shares down nearly 45 percent. This dive in capitalization, shown on the left side of Exhibit 4.7, provides plenty of food for thought.

Of course, a rapidly falling share price because of bad news regarding earnings is not an exclusive feature of the New Economy. Kodak's shares also plummeted when the company announced that a weak euro, pricey raw materials, and high development costs all contributed to third-quarter 2000 revenues being down by as much as $300 million. Kodak's share value crashed (see right side of Exhibit 4.7).

What is special about New Economy companies is that the market mood can change very fast. One of the contributing factors to the demise of Priceline.com has been the dot.com jitters. Market psychology increased the blow to Priceline, and by extension to almost every other Internet company. This created a vicious cycle. Not only did it trigger big doubts about Priceline's core business, but it also raised questions about the company's ability to expand into broader markets.

As a litany of problems has hit the bellwether dot.coms, Priceline.com is by no means alone in its woes. Another Internet incubator, CMGI had less

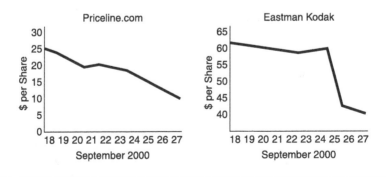

Exhibit 4.7   The Market Is Not Forgiving Poor Results from Old and New Economy Companies

than $100 million in revenues in 1998 when it embarked on a $13 billion acquisition binge. The acquisitions were mostly paid in stock, when its shares had a stellar performance. However, with its price down 90 percent from its peaks, CMGI's growth-through-acquisition strategy tanked.

What happens when dot.com start-ups run out of cash is dramatized by a case in the United Kingdom. On September 29, 2000, Powernet Telecom, the Internet company that had been valued at £100 million (U.S. $143 million) in the *Sunday Times'* Rich List for 2000, closed its doors on staff, telling them it could not pay their wages. Powernet management called in the police to escort angry staff off the premises and informed other staff by e-mail that they would not be paid. A second e-mail said that police would be called if any equipment left the building. The heart of the matter in this, as in so many other cases, has been that as market sentiment changed, dot.coms found it more difficult to justify their existence and some have been plainly incapable of managing themselves. As a result, they are going bust.

Since January 2000, more than three dozen Internet start-ups in the United States have shut their doors, and some 17,000 dot.commers have lost their jobs. A host of telecom companies missed their financial targets in 2000 because of overborrowing and overleveraging, a fact already brought to the reader's attention.

Is a dot.com's survivability assured if it has a rich parent from the Old Economy? The answer is not always positive. Much depends on the parent company, its willingness to continue financing as losses mount, and its strategic plans for the dot.com subsidiary. A growing number of brick-and-mortar companies are launching dot.coms by adopting a brick-and-click strategy.

Some experts believe that the expanding frontiers of Internet commerce are like the Gold Rush in nineteenth-century California. Setting up a domain and setting firewalls is like claiming a homestead that one surrounds with barbed wire. Despite cryptography and other devices used to increase security, the Internet has recently been exposed by events such as the denial-of-service attack that disabled Yahoo!, the breaking into of the highly secure Citibank database that siphoned out $24.5 million, and the troubles Microsoft faced in late October 2000.

By March 2001, after the market punished the technology, media, and telecommunications (TMT) sector for its excess valuation, some investment analysts suggested that their clients should begin to follow the new *B2B,* namely *back-to-basics*. Quality and consistency of earnings have again become the keys to successful portfolio performance. I think they should have always been that way.

The downturn in stock valuations also brought with it a downsizing of forecasts in terms of market penetration. Just prior to the NASDAQ meltdown of 2000, several analysts had projected that before this decade is over, 40 percent of business and 15 percent of retail trade will come from Internet-related services. By March 2001, even longtime I-commerce boosters were questioning such growth assumptions. They wondered if Internet commerce will capture more than 5 percent to 10 percent of all retailing revenue, not the 15 percent that was earlier expected.

Neither the euphoric figures of 1999 and early 2000 nor those pessimistic of late 2000 and early 2001, have any great substance in them. The downsizing reflects the fact that by early 2001 it became fashionable to view the on-line business-to-consumer market as a wreck. The *real wrecks,* however, are those companies that do not pay great attention to product appeal, quality of management, financial staying power, and organization. Good organization is a prerequisite to sound business.

Ultimately, as with all capital spending, the strength of technology investment depends on its contribution to the bottom line. In its fourth quarter 2000 earnings announcement, GE claimed it would generate $1.5 billion of operating margin benefit thanks to the Internet and digitization. With cost savings of that magnitude, technology investments do not look like a problem.

Notes

1. *Business Week,* September 11, 2000.
2. Monte Carlo, Monaco, March 30/31, 2000.
3. D.N. Chorafas, *Internet Supply Chain — Impact on Accounting and Logistics,* Macmillan, London, 2001.
4. D.N. Chorafas, *Reliable Financial Reporting and Internal Control: A Global Implementation Guide,* John Wiley, New York, 2000.
5. D.N. Chorafas, *Agent Technology Handbook,* McGraw-Hill, New York, 1998.
6. *BusinessWeek,* February 12, 2001.
7. *Business Week,* September 4, 2000.
8. *Business Week,* October 30, 2000.

Chapter 5

The Market Demand for Enterprise Resource Planning Software and Customer Relationship Management

In the late 1990s, the market for enterprise resource planning (ERP) software grew by more than 30 percent a year. Experts, however, expect the ERP market growth to fall to about 15 percent as its upper end becomes saturated. The slack will be taken by other products, such as customer relationship management (CRM) software (see Chapter 5.2), which is expected to boom over the coming years to $35 billion, representing about 30 percent of the total world market for programming products.

CRM programming products are part of what has become known as the Customer Service Level Requirements (CSLR) model, which is being refined for assemble-to-order manufacturing systems. This model interfaces to ERP, although it primarily addresses inventory policy in assemble-to-order environments. Analysts expect that CSLR will assist the functionality already established by other programming products such as ERP, helping to simplify more complex approaches to inventory control currently in use (see Chapter 5.4).

The fact that enterprise resource management systems extend their reach in two ways — toward a cost-efficient handling of inventories and an able management of the customer base — should be welcome from a functional angle. Both issues — customer handling and inventory control — are in the front-line, but the capable use of more sophisticated software demands integration over a broader range of technologies in addition to links to ERP systems.

The synergy between the more classical ERP, CRM, and inventory planning and control may not seem evident until one puts the entire issue into perspective. CRM deals with more issues in the front office than ERP. ERP, to a considerable extent, has targeted back-office chores, hence the need to scale up resources to handle a much larger user community by means of off-the-shelf programming products and to provide a central focus for the entire business that is integrated with the Internet-oriented supply chain and the use of smart materials.

A valid approach is to account *now* for new technical requirements expected in the near future. A case in point is mobile access to ERP systems such as the me-commerce chores examined in Chapter 4. If individual customers and the company's sales force can input an order straight into a mobile phone or other portable device, there is no re-keying to be done, and the error rate will be lower than current averages. Also, the order can activate other parts of the CRM/ERP/CSLR system, such as better-tuned inventory planning and supply chain management.

An evolving issue that the reader should take note of is the pluses and minuses associated with the use of the Wireless Application Protocol (WAP). WAP can check inventories and sales for a particular office or region by units or value, or it can compare historical data to current orders. WAP can help the sales force identify the most profitable customers, but thus far it has received mixed reactions. Therefore, both the business opportunity and the technical infrastructure must be studied.

In principle, mobile access can see to it that the benefits of a company's enterprise resource management software need not be restricted merely to people inside the office. Mobile executives can be given the opportunity to reach online decision support data; they can mine databases while in the field and also add to database content in a two-way communication. This extensibility of ERP functionality is the broader message this chapter brings to the reader.

5.1 New Facilities and Constraints Connected with Enterprise Resource Planning

To better appreciate the evolution of ERP software toward a more complex structure, one should return to the fundamentals. In theory — but only in theory — everything from customer orders to manufacturing schedules and inventory levels reside inside the ERP system and its databases. This is what user organizations hear from many vendors who present ERP as a state-of-the-art product with plenty to offer all its business customers, and as a way to make a quantum leap in the organization's internal information using nothing more than browser-based workstations.

In practice, however, things are a little different. True enough, salespeople can datamine to check production status or inventory level, inquire about deliveries, and handle orders directly. However, innovative companies have found that they need to extend their ERP applications to the Internet by means of Web-based enterprise management (see Chapter 3), making even small suppliers on the other side of the world their supply chain partners. As noted in the introductory part of this chapter, these innovative companies also need to add CRM functionality, inventory planning chores, and other routines promoting proactive participation on behalf of business partners. This has many analytical aspects, including:

- As global transactions get increasingly competitive, suppliers become responsible for monitoring their clients' inventory levels.
- When the client is running low on a given product, the supplier must be able to find it immediately and replenish the stock.

This type of application offers competitive advantages to business partners up and down the supply chain; it also poses important technical demands on ERP programming products. Greater security (see Chapter 4) and robustness are two examples of what ERP clients demand. Robustness requires that the system's architecture supports applications with potentially thousands of users and is able to process heavy transaction loads at any time, from any place.

Users also promote the choice of methods and tools that can easily integrate heterogeneous platforms while providing enough power and the appropriate enterprise services for the application environment of their firm. This is an important message for the developers of ERP software, if one keeps in mind that client demand accounts for 35 percent of the origin of new products and, as Exhibit 5.1 shows, this is by far the most critical factor in new software development.

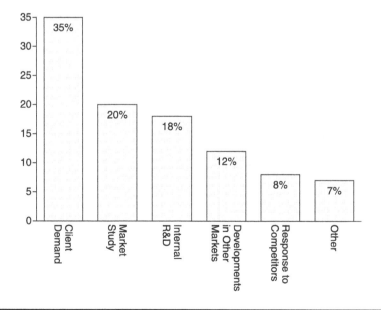

Exhibit 5.1   Origin of New Products in the Software Business

Typically, vendors who do not show sensitivity to customer requests, at any time, in any place they sell, are falling out of the market. Another technical issue vendors should watch for is that organizations want the ERP software to be efficient in session management, transaction services, message queuing, the monitoring of performance, and logging of system events. Provision must also be made for a directory of users and their roles, while the ERP system must be capable of integrating its services to third-party development environments. This includes the ability to handle multiple browsers, support the most popular programming languages, and make it possible to adapt to problems as they develop.

The deployment of an ERP technology that respects the outlined requirements allows a company to automate and integrate important analytical business processes to produce internal intelligence. Analytical business processes that deal with ERP and CRM data help in understanding one's own and one's customers' activity and behavior over time. As in Chapter 3, another piece of necessary software is one that can manage Web applications across multiple servers by simplifying the tasks involved in software scaling, deploying and managing distributed applications, and adding new services and servers that are operationally needed.

A distributed hardware/software environment has no single point of failure, and capacity can be added economically as needed. It also permits taking advantage of the Internet and using a Web-based business model. A job properly done would determine how our traditional business activity maps onto Internet commerce and would decide whether it makes sense to differentiate and customize to reach new customers and create new markets. ERP's role in this is to make transparent issues of schedules and costs, providing information on accuracy and flexibility in managing them. Modeling alternative or emerging Web strategies is crucial in handling the company transition into Internet commerce.

As the careful reader will recall, there is a distinction between the theoretical and practical services that ERP software offers. The reason for this distinction is that few companies have the technical expertise to face the list of requirements referred to in the foregoing paragraphs and turn enterprise resource planning into a competitive advantage. Along with security, this fact explains why only one out of five companies currently uses the full potential of ERP by making its information available to business partners. Exhibit 5.2 presents a three-way classification of open-door policies followed by many firms.

Some strategies, such as the open-door policy for ERP information followed by Cisco, proved to be shrewd and timely ones, but for various reasons it is not yet popular. While to the technologist an open-door ERP solution may sound wonderful, several constraints exist and, to a substantial extent, their origin is in management decisions. To be overcome, such constraints must be analyzed and addressed individually in an effective way.

Senior management may understand that an open-door policy offers value differentiation, but is concerned about confidentiality or proprietary information. The fact that security of networks and databases is not perfect plays a

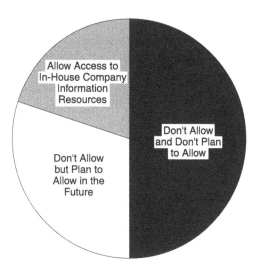

Exhibit 5.2 Statistics on Direct In-House ERM Access by Supply Chain Partners, on Cross-Company Basis

role in this reaction. On the technical side is the issue of communications bandwidth and database bandwidth, which can be a severe bottleneck.

Many companies do not have the network infrastructure to support the large number of customers and suppliers who can access their applications over the Web. Another part of the technological challenge involves connection capabilities, including native drivers; access to stored procedures and triggers; and the ability to create, modify, cancel, or maintain database tables, fields, and views. Still another reference is that of binding user interface(s) to dynamic applications requirements.

Because in the coming years Internet software will be used extensively for the Web range of enterprise resource planning (see Chapter 3), the system must provide support for both advanced HTML (e.g., Cascading Style Sheets, Script) as well as dynamic HTML and XML. The solution must also incorporate the ability to create sophisticated views such as master/detail and table views with grouping, sorting, restricting, and multimedia controls. These technically oriented references also apply to CRM software and other programming products.

5.2 Customer Relationship Management Software and Its Benefits

Internet commerce needs much more than internal data handling software that can be provided through the more classical ERP off-the-shelf packages. As explained in the introductory part of this chapter, an important add-on is the currently commercially available solutions for an effective CRM process. The sought-after goal is that of:

- Providing an effective front office like the customer
- Understanding the customer better than ever before
- Increasing the business the end user does with one's company

Chapter 3 provided plenty of evidence that to succeed in Internet commerce, one must be able to implement an increasingly more efficient solution to the management of one's customer base, integrating business processes and data streams, while improving the effectiveness with which one exploits such information. Like ERP, CRM is an off-the-shelf programming product.

CRM procedures are inseparable from those targeted by ERP. In a credit institution, for example, CRM addresses itself to the task of efficiently managing the front desk and its client relationship, while linking it to the back office and its operational processes. However, not all CRM packages are necessarily easy to use and effective in the functions they set out to perform.

A recent project rated five different packages in terms of cost versus what was perceived as basic functionality. The latter included ease of use, customer handling routines specific to the organization that did the test, ability to link to existing ERP applications, and several other factors. The sum of this rating was expressed in points, 15 points being the highest grade. Because costs matter, each CRM package was priced according to purchase cost and estimated implementation cost. As Exhibit 5.3 reveals, package II rated higher than its competitors, while its total cost was only a notch more than the lowest cost figure.

In this and many other evaluation projects that I have been exposed to, the mining of the customer base has also been kept in perspective. Issues closely associated with the customer base include marketing, sales, after-sales service, and a myriad of other activities, which together ensure steady client handholding. Moreover, because so many companies seek these same goals, an added value would aim to produce customer intelligence that can be effectively used in targeted marketing, and improve the analytics and thereby the decisions made in investing the company's resources in sales efforts.

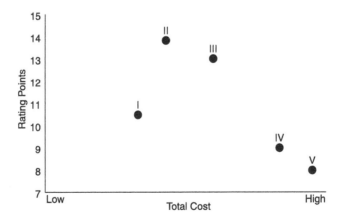

Exhibit 5.3   Rating of Five Different Off-the-Shelf Programming Products Versus Total Purchase and Implementation Costs

Companies that have adopted and that use CRM software have made one of their targets better marketing campaign management across all channels. They do so by using customer intelligence to personalize the marketing effort. Another target is to efficiently disseminate valuable customer intelligence to all people and systems that need it. This assists in optimizing the supply chain based on demand uncovered by measuring penetration and sales and evaluating margins and other management-defined criteria of performance.

CRM solutions, and therefore CRM software, should track both incoming and outgoing customer communications, flash-out types of customer-initiated events, and register direct and indirect responses to business. Communication must be managed in a way that can effectively exploit business opportunities and provide a selective approach to channel integration.

Essentially what is sought after through a CRM solution is the ability to incrementally increase customer account visibility, linking front-desk transactions with back-office ERP information and its supporting software, as well as with legacy transaction processing. This must be done in a way that allows one to get the most out of the supply chain. Such approaches can be instrumental in closing the intelligence gap that exists today in most firms.

One of the persistent remarks made in the course of my research has been that a valid solution will be one that can be effectively implemented in a polyvalent way, in the sense of person-to-person, system-to-system, person-to-system, and system-to-person communications. A flexible approach will also observe the requirements posed by evolving technologies, the management of Internet business operations, and the handling of personalized customer relationships.

The reason for including analytical business processes, as suggested in Chapter 5.1, is found in the need for carefully evaluating messages snowed under heavy data streams. Analyses permit a better understanding of business partner activity and of behavior over time. They also make it possible to evaluate the effectiveness of operational processes such as marketing and service support, enabling a company to move toward personalizing products by promoting customer value and loyalty.

There are, of course, obstacles to this type of sophisticated implementation, including the fact that CRM's integration with ERP software presents problems of heterogeneity. More difficulties are present when integrating CRM software with legacy systems. The problems typically encountered include:

- Complexities in achieving a single customer view
- Issues of data quality and data format
- Multiple incompatible sources for the same data and what to do about the differences
- Often misaligned windows of timing and data availability
- The lack of a methodology for a common approach to design for all data feeds

One of the emerging solutions is that of an *information portal* making it feasible to subscribe, access, publish, and understand business information that is, in principle, of heterogeneous background. This portal is supposed to act as a single user interface to all information and applications as well as to business intelligence tools and analytics.

Undoubtedly, there is merit in this type of seamless access to incompatible data structures, and benefits can go beyond a company extending to its business partners. Allowing customers and suppliers to subscribe to information about products and services, and to make use of a collaborative approach to transact business, is a process that has both direct and indirect advantages. As discussed in Chapter 5.4, however, cultural issues sometimes work against such approaches.

5.3   Repairing the Damage of Disconnects by Paying Greater Attention to Detail

Dr. Henry Kaufman aptly remarks that there are "a growing number of disconnects in our personal relationships, these feelings of disconnect and restlessness are driven to an important extent by the rapidity of change and by a kind of depersonalization that envelopes aspects of our lives."[1] One example is the depersonalization of relations between lenders and borrowers through securitization. Another is the depersonalization of relations between portfolio managers and investors through mutual funds. Outsourcing, too, is a case of depersonalization of relationships, and the same is evidently true in connection with the Internet supply chain.

It may sound ludicrous, but in reality the Internet supply line contributes to disconnects and their frequency. Even the different types of business alliances do not work as expected in terms of handholding. What has become apparent over the last two years is an increasing realization that the global alliances simply are not delivering what was initially expected from them.

To start with, in some sectors of the economy, financial results have been disappointing: Profitability or even breakeven has been difficult (or impossible) to achieve in a number of business alliances, while information technology has presented its own challenges. For example, seamless joining together of networks and back-office systems has been incredibly tough.

Some of the participants in this research suggested that even when technical problems were overcome, conflicting objectives and diverse corporate cultures resulted in unstable conditions. Among telecommunications alliances, for example, Unisource fell apart, Concert continues to disappoint, and Global One has undergone traumatic change.

Similar problems have been experienced by other alliances and joint ventures formed to exploit the opening up of individual national markets. In my opinion, the No. 1 reason for this shortfall is that the CEOs who forged these business alliances did not pay enough attention to detail, nor did they study ahead of time the likely aftermath.

Can the implementation of CRM and ERP software improve the basis of intercompany collaboration? The answer is *maybe* if, and only if, companies try hard. This response will become more positive if one truly understands the customer's call for value in our wares, and one is able to withstand commercial pressure to implement a solution able to manage customer relationships through any and all of the channels created by alliance. This calls for integrating business processes and data streams to increase their effectiveness, and using ERP and CRM to efficiently manage both front- and back-office operational processes.

Paying attention to detail in all matters associated with the customer and his or her business is in no way synonymous with automating marketing through networks and computers. Using customer intelligence to personalize the campaigns is a commendable enterprise, but it is not everything.

A precondition in paying attention to detail is that one understands the application, both in its breadth and in its depth. Companies are right when they buy off-the-shelf ERP and CRM programming products rather than reinventing the wheel. Where they are wrong is that they often think that buying a new piece of software is enough to solve their problem(s). This is not so. Quality of service (QOS) is an example. This is often considered just an engineering and management problem. In reality, QOS represents a complex interplay of three mutually dependent variables: (1) engineering, (2) economics, and (3) customer psychology.

Understanding the interplay between these three variables is critical because QOS is a major differentiator that must be accounted for both in sales activity and in billing for services. The definition of service quality must be broad enough to encompass the needs of all stakeholders — and customers are at top of this list (see also Chapter 12 on General Electric's Six Sigma).

A company's own client contact personnel, manufacturing personnel, and engineering designers are essentially intermediate customers of various support services that the company provides, such as information technology. Experience shows that in the last analysis, intermediate service quality problems result in problems at the business level, affecting one's clients and the relationship one has with them.

Exhibit 5.4 brings to the reader's attention the fact that as far as QOS is concerned, one must watch out for many variables at the same time, and many of them must be controlled in detail. That is what companies that buy ERP and CRM software *hope* to get. What they do not understand is that the deliverables are much more a matter of organizational work and of training than of bought programming products.

The reader should also appreciate that the variables entering into ERP and CRM implementation, and their nature, can overlap considerably. As a result, what impacts one of them will in many cases impact others as well. A wanting infrastructure quality will likely cause problems with data and service quality. The same is true of software quality; hence the interest in choosing the best-suited ERP and CRM solutions. Both individual components of quality and the big picture should be addressed. The solution one chooses must provide an integrated and detailed perspective for managing quality in key processes, products, and services.

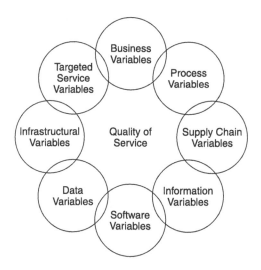

Exhibit 5.4   Quality of Service Depends on Several Variables that Interact with One Another

One should not forget the administrative component of quality of service, nor the environmental influences on quality. A good solution often requires combining the services rendered by two or more software packages. As already mentioned, a traditional project management tool such as Critical Path Method (CPM) must be beefed-up by new project management software — where ERP pays a key role — and by CAD-based engineering tools.

Tools able to address problems stemming from complexity are necessary to allow engineering managers and project leaders to model parallel tasks as well as interdependent activities that, way down the process, may impact upon one another. One of the critiques that applies equally to CRM and ERP is that they do not include innovative model-based methods for managing complex projects. This lack of appropriate support does not allow one to understand interdependent relationships among people and the tasks they are performing; nor does it allow one to break down finish/start barriers between activities in the project.

To my knowledge, there is no off-the-shelf software that allows one to better manage distributed teams than what is available. Yet, if properly used, such software allows one to accelerate tasks that are critically coupled and coordinate others that cut across departmental lines. Beyond current ERP and CRM releases is support for jobs that are nominally parallel or can become parallel as customer requirements and company product designs change.

5.4   The Impact of Management Culture on ERP, Security, and Customization

Nobody would dispute that technology has a dramatic impact on competitiveness in a variety of industrial sectors. Many investors are concerned about the devastating effects the Internet may have on brick-and-mortar retailers, and these retailers themselves see the point and convert to brick-and-click. They are on the Internet although they still trade through their classical outlets. Some traditional brick-and-mortar retailers are actually reaping significant benefits from the Internet as they use it to reach additional customers and extend their product line to capitalize from digitization. Correctly, they see the Internet as the backbone of greater service trade. Companies that are able to use the Web for a number of different applications, and in ways that further reduce their cost structures and increase their opportunities, reap significant advantages. For example, Oracle says that it uses the Net to strip out $1 billion in costs.

It looks as if one is forcing open doors by bringing these points into perspective about the Internet, CRM, and ERP. But one should not forget that the reason for poor utilization — indeed, the most important constraint to the able use of enterprise resource planning software and of the Net at large — is cultural, leading to conditions that are difficult to change. Chapter 5.1 brought attention to the fact that the sharing of ERP information over the Net is not universal. Few companies are accustomed to trusting their business partners with intimate information, and many fear that information-sharing can turn into a competitive disadvantage to their disfavor.

At the top of the list of management fears is the issue of control, or the lack thereof. True enough, by placing strategic data, such as financial reports and manufacturing schedules, online, companies open themselves to security breaches. However, able management would examine both sides of the open access issue: how much the company might lose and how much it might gain by doing so.

For this reason, companies must define *a priori* what information will and will not be communicated to business partners. One way to improve the privacy of a company's proprietary data is to ensure that business partners on the Net sign nondisclosure agreements to reduce the chance of information falling into competitors' hands. At the same time, only select individuals within a business partner's organization should have access to confidential information of other companies in the supply chain, and these people should be equipped with passwords and sign-ons.

Another strategy that improves upon security and confidentiality of information is to thoroughly review the nodes and links of the integrated procurement solution one has put in place. Exhibit 5.5 shows a typical Internet procurement solution and its component parts.

- The weakest link, both in efficiency and in security, is the array of incompatible legacy subsystems at the bottom of the interconnect layer.
- Management is right to be concerned about security when this situation is allowed to persist, but it cannot complain about security and keep this mismatch in place at the same time.

Because of cultural reasons that inhibit an industrial or financial organization from capitalizing on the best technology can offer, the real divide between

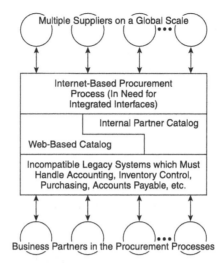

Exhibit 5.5   Integrated Procurement Solutions Are in Great Need of Analytical Approaches Regarding Security and Protection of Privacy

those who are prepared to capitalize on the Internet and those who are not occurs not between companies and consumers, but between the companies themselves. In addition to the question of openness and efficiency, there is also one of skills (see Chapter 3), costs, and of the necessary change in management culture.

Large firms can afford the high fixed costs of persistent, high-speed connections to the Internet by means of their private network, which they endeavor to make increasingly secure. Smaller firms cannot afford such expenditures. They typically have access to the Internet through dial-up lines and their approach to security is rather bare boned.

From both an efficiency and security viewpoint, the leading thought among experts is that until small businesses get high-speed connections at affordable prices, they simply will not be equal players in the I-commerce revolution that is transforming larger companies. Part and parcel of this drive is that products increasingly need to be personalized for each customer, while sales campaigns get sharper. Packaged-good companies and supermarket chains, for example, now target individual shoppers:

- The amount of discounts on each product can be varied according to how much it attracts customers.
- Design characteristics can be adapted to meet a local need, or to start a new market demand.

Neither ERP nor CRM provide direct assistance to this personalization function, although both give a helping hand indirectly. CRM can contribute important customer behavior patterns and product choices, and ERP can provide information on internal processes that necessarily need to be involved in the customization effort.

Also keep in mind that the drive to customization is part of management culture, and, as such, it is forcing a fundamental rethinking about what a company is and does. For example, the new breed of virtual companies avoids building expensive in-house capabilities. Instead, it focuses on partnerships that get together for a new project.

As Chapter 5.3 indicated, software functionality beyond ERP and CRM is necessary because whether the object of customization is consumers or other companies in the supply line (some of which are competitors), the client is becoming the center of the design, manufacturing, and marketing universe. This policy sees to it that design and marketing challenges that lie ahead are daunting. To become customer-centric on the Internet, companies must:

- Perform a complex transformation of their way of working
- Exploit direct links between customers and factories, tailoring products the way each customer wants them

In the motor vehicle industry, for example, the customer is now able to "design" an auto on a CAD machine in the showroom. In just a short time, that customer is able to configure the vehicle over the Internet and get possession of the car within a few days. This is not doable without both CAD software and strong ERP support. Today, it takes weeks to get a customized car because assembly lines are geared to turning out standard autos — as well, there are also cultural barriers to change.

There is precedence to both design flexibility and fast deployment initiatives. The five-day car is a revolutionary concept pioneered by Toyota in the mid-1990s. Toyota envisioned an approach through which customers would pick and choose from a menu of screen options, and then hit a button to send the order straight to the factory. (Toyota has been equipping showrooms in Japan with CAD terminals since 1995.)

Note that manufacturers are not offering customized products through push-button solutions just to make customers happier. They also want bottom-line savings that companies such as Cisco and Dell have achieved. In the auto industry, mass-produced cars sitting for weeks in dealer lots represent a huge investment that yields no return until they are sold. This has been the classical management culture of motor vehicle companies, a culture that the more clear-eyed firms now want to change.

5.5 The Trimming of Inventories Can Be Greatly Assisted by Smart Materials

Auto industry experts venture the opinion that shifting from mass production to direct factory sales can slash car prices by up to 30 percent because trimming inventories would take a lot of cost out of the system. Direct factory sales and fast flow replenishment, however, do require moving at Internet speed in the back end of the business: motor vehicle design, procurement, and assembly affecting both parts and materials suppliers.[2]

Perceptive readers will recognize, between the lines of this statement, that their companies and their suppliers will be out of luck without new, more sophisticated types of software; this means systems that are able to boost manufacturing efficiency and squeeze inventories without running out of product. That is the meaning of keeping up optimization chores at the pace of Internet time.

To appreciate the sense of this reference to real-time optimization and immediate corrective action, one should recall that, to a very large measure, inventories are buffers enabling a smoother production process despite changes in supply and demand. Inventories include final products, intermediate products at the assembly and component levels, as well as raw materials. Typically, currently held inventories relate to different stages of the production process and they can only be optimized in conjunction with production and sales, not independently of them.

Changes in inventories reflect differences between actual and expected demand on one side and production capability on the other. In the short term, the desired stock-to-sales ratio can be assumed to be fairly constant; but in the medium term, it can be affected by volatility in sales, manufacturing, and general logistics. Many ERP packages are wanting in terms of inventory optimization.

Just-in-time (JIT) production and deliveries based on fast flow replenishment (FFR) cause changes in the stock-to-sales ratio. Inventory tightening is reflected not only in income statements, but also in national accounts statistics, including those of finished products, goods for resale, raw materials, and work in progress.

While there are agricultural inventories as well as stocks of precious metals and art objects, the manufacturing and merchandising trades account for the bulk of nationally reported inventories. Macroeconomic statistics from euroland in the 1993 to 1999 timeframe are shown in Exhibit 5.6.

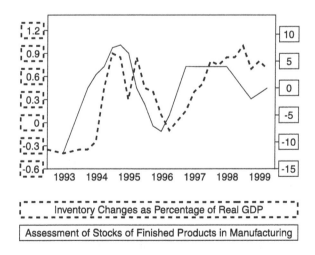

Exhibit 5.6   Inventory Statistics from Euroland: Changes in Inventory and the Assessment of Stocks

It is interesting to note that at the microeconomic level, until the 1950s, no one really worried excessively about production inventories, except maybe during annual stocktaking. Improvements to machining, presswork, assembly, and finishing were piecemeal up until that time period, hence intermediate banks of goods were necessary. But above all, there were no means to measure exactly inventory levels and ongoing demand.

Computers changed that culture. The 1960s were a period of transition, and many experts believe it was the reality of Japanese competition in the early 1970s that spurred, for example, Western car and truck plants to take seriously and examine in greater detail production economics and logistics. Competition drove tooling, presswork, machining, welding, and assembly line technology into higher productivity levels. But the really visible aftermath of competition, computers, and models has been in inventory planning and control and the resulting economies.

Theoretically, inventories are viewed as the moving gear of the global supply chain, highly influenced by B2B and B2C marketing. Practically, however, Exhibit 5.6 proves that this is not the case, at least in euroland. During the 1990s, inventories were at their lowest in 1993 when there was no Internet around and very little ERP. The lesson is that improvements upon current methods call not only for catchwords, but also for a quantum leap in inventory management — from smart production processing identification during manufacturing to systems using smart materials technology, able to monitor the goods flow (see Chapters 8 and 9).

Such monitoring must be accomplished in real-time, with high levels of accuracy at every node, linking the information system of the supply chain. As discussed in Section II, smart materials provide a mechanism that promotes inventory identification, and hence accuracy, at a higher level of confidence. It can also aid in detection of theft and pilferage while informing on procurement needs. *If* materials identification is timely and accurate, *then* a sophisticated model for inventory management can specify a customer service level as percentage of orders filled. This can be accomplished within a target lead-time, rather than by resorting to a penalty cost for orders not filled in time. With this and similar models for effective inventory planning and control, sound management must specify that 90, 95, or 99 percent of all orders need to be filled on time — which essentially means at the 90-, 95-, or 99-percent level of confidence, respectively. The concept of confidence intervals is illustrated in Exhibit 5.7: an example from market risk management.

In Exhibit 5.7, the ordinate is market exposure assumed by a given entity because of interest rate risk embedded in debt securities in its portfolio. The abscissa is the maturity of these securities up to ten years. A similar concept can be used with inventories. Algorithms and heuristics must be applied to optimize inventory levels to meet the specified service with the least inventory cost. These should be included in ERP software, but currently they are not part of it.

Next to the ability to define the level of confidence at which one manages inventory is the need to create a higher-up level of metadata; this is very

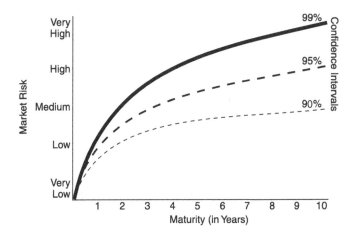

Exhibit 5.7   An Example from Market Risk Management: Assumed Risk at Three Levels of Confidence

helpful in the implementation of enterprise resource planning. Few organizations, however, have done the preliminary work or put in place incentives to acquire and apply the appropriate skills necessary to generate and handle metadata (e.g., dynamic directories). (More about this in Chapter 7.)

The benefits to be derived from adoption of ERP, CRM, and other programming products in conjunction with Web-based solutions depend on many factors that are partly within and partly outside a company's control. These factors include the development of cost-effective technology and applications that allow enterprises to adopt online business solutions as well as:

- Availability of new technology standards facilitating easier integration of multiple vendors' wares and applications
- Performance and reliability of the Internet connection as online usage grows
- Better approaches to security and authentication concerns regarding transmission of confidential information over the Net
- Laws that penalize attempts by unauthorized users, or hackers, to penetrate online security systems

In 2000, there were voices suggesting that use of the Internet might decline if gathering of information about I-commerce users, without their knowledge or consent, would result in increased concerns about privacy. The opposite view is that too much concern over privacy can lead to federal and state governments adopting restrictive laws or regulations relating to the Internet.

Legislation regarding privacy and security is an exogenous factor. An endogenous factor is potential bottlenecks because of the inability of companies to attack the limitations of their legacy systems and processes. This results in the sub-utilization of enterprise resource management solutions and the inability to meet forecasts about rewards from enterprise resource planning systems, customer relationship management software, and supply chain management systems (SCM).

Because they still work with Paleolithic IT, some companies find it difficult to answer, in a factual and documented manner, *when* and *how* questions associated with implementing enterprisewide solutions. Another reason is that the infrastructure of many firms was designed for brick-and-mortar operations — not for Internet commerce. As business transactions are increasingly conducted electronically, the weaknesses of Old Economy structures become bottlenecks. It is no less true that not all companies are agile in making return on investment (ROI) studies, and this limits the clarity of their choice among alternatives.

5.6 Return on Investment, Penalty Cost, and Enterprise Resource Planning

In mid-2000, a research project found that 80 percent of companies could not compute the total cost of ownership for their ERP solutions.[3] Another project surveyed 36 different ERP implementations and the majority admitted they had done a very poor job of mapping out and tracking what really happened in their organization; hence, they obtained precious little out of implementing ERP software.

When this type of mismanagement happens, the fault is not with the programming product itself and its developers, but with the company employing it. To provide themselves with a gauge, even to push themselves toward a more rational course of action, some firms use the penalty-cost model. They program a penalty cost for lost sales, out-of-stock, customer dissatisfaction, etc. into their ERP and use simulation to experiment in order to achieve a better balance — if not ideal inventory levels associated with that penalty.

Some manufacturing concerns that rely on commercial ERP software have a built-in inventory function that incorporates such a penalty-cost algorithm. Their experience has been that the higher the penalty cost they assign to a particular inventory failing (e.g., component stock out), the less likely such events will occur and the better the customer service level.

Other companies, however, feel that this analytical approach is not precise and direct enough to address customer service level requirements. They think that while qualitatively the relationship between penalty cost and service level is more or less obvious, quantitatively they do not know how well their customers are served at a given penalty cost. Also, while one can estimate things such as inventory holding costs, it is difficult to guestimate the penalties in a reliable way.

The pros of the penalty cost method think that their approach can be applied in several domains where ERP is of service (e.g., administrative costs). The principle is that inadequate information systems are a prime reason why administrative costs account for an estimated 15 to 25 percent of total spending in business activities — a share that, curiously enough, has been little affected by computers.

The inadequacy of legacy software in handling administrative chores is a basic reason why ERP and the Internet have a significant potential to trim costs of trivia and administrative duties, transforming current practice in the industry. Companies that have used, in an able manner, Web-based approaches in conjunction with ERP have found they can strengthen the foundation of greater efficiency. This is good news for companies that care about return on investment. Economies of scale is one of the foundations to which I make reference. They are best obtained not from a single very big unit that has plenty of inefficiencies, but from a distributed environment in which costs are trimmed in many units, and these units are made to move in synergy. Basically, this ERP-and-Internet engineered efficiency depends on:

- Providing reliable information to all players
- Supplying the entire chain — businesses, consumers, and providers — with timely data
- Making more learned decisions on a timely and documented basis, through experimentation

Armed with accurate knowledge about alternatives and options, managers can become more competitive. For smaller businesses, the Internet is also providing ways to enjoy thus-far unavailable economies of scale by outsourcing core administrative tasks such as billing, accounts receivable, tax advice, financial management, and information processing, as well as purchasing supplies through specialized intermediaries and exchanges on the Web.

Another criterion that can be used to judge the aftermath of implementing Web-based and ERP software is *productivity*. Productivity is the amount of output produced per unit of input. It is an easy concept to define, but it is very difficult to measure because of two elusive aspects of productivity that defy precise measurement: input and output.

With regard to input, most productivity metrics are usually oriented around counting things such as the number of employees, tons of steel, number of PCs, or checks being processed. If computers are used to produce more of the same product at lower costs, such metrics work. However, when targeting innovation and competitive advantages, rather than simply cutting costs, the old metrics break down.

In a modern economy, output should include not only the number of units coming out of a factory, or of an office, but also the value that has been created. *Value* increasingly depends on factors other than just the number of units; for example, product quality, customization, innovation, time to market, and other intangibles. These are, in large measure, intangibles not handled through ERP and CRM, yet they are vital to management decisions.

Productivity measures are often biased when management fails to appreciate that hardware and software are only two components of a major technology investment. There are also expenditures on training, organizational changes, reengineering, process redesign, etc. In other words, while computers contribute to increased output, the rate of return on technology investments is not linear. One must be very careful with the targets one sets, the metrics one uses, and the conclusions to which one arrives.

Notes

1. Henry Kaufman, *On Money and Markets: A Wall Street Memoir,* McGraw-Hill, New York, 2000.
2. D.N. Chorafas, *Internet Supply Chain — Impact on Accounting and Logistics,* Macmillan, London, 2001.
3. *Financial Times,* July 20, 2000.

Chapter 6

The Supply Chain of ERP Programming Products

To develop effective solutions in complex problem-solving and achieve high-performance system design, one must begin to see interrelationships rather than simply cause-and-effect chains. One must also look for processes of change rather than snapshots. For this reason, while this chapter starts with snapshots for the sake of clarity, it proceeds with interrelationships whose appreciation, in the longer run, will be more beneficial to the reader.

As far as I know, the first users of off-the-shelf ERP software were companies with more than 1000 employees. However, during the past five years, this changed to include companies with less than 100 employees and annual budgets of a few million dollars. What is more, during the 1997 to 2000 timeframe, the area covered by ERP solutions has rapidly increased.

Based on American statistics from six different industry sectors, Exhibit 6.1 presents the ERP implementation trend from 1997 to 2000. On average, ERP implementation in European countries follows a similar trend, but it is not equal in the various countries. Off-the-shelf software penetration is much higher in the Scandinavian nations and in Holland than in Spain or Italy. Statistics also demonstrate that the extent of ERP applications is uneven.

Information from European research projects that focused on ERP among user organizations indicates that the popularity of different key suppliers of ERP software varies. European statistics are shown in Exhibit 6.2, and global market estimates are shown in Exhibit 6.3. The careful reader will notice that a large chunk of the market is held by companies with 1 percent or less of market share, but together they account for 30 percent. In terms of implementation, in the general case, approximately 66 percent of user organizations tend to employ the entire functionality of ERP, while 33 percent use only selected routines, most frequently financial accounting.

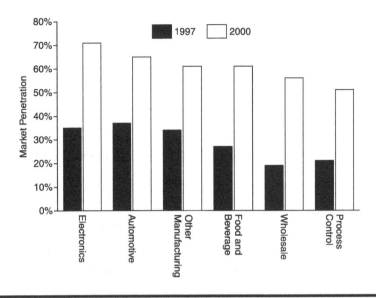

Exhibit 6.1   The Penetration of ERP Software in Important Industry Sectors from 1997 to 2000

Companies that limit themselves to "this" routine or "that" routine out of the package more or less forego one of ERP's main strengths: its assistance in integrating several functional areas. This works to their disadvantage because, everything counted, the most significant contribution of ERP is that it frees human resources that can be used to support killer applications (see Chapter 2).

Another error made by some companies in their strategy with commodity programming products is that they have opted for multi-sourcing ERP software. Subsequently, they have found difficulties in integrating routines from different vendors — particularly so when they target the Internet supply chain and therefore need to effectively communicate with clients and suppliers.

This problem of ERP integration with Web-enabled routines (as discussed in Chapter 3) is present both with intranets and with extranets. The more that Internet-oriented supply chain solutions are adopted, the more ERP multi-sourcing

Exhibit 6.2   ERP Software Vendors and Market Share in the European Landscape

Vendor	Market Share (%)
SAP R/2, R/3	28
Oracle applications	20
Baan	10
J.D. Edwards	7
PeopleSoftware	5
Other vendors	30

Note: Market share statistics are quite different in America and worldwide. For global statistics, see Exhibit 6.3.

Exhibit 6.3   ERP Software Vendors and Market Share in the Worldwide Market

Vendor	Market Share (%)
SAP R/2, R/3	25
Oracle applications	20
People Software	12
J.D. Edwards	8
Baan	4
QAD	2
Epicor	2
Mapics	1
Fourth Shift	1
Infinium software	1
Other vendors	24

increases the challenges connected to supply chain management. Passthrough features therefore become necessary, and seamless integration with Web programming products may be a good approach to a solution addressing problems due to heterogeneity of platforms.

6.1   Value-Added Solutions Improve the Benefits from ERP Software

ERP software comes from such vendors as SAP, Oracle, J.D. Edwards, PeopleSoftware, and Baan, as noted in the introduction to this chapter. Companies go for ERP programming products because it has been found that they are instrumental in tying factory operations to other corporate functions such as purchasing and inventory management. As with most computer operations, the goal is better coordination of internal functions. Whether or not this is being achieved, however, is a different matter.

User organizations that wish to be ahead of the curve are not necessarily satisfied with the current supply chain of ERP software. They do not fail to connect with their vendor(s); but neither are they satisfied with what they get. Here, in a nutshell, is a scenario of what they would like to obtain.

The good news first, starting with the statement that ERP's supply chain applications have enlarged the concept of off-the-shelf routines to include both internal and external functions. For example, having parts ordered for just-in-time delivery, which is not necessarily part of most ERP routines, bridges the gap between ordering, production scheduling, and inventory control. The ideal would have been a manufacturing execution system that reaches the vendor's ERP online, coordinating shop-floor operations between vendor and client, and providing a real-time picture of how the plants are running on both sides of the partnership.

Another improvement to current packages would be the incorporation of autonomous knowledge artifacts. If a problem arises, agents under a knowledge-enriched planning system would analyze its impact. Then they would modify production schedules to make the best use of whatever resources are available at that very moment to meet established plans.

Is there an example of a real-life application of this value-added solution? Sure there is, but not with programming products off-the-shelf. Cisco has one; it is an in-house development that built upon the facilities supported by ERP programming products and significantly extended their functionality.

Other companies also have done add-ons. The message from this value differentiation effort is that both the more sophisticated approaches and their ingenious usage are a level above what is offered off-the-shelf. This does not mean that commodity ERP software is useless. Quite the contrary, it will be crucial to handling tomorrow's steady stream of custom orders from the Internet. However, the customer must take the initiative for further advances, until the vendors come up from under. Typically, each option will have trade-offs that make one approach more desirable (or more comprehensive) than the other. An advanced solution today is the use of system dynamic technologies to create new approaches that are easier to integrate and have minimum side effects.

Further advances are largely based on cross-fertilization among different skills. J.D. Edwards teamed up with Camstar Systems, which specializes in manufacturing execution routines, to help Lexmark International slash production cycles for computer printers by 90 percent. A printer that previously took four hours to assemble now gets made in Internet time: 24 minutes.

No matter what the tool's origin, wise management put its attention on ease of use, simplicity of training, functional capabilities, and on ways to enhance them. The goal is to implement the best available tools to create virtual enterprises, with online links that span the entire design, manufacturing, and delivery chain. As far as human resources are concerned, a good test for a new tool, or off-the-shelf programming product, is the *learning curve* shown in Exhibit 6.4. In principle, no two ERP commodity software offerings have the same learning curve. Differences exist because of the way an implementation is made, the skill of the people doing it, and other factors.

Diversity among suppliers increases the time needed to reach a level of comfort with the new software. If a company can coax its suppliers into a streamlined implementation environment, the learning curve would be compressed. With this, even the most traditional firms could soon be exploring new realms that give them an edge on the competition. Many experts look at the broadening of ERP functionality from the angle of its ability to bring about seamless integration of all vital data streams that flow through a company, including financial, manufacturing, supplier, and customer information.

Cornerstone to a successful approach along this line of reference is the word *seamless*. For more than two decades, since deregulation unleashed fierce competition, large companies have struggled to blend incompatible

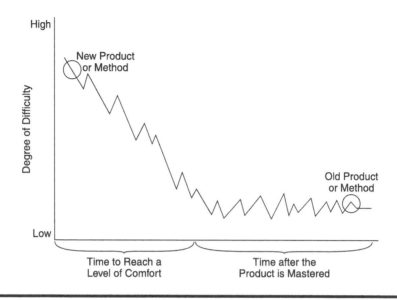

Exhibit 6.4   A Learning Curve Identifies the Level of User Difficulty with New Methods, Packages, and Tools

systems into a workable whole, while spending large amounts of money on custom-made software that frequently failed to deliver what was expected of it.

The difference now is that a new generation of applications software comes off-the-shelf, and it covers many of the basic functions of the procurement–manufacturing–inventory delivery cycle. Examples other than ERP and CRM include Microsoft's Exchange Server 2000 and BizTalk Server 2000, which provide a bridge between applications that may run within, or across, organizational limits.

Exchange 2000 Server is the most recent version of Microsoft's messaging and collaboration server. It provides a single infrastructure for working with messages, documents, and applications to increase productivity of knowledge workers. BizTalk Server provides for a document routing, transformation, and tracking, and is designed to enable companies to integrate and manage business processes by exchanging documents such as purchase orders and invoices.

By sensing current and upcoming business opportunities, vendors increase the breadth and scope of their offerings; still for competitive reasons a company needs sophisticated software add-ons, particularly modules with knowledge engineering characteristics and integrative capability. The strategy underlying this statement is illustrated in Exhibit 6.5.

Many experts put on the negative side of ERP's balance sheet not the lack of advanced type modules that address specific knowledge-intensive needs in management information, but the fact that the successful introduction of off-the-shelf routines may require an inordinate amount of time, skill, and effort — along the line of the learning curve discussed at the beginning of this chapter section.

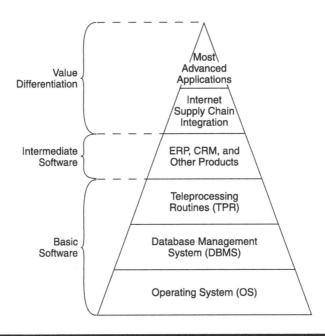

Exhibit 6.5   A Wise Strategy Would Be to Buy Off-the-Shelf Basic and Intermediate Software, but Provide In-House Value Differentiation

True enough, the downside with any software package is that it can require many months — sometimes years — to implement in full. When this happens, it winds up costing several times more than bought software because of the needed amount of corporate reengineering. As Chapter 2 explained, corporate reengineering is the price of entry to the new IT world with its integrative real-time culture. However, ERP does not always require an inordinate amount of time, skill, and effort unless its implementation is inept. The better organized the company is when it buys the ERP programming products, the less will be the preparatory investment. And the wiser the management of the firm, the more it will use this preparation as an opportunity to revamp and restructure.

Plenty of examples point in this direction and help to identify the benefits derived from preparing for the use of ERP products in a consistent, purposeful way. For instance, to get ready for the new solution that liberates it from old data processing chores, Asea Brown Boveri (ABB) has divided its entire purchasing process into the following discrete activities:

- Negotiating with suppliers
- Updating the database
- Issuing purchase orders
- Handling complaints, etc.

It also divided its engineering activities into well-defined functions, and did the same for marketing as well as for finance. This revamping allowed for doing away with overlaps in authority and responsibility between different departments, identified the best links for information transfer, and streamlined management's accountability.

The implementation timetable, however, does pose some questions. To make the new system work, ABB spent three years rethinking its business, rather than turning the entire IT process over to programmers. This decision was sound? Three years is an eon in technology.

The good news is that, once applied, the new ERP solution saw to it that it serves top-management business strategy rather than restricting itself to a lower management profile. Indeed, as I never tire repeating, this cultural change is the top benefit companies receive from enterprise resource planning, customer relationship management, exchange servers, and the other products reviewed in this chapter.

6.2   Implementing the Concept of an Open Vendor Policy with CRM

For starters, an open vendor policy implies that the company is not tied up to any one vendor. It deals with all of them on its own terms — not the vendors' terms; and it knows how to coordinate and manage a multi-supplier relationship. This is not easy, but it is doable and practical — provided that the company has developed and uses an open business architecture and that it builds intelligent interfaces between wares.

Since the mid-1980s when the concept was first developed, an open architecture has been given a variety of definitions, with many manufacturers claiming that their solution is "the only valid one." But at the bottomline, the true meaning of an open architecture is that of an open interface able to integrate the company's business functions among themselves and with those of its clients. The result of an open business architecture is that it leads to better choices in wares, greater cost-effectiveness, and wider competition among suppliers.

In its fundamentals, the business architecture is the study of structure in its broad outlines, generalizable beyond individual platforms. A promising approach to an architectural study that helps open hardware and software options is based on the topology of system components, their characteristics and basic software under which they run individually and with respect to each other, and their ability to share information with other systems and devices of different design.

All these issues have attendant benefits and implications. One of the benefits is that of actively participating in and gaining from the dramatic changes being witnessed in information processing and communications. Developments characterizing procurement strategies can be essentially grouped into four epochs:

1. Single vendor, single machine (1960s)
2. Single vendor, multiple computers (1970s)
3. Multiple vendors, multiple computers (1980s)
4. Open vendor policy for all wares (1990s)

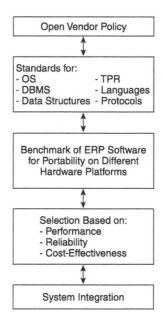

Exhibit 6.6   An Open Vendor Policy Rests on Standards and It Calls for Program Portability and System Integration

As Exhibit 6.6 suggests, an open vendor policy is based on standards, some of them *de facto*. Metrics are also necessary for benchmarking enterprise resource management and other programming products. In the context of an open vendor policy, these benchmarks are made in regard to their portability on different hardware platforms and the relative ease of implementation and utilization.

The platforms supported by the open architecture will be doing the collecting, storing, retrieving, processing, transforming, and displaying of data. This entire system must be studied for reliability and sustainability, and also for cost-effectiveness versus alternative solutions. The concepts underpinning the processing of information are not significantly different from any other production system and could be analyzed in the same manner if information is viewed and treated as a commodity — which is indeed the case.

When in terms of procurement, reference is made to alternative sources of supply of programming products, the essential meaning is engines handling the flow of information. Two data engines are not exactly the same, just as no two cars or no two refrigerators are precisely the same. Exhibits 6.2 and 6.3 have identified the most important suppliers of ERP software in Europe and in the global marketplace.

Any popular programming product has multiple suppliers. Take CRM as an example. CRM software is usually divided into distinct classes, which are interrelated but also work independently within an open architecture. Typically, one vendor dominates in one or two of these classes, and a different vendor or vendors excel(s) in another.

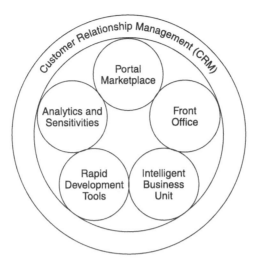

Exhibit 6.7 Component Parts of Customer Relationship Management Software

Some of the reasons for diversity originate in the vendor's own design culture, but the product's specific orientation weighs on the nature of building blocks. In CRM's case, for example, a critical factor is the primary method of communication among devices of choice: WAP phones, other phones, PDAs, Web browsers, fax, e-mail, etc., and also the type of link primarily addressed. For example:

- Business-to-customer
- Customer-to-business
- Business partner-to-business partner
- Sales force reference level

Developers place more emphasis on "this" or "that" approach because it serves in market appeal, although they all try to meet communications management requirements at the front office. Sometimes this involves a multimedia contact center. There are technology choices to be made and these evidently bring somewhat different costs and benefits from one offering to another. Not all methods and technical solutions are the same.

Any complex off-the-shelf programming product can be divided into a number of modules or subsystems. As an example, Exhibit 6.7 outlines the component parts of customer relationship management software. As the preceding paragraphs brought to the reader's attention, different vendors answer the requirement of each one of these CRM modules in different ways.

Here is a quick reference to the diversity of CRM vendors: Portal Marketplace, MySAP.com, Oracle Portal Framework, IBM Enterprise Information Portal, OpenText, Viador E-Portal Suite, Sterling MyEureka, Business Objects InfoView, 2Bridge 2Share, DataChannel RIO, Intraspect, Plumbtree, and Autonomy. Under a horde of labels, one can find the names of vendors specializing in:

- *Front-office packages:* Oracle, Beibel, Vantive, Clarify, Baan, Onyx, Pivotal, Octane, SalesLogix, Applix, Silknet, Chordiant
- *Intelligent business marketplace software:* Microsoft, IBM, Oracle, Net Perceptions, Black Pearl, Broad Vision, Viador, Macromedia
- *Rapid application development tools:* Alpha Blox, Whitelight, AppsCO, AppsMart
- *Analytical-type applications:* SAP BW, DecisionEdge, IBM, Broadbase, Epiphany, Paragren, TriVida

J.D. Edward, CommerceOne, Siebel, Clarify (a Nortel subsidiary), and Vantine are also active in some of these classes. With some notable exceptions, the majority of the companies just mentioned are small; and although their wares may be avant-garde, there is always the risk of survivability. Counterparty risk must be taken most seriously into account in the selection of a package, as discussed in Chapter 6.3 and 6.4. To see themselves through the start-up phase, new software companies should hit two birds with one well-placed stone by:

- Adopting an open architecture that is today favored by a growing number of client firms
- Finding a market niche that has first-class prospects of growing into a unique product

ERP would not qualify as a market niche by any stretch of the imagination, but the different classes of CRM do qualify. According to Goldman Sachs, less than 0.5 percent of inter-company transactions currently take place electronically. This is good news in disguise in terms of market opportunity. From retailing to manufacturing and banking, traditional Old Economy firms are realizing that customer handholding is key to gaining leadership in merchandising exchanges, and Web-based merchandise exchanges and the like can slash procurement costs in a radical way.

A good example along this line of reference is the February 2000 announcement by America's top three car makers regarding a Web-based exchange for parts. Aware of the challenge, automotive suppliers have been doing the same. Morgan Stanley suggests that such initiatives could reduce costs by $2000 to $3000 per vehicle over the next few years. No one knows the exact figures, but significant cost savings seem to be in the books, and part of it would find its way into the treasury of companies producing the right kind of commodity software.

6.3 Request for Information and Request for Offers

The selection of a vendor of commodity programming products should be done in a most careful manner. This is a long-term commitment — not an overnight association. The best methodology for supplier selection is the one done step-by-step. The major steps characterizing the screening and commitment process, at least those I apply in my professional work, are the following:

- Concept of projected implementation
- Request for information (to vendors)
- Study of proposals and preselection
- Prototype of projected implementation
- Request for offers (to selected vendors)
- Selection of two vendors for pilot project
- Final commitment to one of the vendors

Establishing the concept of the projected ERP, CRM, or other off-the-shelf software implementations means establishing black-and-white goals, constraints, and functionality; and also the costs, benefits, timetables, and human resources to be committed to introduce the package into the IT stream of the organization.

If customer relationship management is the goal, then the conceptual description of functional and other specifications will include the operational aspects of the application, including supply of customer data to one or more databases where it is analyzed by business intelligence tools. The aim is to promote an analytic approach to CRM able to produce customer intelligence.

Such a procedure must be extended through a mechanism able to pass customer intelligence to the front office. This will involve business processes and views of business relationships, which must be described both quantitatively and qualitatively. The implementation concept should include a choice among platform(s) on which the projected applications will run — to sustain as far as possible a sense of homogeneity.

The request for information should be addressed among six and twelve vendors, asking them whether (and to what degree) their programming products can meet specifications. Any exceptions or limitations should be noted in their replies. The suppliers' replies must also include precise references to existing (preferably similar) CRM/ERP applications, reliability statistics, and descriptions of available interfaces.

Part and parcel of these replies should be an order of magnitude indication on costs, both of the package and of its implementation, the latter based on similar historical references. Also vital is information regarding client sites, the individuals responsible for each of them, and the after-sales service the vendor has provided.

My policy is to make a pre-selection based on the criteria described in the foregoing two paragraphs. Typically, one out of two vendors is retained for the next round, but the information provided by all of the vendors can be most valuable because it serves to check the feasibility of the more advanced part of the CRM project, leads to comparisons between different sources of supply based on practical responses, and makes feasible some meaningful technical comparisons, which can be quite helpful later on in benchmarking.

As the careful reader will observe, mid-way in this step-by-step procedure is the prototyping of projected applications and subsequent testing. The object of this approach is to obtain qualitative and quantitative results through factual benchmarks. The process underpinning a benchmark is based on a number of hypotheses; its framework is presented in Exhibit 6.8.

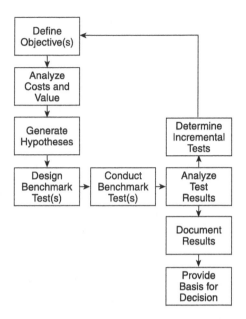

Exhibit 6.8   The Block Diagram Presents in a Nutshell the Application of Any Benchmarking Procedure

Benchmarking can be done both for software and for hardware, but under no condition should hardware selection precede that of the targeted programming product. Software sells hardware; therefore, it should be given preference in the evaluation process and also in investment decisions. In addition, it is wise to keep in mind other crucial criteria that influence a rational selection process, including:

- *Conformance* to the company's internal standard
- *Survivability* of vendor to be selected
- Diagnostics tools and maintenance tools
- Quality of online and on-site support
- *Costs*, which always matter

Every selection process into which one enters — not just for ERP or CRM — must keep in perspective the fact that technology changes, and so does the basis for making decisions. Therefore, the analysis preceding a decision concerning the choice of a vendor and its wares must be rigorous, factual, and well-documented, but also from the viewpoint of projected investments.

In procurement, management should act more from the side of the software functionality it can see and test, and much less from the hardware that sits behind the programming product being chosen. Modern software routines make the hardware practically invisible to the user. These are notions entering both the benchmarking and, subsequently, the Request for Offers.

To make a Request for Offers one should review and reevaluate the outline of objectives, capitalizing on the results of the benchmark and on the fact that one has moved much nearer to the implementation. One must also define the standards used in the open business architecture and the interfaces one would like to see supported. The more focused this report, the better will be the input provided by preselected vendors.

If the Request for Information was a first *tour de force* that provided the base for a preselection, the Request for Offers is the final screening. I usually follow the policy of calling in all of the preselected suppliers; that is, those that survived the first round.

The input from vendors received in response to the Request for Offers also serves several purposes. It allows one to tune the specifications to what is available as commodity software in the market and to proceed with the critical part of the selection process that leads to a commitment.

Both at the level of Request for Information and Request for Offers, there are some sound criteria for evaluating proposals that the reader will be well advised to follow. First and foremost is the ability to tear to pieces the vendor's report as soon as it is received:

- Carefully look for consistency as well as for discontinuities and unsound statements.
- Examine the documentation of the statements being made as well as associated commitments.
- Analyze the statistics supporting the proposal by the vendor, particularly reliability, blocking factors, and other constraints.

The statistics must be right; the conclusions are a person's own. An integral part of these conclusions is the quantitative analysis of the proposal; examination of the responsibilities assumed by the vendor of the programming product; attention to deadlines paid by the vendor; written clauses for corrective action in case something goes wrong; and, of course, costs (see Chapter 6.4) and the vendor's ability to survive (see Chapter 6.5).

6.4　Costs Matter — and So Does Return on Investment

There are two ways of looking at cost: absolute and relative. The absolute cost consists of quoted prices and estimates for implementation expenses. The relative cost is a function of the time it takes to complete each of the steps discussed in Chapter 6.3 and to implement them. How long should the selection procedure take?

My answer to this query is less than six months from concept definition to parallel testing. Half that time is selection proper; the other half is implementation. Altogether, this is about 16 percent of the three years it took ABB, but it is doable. The principle is that the more lead-time one gives for deliverables, the higher will be the costs, the more elusive the benefits, and the lower the implementation accuracy.

Exactly because they pay scant attention to the accuracy of the implementation, many companies have found that high technology can be a mixed blessing. Sophisticated systems that are inserted into poorly organized firms can reduce rather than raise productivity. This is why information systems planning has become a strategic concern in many corporations. The successful implementation of ERP and CRM depends significantly on how well the following were performed:

- Prerequisite study of the implementation area
- Reengineering of the company's information technology
- Training of systems specialists and the users on ERP functionality

The activities identified by these three bullets should be done in parallel with the search procedures discussed in Chapter 6.3. At the same time, the existence of these functions documents that the cost of the ERP software will only be a fraction of the total cost of its implementation. Organizations can expect to incur much larger costs in reengineering, training, and consulting than the cost of the package alone.

As I never tire repeating, costs matter. Therefore, not only should one watch every dollar like a hawk, but one should also evaluate the return on investment (ROI). Greater productivity is one type of return, but it should be documented, not an abstract notion. For this, the prerequisite organizational work must determine the activities in which managers and professionals spend their time, and the improvement(s) contributed by the implementation of ERP or CRM to these activities.

This means providing a solution that addresses these activities in an able manner; determines if the users properly employ the functions of the system, and how frequently they are doing so; and calculates the time saved per person by using the ERP or CRM solution. To avoid incurring extra costs, data collection should be integrated into the day-to-day operation of the bought system.

Higher productivity will not come on its own. Recall that work expands to fill the amount of time available for its completion; but work does not expand to engulf the facilities provided by the equipment that is available. Therefore, idle time is easier to identify at the equipment level. If the right organization work is done, ERP software amplifies a wide range of executive communication and control capabilities. This is why the software influences many operations that previously remained immune to classical data processing.

In the New Economy, measuring ROI in a factual manner calls for establishing a new set of cost standards. When computers were confined to back-office tasks, the computation of ROI was generally possible based on labor savings, or cost displacement. However, when computers, communications, and sophisticated software are used to implement transactional and message systems, ROI can only be measured as a function of improved transactional efficiency, turnaround time, better documented management decision processes, elimination of "management fat" in an organizational sense, and speed of new product delivery — hence time-to-market — as well as rapid inventory turnover, faster billing/receivables, and higher customer satisfaction.

The range of these activities and the diversity of their nature show that quantifiable justifications on cost savings are more difficult to pin down. But at the same time, failure to automate carries a high survival risk. Among the reasons that technology investments must be rewarding is to encourage further development. Return on investment should give the project a reward for the additional effort being put up and leave it with a fair share of profit if its performance is satisfactory. Both short-term and long-term ROI horizons are important.

- Long-term evaluations ensure that the paybacks of the investments are visible in the years to come. If they are not visible, this means the results were not transparent, and in all likelihood they were not satisfactory. There must be a sound pricing of both expenses and benefits that allows one to compute ROI.
- Short term, the rewards of the project teams must be linked to their immediate return. This is important information, as an incentive.

Whether one buys off-the-shelf software or develops it in-house, a business enterprise does not undertake a project just for the fun of it. Management requires, or at least it should require, deliverables that are timely, robust, purposeful, and of high quality — and also cost-effective.

One of the better examples of the cost-effectiveness of technology in the longer term is shown in graphic form in Exhibit 6.9. It concerns a computer company that, at the height of its power, knew how to put its own and other firms' technology to work to steadily improve the bottom line. This is the sense of practical implementation of a ROI policy.

If one really wants to get results out of the money spent on technology, then one of the messages of group-level IT strategy should be that of ensuring ROI standards and seeing to it that they are observed. One of the best goals

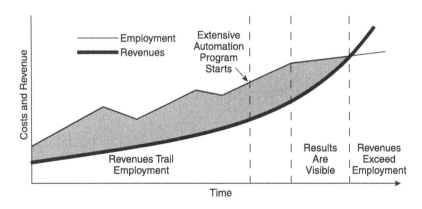

Exhibit 6.9 Putting High Technology to Work on a Steady, Return-on-Investment-Oriented Basis

attained through ROI is that because evaluation is done by the user organization, information technologists must run fast to reach the established ROI objectives in time.

Another favorable aftermath of a high enough ROI is the price put on the *quality* of the system solution — which tier-1 organizations evaluate through quality circles. Still another important aim is cost-consciousness, leading to better-tuned standards of performance and to much greater attention being paid to deliverables.

ROI standards at the level of 20 to 22 percent, at least, help in yet another way. They assist senior management in appraising the existing corporate strategies and programs for improving the software development environment, hardware procurement, and other associated processes to implement technology. Any CEO worth his salt would want to see if these strategies and programs are yielding useful results and if they can be fine-tuned in view of current corporate goals and circumstances.

If ROI is low, the failure may be on the side of the software's functionality, in the accuracy of its implementation, or in the company's *readiness:* a low ROI should lead to assessing the state of organizational readiness for change because this is a main driver of ERP assimilation. The board and the CEO are well-advised to assess each department's attitude. I often determine the history of the organization's reaction to technology through the ROI established in IT.

The implementation of enterprise resource planning and customer relationship management software is a good example because, speaking from experience, the areas where the highest return on investment can be obtained are in logistics and in marketing — more precisely, in relationship management inside and outside the firm. In addition, relationship management lies in an unstructured domain of IT implementation. Hence, it takes more ingenuity and hard work to get results.

At the same time, many of the issues being handled in logistics and marketing are strategic and they require plenty of knowledge — not just classical data processing skills. Knowledge-oriented activity is not the area in which most effort is currently placed in the majority of companies. The larger number of investments — and of available skills — are currently spent on non-exciting low technology, addressing fully structured operations.

6.5   Vendor Credit Risk and the Wisdom of Writing One's Own Contract

An alternative title to this chapter might be "How Not to Be Taken for a Ride by Your Vendor." Vendors of computers, communications, and software often take their clients to the cleaners because their contracts can be tricky. Therefore, the management of user organizations should read them carefully together with a lawyer. Vendor relationships can turn disastrous. Several reasons might lie behind unfavorable developments in vendor-client relationships, including:

- The platform or its software may underperform.
- Joint efforts promised by the vendor are understaffed in skills.
- Timetables are repeatedly extended, increasing costs and generating friction.

Another risk that user organizations do not always perceive is that vendor companies can fail, taking down the precipice with them, the ongoing project, or even an up-and-running application. Among background reasons for vendor failures are poor management of the vendor company, insensitivity to market trends and tastes, high product costs and administrative expenses, and out-of-focus product line(s) and lack of renewal.

User organizations, too, are not immune to failure of joint implementation efforts. Among the most persistent reasons why manufacturing companies, merchandising firms, and financial institutions get in trouble with technology are: the failure to observe an open vendor policy and capitalize on it (see Chapter 6.2); and the inability to put in actual practice cost-effectiveness rules regarding *their* information technology (see Chapter 6.4).

Sometimes, deficiencies on the side of the user organization poisons the vendor relationship and the joint project. An example is long implementation timetables. No matter the background reason, long timetables have the net results of:

- Making the commodity software products obsolete before they are actually in use
- Increasing the cost of ERP applications well beyond approved levels
- Creating friction between the vendor company, IT organization, and user departments

Behind some of these issues lies the fact that in information technology the innovation cycle has been reduced from 10 to 15 years to less than two years, and it continues to shrink. Not only is rapid technological evolution a permanent fact of business life, but user organizations are tremendously exposed to the failure of their vendors to deliver new releases (see Chapter 7) with meaningful improvements in functionality.

For this reason, it is wise to establish internal rating criteria for vendors. Other things being equal, I will look quite favorably at a company that is a dominant leader with a clear history in the software sector and with strong growth prospects. My preference is for a company that is profitable or on a documented path to profitability, that has a strong cash position, and that has attractive wares.

Acceptable can also be a notch lower than that in software vendor quality; a company with good growth prospects, even while being a dominant sector leader, faces some problems the market expects to be resolved. This company should have, in principle, reached profitability or be about to do so. What this leads to is a notion of *credit risk* associated with the vendor and one's relationship with the vendor. This credit risk is omnipresent, whether or not it is recognized.

Credit risk should be hedged, and this can be done through a derivative financial instrument; for example, an option triggered by the vendor's failure. Bankers Trust had done so in the early 1990s, after it found that its exposure to DEC's failure because of IT commitments was greater than the credit line it had given to DEC.

No company should underestimate the massive amount of exposure to the vendor's failure. Here is a precise example of what I mean by taking insurance on the likelihood of the vendor's failure. A New York-based financial institution established that its exposure to the failure of one of its major vendors stood at $400 million for hardware and $1 billion for software. This was the money at stake for one vendor alone, out of two key sources of supply. Interestingly enough, this $1.4 billion far exceeded the $400 million of loans to that vendor. The bank bought insurance to cover itself from the vendor's failure risk. By paying $7 million per year, the insurance gives this bank a windfall of $700 million in case that vendor goes under.

If one single financial institution faced a $1.4 billion exposure in case of its vendor's failure, what would be the exposure nationwide? It is estimated that over $9 trillion has been invested in America in computer software alone. The majority of this software is written for proprietary operating systems, but a big chunk is packages; yet very few companies are clear-eyed enough to take urgently needed insurance.

Credit rating is also important. I would keep away from vendors facing significant issues relating to intermediate-term outlook, even if they do have a business model that fundamentally works. On this principle, I would never call to my Request for Information a company with which significant uncertainties or reservations remain.

This screening from a business perspective will avoid making questionable software partnership choices. Credit risk should not be confused with a vendor's technical strong points: open architectural approach, sophisticated solution(s), attractive applications features, extended portability, advanced technical skills in consulting, and first-class development and maintenance organization. Credit risk has to do with the ability to survive the tough software competition, which is here to stay.

The message to convey to the reader is that beyond the selection of package(s) and tool(s) that best meet(s) one's requirements, one should address how well a potential vendor will meet one's longer term needs of a business partnership; that is, the sense of determining the long-term stability and viability of the potential vendor. The concept of credit risk leads to another set of very important issues: the challenge of contracting ERP, CRM, and other programming products on one's own terms. My advice is: Write your own contract, and have one type of contract for all vendors.

A user organization of computers and software is well-advised to seek competent legal advice in contracting software and hardware by involving the firm's corporate legal counsel or outside lawyer up front. A professionally prepared legal document requires a lot of work, but it will bring far more comfort to the user organization some years down the line than buying wholesale the vendor's presentation of legal clauses — which, to be sure, will be in one's disfavor.

There is a saying in the United States that says that "the client is always right." One of the important clauses to be included in a contract is that of the source code. Usually, the software vendor will give the customer the object code. That is common practice. However, in case the vendor fails, the object code will not help and one will be left high and dry.

My policy is to require the vendor to deposit a copy of the source code and all the documentation at the buyer's notary public. The contract should specify that, while this is the vendor's property, if the software company goes under, the source code becomes buyer company's property. Such a clause, incidentally, helps in inviting start-ups to the Request for Information because it ensures that there will be a continuity in software updates.

The No. 2 rule that I use in vendor negotiations is never to pay list price. A company should use its clout to negotiate significant discounts. The No. 3 rule is to introduce a reliability clause that would pay downtime expenses. The vendor should guarantee at least 99.9 percent reliability. All of this is an extension to taking insurance with regard to the vendor's failure. Among the steps in calculating vendor's risk are a:

- *Worst-case scenario* for each vendor, within the hardware/software capitalization perspective
- Decision on the sum to be assured through reinsurance by balancing premium versus risk
- Polyvalent reinsurance plan, which is often done by buying options

This chapter section has explained why a company should take insurance in case the vendor goes under, and has described the kinds of contractual clauses necessary to establish continuity in software support. The windfall from the insurance plan will finance the massive restructuring job. A hedging scheme will likely cost about 1 percent of insured value, and companies with experience in this strategy say that it is worthwhile.

Chapter 7

Implementing Successive Releases of ERP Systems

The software industry is renowned for using non-standard terminology in describing its wares. Therefore, it is necessary to define the terms that will be used as well as establish the difference between a *new version, major upgrade,* or *minor upgrade* of a programming product. Quite often, for commercial reasons, these terms are used interchangeably.

If a *new release* of off-the-shelf software, such as ERP or CRM, represents only a *minor upgrade,* this will typically involve correction of errors, bug fixes, removal of patches, or weeding out some of the inefficiencies. By contrast, a *major upgrade* will typically involve novel functions. It may also account for regulatory changes regarding financial reporting and other requirements.

While each vendor tends to use its own terminology, the way to bet is that a major release sees to it that any successive version of an ERP system (or any other type of commodity software) will tend to be significantly different than its predecessor. The core product itself is affected and, quite often, this impacts on the user organization all the way from system skills to central memory and other technical requirements.

Both the aims and problems associated with new releases can be better appreciated through a quick look at the history of ERP software. When in the late 1980s/early 1990s, ERP hit the market, its different vendors concentrated their efforts on capturing as much of market share as possible by steadily enlarging the scope of their offerings — and through this strategy, their customer base.

ERP was not invented overnight. One of its predecessors was MRP II, originally designed to manage a production facility's customer orders, scheduling plans, and inventories. The need to integrate the sales book with in-process goods and inventory data came as a logical next step. This was a new release. As seen in Chapter 1, other releases took care of accounting routines, financial information, and human resource planning.

The need for steady innovation can be appreciated by the fact that while most of the 1990s witnessed booming ERP sales, by 1998 the market slowed down with revenues from selling new software licenses declining. One reason was that client companies needed to solve their Year 2000 (Y2K) problems. Another reason was that the ERP market itself started becoming saturated.

By adding new functionality to commodity software, successive releases are often instrumental in breaking through the saturation barrier. This, however, might lead to complexities on the implementation side as well as the lack of skills in solving them. One of these complexities is the so-called *multi-site* enterprise resource planning applications, where at each site there are different choices due to different criteria for evaluating the alternatives and proceeding with a valid solution (see Chapter 6).

New releases are also necessary to match the requirements posed by advancing technology. An example is the need to incorporate into the package support for the Product Markup Language (PML), which is an extension of the Extensible Markup Language (XML) — itself a development of the Web's HTML.[1] PML is discussed in Chapter 7.6; its functionality serves in handling smart materials, as it is on its way to becoming the standard language for describing physical objects. Smart materials is the theme of Section II.

7.1   Distributed Processing Increases the Challenge of Implementing New Releases

Implementing a new release was somewhat simpler when computer processing was centralized in huge hospital-looking buildings, with large internal glass windows to permit visitors to see the marvels of a machine with attendants wearing long white robes. While it had many other defects, particularly in downgrading efficiency and reliability, this concentration of data processing somehow simplified the change of a release. But in the 1950s and 1960s, new releases were scarce.

Today, it is different in many ways; the pace of releases and upgrades has accelerated while in the same user organization there may be multiple sites, and some of these IT sites are largely independent of the others. Therefore, a significant amount of coordination is necessary. Sometimes, release changes at one site limit the available choices or affect the performance of the system at another site. User organizations are therefore well-advised to plan multi-site ERP and CRM implementations very thoroughly. They should do so *before* committing themselves to a given commodity software solution and its successive releases.

The main handicaps in implementing successive ERP releases concern background technical reasons, ranging from heterogeneous hardware platforms and OS/DBMS choices at user organization premises, to limited skill for keeping the system up-to-date at each site. Even if in the past years or months, the problems of heterogeneity of platforms and basic software were temporarily solved, they resurface with a new release, leaving companies to perceive migration as difficult, time-consuming, and costly.

New releases of commodity programming products, whether basic software or applications, are in fact a double-edged sword. One reason why the migration process takes so long to execute is the attention that needs to be paid to each existing heterogeneous platform. Another reason is wanting coordination and the traditional policy of many IT shops to move at slow pace. Indeed, the latter reason, more than any other, sees to it that some migrations to a new release receive bad reviews.

Whether one is talking about ERP, CRM, or any other programming product, multi-site coordination is the keyword. Keep in mind that many ERP-supported business functions are increasingly executed simultaneously, interactively, and in real-time. This requires business and systems staff to work in close collaboration with both the vendor and the different implementation sites, and to address all types of implementation issues in a rigorous way, including problems surfacing in one site but not in others.

People who have, on a number of occasions, gone through the experience of implementing new releases are commenting that, in their judgment, some of the complexities in ERP software releases emanate from the highly generalized nature of the off-the-shelf applications and from the fact that user organizations move to personalize these routines. This sees to it that diversity and therefore complexity increases, the more so if instead of a parametric customization, the user company alters some of the software. Good systems sense suggests that such alteration should not be made. Off-the-shelf software should be used *as is*, subject only to parametric customization, and the latter should take place only if such a facility is available by the vendor.

To help in evaluating the wisdom of adopting a new release, Exhibit 7.1 suggests a selection procedure for off-the-shelf programming products. Typically, a company has a list of top-ten functions it would like to see supported in a more efficient way than the one currently available. These come first in the evaluation. They are followed by key performance criteria.

The ERP package, whose most recent upgrade is mapped in terms of effectiveness in the radar chart, was installed at five major sites of the EPSILON company (a ficticious name, but a real entity). Each site, identified I to V, tested the aftermath of the upgrade and came up with a rating reflected in Exhibit 7.1.

As the reader can appreciate, these ratings were diverse. At sites IV and V, for example, the cost of installing the new release hardly broke even with expected benefits. The question was therefore posed: should EPSILON install this new release or forego its benefits?

- The change of a release has significant costs associated with it.
- These should be justified by an increase in functionality and performance.

Notice that this method is also applicable in the original selection of an ERP package and not only in evaluation of adopting successive releases. In

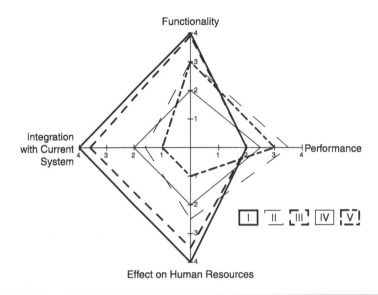

Exhibit 7.1   A Radar Chart for Evaluating Five Different Sites of ERP Packages and Their Upgrades, Based on Four Factors

original selection, the cost/benefit comparison will be against the current method.

Management should appreciate that migration between successive releases of ERP software is often a challenge. Even if one of the aims of new releases is that of improving business processes, one should have evidence that the upgrade is indeed benefiting the organization. Such evidence is obtained by pinpointing important business processes for which measurable results can be obtained.

By being careful with regard to cost-effectiveness, users can influence ERP vendors to add more functionality or to improve the efficiency of their releases. At the same time, vendors should be keen to test projected upgrades with user organizations. It is appropriate that the evolution of ERP solutions is influenced by changing market conditions, but there is a whole list of criteria to be observed, including better service-oriented approaches. Even if many organizations do not migrate the moment a new version becomes available, in the longer run they are motivated to adopt the new release for technical reasons and business opportunities.

At the level of user organization, not only does the current application's complexity need to be evaluated through benchmarks addressing the new release, along with expected benefits at each site, but future requirements must also be taken into account, given the evolution of demand for products and services. For cost/benefit reasons, it is my policy to track the cost of the initial installation of an ERP system and of its subsequent releases. This can be done through a simple chart similar to the one presented in Exhibit 7.2.

■ Functionality and performance criteria of the new release should be established by the company already implementing the programming product.

- What the vendor says may be indicative, but it is not the bible. Both criteria and benchmarks should be the company's own.

It should as well be appreciated that an open architecture (see Chapter 6) presents better opportunities for an evolutionary process that is easy to implement and assists in establishing a business differentiation. Not only does an open architecture ease the original integration task of commodity ERP software, but it also, other things being equal, simplifies the installation and operation of new releases.

Notice as well that with practically every new release, ERP, CRM, and other programming products can be configured through conceptual models linked with the repository of the system currently in use. That is why, to a very significant extent, rigid concepts customary with mainframe solutions are no longer welcome. What is needed is flexible targeting concepts that fit well with new releases and parametric customizing techniques.

The use of modeling tools can help in migration to a new release because they can assist in functional definition and in setting performance criteria. The existence of a development database makes it possible to have detailed documentation both at the business and technical levels. It also provides a good linkage to further upgrades.

I insist on these issues because the problem of upgrading is scheduled to become even more pronounced in the coming years because a significant number of ERP and CRM application users are moving out of their current monolithic releases to take advantage of new functionality as it becomes

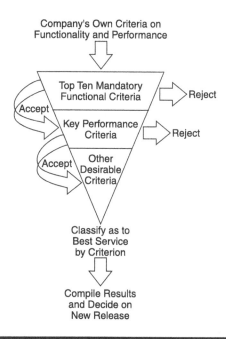

Exhibit 7.2   Characteristic Features of Commodity Software Should be Analyzed Prior to Its Selection, and the Same Is True of Subsequent Releases

available. While one is not obliged to adopt them, new releases are part of the natural evolution of ERP applications and aim to incorporate Internet enabling techniques that drive the requirements for continuous integration of new routines. They also help in substituting aged in-house legacy applications, which should have been weeded out 10 or 20 years ago.

7.2 Metadata and Metaknowledge: An Upgrade No Company Should Forego

No technology, no new product, and no upgrade is worth anything if it does not deliver value. Value is created either by linking technology to marketing through innovative, more efficient products and services, or by increasing internal performance and therefore swamping costs. At the junction of these two organizational breakthroughs lies the concept of *meta*.

Meta is a level above another more basic level, and therefore it is strong in semantic content. Exhibit 7.3 provides two examples: the one from banking, the other from inventory management. The amount of money written on a check is the lower information level. Date and place of issue is meta to it. Still higher up is the control level, which delimits date of validity and maximum acceptable amount.

Metadata is important in many activities. Inventory management is another example. Metadata to raw inventory levels includes a directory of inventory locations, minimum and maximum per item, and level of confidence for automatic reordering. This is important for marketing and for optimization. Such metalevels are specific to the item; hence, so much can be gained if, as will be seen in Section II, each item is able to:

- Automatically identify itself
- Transmit its ID and position to other entities

Making the grand statement that technology has the potential to significantly improve productivity and bring benefits beyond present-day practices means

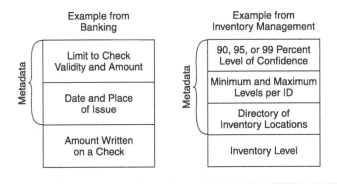

Exhibit 7.3 The Concept of Metadata Is Not Well-Understood, Yet It Is Fundamental to Modern Computer Applications

that one can obtain tangible results from its implementation. *Metalevels* allow one to fine-tune inventory planning and control. How this connects to services provided by smart materials is explained in Chapters 8 to 11.

These two examples — checks and inventory level — assist in explaining that *metadata is data about data*. As such, it is critical for the effective management of data resources and also for defining the best structures to be adopted in connection with logical and physical databases. ERP and CRM software should be strong in metadata support, but usually it is not. Therefore, one should not miss the opportunity to implement a new release using metadata.

A different way of looking at this subject is that the focal point of databases is their organization, utility, and service in a marketplace that is steadily becoming more competitive and more demanding. The contribution to one's database should be a major criterion in the selection and use of ERP and CRM programming products. Emphasis must be placed on applications that exploit knowledge-enriched database solutions — and this means the able handling of metadata and metaknowledge.

Technically speaking, *metaknowledge* contrasts with *object knowledge*. Object knowledge is basic level. For example, typical logic programming is an expression of object knowledge. In contrast, in a way comparable to what was just explained about metadata, metaknowledge is of a higher level, which includes generalizations and constraints. Metaknowledge — that is, knowledge about knowledge — is essentially constraint-type knowledge. The notion of *constraints* is very important because it controls the inference processing mechanism in humans and machines.

In practical implementation terms, metaknowledge can be instrumental in the transformation of behavioral views, procedural and other patterns, and operational frameworks. Knowledge management systems need both metadata and metaknowledge. This is true whether one is talking about computer-based artifacts or about manual handling. Currently, there are no efficient solutions for manually handled information; therefore, a computer-based advanced metalevel functionality is most welcome. Data traditionally stored in databases may only represent 10 percent of the information assets of a company. The remainder is usually stored nondigitally as documents, faxes, paper files, drawings, or photos. The challenge is how to use metaknowledge in connection with the latter. The answer is to classify this type of information in a way that end-users can access as part of a global resource (see Chapters 10 and 11 on classification). This being done, further duties can be assigned to a knowledge management system. Knowledge mapping extends metadata concepts to classifying and retrieving nondigitized information.

Exhibit 7.4 explains this interaction between higher and lower levels by introducing the concept of *macroscopic* and *microscopic* views. The metalayer is based on macroscopic knowledge, which is conceptual and might even be fuzzy. The microscopic level consists of detail, with elementary data types that can be recombined. The two are linked by *inheritance*, which is dynamic, instantaneous, and perishable.

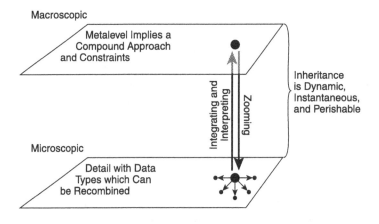

Exhibit 7.4   The Metalayer Is Based on Macroscopic Knowledge, Which Is Conceptual and May be Fuzzy

Readers familiar with object-oriented databases[2] and object programming will recognize that this is the reference underpinning this discussion. It is preferable that ERP and CRM programming products be object-oriented. If the programming product being used is not, and its vendor brings out an object version, then one should do what it takes to implement it.

Both ERP and CRM functionality can benefit from metalevels, above the level of detail that constitutes the object of this examination. Supported by the metalevel, a macroscopic view would allow one to focus on component parts (through zooming) and to examine the integrative view of detailed elements. In principle:

- *Microscopic* knowledge is focused on one domain in which there is little or no contradiction. An example is the handling of a specific financial product, such as letters of credit. The specialist's microscopic knowledge is important not only to ensure the proper debits and credits, but also to calculate the risk being taken by the bank — and therefore the product's pricing.
- *Microscopic* knowledge is often considered "obvious" to people with experience in a given limited domain. Although microscopic knowledge typically addresses a narrow field, there are several difficulties in data and knowledge acquisition. Also, while there is only one or at most very few established patterns in connection with microscopic knowledge, there exist at times less than realistic approaches to reasoning.

Contrasted to this, management knowledge is *macroscopic*. It concerns the grand design as well as projections, extrapolation, inference, deductions, and inductions. Macroscopic knowledge deals with *soft data* (e.g., forecasts) and *hard data* (e.g., statistics). However, forecasts are part of management knowledge, while statistics and historical evidence are the province of microscopic knowledge. Soft data comes at a certain level of risk; projections valuable in planning may not materialize, but as long as one understands that this information may be fuzzy, vague, and uncertain, one can derive benefits from soft data.

Macroscopic knowledge is not a collection of microscopic knowledge, such as summing up a supermarket bill. It comes from a long experience crystallized into qualitative rules. This requires the institution, operation, and maintenance of a corporate memory facility. All these are reasons why a new release of ERP, CRM, or other programming products that uses object orientation, metadata, and metaknowledge should not be missed.

7.3 An In-House Standard for Multi-Dimensional Software Evaluation

The functionality of ERP, CRM, and other programming products is to a large extent driven by market forces. More precisely, it is driven by market pressure to interchange information among different entities and therefore heterogeneous platforms, and to make seamless the difference between transaction processes under multiple transaction handling routines. There have also been initiatives that tend to establish some sort of wider areas of business meaning that have important implications for both ERP vendors and for their customers.

These changes to the traditional way of implementing commodity software epitomize the use of advanced technology as a major force in competition. They are instrumental in bringing about a wider reach by computers and networks, not just because they are adding more leverage, but also because new tools allow one to employ information technology to reengineer chronically stagnant organizational resources. This is another perspective under which new releases should be viewed, like the example in Chapter 7.2.

In the process of this faster and deeper change, the rapid cycle from design to manufacturing and sales is becoming an evermore integral part of our way of operating. The core of a company's global strategy is to use IT to help itself and its customers take advantage of global markets. More and more, the entire process of computer usage is geared to that philosophy which, however, must pay plenty of attention to human capital, including recruitment, training, and compensation.

What has been learned from recruitment of college graduates in the United States in the spring of 2000 reinforces the attention that needs to be paid to these three areas. The better engineering programming products — ERP, CRM, and others — pay attention to the upgrading of human resources and to productivity. The more sophisticated they are, the more they require retraining human resources, and this is to the benefit of everybody, including the IT specialists, the end-users, and the company as a whole.

A company benefits because as Internet commerce becomes more popular, direct marketing channels and conventional customer service are no longer sufficient to meet the demands of an increasingly disparate customer base. More than ever before, in the coming years the key element will be effective communications, and this requires the more advanced type of software.

The effectiveness of communications is characterized, as a condition, by value differentiation in the any-to-any network link such as the one provided by the Web — at any location. At the front-end comes the role of CRM enabling a customer contact center, which incorporates different forms of customer contact channels: video, e-mail, fax, mail, and kiosk. But the front-end must be supported by back-office information, which emphasizes ERP's role.

■ A new release of ERP or CRM that integrates the two packages should, in principle, be implemented.
■ In reaching the implementation decision, however, it is always good to examine cost/benefit (see Chapter 7.1).

In principle, but only in principle, productivity in customer contacts can get a boost if one is able to achieve a state-of-the-art contact center while avoiding the many integration problems along the way. This leads to the critical variable in a new release decision: the integration process that adds to the project challenges faced by the implementers of ERP and CRM.

Effective solutions to integration problems have become more complex because of the abundance of platforms, which adds to the challenges posed by their heterogeneity. Some good advice for getting ready is to learn about the problems that one's peers are facing and the solutions that they have been implementing.

Although neither the nature nor the scale of the solutions being sought is comparable to the challenges faced in the 1970s with management information systems (MIS) and decision support systems (DSS), and in the 1980s with expert systems,[3] there are some similarities; therefore, one can take advantage of the lessons learned at those times, including the ability to analyze facts and figures, the need for recommending dynamic solutions, and the method-ology for evaluating alternative possibilities.

One recalls that with DSS, after the advent of the spreadsheet in the early 1980s, it was the end-user who suggested situations and wanted *what if* evaluations as an answer. Spreadsheets helped in doing such evaluating in an easy and comprehensive way. In contrast, with expert systems, the intelligent software suggested and evaluated different situations, giving advice that was properly documented. In this sense, the expert system identified relevant cases, evaluated alternatives, and constructed a path to the solution.

This procedure has once again become crucial in developing a next-generation call center capability in Internet commerce, something CRM should provide. The need to make such an approach the most sophisticated is at the top of many organizations' agendas, even if the road to success is a difficult one because, as already mentioned, it involves:

■ Integrating and deploying ERP and CRM solutions to establish a multi-site, multi-functional, multimedia capability
■ Deploying resources in a way that ensures a smooth and harmonious approach to client handholding, as well as to closing sales transactions

Companies with experience in this integrative domain suggest that the able use of Web technology can make significant contributions to an interactive handling of problems and solutions and to the making of requests for offers, as well as ensuring proactive real-time voice and video communications. Agents can play a key role in reaching this goal.

Vendors of ERP, CRM, and other programming products should be eager to develop systems that see to it that the artifact learns from the work it is doing. With *learning systems*, there is an interaction between the knowledge bank and the user of the interface, which contributes to the system's maturity. This process involves reasoning methods and rules able to grow by successive knowledge intake.

As experience with Web-enabled call centers is further developed, the real question is that of a global view that can improve the company's competitive edge. This is a natural extension from *what if* to *why if*, leading toward the development of a strategic information system able to help all managers and professionals in the organization, as well as business partners in the supply chain.

In conclusion, from the beginning of quantitative aids to management, computer supports have been identified with personal decision-making. At the bottom line, this is the aim of personal computing — to which the typical inertia and misinformation of classical data processing is anathema. Like DSS and expert systems in the 1980s, CRM and the new generation of ERP must be characterized by rapid development of value-added functions, putting a premium on being able to handle *ad hoc* and very quickly the needs that are developing on the end users' side. New releases upholding these principles may well be worth their salt.

7.4   Increasing the Pace of Implementation of Sophisticated Systems

Chapter 6 underlined the fact that the time it takes to implement a new programming product, or a new release of one already in production, and the cost of this operation correlate positively with one another. Studies have shown that this correlation coefficient is not equal to 1; it usually varies between 0.75 and 0.85, but this is high enough to make clear-eyed companies run faster to demand rapid implementation timetables and cut down on implementation costs.

Sometimes a crisis is instrumental in demanding a rapid implementation phase. On October 27, 1997, the economic and financial debacle in East Asia sparked stock market activity that sent trading volumes to a high-water mark high. The NASDAQ stock market received a record 20 million hits in one day at its Internet trading site, nasdaq.com. As a result, NASDAQ urgently needed additional servers to handle this large increase. At NASDAQ's request, Dell built and shipped eight custom-configured, fully tested server systems in just 36 hours. Three days later, NASDAQ was using the servers to conduct its online business without any visible flaw.

This rapid action provided NASDAQ with a systems solution of state-of-the-art technology, within a timeframe that no other computer vendor has thus far matched. The record-breaking implementation was achieved by a joint Dell and NASDAQ sales, procurement, and manufacturing team working together to understand and analyze, and then rapidly respond to, customer requirements.

That same year, 1997, Wal-Mart, the world's largest retailer, wanted to enhance its shopping experience by building multimedia kiosks where videotapes and compact audio discs could be previewed before a purchase. To do so in time for the 1997 Christmas shopping season, Wal-Mart needed thousands of custom-configured computers in a matter of weeks.

Through its build-to-order manufacturing process, Dell built and shipped 6000 systems to nearly 2000 Wal-Mart stores across the United States in just six weeks. It custom-configured and tested 2000 desktop PCs and 4000 servers with proprietary multimedia software. Other responsibilities included loading this proprietary software and testing the installed systems on-site to simplify implementation and maintenance.

These references are eye-opening when compared with the slow-going policies of old EDP, which continue today particularly in mainframe environments. While something can be done fast at time t, it is usually done at time $10t$ because there is no stiff timetable for deliverables, and there are no penalties associated with breaking the timetable if there is one. The way to bet is that:

- At time t, the quality of results will be superior to that obtained at $10t$.
- The costs at time t will be a fraction of those incurred at slow-pace $10t$.

Often operational requirements simply do not permit a leisurely approach. In World War II, two of the three American carriers that reached Hawaii after the battle of the Coral Sea were severely damaged. The naval engineers said they needed *two* months to again make them seaworthy. Admiral Nimitz gave the engineers three days to put the carriers back in good working order, and the engineers met the challenge. CEOs should learn from what Admiral Nimitz achieved.

The plot in Exhibit 7.5 makes interesting reading. It maps the performance rating of four similar projects concerning the introduction of new commodity software. This package was implemented in different companies of about the same size and line of business. From A to D, the relation between rating and cost could be approximated through a line that suggests significantly greater costs, hence diminishing return for lower and lower performance.

- Project B took one-and-a-half times longer than project A, and its cost was 53 percent higher.
- Project C required about 80 percent more time than A, while a 2-to-1 ratio prevailed in cost terms.
- Project D took about twice the time of A, and its cost was 260 percent higher.

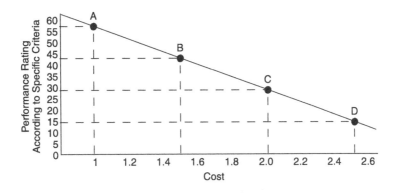

Exhibit 7.5   A Cost/Performance Evaluation of Four Similar Software Projects Implemented at Totally Different Timetables for Deliverables

This being the case, why is management control over implementation timetables so weak? A recent study has found that top management is confronted with two problems that it finds difficult to overcome:

1. Its own *computer illiteracy,* which does not permit to exercise rigorous internal control, as in other domains, and
2. A deliberate *go-slow* software development and implementation policy, done mainly for reasons of job security

In some of the projects visited in the course of this study, management made the reference that analysts, programmers, and CIOs were taking about 200 to 300 percent more time than really needed to develop and implement new computer programs. A recurrent reason for this deliberate go-slow policy is that they think that by so doing, they have better job security. Precisely the inverse is true.

Only the best-managed companies move really fast in software development and implementation timetables. In the course of my research, a British bank said that as far as derivative financial products and treasury operations are concerned, the minimum effective time for new software is one hour, and the longest acceptable time is three months, for a team of two people.

Along the same frame of reference, an American bank stated that a good deal of software produced for new financial products is typically done in two hours. If the project takes two weeks, it is already too long. These timetables run contrary to what I indicated in the preceding paragraphs as the more general current practice, where software development takes three years — and sometimes more.

Equally wrong is the use of old platforms and obsolete basic software to implement new applications. In the early 1990s, a Swedish credit institution, Skandinaviska Enskilda Banken, programmed a first-class client relationship management project on a mainframe using the hierarchical IMS database management system. The result was an unacceptably long response time because by using a hierarchical approach, the program needed to do 100 database accesses for each transaction rather than the more typical 7 to 10. Even the best CRM or any other programming product can be killed by this straitjacket of an obsolete DBMS. New applications and new software supporting them require high technology, not wares that gave up their souls a long time ago.

Particularly long are the software development and implementation timetables for mainframe routines. For example, in 1989, Sweden's Nordbanken started a new loan system written in Cobol and based on DB2. The development plan had foreseen:

- 600 man-years of work, with the first subset of deliverables expected to require three years for a team of 20 people

Four years down the line, in 1993, even that first subset was not yet ready. In contrast, Securum, a go-go Swedish financial company that was the liquidator of Nordbanken's bad loans, did the loan system on a client/server. This loan program was done by one person and required only 500 man-hours.

Securum's stellar performance needed less than one hour for one year of Coboloid work on mainframes. This is also a first-class example of Securum software strategy. Said a senior executive in the course of our meeting in Stockholm, "If we have a chance to survive, we must keep costs rockbottom and move very, very fast in a fluid market. We must have very sophisticated information technology tools at our disposal."

This is what every senior executive should tell his people; he or she should pay them well and then expect them to produce deliverables of high quality in short timetables. Securum's strategy has been based on two pillars: (1) rapid software development timeframes and (2) low design and implementation costs for information technology. The company's software endowment was done on a client/server with a small development team, rather than in five years with a large development group as demanded by the mainframers of the old Nordbanken.

7.5   Commodity Software and Tools for Advanced Business Solutions

Chapter 7.4 emphasized the point that advanced software solutions are crucial to industrial competitiveness and therefore they should move fast, targeting first-class results. Sophisticated software can be instrumental in improving the quality of one's business and the firm's reach. The emergence of software intelligence, coupled with high-speed communications, offers new and dramatic possibilities for the development of innovative products.

Statistics are increasingly convincing that high technology has the potential for great and far-reaching impact on personal productivity. At the same time, good management sense sees to it that one must define the exact roles to be played by the various actors in the high-performance program, doing so in world-level context by using the Internet. Computers and communications are a global market.

- A dynamic program is necessarily driven by *user needs*. This program must be results oriented and aimed at establishing industrial and financial leadership.
- Such a program must also be able to create domestic and international market conditions favorable to the development and maintenance of a competitive supply chain.

These are the goals to reach with ERP, CRM, and other programming products, not just in one location but throughout the network of a company's operations. This must be done efficiently while providing valid answers to a number of viewpoints, even if these viewpoints have partly complementary and partly conflicting requirements.

In a distributed environment, a number of different points of view must be supported at record speed. The information-handling function addresses data modeling and data flow, as well as data manipulation constraints. The computational side of the equation focuses on the structure of application components and the exchange of data and control among them. A properly studied methodology should target the streamlining of procedural and implementation chores.

Take as an example the process of adopting successive releases of bought software, referred to in the early part of this chapter. A method that I have found rewarding is to keep track of the time and cost of implementation of successive releases, both for internal control reasons and for post-mortem discussion with the vendor on its (usually optimistic) forecasts.

Exhibit 7.6 is a cost plot. The performance classification criteria are those of the company. For comparison purposes, it is sufficient to note the difference in terms of functionality and cost associated with the implementation of each release. As can be seen in the graph, bringing the next release into the mainstream required nearly 30 percent of the cost of the original implementation — but performance significantly improved. Over time, however, it was possible to reduce the implementation costs of new releases.

This balancing act between cost and functionality brings into perspective both engineering and managerial viewpoints. The latter concerns the mechanisms

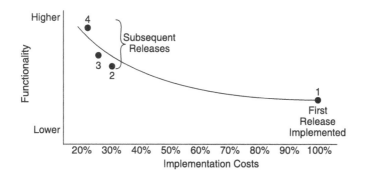

Exhibit 7.6   A Convenient Method for Keeping Track of Initial Cost of Programming Product Introduction and of Subsequent Releases

that provide transparency in terms of functionality and cost. Often, a significant cost chapter is that of handling constraints imposed by the technology from which the existing IT system is constructed. A longer-term cost viewpoint should look at optimization under specific cost-effectiveness considerations approved by the board.

To accomplish what was implied by the preceding paragraphs, one must have and use in an able manner powerful software tools. The old practice was that people who are interested in advanced IT projects often engage in relatively complicated developments because they use old tools and fail to take advantage of prototyping. This attitude implies that such people are not very interested in first-class applications.

New, more efficient software tools are urgently needed for rapid development because business thinking about software undergoes radical change over time. Company management is increasingly forced to make difficult choices about where to spend precious software dollars. A tool per se (e.g., object-oriented programming [see Chapter 7.1]), will never turn poor programmers into good ones. The opposite, however, is true. Poor tools will snow under the skills of good programmers, delay the expected deliverables, and contribute to budget overruns.

One should not forget that at the other end of the implementation spectrum are users of tools who may not quite understand the new application, and therefore continue in their way of thinking with the old method. Typically, this is too traditional. End users who are not particularly computer literate have no drive to get out of legacy systems or to employ new software that addresses their problems in a more effective manner — unless they are appropriately trained and understand the functionality made available to them.

Better development methods and better tools are urgently needed because there are also limits to the number of people who can effectively work together on the same project. One, two, or three people are acceptable but, as Exhibit 7.7 shows, with four or more people, personal productivity is sharply reduced. When the development team has ten or more people, a frequent phenomenon, productivity is at rockbottom.

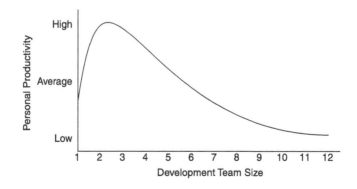

Exhibit 7.7   Programmer Productivity as the Size of the Development Team Increases

There are also constraints regarding the number of people who have the ability and aptitude to be software professionals. Today, England is already lacking 40,000 software workers. Germany has about the same statistics, although some estimates bring this number to 70,000 vacant IT posts. In the United States, vacancies in software engineering are much higher. Therefore, in late 2000, the U.S. Congress passed a law authorizing exceptional immigrant visas for 199,000 skilled analysts, designers, and programmers.

One has to face the fact that both corporate and national competitiveness in the New Economy depends significantly on tapping resources of well-trained people. These are the specialists who will develop imaginative programming products and their subsequent releases. The problem created by a shortage of skilled personnel is serious because a lack of qualified software workers can:

- Lead to a slowdown in the introduction of new products and services
- Make virtually impossible quality upgrades in programming products like ERP and CRM

As it cannot be repeated too often, innovation has historically been one of the key competitive advantages of many dynamic companies, but innovation requires more and more sophisticated software. There are, for example, some 300,000 lines of programming embedded in a cellular phone. Somebody must write them.

Experts suggest that millions of lines of software code will also be needed for future automobiles. New banking products will contain millions of embedded lines of programming. New developments see to it that the demand for software rises steadily over the years. Part of the shortage in qualified technologists comes from the fact that in most firms senior management has been slow to realize that a modern company is software enabled and software intensive.

This means that management has not seen software development and maintenance as one of its core competencies. Indeed, on the surface, Old Economy companies do not appear to be in the business of making software, yet the products and services they sell are more computer reliant than ever before, and they will be even more so in the coming years.

7.6 Product Markup Language for the Smart Materials World

This chapter makes several references to the need for better tools, beginning in the introductory remarks, which brought to the reader's attention the Product Markup Language (PML) for describing physical objects. PML is based on the eXtensible Markup Language (XML), which is a development of the Hypertext Markup Language (HTML), the common programming tool on which most Web sites are based.

HTML enables any user to surf the Internet from a desktop. But whereas HTML tells the computer how information should be displayed, XML goes a step further by instructing the computer on what kind of information the user is viewing. Microsoft has developed Visual Studio.NET, which is an XML-based tool. It is both a programming model and a means for rapid application development. The object of Visual Studio.NET is to make possible easy delivery of highly distributed programmable services running across stand-alone machines. These can be located at corporate data centers or in the Internet environment. This is commendable, but it is not enough with smart materials. MIT's PML goes further:[4]

- It helps in building-in layers of increasingly specific data to describe physical objects, their configuration, and their state.
- It provides instructions for machines that process or alter a product, such as motor vehicle processors, microwaves, machine tools, and other equipment.

Together with the Electronic Product Code (discussed in Section II), PML satisfies the basic components needed to automatically link information with physical objects. In other terms, it provides urgently needed connectivity between the physical network and the logical or digital network.

PML functionality is found beyond handling static data. This choice was made in appreciation of the fact that there is a need to communicate *dynamic data:* that is, information that changes as a product is being used, ages, or is consumed. Examples are changes in weight, volume, temperature, moisture, pressure, and other variables being tracked through metrics. In principle, a company should not forego a new release that includes PML.

The design of PML accounts for the fact that future applications will most likely need to include software that describes how an object behaves. For example, a PML file may contain the program that says how fast a resource will be used before it needs to be replaced — or how fast a production process will run out of inventories, given available levels and current consumption.

In connection with smart materials applications, there is also a need for an Object Naming Service (ONS) that ensures that the physical network and the logical network can effectively work together. The object is to provide universal connectivity between objects in the physical world and their digital mapping. Some of the challenges currently addressed by researchers at MIT's Auto-ID Center include *how* PML will:

- Handle both static information and streaming, dynamic data from physical sensors
- Accommodate individual objects, bit object hierarchies, assemblies, and aggregates
- Facilitate distributed management of product and process information at central locations, such as factories, warehouses, and sales outlets

- Provide for security (preferably embedded in the language) to ensure that proprietary information is protected

Still other challenges are making feasible ways and means for software changes and upgrades to take place simultaneously and immediately; guaranteeing that products are linked with the most up-to-date data; enabling real-time access to critical information; channeling online recycling instructions; and including multifunctional timestamps at product and process level. Full support must be provided for scripts and scenarios, device drivers, control systems, and the intelligent management of an environment.

A major challenge is that of software testing in connection with applications that can be as diverse as the administration of a supply chain, enterprise resource planning, customer relationship management, and other implementations in-the-large, and also novel applications in-the-small, such as smart appliances, automatic check-outs, theft deterrence, focused advertising, instant service manuals, and dynamic pricing.

Finally, whether talking about new tools or old ones, development toolkits or entire applications, programming products or in-house routines, always keep in mind that software testing is an indispensable part of software development, implementation, and maintenance. It consists of executing a program with the intent of finding errors, omissions, and bottlenecks in the code. Only exhaustive testing can give some assurance about the absence of errors in a computer program.

If for some test the software behaves incorrectly, then it is either inexact or it contains errors. However, if it behaves correctly, this does not mean that it is free of errors. All it means is that the errors were not found. To repeat this statement: if the tested program behaves correctly, this only shows that with the test method and the test data being used, it works.

It is precisely because of this uncertainty between the part and the whole, the visible error and the hidden error, that exhaustive testing is done to establish a degree of confidence that a computer program does what it is supposed to do. This is accomplished by means of test cases involving description of the input data and of the correct output for that set of input data.

The best policy with test cases is that they are written to explore both normal conditions and outliers; for example, invalid and unexpected input/output conditions; twists in the processing sequence, which are unlikely but possible; loops that might not have been evident at first sight; and other events of relatively low likelihood but still able to upset a computer program.

Test cases should cover all the syntax and semantic rules of the language. In the special case of PML, they should incorporate dynamic data; and in all advanced software cases, they should generate opportunities for errors in all contexts in which the program is expected to run. A test case is thought to have passed its testing process if after compiling and executing, the generated output matches the expected output not in one but 100 or more repetitions.

In conclusion, one of the main problems in software development, testing, implementation, and maintenance is the impossibility of ensuring a 100 percent coverage of the system undergoing the sort of critical examination being espoused. In science, one is more sure when one rejects a case (or a theory) than when one accepts it. Any acceptance is tentative because it only means that thus far no reason(s) have been found for rejection.

Notes

1. D.N. Chorafas, *Visual Programming Technology*, McGraw-Hill, New York, 1996.
2. D.N. Chorafas and Heinrich Steinmann, *Object-Oriented Databases*, Prentice-Hall, Englewood Cliffs, NJ, 1993.
3. D.N. Chorafas and Heinrich Steinmann, *Expert Systems in Banking*, Macmillan, London, 1991; and D.N. Chorafas, *Simulation, Optimization and Expert Systems. How Technology is Revolutionizing the Way Securities are Underwritten, Analyzed and Traded*, Probus, Chicago, IL, 1992.
4. See also PML's contribution with smart materials, in Section II.

ORGANIZATIONAL PREREQUISITES FOR SMART MATERIALS, AUTOMATIC IDENTIFICATION, AND QUALITY ASSURANCE

II

Chapter 8

The Next Frontier in Technology and in Supply Chain Management: Automatic Identification

Nobody will dispute the need for identification in human society. Everyone has a name and identification (ID) card. Many of us who travel internationally have a passport with name, vital vitae, and a photo. But this concept of accurate identification, article-by-article and entity-by-entity, has not yet taken hold in the physical world in a universal manner.

During the past few years, microchips have started to be used as identifiers. Silicon ID has been embedded in employee identification tags worn around employees' necks. These chips communicate to a corporate system that registers when employees arrive in the morning, when they leave in the evening, as well as where and for how long they went from one department to another or for lunch.

Some experts think there may come a day when chips are not just worn around the neck, but are actually implanted under human skin. This sounds like science fiction, but it is not impossible given that the tagging idea has already taken hold, albeit for inanimate objects. One opinion I have heard in my research is that as more and more objects have chips that act as identifiers, transmitters, and receivers, industry will essentially be endowed with a sort of global positioning systems (GPS) that will allow companies to track their assets at all times through the use of ID tags and satellites.

People and companies promoting this solution speak of benefits ranging from real-time inventory management to the control of assets, including, through steady tracking, a significant reduction in stealing of property. Other possibilities are also under examination, such as smart highways that can communicate with cars already running on them or ready to gain access.

It has been a deliberate choice not to enter into futuristic discussions in this text. Instead, the present chapter focuses on what is currently available or what will be available in the near future (for example, the use of automatic identification (auto-ID) in connection with Internet commerce, online supply chain requirements, and other applications from which there is benefit at an affordable cost). Auto-ID becomes more important as one begins to appreciate that people live in a physical world with physical objects that need to be uniquely identified to face the challenge of connecting the physical world to the virtual (data) world.

Here is exactly where the concepts of classification and automatic identification come into play. The next wave of change in the supply chain will see to it that the notion of handling inanimate objects will evolve as radically as it did with Henry Ford's assembly line at the beginning of the twentieth century. The first message this chapter conveys to the reader is that we are at the threshold of a major transformation.

- The revolution currently under way in merchandising and distribution parallels that of the assembly line in terms of depth and the likelihood of its being widespread.
- At its roots is a unique identification code for each individual item that is embedded in products, printed in packages, and used to store, transmit, and receive information to or from a reader.

In the post-PC era, $100 devices with resident agents and telecom gateways will receive and read the signal, translate the code, pass information to a computer directly or through the Internet, and generally share the received data stream with other intelligent entities. Such a system will permit multiple materials, platforms, and software modules to talk to each other while other software modules execute fully online accounting and logistics operations without human intervention. This will have a direct impact on the implementation of enterprise resource planning (ERP) and customer relationship management (CRM), as well as on Web-enabled solutions.

8.1 The Concept of Identification in a Physical World Is in Full Evolution

Section I has given evidence that, historically, the notions underpinning a supply chain did not change until the Industrial Revolution altered the means of transportation, making possible large transfers of heavy material over long distances. Trains and automobiles were nineteenth century developments. Then in the twentieth century came air cargo, air travel, computers, and networks, along with the notion of "communicate; do not commute."

In its first 100 years, and until the advent of computers, the Industrial Revolution did not particularly benefit the handling of information. Even after the commercialization of computing machines in 1954, the old bookkeeping methodology was retained. Any-to-any automatic linkages to all key nodes of the supply chain did not happen until the advent of the Internet that provided a total transformation. There is an aftermath from four decades of delay (1954–1994), which can be summed up by:

- As long as old concepts dominated, information about current status and future trend, therefore *visibility*, has not greatly improved — and this lasted during the first 50 years of computer usage.
- To the contrary, there has been a kind of reduced visibility — if not outright lack of reliable information — about future demand as the complexity of business increased with deregulation, globalization, and innovation.

A key reason for this persistent deficiency in visibility has been the latency in feedback from consumers and small businesses toward the main suppliers of goods. The Internet changed this perspective. It is expected that by 2002, about 2.2 million businesses will be connected to the Net and benefit from its any-to-any information services.

To appreciate the impact of this vendor-to-client connection executed in real-time, and client-to-vendor online feedback, one must keep in mind the negatives from lack of information, and even more so from misinformation. Reduced visibility at the sales end affects production planning and inventory control by creating uncertainties that lead to volatility in production schedules.

The hope is that smart materials will add to the Internet effect, increasing the ability to keep the information pipeline open, smooth the ups and downs of production planning, and allow for efficient management of inventories. It needs no explaining that smoother production and distribution schedules have a multiple effect; they lead to greater customer satisfaction, improve a company's competitiveness, help to swamp costs, and improve quality assurance.

Collaborative forecasting between the different players assists the back end of the supply chain in a significant way. It allows for targeting collaborative purchasing agreements, like that of Ford, General Motors, DaimlerChrysler, and Renault-Nissan, which represents a market of $250 billion per year and an estimated 10 percent savings in costs. An efficient two-way flow of information also improves the ability to compress the supply chain; the aim is not only to reduce costs, expenses, and timelags, but also to capitalize on supply chain dynamics.

Experts believe that improved supply chain dynamics will make the business partnerships' behavior much more predictable. But new and better solutions will not come easily. Entire supply chains will have to thoroughly analyze and revamp their logistics, a task that requires a significant effort in classification and identification (see Chapters 10 and 11). Otherwise, the effects of cross-industry purchasing agreements will be minor, while agency costs because of friction and confusion will be big.[1]

An example of how far one can go in reference to needed restructuring of physical resources, and the fact that legacy solutions are not fit for Internet-enabled business, is provided by the auto industry. Some experts think that if the motor vehicle industry had been invented at the start of the twenty-first century, it is most probable that the current structure would be dismissed as unworkable. Among other organizational defects, it features massive capital investments with low return on investment, and a continuing global over-capacity of some 20 million units.

One of the organizational defects that auto industry experts identify, and which has not been corrected with ERP, is vertical integration — because motor vehicle manufacturers want to produce virtually every nut and bolt. Only recently have the better-managed motor vehicle producers decided that their core competencies lie not in seats, suspension systems, or even chassis, but in styling, design, and marketing.

This urge to concentrate on core activities has as an aftermath a cultural change of significant proportion with identification of inanimate materials as a pivot point. Its impact is by no means limited to auto manufacturers, but extends to all firms. In practically every walk of life, companies do not really have a choice about radically restructuring their logistics. At least the more clear-eyed among them understand that there is a shakedown coming that will put to the test their financial staying power and see to it that their margins are dramatically shrinking.

The Internet adds its own weight to the restructuring of logistics. Real-time links between business partners have the effect that some supply chain intermediaries are being targeted for extinction. Their only hope to survive is greater efficiency, which capitalizes on universal visibility of information rather than antagonizing the wave of change, and also fully accounts for new patterns in regulatory issues, including taxation.

However, there are prerequisites to converting prevailing concepts about logistics restructuring into actual practice. One of these prerequisites leads to the issue of identification, more precisely that of auto-ID, in the physical world. Not only do logistics models need rethinking, but there is also the added flavor of a restructured accounting system able to respond to online supply chain challenges in an effective manner.

The careful reader will note the repeated emphasis on *identification,* but not *authentication.* Authentication is a very important issue for security and protection reasons, but it is not the subject of this book. Security is also an issue to which plenty of effort must be dedicated, with the goal to analyze strengths and weaknesses of current applications and ongoing projects. Assuming that one is comfortable with the level of security characterizing a particular system:

- All items automatically identifiable in the supply chain should have their accounts updated online, whether they are in storage, in transit, or in use.

- Online accounting brings along the need to radically revamp the concept of the voucher, which with auto-ID becomes associated to an electronic tag (e-tag).

Such a voucher/e-tag relationship is novel, and it carries all the way to the journal and the ledger. Ledger updates should be auditable online by all authorized persons or artifacts, with the journal serving as the reference platform. For item-level payments this, most evidently, cannot be done the old manual way. Inefficiency will be high, delays will make a legend, and costs will be prohibitive. It must be done in real-time through *agents*.[2] A great deal of the restructuring of accounting, and its impact on logistics, is encapsulated in this short paragraph.

8.2   Identification Is Key to Introducing Smart Technology into the Supply Chain

The concept of using *smart technology* in the supply chain for identification purposes is new. Yet, practical applications are not that far down the line. Some companies, such as Gillette, plan to start implementation of chip-based auto-ID by 2002, and they foresee a generalization of smart technology applications by 2005. International Paper has a joint project with Motorola, and other companies are actively engaged in a process of exchanging ideas, sharing vision on the course smart technology will most likely take.

But what is meant by smart technology? The simplest way to answer this query is to say that it represents the development of low-cost and low-power solutions that permit the use of smart material in the best possible way. What does smart material stand for? Any sort of material that one uses is an object one can classify and identify. It may be raw material, semi-manufactured goods, or ready products. It may be in process at the factory floor, stored in a warehouse, or in actual use in the home or office.

If this material, wherever it happens to be, has the means of knowing itself, or at least the class to which it belongs and its serial number, then it can be thought of as being smart; all the more so if it can receive messages from this material and respond in real-time to queries about its routing. This is the sense of *automatic identification*, which is based on very low-cost chips.

As Exhibit 8.1 suggests, auto-identification is the merger of two technologies: classification and identification (see Chapters 10 and 11), and semiconductors. Classically, inanimate material has been identified as a group: computers, chips, tables, chairs, razors, pencils, or other objects. Some of this material, typically the more expensive, has a serial number — therefore, individual identification. Autos, all sorts of motors, and personal computers are examples. This serial number, however, has the following limitations:

- It is typically issued by its manufacturer; it is not global.
- It is imprinted on a piece of metal attached to the machine; it cannot communicate its ID.
- It helps very little in inventory optimization, where the class to which the item belongs (not the individual item) is tracked.

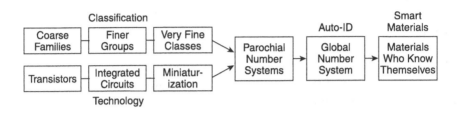

Exhibit 8.1   The Concept Underpinning Automatic Identification Is the Merger of Two Technologies

Both globality and auto-ID are important. Yet, despite big pronouncements such as the Universal Product Code (UPC), there has been a distinct lack of valid identification methods and procedures. In a globalized economy, this is a major drawback. Half-baked approaches such as UPC are not enough. Identification should have universal characteristics with synonyms and acronyms avoided as much as possible. This is not easy, but it is doable (see Chapter 10).

Classification is a prerequisite to a global ID system. Once a piece of material, any material, has been properly classified, it can be uniquely identified; and with low-cost technology, it is possible to go to the next step: automatic identification. What one needs to add to this material is a very inexpensive chip with an antenna; therefore, the ability not only to store the ID number but also to communicate it to other entities: materials or people.

A more advanced implementation stage of smart materials will go beyond communication and require some sort of computation. This will be available everywhere in abundance at very low cost during the coming years. The same is true for efficient, user-friendly personal access to databased resources to be used by smart materials and by people.

Individual item identification, chip technology, antennae, and direct access to databases are the pillars of the emerging and growing domain of smart technology. Several experts now consider the concept of smart materials as indivisible from the next major productivity strides — a process sure to impact, in a most significant way, enterprise resource planning. In all likelihood, ERP as it is known today will be turned on its head with smart materials. The same is true of CRM. Rather than using a long-established production plan, a manufacturing process will depend on the products it makes to organize their own processing and assembly operations. This may come about because smart materials can provide the manufacturing and distribution system with much

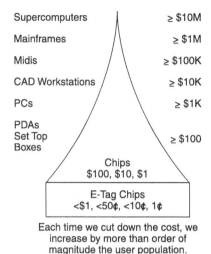

Supercomputers — ≥ $10M

Mainframes — ≥ $1M

Midis — ≥ $100K

CAD Workstations — ≥ $10K

PCs — ≥ $1K

PDAs Set Top Boxes — ≥ $100

Chips $100, $10, $1

E-Tag Chips <$1, <50¢, <10¢, 1¢

Each time we cut down the cost, we increase by more than order of magnitude the user population.

Exhibit 8.2   The New Pyramid of Computing at the Beginning of the Twenty-First Century

more information than the UPC's limited product-type data. There are, however, major organizational challenges to be addressed prior to this happening. For example, one must answer in a globally valid sense the following query: when does a given material become a thing for which auto-ID is necessary or at least makes sense because of foreseen developments?

To a large extent, the response is related to use, cost, and projected effectiveness. Gillette plans to identify every razor blade when the cost of an e-tag drops to 1 cent, which it eventually will. Exhibit 8.2 gives a bird's-eye view of the pyramid of computing devices and their costs, as it presents itself at the beginning of the twenty-first century. Computing devices are unique in the range of costs: those at the tip of the iceberg cost millions of dollars; at the base, chips are available for a few cents.

The perceptive reader will appreciate the opportunities that the bottom of the cost pyramid presents in terms of identifying inanimate materials. A global Electronic Product Code (EPC, ePC) based on the technology just described will lead to smart tags able to identify a practically unlimited number of individual items, as well as aggregates of goods such as assemblies, collections, or storage locations.

Individually, each of these goods will be able to transmit much more information than type and price. This information will help to create an intelligent infrastructure leading to far better inventory management and near-instantaneous customer checkout in retail environments — without human intervention.

What the reader should retain from this discussion is that the implementation and use of smart tags is not only technically feasible, it is also commercially practical once the price of manufacturing and applying smart tags drops to a few cents each. More demanding, however, than the design of the single chip is the ability to fulfill system prerequisites. One of the challenges is the *architecture* to be used. Without doubt, a global system of automatic identification requires an open architecture, and an open mind about the nature of e-tags and their communications chores.

The tougher part of the smart materials revolution will be cultural because organizations are made of people and people tend to keep old habits. Both an open architecture and an open mind are made necessary by the fact that the global supply chain is the largest network in the world. It is operating all the time, seamlessly to most people, and it is at the same time sophisticated, random, and complex.

When they serve a larger scope than the local retailer, supply systems tend to become self-sustaining entities with totally distributed command and control characteristics. One of the marvels of stand-alone supply systems is the way that big cities, such as New York, London, and Paris, feed themselves without any bureaucrat pulling strings from a Kafkasian castle.

Experts believe that the impact of smart supply systems on the economy is going to be so profound that when these systems change, the real world as we know it will change with them. Therefore, a major challenge in the coming years is to identify how the virtual world of supply systems connects to the real world of physical entities (humans and machines) and how the two influence each other.

As Exhibit 8.3 suggests, the real world of entities and the virtual world of data are coupled together. Classically, these links have been *ad hoc* and mostly local. However, the Internet has changed all that because it provides a global interconnection capability. As a result, more and better organized online interfaces are in development — some planned, others self-generated and self-sustaining through I-commerce — although many of the latter are still weak. The next wave of change, which most likely will make these interconnection links stronger, is auto-ID. This is expected to provide a bigger step forward in coupling interfaces than seen thus far with computers.

As technology advances and sophisticated solutions come at reasonable cost, it is unavoidable that the interfaces between the real world and the virtual world will change. Most links are provided today, by and large, through Old Economy solutions. However, to have these two worlds — the

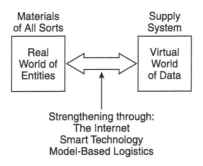

Exhibit 8.3   The Link Between Real and Virtual Worlds Has Classically Been Weak, but Technology Helps to Strengthen the Tie

physical and the logical — seamlessly merge their services, the New Economy will have to reinvent the sense of linkages, their nature, and the way they are used.

In conclusion, auto-identification by smart materials and the ability of all entities to communicate their information or ask for other datastreams will revolutionize current concepts. Nothing has yet been seen concerning the real magnitude of the oncoming change and its management. Sending and receiving data by inanimate entities will cause changes in the physical world beyond those experienced during the past 60 years with computers and give a big boost to Internet commerce because I-commerce will be at the core of streamlining the total supply chain.

Today, Internet commerce still represents approximately 6 percent of the U.S. economy's supply chain, including dealing in shares and therefore in virtual commodities. In other countries of the Group of Ten, this figure is smaller, which documents that I-commerce has a long way to go to serve the global economy. Any solution should consider the broader perspectives of globalization, deregulation, innovation, penny e-tags, and universal broadband communications — both in setting goals and in reaching them.

8.3 Goals to Be Achieved Through Automatic Identification

There are four major components in the solution targeted by MIT's automatic identification project: the ID code, ID system, Internet directory, and language. The latter is the Product Mark-up Language (PML) discussed in Chapter 7. The implementation of auto-ID has put forward several objectives, each with characteristic contributions to greater supply chain efficiency, including:

- Enrichment of product information
- Ordering via the Internet
- Fast replenishment in the shop
- Automatic check-out and online debit
- New ways to strengthen customer loyalty
- Product customization to each customer's needs

Perceptive people in American industry believe that these are not far-out objectives. They are doable in the coming years because the technology is available. Therefore, several companies have already espoused MIT's implementation plans. For example, as already mentioned, the timetable projected by Gillette is very short; by 2002, the smart materials application will be under way, and by 2005, Gillette will begin wider implementation of auto-ID.

There are several reasons why companies stand behind the auto-ID project. Today, marketing is badly served through current product identification. The bar code-based Universal Product Code is over 35 years old, and it does not perform that well. Another catchword, electronic article surveillance (EAS), is about 30 years old, and it can only handle some 20 percent of all products.

There are also other shortcomings with current methods that make them unfit for twenty-first century challenges. Non-smart tags approaches, like bar codes, are not able to guarantee that the sales area is refitted with goods in real-enough-time. Current statistics indicate that a shopper in the United States finds that 8 percent of the items he or she wants are not on the racks during the week. This is raised to 11 percent on weekends.

In contrast, with smart tags used by all items on display, replenishment will be done automatically. Floor intelligence will be informed by rack intelligence on items whose frontline inventory is thinning. But able use of auto-ID obliges one to rethink the entire design, packaging, and merchandising process — as well as to seamlessly integrate the new system's components with those already in place. Otherwise, there will be crevasses in process management.

Take the ID code as a first example of a basic component of the automatic identification system. The need for a global approach is promoted by the fact that since the early 1970s, the UPC has helped in better management of retail checkout and inventory upkeep, but it is now reaching (or has reached) the limits of what it can do. For example, it does not carry enough information to universally distinguish individual articles within a group of products. Competitive pressures see to it that the required level of detail is individual identification, achieved in a dependable manner. Another requirement is descriptive information with limits for items such as medicine and packaged foods. Medical and food products must indicate *where* and *when* they were made, *what* they contain, and the expiration date. As new diseases show up, ID information requirements increase significantly — as is the case in tracking beef and beef derivatives to their origin because of mad cow disease.

Other individual product information demanded by regulatory authorities is how the goods were prepared, how each item should be used, how it should be sorted for recycling efficiency when discarded, and other items that simply were non-existent at the time the UPC was designed. New managerial requirements also see to it that many products are identified through a unique name beyond the serial number, to include commercial characteristics and origin (see Chapters 10 and 11).

Solutions to this glut of individual information will be provided by the Electronic Product Code (EPC), which within its 96 bits integrates the UPC (see Chapter 9); whole low-cost chips make available 1 kbit of storage. EPC is still in development and MIT's Auto-ID project works with both its sponsor organizations and the Uniform Code Council to:

- Reach consensus with those who manufacture, transfer, and use goods up and down the supply chain
- Establish a standard numbering protocol through the assignment of values to EPC's partitions

In my judgment, an able solution to the problem posed by the second bullet poses a further-out identification problem, as will be seen in Chapter 10. Neither is the ID code the only challenge. While the EPC may currently be a focal point of attention, another team at MIT works on how the ID system would tick as a whole. A vital part of the new system is the tag-and-reader identification, keeping in mind that the impact of a good solution will be felt all the way from the design and networking for single reader stations to mass production and usage of low-cost/high-performance e-tags.

Part and parcel of the ID system study is ways and means through which the EPC embedded in an item sends a signal to the reader, the reader's ability to receive and process the message, the dependability of this communication process, and the aftermath of both material flow and inventory management (for example, the action to be taken after the product has been removed from the shelf).

Both foreground and background of such communications processes need to be studied. As an example, the present-day UPC is typically read by a scanner by manually swinging across the bar code. A more effective solution is that EPC communicates its information, including its unique ID, without human intervention. For this, each smart device must be able to automatically identify itself to a machine — an information exchange that must be studied in all its ramifications. It is the e-tag's business to communicate with a reader. The reader will be a device attached directly to the Internet, or indirectly through a gateway.

This is no far-fetched deal because the technology already exists for e-tags, their readers, and automatic information transfer between inanimate objects. From a system viewpoint, however, more is necessary in terms of directory assistance, for the dual purpose of:

1. Optimizing the cost of the solution being sought, while minimizing the cost of each e-tag
2. Providing, since the drafting board, means for maintaining flexibility and extensibility of the projected solution

Database mining will be key to fulfilling both objectives, hence the interest the MIT project brings to the use of an Internet directory and its real-time usage. Simply stated, after interpreting the auto-ID, the Internet directory will provide the information necessary to channel the message to the appropriate server. This server will contain appropriate product and package information to permit holding less data on the e-tag than otherwise necessary, therefore reducing local, item-by-item cost.

One option is the case of a data-poor EPC, where apart from a universal serial number providing a unique ID, no other information needs to be contained on the e-tag itself — because such data will be stored on the Internet server. The tag will only need to communicate a unique address that is linked to the server, where much richer information resides. At the other end of the spectrum of possible solutions is the data-rich e-tag that, under current technology, can contain 1 kbit of data, including regulatory and managerial information requirements.

The e-tag's advantages lie in the data-rich side. With 1 kbit of storage, very low-cost chips provide many more identification possibilities than are possible with bar codes. Also, unlike bar codes, they can be read from any angle, do not need to be in a reader's line of sight, and allow that information to be updated *en route*. Precisely because of capitalizing on such features, auto-ID aims to ensure the interconnection of networked physical objects in a way that is automatic, seamless, extensible, low cost, dependable, and characterized by standards (see Chapters 8.5 and 8.6).

No doubt, and as also seen in Chapter 7, any communications-intense solution brings to the foreground the need for defining the *language* that will allow e-tags, computers, software modules, and other nodes to talk to each other. The careful reader should recall that HyperText Markup Language (HTML) is the common means for most Web sites.[3] Also discussed were the Extensible Markup Language (XML) and the Product Markup Language (PML):

- HTML instructs an Internet device how information should be displayed.
- XML tells the computer what kind of information it is viewing in a particular instance.
- PML, MIT's own development, is based on XML and allows inanimate objects to talk to one another.

As added value to the supply chain, this HTML, XML, PML sequence makes sense because the way to bet is that most smart material applications will rely on the Internet, particularly so because the Net is liberated from the confines of the personal computer. Eventually, everything will be tagged and everything will be online, with the Web playing the role of the wider system.

It is expected that this solution will increase the accuracy with which products move through the production floor, are warehoused, marketed, sold, and served after sales. Beyond better balancing, lower operational costs, and fewer errors, the supply chain will benefit from a significant reduction in manual intervention, therefore realizing much greater cost-effectiveness than is possible with today's classical means.

The hope is that a synergy between a global electronic product code and auto-identification will lead to a very significant improvement in inventory management. Supported by new technology, the evolving system will allow industries to recover billions in lost sales every year while cutting inventory costs. An ongoing challenge will, however, remain; that of making the electronic tags cheaper and cheaper to produce and implement. The underlying concept is *penny tags* that could place silicon chips on any material object at a cost that is perfectly affordable.

8.4 Why Automatic Identification Means Major Changes in Business Partnerships

The advent of an auto-ID system will promote further development of online commerce. I-commerce will get a great boost *if* and *when* current inefficiencies dating back to Old Economy solutions are overcome. Therefore, there is plenty of scope in studying the further-out impact of auto-ID, as well as in providing a steady stream of improvements.

From customer relationship management to enterprise resource planning and distribution chores, e-tags will in all likelihood underpin the new logistics. The expectation is that smart products and smart packages will bring massive efficiencies to the global supply chain, starting with the assistance they can provide to manufacturers in assembly lines as well as in tracking inventory and foiling counterfeiters. Other applications include integration with ERP and CRM software to promote customized products, new production paradigms, use of e-tags in robotics, and warehouse management.

These are fairly realistic and worthwhile objectives, as opposed to some others that do not particularly make sense (for example, the *smart fridge)*. This refrigerator can see what it contains and, if it does not see a certain item, it asks its owner whether he or she wants to order it; then, if yes, it orders it directly from the manufacturer online. Researchers working on smart materials are well advised not to use such examples in their presentations because they make a mockery of the entire system.

The integration of the facilities provided by e-tags into new releases of ERP and CRM software is, in my judgment, fairly urgent because the first smart materials and smart packages are scheduled to roll out by the end of 2001 or shortly thereafter. They will permit manufacturers to track individual products and packages as they move from the assembly line to delivery trucks, and from there to store shelves and checkout counters.

The way to bet is that these first applications will be prototypes, on whose success will depend further implementation. Success will necessarily rest on how well this new departure will integrate with current manufacturing and marketing methods weeding out discontinuities. Therefore, both ERP and CRM software must be revamped to make such integration feasible.

If I ran a manufacturing company, the first implementation of e-tags I would do would be in-house in connection with production processes and inventory management. In this I would co-involve not only the MIT project developing smart materials and its business partners, but also ERP vendors. If one is serious about auto-ID, then one must start integrating its concepts and facilities at the design and prototyping stage.

Projecting and associating the EPC to a given product should be part of computer-aided design (CAD) software.[4] A similar statement is valid in connection with ERP solutions, which will see the product, its components, and its assembly through the manufacturing process. Using e-tags in connection to ERP will quite likely require a major update of ERP software (see Chapter 7).

Even so, it will be worth the investment because production is a controllable environment, and one can apply experimental design methods similar to those used by General Electric (see Chapter 12). The final test of any new notion is, Does it work? To prove it does work, the test must co-involve the worlds of inventory management and scheduling of manufacturing lines.

If the auto-ID concept successfully passes in-house testing, then it will parallel one of the greatest twentieth century developments — Henry Ford's assembly line. By installing a moving belt in his factory, Ford enabled employees to build cars one chunk at a time. This produced efficiencies of such scale that in 1915, Ford was able to eliminate 65 percent of the price of an individual Model T.

The fact that such huge price reductions upset the scales of competition and made automobiles accessible to a large population of consumers is well-known. Another significant aftermath is the process of mass production that affected a much broader range of industry than motor vehicles *per se*. What about marketing operations and the integration of the e-tag with CRM software?

A sound management principle is that if the in-house test through manufacturing gives positive results, then e-tags should be subject to experimental design for tests in merchandising, from marketing to distribution and after-sales service. This is where e-tag integration with CRM software makes sense. Starting with marketing, as several projects today do, is like putting the cart before the horse. Problems that will invariably arise will be pushed upstream.

Provided that both the manufacturing and marketing tests of smart materials are successful, their paradigm shift will be *online customization* at an affordable cost. Smart online customization to client requirements will turn the supply chain on its head. Sophisticated new logistics, global supply chain, and auto-ID work in synergy, as Exhibit 8.4 suggests. To appreciate what may

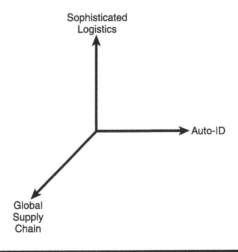

Exhibit 8.4   The Frame of Reference of Smart Materials that Contributes to the Pace of the New Economy

come out of this synergy, one must remember what has already been said: that the global supply chain is the largest network in the world, bringing together the virtual world of logistics and the real world of manufacturing.

With smart materials, agile seamless interfaces and the ability of inanimate agents to communicate among themselves will automate operations that are still manual, despite 50 years of using computers. Account must also be taken of the opinion of many experts that the current limited flexibility of manufacturing systems is not the main barrier to online customization of products. The most important blocking factor is the manual fulfillment of customized orders. In the factory and in the office, people must still sort, track, package, and ship customized requests. This is prohibitive in terms of costs, especially for packaged goods and products with very thin margins.

People who participated in my research stated that this fact alone is evidence that ERP and CRM failed to deliver what they promised. For many companies, this is indeed true; but the answer to the query as to whether the failure is on the software or implementation side is more complex because many ERP and CRM applications are below a reasonable standard of performance (see Section I).

To help in better e-tag integration with CRM and ERP, as well as in upgrading these programming products, here in a nutshell is the scenario that will most likely characterize a thoroughly restructured logistics process. A customized order will be received over the Internet; it will be assigned an electronic product code and scheduled for production; the EPC will be embedded in a smart tag attached to the item; and a low-cost chip will literally be printed on the package. From this point on, the identification/communication process will take on, so to speak, its own life.

- The smart tag will communicate its needs to smart machinery.
- It will tell to whom it should be shipped as well as other delivery details.
- Knowledge artifacts will optimize the routing, issuing appropriate instructions.

Prerequisites are evident in implementing this kind of on-demand solution. In addition to the assignment of an exclusive ID number with self-communicating capabilities to each object, there is a need for modeling, simulation, and optimization to help in handling physical and logical (virtual) items. Experts believe that multi-modal information tracking needs to be both statistical and analytical.

The new logistics system must be designed to answer the basic goal of allowing inanimate objects to communicate with each other and with people on their own initiative. Because this solution should be global, there is a requirement for standards. The drive to normalization leads to other issues, such as the necessity for international agreements and the evolution of generally appealing tools and ID methods — beyond the standards *per se*.

8.5 The Need for a Sound Policy Regarding Technical Standards

To introduce the concept underpinning the need for global standards in a rigorous manner, one can start with a definition of the word *standard*. Etymologically, the term means any figure or object, such as a flag or banner, used as emblem or symbol of a community or military unit. A standard is also a reference, a norm, something established for use as a unit of measurement (e.g., the meter), technical characteristic (e.g., the Internet Protocol [IP]), or quality of material (e.g., the proportion of pure gold and base metal).

A standard is something recognized as correct by common consent, approved custom, industry agreement, rule, or regulation. As such, it helps as a guide in the domain where it applies because it is regarded as a goal or measure of accuracy. Because it is viewed as a general reference, a standard tends to be associated with a *model*.

- Without standards on which to rest, no new product would survive the market's test for a long time.
- Any product and any process needs a generally accepted frame of reference, targeted by setting standards.

Standards, and therefore *norms*, can be established by professional bodies or *ad hoc* by market leaders. In its heyday, IBM imposed the mainframe standards, particularly ones connected to its operating system MVS. Today, a standards setter in operating systems is Microsoft; in microprocessors, it is Intel. Standards set by professional bodies can be national or international.

International standardization efforts usually begin after a certain product or process reaches a degree of maturity. It is not just a matter of chance that since the 1950s, standards have typically been dominated by technology, and they are by and large *de facto* type standards. This happens for two reasons. First, immediately after the development of a new product or process, the time is not right to exert controls and norms by inter-industry bodies. The risk is high that standards will be half-baked and they would stiffen a still-primitive new product, ossifying it in terms of future development.

Second, the people who are supposed to be the standard-setters do not have — at such an early stage — a clear image of what the norms should be. This has happened with a variety of products. By the early 1920s, for example, the architecture of automobiles became standardized and has not been altered significantly since then. Some experts suggest that this normalization has hurt both the motor vehicle industry and the consumer.

Standards characterizing communications and computer systems have often been controversial. For example, by the early 1970s, a standards effort has been directed toward integrating computers and communications by subordinating different developments to national and international standards influenced by "this" or "that" vendor. IBM's System Network Architecture (SNA) and DEC's Digital Network Architecture (DECNET) — both dating from 1974 — are examples. Neither lasted more than 20 years.

When they were released as *de facto* standards, both SNA and DECNET provided networking for terminals and host computers, including the distribution of processing functions, but they did not directly address the problem of universal interconnectivity in a heterogeneous environment. However, the concept that equipment from different vendors should work in a seamless way throughout a network, beyond the level of plug-compatible devices, was not alien at the time.

In the late 1970s, the International Standards Organization (ISO) put forward a seven-layer model of network architecture, known as the reference model for open systems interconnection (ISO/OSI). Correctly, this system architecture did not involve specific hardware implementations, and it was linked to no vendor in particular. Its goal was the structure of protocols needed in data communications. The layers in the OSI reference model have been associated with different levels of interaction enabling the network to work as one body. The protocols for each of the seven layers are communications rules, and interfaces were included for each two successive layers to talk to one another.

The ISO/OSI model lasted about 20 years. Some governments, like that of Japan, turned it into a national policy on technology. But it is no less true that shortcomings revealed themselves quite early; for example, since the beginning of the 1980s with local area networks. At the same time, vendors with established system architectures did not pay attention to ISO/OSI's layered structure. IBM used to say that SNA is compatible end-to-end but not layer-to-layer with ISO/OSI.

Other ISO/OSI limitations are related to intelligence of the attached device, and of the network as a whole. In the late 1970s and early 1980s, devices were not intelligent; the practical use of expert systems in industry and banking was still some years away[5] and there was no perceived need for automatic identification. Yet, some companies (e.g., Ford in the United States, Osram in Germany, and Italcementi in Italy) felt the need for a classification and identification system that could help all the way from production planning and control to inventory management, marketing, and customer service (see Chapters 10 and 11).

For the most part, these have been individual initiatives by companies that care to improve management of their production processes, inventories, and sales efforts. In a global sense, standards for identification have been until recently an issue on the back burner. However, this concept was not alien to ancient civilizations. "Guide the people by virtue and regulate them by *li* (sense of propriety), and the people will have a sense of honor and respect," Confucius used to say. He insisted on the rectification of names, calling a spade a spade. His logic was based on *If, Then* arguments:

- "*If* the name is not rectified, *then* the whole style of one's speech is not in form, and orders cannot be carried out."

- "*If* orders are not carried out, *then* the proper forms of worship and social intercourse cannot be restored."
- "*If* the proper forms of worship and social intercourse are not restored, then legal justice in the country will fail."

Confucious also used to say that "when legal justice fails, then the people are at a loss to know what to do and what not to do." In business and industry, people and companies are often at a loss to know what to do and what not to do when the resources that they manage are not properly classified and identified. To correctly identify the machines, spares, tools, accounts, and even concepts being used, one must first classify them. This calls for a rigorous methodology (see Chapter 10). It also requires standards.

The need for standards is most often felt when dealing with complex systems in which transparency becomes important, and it cannot be efficiently supported without a properly studied process of normalization. As Exhibit 8.5 illustrates, the more global and more complex the network, the greater the need for standards. A similar statement applies to databases and any other technological system.

Norms and standards, however, must be requirements-driven and not technology-driven. Some experts think that much can be expected during the next five years in this direction of revived interest in standardization, but I am not so sure because a standardization effort of the magnitude being discussed is unprecedented — and there is on hand no experience as to how to proceed when confronted with a global level of complexity in norms. To the contrary, there is experience suggesting that reaching international accords is, at best, a slow-moving enterprise full of potholes and traps.

There is also present the need for added value, which will further differentiate a standards-based auto-ID system from its predecessors. An example

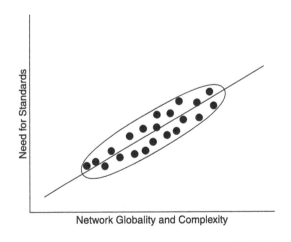

Network Globality and Complexity

Exhibit 8.5   Managing Network Globality and Complexity Has a High Correlation Coefficient with Standardization

is the ability to identify authentic products from fakes. In one meeting, I was told that with smart tags distributors and retailers would be able to confirm with accuracy whether or not the goods on their shelves are authentic. This statement is too simplistic for my taste, because counterfeiters are not dumb.

- Only the producer has access to detailed information about *when* and *where* each of his products was made, for *what* purpose, and of what specific type.
- But what the producer does not know is how many illegal copies of that product have been made, when, and by whom, or where they are now located and to whom they were sold.

Automatic transmission of product ID to the producer still leaves the tracking of counterfeits as a problem of colossal dimensions. I experienced it in the 1960s as a consultant to senior management of Omega, the Swiss watch manufacturer. Little has changed over these 40 years. Eventually, keeping life histories of every vendor's products and sales outlet's inventory will require *petabyte* (millions of gigabytes) databases and very powerful mathematical tools capable of determining the diameter and specifics of directed multigraphs.

This megaproject, which is not currently targeted, may be worth the effort, but solutions are not for tomorrow. Only the need for it is sensed. According to a study by the International Trade Association, the impact of product counterfeiting in terms of losses on the annual revenues of American companies alone mushroomed from $5.5 billion in 1982 to $200 billion in 1992. Exact data for the subsequent years is missing, but the educated guess is that it keeps on rising.

8.6 Bit-Level Standards and Infrastructural Developments

Today, databases are global, they are available interactively, and they are accessible from a large variety of end-user devices. Routinely, one connects to database systems through means that range anywhere from nomadic portable to big multi-million dollar machines. These devices are linked together through a network that knows the circuit end-to-end, but is often blind regarding the identifications of other real-world entities mapped into the database.

A change may come with e-tags. Standards are necessary to make identification effective. More precisely, there is need for two sets of standards: one for the network of *items* and one for the network of *bits*. Any study on standards concerning items and bits must account for the fact that today identification is both expensive and inefficient because it has not been properly researched after the advent of the bar code some 35 years ago. We also should not lose sight of the fact that classification is a prerequisite to efficient identification and would be a daunting task on a universal scale (see Chapter 10).

Bit-level standards and network standards relative to electronic product code systems should account for EPC's targeting a global implementation. Why is it necessary to establish standards on two levels? The answer is because we are faced with two challenges:

- The *network of items*, handled through Internet, intranets, and extranets. Here, the pivot point is the EPC which, as seen in Chapter 9, integrates UPC, ISBN, and all other codes. The careful reader will recall from the discussion on EPC made thus far that it will eventually label components, assemblies, systems, packages, containers — any commodity.
- The *network of bits*, which is a new concept and is generated from the network of items.

The fundamental issue underpinning the network of items and the network of bits is the ability to auto-identify, which requires an architectured solution able to serve, in an efficient manner, the post-PC era and its $100 hand-held devices that use agents and are object-centric. A layered architectural solution is shown in Exhibit 8.6.

Both nomadic agents operating hand-held devices (see also Chapter 9) and other job-specific agents in network nodes will be needed to serve the wider global business perspective. Some knowledge artifacts will be user oriented. The focal point of others will be in logistics, accounting for the fact that the EPC code is designed to handle any material — components, assemblies, systems, packages, containers — through a unique ID approach, while at the same time interactively incorporating current coding standards exchanged on the Web.

In systems terms, this polyvalence in identification procedures leads to another issue that has to do with advances in Internet infrastructure. Stated in simple terms: how much bandwidth should one expect in the coming years at an affordable cost? Will this bandwidth be cheap enough to encourage intensive

| Wider Business Logic |
| Interactive Logistics |
| Nomadic Agents |
| Objects |
| Intelligent Devices |
| Basic Services |

Exhibit 8.6   A Layered Architectural Solution Must be Able to Respond to Both Human and Smart Materials Communications

communications by low-cost items? Will available protocols be able to handle an expanding range of applications, links, and physical layer requirements.

Because of the law of the photon, which says that bandwidth doubles every nine months at practically equal cost, the answer to these queries tends to be positive. However, there is another challenge of a technical nature and it has to do with establishing and upholding universal type design criteria such as adaptability, scalability, efficiency, and quality of service.

None of these four criteria, by itself, appears to be an impossible task. Their synergy, however, tests the limits of current know-how, as the applications domains expand and there is talk of about 10^5 more connectivity than what there is today. The principle I learned in the early 1950s at UCLA is that when something changes by an order of magnitude, the way one looks at technical and managerial solutions should also change.

The difference associated with new challenges is five orders of magnitude, which is an immense challenge. It impacts on smart materials all the way from design to delivery and maintenance. A good example is quality of services (QOS). The upgrade of quality of service should be made through a quantum jump, similar to Six Sigma explained in Chapter 12.

Nobody should take lightly the level of quality necessary to confront this change by 10^5 in connectivity. System designers must concentrate on the solution space defined by the frame of reference in Exhibit 8.7, keeping in mind that some of the changes in concept and in approach need to be radical. For example, the Internet currently works hop-by-hop. There must be a much better infrastructure than that for quality of service, including solutions capable of any-to-any interoperability, and mobility, given wireless access.

Because in all likelihood the budgets necessary for systems conversion will be large, experts advise that the big amounts of money currently spent by carriers on upgrading an extending existing twentieth century infrastructure

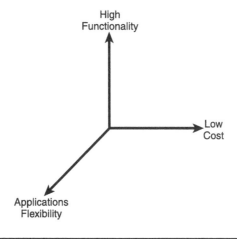

Exhibit 8.7   A Frame of Reference in the Development and Implementation of 10^5 Greater Connectivity

must be reevaluated with both innovation and integration as goals — or even outright redirection of design and implementation. It is just as important to account for new departures in applications, including the concept of disaggregated devices discussed in Chapter 9.

Notes

1. D.N. Chorafas, *Internet Supply Chain — Impact on Accounting and Logistics,* Macmillan, London, 2001.
2. D.N. Chorafas, *Agent Technology Handbook,* McGraw-Hill, New York, 1998.
3. D.N. Chorafas, *Visual Programming Technology,* McGraw-Hill, New York, 1996.
4. D.N. Chorafas, *Engineering Productivity Through CAD/CAM,* Butterworths, London, 1987.
5. D.N. Chorafas and Heinrich Steinmann, *Expert Systems in Banking,* Macmillan, London, 1991.

Chapter 9

Advances Underpinning Development and Use of the Electronic Product Code

Costs matter. A practical implementation of automatic identification might not have seen the light of day if not for the technology advances that make feasible very low-cost auto-ID chips. No matter how important the reasons for smart materials might be, the ratio of the ID chip's cost to the cost of the material to which it is applied remains an important criterion of any implementation decision.

In mid-April 2000 when Motorola announced its BiStatix chip (see Chapter 9.2), it tagged to it no exact price. The industry, however, felt that as a start its cost would be well below 50 cents, although still above 10 cents. Market participants with whom I spoke suggested their interest in BiStatix will be in inversely proportional to its price, targeting below 5 cents within a relatively short time span, and being eventually priced at the 1-cent level.

The Electronic Product Code (EPC) and the chip on which it will be stored define the functions assigned to e-tags and the automatic identification process at large. A system solution involving e-tags has also been studied from the viewpoint of providing cost-effective approaches at the reader's end. It is to the credit of the MIT auto-ID project that system specifications are being chosen, whereby e-tags receive from and relay information to a computer through an antenna, and ink can be drawn on the material's surface to make the entire box an antenna, if this proves necessary.

To receive and transmit, the chip needs two antennae, roughly arranged in the manner shown in Exhibit 9.1. Capitalizing on identification and communications facilities, this solution makes possible real-time tracking of all

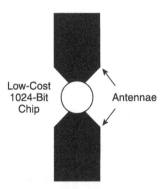

Low-Cost
1024-Bit
Chip

Antennae

Exhibit 9.1   Motorola's Bistatix Chip Requires Two Antennae to Receive and Transmit Data

materials in storage or in transit at any point in the supply chain. Information becomes readily accessible not only on ID, but also on availability, volumes, servicing levels, and other variables important to front-office operations, and therefore closely connected to customer relationship management.

Immediately following the announcement of BiStatix, International Paper was the first company to announce that, in a joint project with Motorola, it will use the chip in some of the 8.5 million tons of corrugated crates, glossy perfume boxes, and other packages that it produces annually. The goal is to vastly improve upon current UPC approaches by providing greater visibility of each item and continuity of supply chain information.

On precisely the same premises, Gillette suggested that it targets a 1-cent chip embedded on top of every razor blade. With an estimated 2.0×10^{10} razor blades manufactured each year, Gillette's unique item-by-item identification requires 34 bits for auto-ID — or roughly one third the storage currently available on the BiStatix chip.

Managing the whereabouts of each unit is critical to control of the supply chain, according to Gillette. But as discussed in Chapter 8, able use of auto-ID obliges us to rethink the entire identification/classification concept (see Chapters 10 and 11), as well as the packaging and merchandising procedures, among other vital elements of a total solution. It also brings into perspective the need to:

- Design the electronic product code independently of current constraints in technology, while still capitalizing on what is technically available (see Chapter 9.1)
- Integrate into the solution to be retained both ERP and CRM business processes, to enhance application building and provide a roadmap to guide the hand of designers and implementers

Essentially, this means integrating CRM front-office transactions with back-office ERP and legacy transaction processing in a way that promotes the supply chain, provides for efficient inventory management, ensures better quality of service, automates delivery operations, and generally closes the current intelligence gap in business and industry. The most promising application of EPC should, in my judgment, be seen within the perspective of a whole range of sophisticated solutions.

9.1 Objectives of Wider Implementation of Electronic Product Code

The kernel of a new, more effective solution based on smart materials and the restructuring of global supply chain operations is enabling management to be efficient and effective. The contribution of e-tags and of the EPC should be seen from this perspective. One can better appreciate the range of possibilities presented by a chip-based naming scheme for physical objects if one thinks in the following terms: 1024 bits of information in an e-tag with antenna will soon be available at less than 10 cents.

An enrichment of product code through semantics would provide the infrastructure that enables organizations to build an effective online business. Product profiling, transaction processing, targeted marketing, and merchandising can integrate to create a comprehensive, customized system. Because the antenna transmits the bits stored on the chip and also receives information, the ground is there for any-to-any, two-way communication — which revolutionizes the whole concept of logistics.

Some manufacturers and merchandisers believe that a system based on these premises will start full-scale implementation by 2005 — just a few years away — thus greatly facilitating information exchange among inanimate objects. Once the methodology is in place, this solution will provide for extensibility of the code and assist in the definition of all kinds of materials beyond the level of an original classification (see Chapter 10.4 on further definiens).

As this online interactive system comes into place, a CRM applications architecture will help to bring together the main building blocks of an integrative solution able to support a wealth of business processes. The applications system can serve as a roadmap to guide the development and deployment of the solution, which, according to some estimates, will be the hallmark of the first decade of the twenty-first century.

The reference to a roadmap for implementation is intended to ensure that it is a well-thought-out order in which ERP and CRM processes can integrate in a smart materials environment. The study must cover not only the systems architecture, but also the risks associated with its implementation and the alternatives that exist in managing them. Critical elements in this type of study include:

- The grand design of an architecture capable of incorporating ERP, CRM, and intelligent business processes
- Specific issues relating to each industrial sector to be supported in a flexible manner parametrically under the business architecture

- The ability to relate e-tags to applications such as financial management, direct customer service, and fast flow replenishment

Details are important inasmuch as new departures in system solutions are fundamentally iterative and one must know in advance where each iteration might lead. Subsequent improvements will be driven by the repetition of tasks and the feedback these provide, as well as by the availability of new technology.

Sometimes, the results of iterations are predictable and one can plan what to do with them. However, there may also be deliverables that are unpredictable or impossible to anticipate. Therefore, companies intending to use smart materials must first and foremost learn how the e-tag model can be employed experimentally to:

- Portray solution trade-offs
- Prioritize design issues and determine where to concentrate efforts
- Establish the rate of convergence of each of the problems that will unavoidably arise

Just as valuable is the ability to decouple complex problems into issues to handle. This requires attention to minute detail, starting at the level of electronic product code. The researchers at MIT's Auto-ID center have indicated that there were two major considerations in code design: bit count and partitioning.

A primary reason for partitioning the electronic product code has been to facilitate namespace search. Another reason is that this makes feasible the incorporation of UPC, EAN, SCC-14, SSCC-18, UCC/EAN-128, and ISBN into EPC, thereby providing a basis for a soft transition from the old code to the new without upsetting product code approaches currently in use. EPC has four bit partitions:

1. *Header*, 8 bits: contains metadata (see Chapter 7) to explain the code's organization to the reader
2. *Manufacturer*, 24 bits (a UPC concept): enables 64 million unique identifications
3. *Product*, 24 bits: stock keeping unit (SKU), also UPC; with 64 million unique IDs
4. *Serial number*, 40 bits: provides for 1 trillion unique identifications

The statement was made during the Smart World Conference (April 12–13, 2000) that 40 bits are plenty for a serial number, keeping in mind the fact that EPC aims to ensure auto-ID through a unique name. The statistics in Exhibit 9.2 were given as to the number of bits necessary for unique identification.

In a sideline discussion at this conference, it was noted that since we do not plan to automatically identify every grain of rice, 40 bits seem plenty for

Exhibit 9.2 The Number of Bits Necessary for Unique Identification

Bits	Number	Things
23	6.0×10^6	Automobiles, per annum
29	5.6×10^8	Computers, in use
33	6.0×10^9	People, total 1999
54	1.3×10^{16}	Grains of rice, per annum

ID of every person living on Earth, should the United Nations or some other big overhead organization one day decide to do so. This is a questionable argument because of the intricacies involved in parallel classification/identification that might eventually involve a myriad of inanimate objects.

The solution that is chosen, including its strong and weak points, must be viewed with respect to both current and future implementation goals. The goal is to make inanimate materials smart; and for this reason, 40 bits allocated to the serial number are, in my judgment, not enough. To explain why, one must make two different hypotheses. One is that the serial number works in tandem with the 24 bits of manufacturer code. The other is that the 40-bit serial number is independent of the vendor; hence, it is a global serial number. If the serial number is per manufacturer, then there will be in the system many copies of the same serial number identifying different items. This will pose a horde of problems, not the least being to properly assign a code per manufacturer, without forgetting its subsidiaries, independent business units, and other entities under its wing. Even if this was doable at an acceptable level of accuracy and within a reasonable timespan, which should precede final EPC design let alone implementation, it may get unstuck somewhere down the line because of mergers and acquisitions.

Speaking from personal experience with item identification, product quality varies tremendously from one country to another — even from one factory to the next of the same company within the same country. It is therefore important that *origin* goes down to factory-level detail. It is no trivial problem to define and identify a factory.* Alternatively, if the serial number is global, which should be the case, then 40 bits is peanuts. It would not last long as a solution.

Short of having a central office assigning global serial numbers (an awful approach), the bit field must be large, albeit partitioned into smaller chunks. Chapter 10 suggests distinguishing between:

- `<basic code>`
- `<suffix>`
- `<origin>`

---

* In the 1970s, I had a project of this kind with Osram in Germany (now Osram-Sylvania in the United States), and I am talking in a documented manner (see also Chapters 10 and 11).

The `<basic code>` is a running number; `<suffix>` provides greater detail; and the concept `<origin>` is polyvalent because, apart from the aforementioned problem of variation in quality, it can also serve in the context of taxation. In fact, tax issues more than anything else have been at the beginning of the notion of `<origin>`, in the Osram project.

A good paradigm of a unique global identification code (EPC or any other), and the challenges that it raises, is what currently goes on with the assignment of Internet Domain Names (see Chapter 9.3). A good deal of the innovator's dilemma is related to how the *next events* will impact on what he or she is currently designing. Flexibility is always at a premium but sometimes it conflicts with other design criteria.

The current context of disjoint identification tags represented by UPC, SKU, IDS, and other codes has a silver lining. With a piecemeal approach, the probability of error is kept relatively small because limited portability standards see to it that these codes operate as discrete islands. In contrast, a universal EPC associated with smart materials and processed with *any* transaction, at any time and any place, presents the likelihood of a higher error quotient. Error control should be added to the objectives of EPC.

As discussed in Chapter 10, the `<basic code>` of the Dimitris Chorafas classification and identification system includes parity check. The code of smart materials should definitely feature an error control facility. Furthermore, and as already emphasized, the goals of classification and identification should be addressed separately — although the resulting codes must correspond one-to-one to each other and work in synergy. The stated goal of EPC is to *minimize* information content, product categorization, data storage or bit count, and computational requirements.

This is like killing four birds with one well-placed stone. To a substantial extent, these are conflicting requirements; in addition, they are not served that well with EPC as it currently stands. Entropy suggests that one can minimize information content by maximizing product categorization (classification) — and therefore organization. And one can minimize data storage at the local smart materials level by significantly increasing network-wide computer access and remote computational chores.

9.2 Can a Very Low-Cost Chip Change the Supply Chain Dynamics?

First and foremost, keep in mind that the electronic product code will address everything from products to packages, containers, and pallets. The products themselves will range from bolts, nuts, and fasteners to electric motors, gears, diesel engines, airplanes, and ships or locomotives. The packages can be cases, boxes, bundles, bags, rolls, baskets, bins, pallets, trucks, or storage rooms. Experience suggests that a statistically valid sample of this immense variety must be studied prior to committing to a new code.

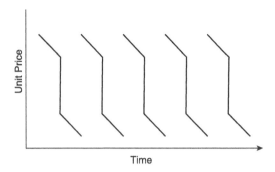

Exhibit 9.3   The Price of New Chips Drops First Slowly, Then More Rapidly, and They Disappear as Their Replacements Come Onstream

In many cases, a bottle (e.g., that of a perfume) will be in a box. Will the perfume and the box have the same or different serial numbers? This is a different issue than company and factory identification and, here too, the solution is not simple. As discussed in Chapter 10, the issue of *suffix* has to do with this query. The challenge is one of *a priori* weeding out *entropy*, because in the final analysis the EPC should be a very *short* ID for several reasons: transcription, transmission, and error probability among them.

A problem closely associated with organization is that of a low-cost chip. Since the invention of the first microprocessor in the early 1970s, the value of chips has always been influenced by their ability to reflect the users' near-term and longer-term needs at an ever-decreasing cost per operation (Moore's law). New microprocessors are introduced at a relatively higher price; this price drops slowly at first, then more rapidly as replacement(s) come on stream. This transition is shown in Exhibit 9.3. The ability of the semiconductor industry to renew its products and itself at a rapid pace ensures:

■ Higher and higher chip functionality
■ Availability at lower and lower cost per operation

Such development has characterized the history of semiconductors for nearly three decades. Significant advances in technology are instrumental in sharply reducing the cost of electronics, but they do not do this single-handedly. Their ability to influence a product's fortune is directly proportional to organizational skills employed by the company. The other major contributors are the markets and their steadily growing appetite for services provided by chips.

The market effect is so valuable because to really reduce the chip's cost and make it affordable for a golden horde of new applications, one has to increase the user population by an order of magnitude. There must be a mechanism for accomplishing this task, and this mechanism benefits greatly from organization.

Some experts refer to this market effect as the *strategic value* of semiconductors. Down to its fundamentals, strategic value is difficult to assess without

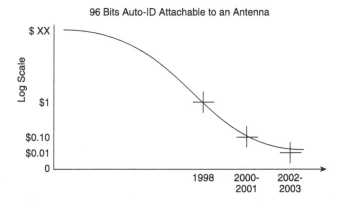

Exhibit 9.4   The Falling Cost of Embedded Identity Chips (Auto-Id) Attachable to an Antenna

considering the utility of resulting solutions. Utility demonstrates itself in personal productivity (which to a large degree is measurable) and quality of life (which is difficult to quantify, except as the more mundane standard of living). It is perceived utility that makes the market size grow. Market size and lower cost correlate, and this adds up to favorable cost projections for electronic tags, as Exhibit 9.4 demonstrates. However, if utility falls behind, or the supply chain does not catch up, then chip prices stop falling.

Because experience with the use of e-tags is not yet available, estimates about their utility look like a ripple wrapped in an enigma, yet such estimates are the pivot point in judging technological advances. Perceived utility promotes market demand for sophisticated electronics at an affordable price.

Nanotechnology is another colossal market for low-cost microprocessors because of demonstrable utility. *Nanomedicine* is a rapidly growing research area that uses tiny machines to repair the body on the molecular level. Scientists also use special micro-imaging techniques to analyze the outer shell of viruses (e.g., the one known as HK 97). They study its use to repel attacks from the body's immune system and the environment. This, too, is perceived utility.

Other applications of nanotechnology focus on inanimate materials and the way their potential can be exploited. Experts believe that *nanotechnics* will enable computing power at a high multiple of what is currently available. For example *atomic writing* on titanium oxide is expected to make practical densities of terabit per square inch. I insist on these issues of perceived utility because that is how the Motorola chip should be viewed — the tip of an iceberg of which we are far from knowing the exact dimension, but think that it is going to be very big.

These references are important because it has been a consistent characteristic of chip design that the applications architecture must focus on values beyond immediate usage needs, therefore involving potential utility. Having defined this broader perspective, one can now focus on immediate developments. The Motorola BiStatix chip is printed on paper with some carbon and a grain of sand on it. The chip is basically simple, but it can be programmed, and it can be printed on any paper substrate, including vendor boxes.

Functionality and flexibility count a great deal. The BiStatix chip looks like an ink blot on paper made of silicon the size of a pinhead. It sits between lines of carbon-laced ink that serve as a pair of antennae (see Exhibit 9.1). The chip and antennae are attached to a stamp-sized platform. As it is passes in front of an electronic reader, the smart tag powers up.

What attracted my attention during Motorola's presentation at the MIT April 2000 conference was the flexibility of the solution. The electronic antennae are printed in conductive ink with carbon. Radio signals from an electronic reader boot-up the chip, which receives or relays information to a computer and then to the Internet. As mentioned, this chip is a 1-kbit read/write device, with overriding design criteria: low cost and one size.

The cost of the chip and the cost of the solution do correlate, but there are other costs to a solution in addition to the chip itself and therefore it is wise to integrate all other costs, including those of restructuring the supply chain, chips readers/writers, and software. All expenses must be recovered to enhance a new product's market appeal and make it a viable proposition.

After the announcement of the Motorola chip for automatic identification, in a sideline discussion at the April 12-13, 2000 conference, it was suggested that adding all the costs of a solution would tend to bring the bill to about 50 cents per item. To shrink it down to 10 cents, it will be necessary to rethink the entire identification process and streamline the applications. And then the entire process must be reinvented once again to be able to approach the next goal of 1 cent.

Reinventing the application of e-tags is a rewarding exercise because the three most important elements for the success of auto-ID are: cost, cost, and cost. Because the history of the silicon revolution is indivisible from cost-effectiveness as perceived by users, Motorola's focus has been the lowest possible cost with contact-less sensors. In the near term, the R&D goal is to eliminate the antenna; and in the longer term, to find a silicon alternative.

As discussed in the introductory remarks to this chapter, International Paper and Motorola have agreed to implement the auto-ID chips in the packaging concern's boxes, eliminating bar codes and ultimately bringing the entire manufacturing supply chain online. This real-life test capitalizes on some of the new chip's features:

- Tags can be read after being mishandled, and they can be read at any angle.
- Ink can be drawn to make the entire box an antenna.
- Chips provide for real-time tracking at all points in a supply chain.

Potential users of smart boxes include International Paper's largest consumer-products customers. Three of them — Procter & Gamble, Unilever, and Philip Morris — are partners with International Paper in the MIT project of auto-ID, which also includes several other well-known firms. It is hoped these tests will provide detailed insight into the potential use of auto-ID and therefore lead to a dependable system design.

9.3   Challenges Associated with Domain Names and Their Assignment

A hypothesis is a tentative statement made to lead to the investigation of a certain issue or permit experimentation on a given problem. Making the hypothesis that very low-cost chips, like BiStatix, will become one of the motors of the New Economy, will underpin a wide implementation of EPC, and will promote supply chain dynamics, leads to the next salient problem: the global naming service that will permit efficient smart material-to-any smart material communication, at any time and in any place.

This is a challenge not very different from that of *domain names* on the Internet. Many entities — from government agencies and the Organization of Economic Cooperation and Development (OECD) to user groups — have become involved in Internet domain names because it is an issue of critical importance to I-commerce. The presently available Domain Name System (DNS) has done a good job of solving the problems for which it was designed to deal. It also demonstrated the capability of extending beyond its original, more limited aims. With some 250,000 servers keeping track of millions of sites for billions of clients, the DNS is the largest distributed database in existence. However, these numbers are peanuts compared to smart materials' communications challenges — already people complain that DNS is the root of some annoyance in the networking world.

To provide a level ground for the reader, a brief explanation of what lies behind Internet addresses or domain names is in order. These are composed of four fields, each consisting of numbers ranging from 0 to 255, separated by dots. From this results over four billion attached devices, usually computers, that can receive an individual address of the type:

$$126.225.49.50$$

The first couple of fields show in which zone of the Internet (subnet) the computer is located. One can conclude that two computers with the numbers 126.225.49.50 and 126.225.49.28 are located in the same vicinity. The last digits represent the host number.

There are problems with this arrangement, both short range and long range. A longer range problem is the evolution of the address system (more on this later). An immediate challenge is remembrance of the address number by everybody. There is no question that computers can handle address numbers, but people do not necessarily remember the different number sequences. This has led to the notion of *name-servers*. Based on tables, these translate *host-numbers* into *host-names*.

Separated by a dot (.), a host-name involves two fields: computer and zone. This host-name is compiled of words that describe the location or purpose of the computer. The zone is identified at the end: .us (United States), .uk (United Kingdom), .de (Germany), .fr (France), .ch (Switzerland), .ca (Canada), etc.

Quite likely, the Internet's founding fathers assumed that companies, academic institutions, governments, and other entities would want to register under a geographically significant classification. This had the added advantage of making feasible the existence of a local authority. In the United States, the Internet Assigned Numbers Authority (IANA) established rules for the .us domain that required state and local domain names to be included in each full name. Other countries do not have such a rule.

The next-to-last field is the organization, organizational domain, or Top Level Domain (gTDL). There are fairly strict limitations on the type of entity that can use them. Common organizational identifications include: .edu (educational), .com (commercial), .gov (government), .mil (military), and .org (other organizations).

These tell a lot about the origin of the Internet. They are primarily valid in the United States, but are also used in several other countries; however, not all countries use the same mnemonics. The Japanese, for example, use .ac for academic institutions rather than .edu.

Some of the gTDLs have become bottlenecks, particularly in I-commerce. In the late 1980s, the Internet was not used for commercial transactions. When the rules changed, the .com designation was the only gTDL that most commercial Web sites considered. Clearly, this has become too narrow a solution.

Another issue to keep in mind, because of its relevance to the Internet supply chain, is that there is a prerequisite to having and using homogeneous Internet addresses: somebody must be responsible for assigning them. These addresses are attributed by a central service: the Internet Registration Service. Keep this in mind as the text discusses ICANN (in the next several paragraphs) and ONS (in Chapter 9.4).

In principle, nobody would dispute the need for global portability of Internet address numbers. This is nearly everybody's concern, but there is disagreement on how to implement it; and the result has been stalled plans by the Internet community in terms of creating an independent number registry.

The board of the Internet Corporation for Assigned Names and Numbers (ICANN) is the body that oversees the system of domain names. For any practical purpose, its role is a cross between a standards body and an assembly of representative organizations and private people who have something to do with the Internet. Nine of its members have been chosen by three supporting entities that represent the Net's stakeholders, such as Internet service providers (ISPs) and networking engineers. Five additional directors were elected in October 2000 by the at-large membership, meaning all citizens older than 16 with a verifiable e-mail and physical address who had signed up as ICANN members.

Another four directors are scheduled to be chosen in a subsequent election. To a large extent, the number of people who sign up as members of ICANN in different countries depends on how much attention the media pays to this election, as well as on the Internet's penetration among businesses and consumers.

No matter how its members are selected, the board of ICANN and its advisors must confront the fundamental problems of addressing identifiers and pointers. As with databases and smart materials, domain names must be globally unique. Increasing the number of credible gTDLs may ease the pressure on dot.com address availability, but it will probably not solve the challenges being discussed.

Many experts today ask if it is really necessary to use domain names for navigation. They suggest that new departures are necessary, capable of making a dramatic difference as the Internet's user population continues to grow. New departures, however, do not appear to be around the corner. Hence, new projects such as auto-ID must develop their own solutions that permit them to deliver results. This is the focus of Chapter 9.4.

9.4   Beyond Domain Names: The Object Naming Service by the Auto-ID Project

The Object Naming Service (ONS) discussed in this chapter section is an MIT development project. Its incorporation into the auto-ID system has a great deal to do with the portability of Internet address numbers. The evolution of smart materials applications will be constrained by a lack of portability of IP addresses and of means for Web sites to retain their unique routing numbers. This could lead to:

- Fragmentation of the global Internet implementation domain, and hence of the supply chain
- Users being more dependent than ever on their Internet service providers (ISPs)
- Smaller ISPs becoming feeder lines to their upstream partners in the Net

A major drawback to the lack of portability is that it makes it difficult for corporate users to change their ISPs, and it locks smaller ones into the larger ones that hand down IP addresses. Internet engineers usually answer this argument by saying that the need to aggregate addresses to ease routing makes the lack of portability unavoidable, at least for the moment.

This is, however, a response that is difficult to swallow in the context of smart materials endowed with any-to-any communications capabilities and (eventually) acting as microcomputers. One must always think about what comes next. Even PCs are no longer looking like the personal computers of the 1980s and early 1990s. New functionalities, shapes, and styles are now available, thanks to the ever-shrinking size of the logic and the elimination of previously required interfaces such as serial and parallel ports. Computing devices mark themselves. They can be submerged into automobiles, home appliances, and entertainment systems; they do not need to be standing out in the open.

Therefore, when thinking of communications solutions that stand a chance of remaining valid in the next 10 or 20 years, one must step outside conventional wisdom, taking approaches able to lead to breakthrough solutions that can provide new features and capabilities. These will revolutionize the Internet or any other network. One must also be ready not only to make this change step, but the next one, and then the one after that.

We are not yet out of the woods with Internet domain names and global portability. One of the reasons for lack of agreement on the best possible course is the technical challenge represented by new departures. However, an even bigger reason is money, particularly questions having to do with taxation. In its proposals, which date back to April 1997 but have yet to reach the end of the tunnel, the OECD has suggested a series of action points for governments, including benchmark pricing for domain name registrations.

In other words, according to the technocrats — or at least some of them — domain names might become the pivot point for Internet commerce taxation, like an IRS number, no matter what sort of hurdle this represents in systems terms as well as from the end user's viewpoint. Governments, OECD said, need to recognize that the Domain Name System (DNS) is of critical importance in their own legitimate activities, in terms of taxation, compliance, and protection of minors.

This thesis says that databases of DNS registries not only perform critical functions in sign-posting information highways, but they are also the only identification records available for governments, businesses, consumers, and parents. The role of governments is to ensure that the administration and operation of the DNS is stable, that there are no hidden ripples in the system, and that competition occurs in a fair and open manner.

There is, of course, some basis for these arguments. Most essential is the fact that, to a considerable extent, they apply to the Object Naming Service (ONS) for automatic identification, the goal of which is to tell computers where to locate information on the Internet; for example, information about any object that carries an electronic product code. ONS must integrate seamlessly into the Internet domain name system. Therefore, it cannot avoid the problems facing DNS.

Precisely because any-to-any communication by smart material requires a structured information environment, the auto-ID project at the Massachusetts Institute of Technology developed the concept of the structured approach discussed in this chapter section. Its aim is to make it feasible for Internet routing computers to identify where the pages associated with a Web site are stored. Specifically:

- The ONS will be used every time information is needed about a physical object.
- The DNS will be used every time a Web site is accessed.

In other words, and beyond the objectives of the Internet's domain name system, the projected object naming service must provide a steadily increasing range of information about an object, based on its EPC and other data stored on the very low-cost identification chip. The auto-ID project claims that ONS will be operating like a telephone book in reverse, taking as input the EPC code and returning a Web address (or Uniform Resource Locator [URL]). That

URL references the Web site where all information about the object resides, making it possible to store large amounts of data on the Internet rather than on the object itself. From an Internet system viewpoint, this evidently poses a number of other challenges — among them, cost allocation, broadband availability, and the likelihood of blocking (affecting traffic and leading to delays).

Because there will be a myriad of smart materials, it is quite likely that ONS will need to be both larger and more polyvalent than current DNS. And because of the mission assigned to ONS, its design is a challenge. As a naming solution, it must be capable of quickly locating data for every single one of the trillions of objects that could potentially carry an EPC code.

Ironically, more challenges will come along if ONS succeeds in this mission. Some experts believe that if it succeeds with auto-ID, ONS will become an e-mail system between people and inanimate objects, as well as between smart materials themselves. Therefore, from the drafting board, its design must foresee the fact that it would receive and deliver billions of e-mails — every day, the world over; and reliable and efficient technical solutions of the nature being discussed must be developed and successfully tested before statements can be made that by the end of this decade we will be on the threshold of a world in which conversations between inanimate objects lead to unprecedented efficiency, great savings, and productivity levels beyond what is known thus far.

Let me add that the current object naming service is a prototype, residing at objid.org. This service cannot be reached at present through standard Web browsers. It needs software that is compatible with EPC, and it is used in the realm of the R&D effort currently under way in the auto-ID project.

9.5 Mobile Commerce, Internet-Enabled CRM, and Smart Materials

Start with the projection made by mobile equipment manufacturers and operators who are rushing to take advantage of the demand for mobile commerce systems. This forecast, which is often heard in technical meetings, says that:

- By 2004, businesses will be using mobile technology to produce annual savings of $230 billion.
- By 2010, mobile commerce will be the second-largest industry in the world behind healthcare.

Both forecasts give overly optimistic messages; but even if the market for *me-commerce* (see Chapter 4.4) is half that size, the Internet will have to provide real-time, broadband, continuous access to satisfy the new breed of wireless customers. Over and above an able solution to DNS and ONS problems, as discussed in Chapters 9.3 and 9.4:

- Smart materials will be part of the game, if not at the center of it, largely as disaggregated devices (see Chapter 9.6).
- Technical solutions will have to deal with many types of gateways, networks, protocols, and devices.
- Knowledge artifacts will most likely repackage, in real-time, the digital content for users.

The technical challenges are so numerous that tier-1 companies are establishing research and development centers to ensure their presence at the cutting edge. Part of the cutting edge is the integration of the business environment with customer relationship management, a process recently referred to as e-CRM or Internet-CRM (I-CRM). In the background is the concept that bread-and-butter customer relationship management will no longer suffice to run a successful Web site.

Industry analysts and software vendors suggest that I-CRM implementations are long overdue, but they have been neglected as businesses struggled to translate their traditional customer relationship practices into the online marketplace. Smart materials bring Internet-intense CRM to the foreground because they will eventually be accessed by a larger number of customers and be able to communicate through the Internet. The forecast is that the chains of customer communications will be extended to reach the level of smart materials, and that manufacturers and merchandisers that wish to be ahead of the curve, will be obliged to exploit the opportunities presented by auto-ID.

Starting at the drafting board, auto-ID capabilities of smart materials can significantly decrease time-to-market of new products and achieve first-mover advantages in competitive situations. One such concept is that of using auto-ID to share a design infrastructure in which it may be possible to tie together dozens of engineering workplaces, powerful server farms, and sophisticated design methods.

This would be a major step toward creating *virtual design teams*, by enabling engineers scattered around the world to collaborate more effectively than currently possible. Smart materials, and the right resources, may empower major innovation such as a Design Chain Management (DCM), thus redefining how products are developed in the networked economy, and how they are outsourced in a global landscape to take advantage of local efficiencies.

According to the same grand design at the marketing end of smart materials, I-CRM will use Web channels and business intelligence software to improve the understanding of customer behavior. A similar statement can be made about an intelligence-enriched ERP, to make possible dynamic production planning and inventory management.

Exposed to the business opportunity offered by the 1024-bit chip at the cost of around 10 cents, a European auto manufacturer suggested that it can see plenty of logistics applications that would help to improve current client service. These include the auto's identification book, information on the owner, data on optional characteristics of the vehicle, and the guarantee and its usage.

The motor vehicle manufacturer also said that the sales order itself can be served by smart materials, with online transmission to the company's production planning and control system, using the Internet. The same is valid for purchasing lists and supply chain solutions.

The implementation of choice of another company, with which I discussed possible applications for smart materials, fell on smart vouchers. A smart voucher may significantly simplify data handling for compliance purposes (for example, foreign exchange (forex) transactions). In some countries (e.g., Italy) banks are required to make five registrations of a forex transaction:

1. Matrix of accounts of the reserve bank
2. Unique information archive (also required by the reserve bank)
3. Registration with the Ministry of Finance
4. Analysis of forex transaction for whitewashing
5. Execution of the transaction proper by the bank

A smart voucher, according to one credit institution, will automate the input to all five sources, relieving extensively what is basically heavily manual work despite nearly 50 years of computer usage. Smart vouchers will also be instrumental in enriching register information with analytical dimensions at practically zero cost.

9.6 Microsoft's Concept of Disaggregated Devices

Closely connected to the challenge of mobile commerce and the opportunity of auto-ID is the concept of disaggregated devices — a new development by Microsoft. In the background is the fact that evolving sophisticated applications see to it that not only product codes, item intelligence, bandwidth, and routing algorithms must be thoroughly revamped; but also the concept of interfaces and the way interfaces are used. In the past, the user interface was attached to a specific application. In the mobile world, there is need for both more general and more versatile solutions.

Along this line of reference runs the current project by Microsoft Research. Its theme, *disaggregated devices,* targets a new-generation technical solution that is not directly connected to a computer — as is the usual case at present. The user interface of disaggregated devices is an *invisible shield* and a *sensor,* which at the same time connects and protects the user, permits access to information, and communicates with people in seamless ways.

At the root of this project lies the fact that everything we carry has the potential of becoming a sensor and user interface (for example, watches, pens, and clothing). To gain greater perspective, imagine that this "everything" is smart, it is automatically identified, and it is able to communicate. Simple local processing, according to Microsoft, calls for the observance of two characteristics: peak detector, with low duty cycle and low bandwidth; and raw signal, transmitting user identity and additional user data.

The reader will appreciate that these conditions are observed by smart materials and, through them, they can be extended two ways: toward enterprise resource planning and toward customer relationship management. The development of an implementation of disaggregated devices, however, demands more than what Chapter 8 and this chapter have discussed about the current status of smart materials; namely, the definition of value-added characteristics: power, sensory media, computation, and bandwidth. One of the major concerns is partitioning, and the following questions need to be answered:

- How much computability locally?
- How much communication capability?
- How often the power supply should be changed?

Each alternative has advantages and presents constraints. Local computation requires local power. Remote computation calls for greater bandwidth. Both must be supported by a replenishable and reliable power supply; which will be the best power source?

Some of the disaggregated devices (e.g., shoes) will replenish their power supply; but others will not, and they will have to be supported through batteries. Power requirements under different applications scenarios is a crucial variable in system design. The same is true of channel capacity. Bandwidth requirements vary by type of application. In terms of raw channel capacity, moving requires 12 bps, talking requires 16 kbps, listening requires 88 kbps, and seeing requires more than 1 mbps.

Microsoft projects that forthcoming applications will require orders of magnitude more connectivity than presently available. Other tier-1 vendors have come to a similar conclusion. Therefore, they are currently rethinking available channel capacity and projected bandwidth requirements. Many experts see significant growth in bandwidth as this type of application becomes popular.

What several projects working along this line of reference have found is that system partitioning holds many surprises. As the computers and communications system of disaggregated devices are partitioned, many other subjects we did not think of pop up, and more choices must be made. For example, with regard to connectivity, designers must decide about adaptive transmission levels, duty cycle control, and network hierarchy, if any.

With disaggregated devices, one of the challenges is the fact that user interfaces act as a control system and therefore require both sensors and actuators. They also call for solutions that must be possible to personalize. Reliability is also a major requirement. Experts think that some entities should be designed for an unlimited lifetime (for example, sensors, processors, and wireless communications).

As far as human use of disaggregated devices is concerned, it should also be possible to consolidate off-the-shelf bandwidth and minimize power on-the-body. Microsoft's project adds to these requirements some issues related to software. Software functionality and bandwidth correlate, local computation calls for a local power supply, and remote computation increases the bandwidth and connectivity requirements.

The software developed for disaggregated devices, Microsoft advises, must be intelligent. It must be aware of the physical world characterized by time, space, and events. The level of software sophistication should be high enough to appreciate that things are not always in the same place. Agents must inform the user that his or her actions have costs; communication and computation requires power and bandwidth, which come at a price — over and above the price of transactions done in Internet commerce.

The subjects discussed in this chapter demonstrate that there is not one but a whole constellation of issues in R&D that will influence significantly the way we do business, as well as our standard of living. Companies planning to take advantage of these developments, however, have lots of homework to do. Much better organization than what is currently available can be achieved through a rigorous classification effort, as documented in Chapter 10.

Chapter 10

The Chorafas Classification/Identification System for Supply Chain Requirements

Down to its fundamentals, an *identification* code, such as EPC, is a composition of numbers (binary, octal, decimal, hexadecimal, or other), letters, or other symbols used to identify a physical or logical entity (for example, a motor vehicle, a book, a razor, or an information element (IE)). A *classification* code is prerequisite to identification because it enables an item to express its relationship to other items of the same or similar nature. As shown in Exhibit 10.1:

- Identification (ID) should be a short number designed for cost-effectiveness and error-free data transcription and transmission.
- The classification code (CC) is semantic and taxonomical. It should be a databased descriptive structure, the goal of which is to provide detail and remove ambiguity.

The rationalization of identification and definition of all materials, as well as of the internal structure of a database, is at the very heart of every classification system. A flexible and effective organization can be instrumental in putting into application the opportunities presented by rapid developments in technology. As discussed in Chapters 8 and 9, one of these developments is very low-cost chips able to serve as ID elements. This has important implications on the nature of input and output: *where* transactions happen, *how* they are recorded, and *when* the database is updated.

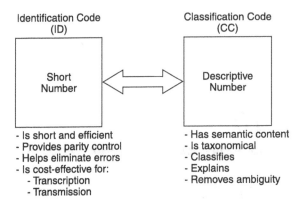

Exhibit 10.1 . Identification Code and Classification Code Are Twins, but Each Fulfills Different Objectives

Years of practical experience with development and implementation of identification codes and classification codes have demonstrated that one single number cannot perform both functions. Efficient coding is a problem of specialization. To develop a cost-effective coding system, it is necessary to select the most compact, complete, and methodological solution, and to implement this solution in the population of physical items, or information elements, that will be stored in mass storage media and retrieved interactively online.

Over the past 30 years, the services provided by the applications described in this and the following chapter have evolved into general facilities used routinely by administrative and technical personnel in well-known companies. Cornerstone to the original classification and identification code design and its evolution is the fact that it has been possible to take advantage of technological developments that make possible low-cost but sophisticated applications.

A computer-based coding system able to provide the needed dependability is a difficult and challenging undertaking, particularly because little exists today in terms of a theory able to meet identification and classification requirements in a more or less universal way. The problem with organizational work concerning data management in its broadest sense starts exactly at this point of missing skills and half-way methods. This chapter presents the solution that I have developed over long years of practice in collaboration with leading enterprises.

The reader should keep in mind that the methodology discussed in this text, its practical implementation, and also the basic principles on which it rests are documented through long-standing working conditions in industrial concerns and financial institutions. Therefore, they are practical. They do not exist just in test environments, but support important facilities that have enhanced productivity and enabled deadlines to be met.

10.1   The Concept Underpinning a Classification Code

A code can consist of characters such as letters, punctuation marks, or numerals. Identification through characters such as punctuation marks is the least suitable for data communication and data processing. The use of letters has a greater coding capacity per character position than decimal numbers because alphabets consist of more than ten different characters. The *radix*, or base, for a numbering system based on the English alphabet would be twenty-six.

Codes composed of letters alone can thus be shorter than purely decimal numerical codes; but even better, one can develop a radix 32 code that is expressed in binary form and is used on a strictly numerical basis. With this coding, the pseudo-alphabetic characters A,B,C … X,Y,Z serve as an extension of numerical signs to reach 32 positions. This solution has been adopted by the Dimitris Chorafas System (DCS), and it helps shorten the field size in terms of transcription, storage, and transmission.

The classification code is a different ballgame. In its background is organization and semantics. In a classification system, items of similar type must be grouped into homogeneous categories using their similarities and the relationships developing therefrom. This is primarily a *taxonomical* approach, and it has been chosen to underpin the classification part of DCS.

Taxonomy is an important organizational principle, but it is not everything in terms of a rational classification. Left to its own devices, a collection of sources such as machines, books, drawings, reports, or other entities will not contribute original research or invent anything. However, if these entities are efficiently classified, this will save time that managers, engineers, designers, and other professionals would otherwise waste in seeking buried or widely scattered information. This is where the economies of a classification system come in.

Different families, groups, or classes of physical items (and data) have distinct classification needs in terms of detail. Therefore, as will be seen through practical examples, a taxonomical organization may not end in a one-to-one correspondence between the items being classified and the corresponding identification code. In this case, the solution is to use *further definiens*[1] to reach a level of detail able to provide an unambiguous link between classification and identification for each and every item.

This one-to-one correspondence is vital in facing engineering challenges, but it is also valid for other data. Accounting is a prime example. The handling of accounting information is one of the oldest computer applications. It is also one of the least well-structured operations in terms of input, output, and databasing because client accounts, supplier records, files of purchased items, and manufactured goods inventories (to name a few) have common information elements that are structured in different ways — with the result of being incompatible among themselves. Two issues stand out:

1. One cannot provide homogeneity without a classification and identification system that should itself be homogeneous. This has as a prerequisite taxonomical work.
2. If a classification must reflect all the special interests of all its individual users, it would have to embody information of no particular interest to many of them — but of interest to others.

The answer to the problem posed by these two issues is to have a prime taxonomical classification with the highest possible common factors of general interest, without making the solution top-heavy in a coding sense. This means delegating the individual user's *special* concerns to a secondary classification made by means of further definiens. The key to a valid classification system design lies in a few basic rules:

- Observe the logical structure and general requirements of the population under study.
- Establish and observe classification rules and the process of ordering that these imply.
- Properly define entity characteristics so that the resulting codification can be tailored to a user's needs.
- Assure the right place (and only one place) for each physical item (or data) in the population being ordered.
- Provide for further expansion of the system being developed as the applications domain itself enlarges.

There are also identification rules that must be followed. First and foremost, the identification code must be short for economical transcription and transmission purposes. It must be linked to the classification code in a way that allows one to distinguish between user requirements (technical, commercial, other) concerning the same item. In addition, it must feature a parity check for error control (something both UPC and EPC are, thus far, lacking).

With manual processing, these rules have not been thoroughly appreciated. Perhaps the greatest failure has been the general tendency to try to combine identification and classification into one and the same code. When this happens, the resulting code is too long and cumbersome; and neither the classification nor the ID work is well done. Neither is it a good solution to leave the prerequisite classification work for later or to forget it altogether. Given the large amount of available data, it is often physically impossible to search for overall similarities without the prerequisite organizational work. There is typically a substantial number of related items with many and varying characteristics. Difficulties in data management are often compounded by the lack of a methodology that permits one to put in effect a straightforward classification process.

The top priority is, therefore, one of organization and methodology. Provided that organizational prerequisites have been fulfilled, computers offer the chance of seamlessly targeting data retrieval objectives. Keep in mind that the proper organizational work involving classification and identification is not easy. An example from industry helps to demonstrate what this means. Today, two methods predominate in the classification of technological products: one is based on nomenclature, the other on design features.

Both start from recognition of the fact that undisciplined nomenclature causes waste in a multitude of ways. To avoid such waste, attempts have been made to establish *standards* (see Chapter 8). However, over the last half century, standardization and streamlining have been often handicapped, and methods have proved unreliable when names, codes, and numbers have been allocated by more than one person or department.

Efforts to ensure a unique *name space* by leaving gaps in a numbering system to be filled out later (as the need arises) have invariably failed. These are half-baked approaches leading to dead ends. Over a short time period, the impass is resolved through patches and different types of twists; but in the long run, the situation becomes chaotic. In contrast:

- A serious, fundamental study for indexing and retrieval of information elements takes the proverbial long, hard look regarding the evolution of a coding system.
- The prerequisite organizational work weeds out remnants from obsolete, manual information retrieval approaches that are complicating the development of universal, analytic indexing and searching.

The user's needs for information retrieval should be at the top of the designer's priorities. Retrieval characteristics derive from the evaluation not only of what is required now, but also of what will most likely be needed in the future. Neither should this study lose sight of the fact that indexing and retrieval are separate, although closely related, activities in an information handling system.

Indexing is facilitated when the facts characterizing an information element are identified, classified, and stored according to a valid methodology. The rules for storing these facts must be recorded, streamlined, and made readily available to any authorized computer-based system or individual using it. For retrieval, the general store of information elements must be searched, and a specific word, topic, or subject in a request pinpointed in storage. For example, indexing of texts (books, papers, articles, etc.) can be accomplished chronologically, by subject, by author, or by publisher.

In conclusion, once properly developed, a classification/identification system becomes a pivot point in technical information, management information, and internal control. Exhibit 10.2 exemplifies this reference by presenting the ideas just discussed in a coordinate system. As the reader can appreciate, identification is the pivot point of the three-dimensional representation that:

1. Supports the classification code and, by extension, the distributed database structure
2. Permits effective data management for engineering, production, marketing, accounting, logistics, and other reasons
3. Provides semantic links holding together geographically or functionally distributed sections of the global database

Without well-thought-out solutions to the issue of coordination between classification, identification, and database management, efforts to weed out unwanted duplications on information elements will be futile; database

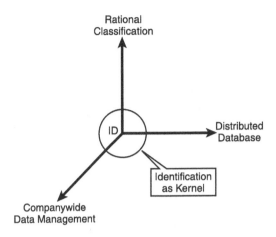

Exhibit 10.2   Solution Space for Database Organization Answering Distributed Intelligence Requirements

integration will remain a vain exercise; and the corporatewide simultaneous update mechanism will be impossible to support. These events will make database disintegration a distinct possibility. Classification and identification are not ends in themselves, but means in making the information management job more rational.

10.2   Benefits Resulting from Architecturing an Identification Code

The point was made in Chapter 10.1, that with DCS, each classification number has a dedicated identification code in one-to-one correspondence, and that an ideal ID code must be short and unique. One can enrich this reference with the statement that this uniqueness should respond to functional requirements. The problem that arises most often is that there are conflicting functional criteria. What suits one department is not necessarily what another department wants to have.

There is also another challenge. Some of the functional requirements change over time, particularly those connected to marketing. In contrast, engineering drawings are rather stable; when they change, a different product is born. Based on these premises, the identification number of DCS has been divided into three parts, in order of priority:[2]

1. basic code, <bc>, for engineering characteristics
2. suffix, <s>, for commercial requirements
3. origin, <o>, for identification of the factory where the product is made

To better follow the rationale for this three-way division of ID, one should bring it into historical perspective. DCS was first developed in 1969 to serve the needs of Osram GmbH, a German lamp company that now operates in the United States as Osram-Sylvania. Osram had its base in Munich and Berlin. When the groundwork of the parallel code system was completed, an argument developed between the design engineers and the commercial executives. What is a lamp? Or, more precisely: *How should a given product be identified?*

The most concise answer is that a product should be identified through its technical characteristics. However, the commercial people argued that issues such as trademark, packaging, and some additional information (e.g., stamps put on a product) constitute equally valid references that must be coded; they cannot be omitted. As well, the argument was advanced that a coding system either satisfies every end-user's requirements, and thus stands a good chance of being adopted by everybody; or it does not, and therefore it never establishes itself, let alone becomes universal; it remains parochial.

The problem is that, in the general case, nobody has really thought out the answers well — despite the fact that on a number of occasions research demonstrated that much of today's confusion in item coding by a typical firm originates in the matter-of-fact discrepancy between the engineering identification and sales identification of the same item.

Not everyone who works on the development of a coding methodology appreciates this principle. Even standards' bodies fail to observe it. Yet, since 1969, I have been able to ascertain this discrepancy a hundred times and did so with several companies — both those that have been successful in their efforts to classify and identify their wares and those that failed despite the time and money they spent on ID.

While the specifics of the work done for classification and identification reasons vary from one case to another, the bottom line is that the queries being asked are the same: What is a product? What is a factory? How should they be defined? How should they be identified? Fast and dirty answers will not do because they will not pass the test of time. It is not easy to identify a product, any product.

The research that I did both before and after DCS provided plenty of evidence that identification code and classification code should work in parallel with one another. Translating a given code into another, within a given industrial operation, has always caused delays, difficulties, and mistakes. A new code system should avoid such deficiencies. Exhibit 10.3 identifies the nuts and bolts of the adopted solution:

- The basic code is allocated on the basis of the technical characteristics of an item (or data) as outlined in the classification code (taxonomy and <bc> oriented further definiens).
- The suffix <s>, which complements the basic code, identifies commercial or secondary characteristics of an item (or data), depending on the family in which that item belongs (see Chapters 10.3 and 10.4).
- The origin <o> indicates where an item was made (multiple production sites is a frequent case with globalization), or where the item is installed (this is the case with machines).

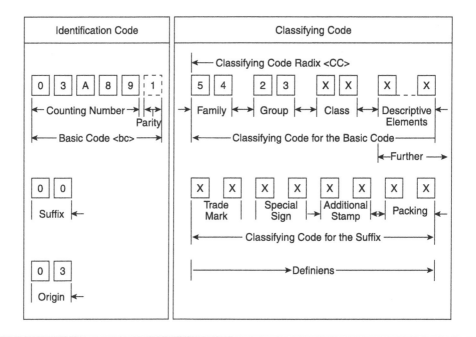

Exhibit 10.3   A Closer Look at the Structure of the Parallel Code System

Both suffix and origin depend on and complement the basic code. Neither can stand on its own. Furthermore, if the origin is to be shown, the suffix must precede it. Item identification can be done through the basic code alone: five digits plus parity for a total of six; or through ten digits: <bc>, plus 2 for <s> and 2 for <o>.

The power of this coding solution is significantly increased through a higher radix than decimal. I have mentioned radix 32 as a possibility. In Osram's case, the hexadecimal system (radix 16) was chosen. One can take a quick look into this approach and the possibilities that it offers in coding.

A radix 16 requires an equal number of distinct digits. This consists of 0…9 and A…F, used not as alphabetic characters but as numbers (10 to 15). Because $16 = 2^4$, each number 1…E is written through four binary digits. Hence, in binary form, the basic code has 24 digits, including 4 bits for parity. But for man/information communication, it is written in a six-digit (five + parity) hexadecimal form. This simplifies reading (see Exhibit 10.4).

Selection of the identification number structure has reflected a concern for transcription and transmission requirements; it has been purposely chosen as a short number with a parity check. The use of a five-digit (plus parity) hexadecimal notation offers the ability to identify more than 1,000,000 items in a continuous assignment of numbers in <bc>, as no classification work needs to be done by the ID structure.

This identification potential is impressive, as in actual application only the difference in technical characteristics reflects itself into <bc>, and leads to a difference in the basic code. Nontechnical issues are presented by means of

Suppose that in binary notation, the identification number is:

Counting Number	Parity
1̲0̲1̲0̲0̲0̲1̲1̲1̲1̲1̲0̲1̲0̲0̲0̲0̲0̲0̲1̲	0̲1̲0̲1̲
20 bits, 5 hex	4 bits, 1 hex

In hexadecimal form, this is written:

1010	0011	1110	1000	0001	0101
A	3	E	8	1	5

Exhibit 10.4   Six-Digit (Five + Parity) Hexadecimal Form

the <s>. Typically, the suffix employs two hexadecimal digits, and so does the origin. In hexadecimal code, this assures 256 possibilities for each.

The careful reader will appreciate the flexibility of this solution. If necessary, the identification capability of the basic code can be increased in either of two ways: by adding an extra hexadecimal digit to the left, bringing the identification potential to over 16,000,000 positions; or by switching to a number system of radix 32, thus making available roughly 33,500,000 positions with five digits plus parity. Neither change will upset the numbers thus far allocated because either (and both) expansion(s) constitute(s) a system development within the chosen range of coding flexibility:

- A five-digit (plus parity) hexadecimal number is a subset of a six-digit plus parity hexadecimal number.
- A five-digit hexadecimal number is a subset of five-digit number radix 32.

A two-digit <s> and a two-digit <o> benefit from the second alternative: radix 32. The identification possibilities increase for each to 1024. Alternatively, the two-digit hex of <s> and <o> can be increased to three-digits (first alternative). Exhibit 10.5 presents the digit structure for radix 16 (hexadecimal) and for radix 32. The overall system for identification code is flexible, easy to apply, streamlined, and efficient.

10.3   Developing the Classification Part of a Parallel Code System

Classification can be done either linearly, through a roster, or in matrix form permitting two entries to a taxonomical pigeonhole. The linear order of classification has a major weakness: the difficulty of inserting other items in the list (or deleting them) without upsetting the order. Even if care has been taken to provide spaces for future growth, no one can foresee the precise number of spaces needed during, say, the next 10, 20, or 30 years — which is a reasonable lifetime for a new classification system.

Exhibit 10.5 Digits of Radix 16 and 32

Decimal	Radix 16 Radix 32	Decimal	Radix 32
0	0	16	G
1	1	17	H
2	2	18	J
3	3	19	K
4	4	20	L
5	5	21	M
6	6	22	N
7	7	23	P
8	8	24	R
9	9	25	S
10	A	26	T
11	B	27	U
12	C	28	W
13	D	29	X
14	E	30	Y
15	F	31	Z

Note: I, O, Q, V are omitted to avoid confusion: I, O with one and zero; Q with O; V with U.

Therefore, the decision was taken during the design phase of DCS to use a matrix basis for classification. This matrix, shown in Exhibit 10.6, observes a taxonomical order. It is doing so at the first levels of detail: *family*. Each pigeonhole in this matrix can be expanded to another 10 × 10 matrix for *groups* (second level of detail); and each group pigeonhole can be expanded to a 10 × 10 matrix for *classes* (third level of detail). The architecture of the classification code is therefore family, group, class (plus further definiens discussed in Chapter 10.4).

As has been the case with the choice of an ID code, this classification solution is flexible. The 10 × 10 matrix can be expanded to 16 × 16 or 20 × 20, if necessary — but I do not advise doing so at the start. Classification results are more polished when one begins with a limited number of options. *Family* is identified by two decimal digits: from 00 to 99.

The example shown in Exhibit 10.6 is the one retained and applied at Osram, and is further discussed in subsequent chapter sections. Note that everything used by the company has been classified: from products, machines, instruments, and other assets, to human resources and management reports. In the manner explained in preceding paragraphs, each family has been divided into 100 classification groups, and each group into 100 taxonomical subgroups or classes.

The way to proceed with the classification is shown in Exhibit 10.7. Suppose that the product of this company is motor vehicles and there are three product lines: trucks, buses, and personal cars. These are families. Each family (in this example) has three main groups of vehicles. In the general case, taxonomical work has hierarchical characteristics.

The reader will observe that a classification problem exists with minivans and station wagons, which might use the same platform. This is a problem to be sorted out in the classification work whose taxonomical nature is exemplified by the legend of the exhibit: supertypes (families), subtypes

Exhibit 10.6 The 10 × 10 Family Matrix for a Lamp Manufacturing Company

			Raw Materials and Semi-finished Products			Finished Products				
	Human Resources	Assets Except Machines	Glass/Chem.	Wire	Others	Incandescent Lamps	Discharge Lamps	Hybrid	Machines	
	0	1	2	3	4	5	6	7	8	9
0 Top Management					Management Information/Financial Results					
1 S.I.P. Optimization					Sales-Inventory-Production					
1 Order Analysis	Order Analysis	Sales Forecasts	Transport - Logistics	Warehous. - Inventories	Customer Records	Regional Records	Product Records	Quality Records	Production Plans	
2	Hired Services	Real Estate (Land And Buildings)	Chemicals (Basic Elements)			Stems		OtherAssembled Inner Parts	Parts (Incl. Spares)	
3		Furniture and Fixtures	Chemicals (Derivatives)	Other Wires		Incandescent Lamps Except 54-59	Discharge Lamps Except 64-69	Other Finished Products Except 74-79	Assembled Parts	
4	Salaried Personnel (Executive/ General)	Utilities (Electricity, Gas, Water, Information)	Formated Glass	Tungsten Wires	Shaped Pieces	Incandescent Stem Type Lamps Without Spec. Request To Location/Meas. Fil.	ABC Discharge Lamps	Accessories	Machines For Semi-Finished Products	
5	Hourly Personnel (Direct/ Indirect)		Tubular Glass	Molybdenum Wires		Incandescent Stem Type Lamps With Spec. Request To Location/Meas.Fil.	Glow-Discharge Lamps	Lighting Fittings	Machines For Finished Products	
6	Storage Transfer		Full Glass	Leading-In Wires	Stamps	Incandescent Bead-Mount-Type Lamps			Machinesand Tools/ Common Use	
7	Quality Standards	Consumable Materials		Coils	Packaging Materials	Incandescent Lamps With Quartz Bulb			Instruments (Measuring, Testing, Control)	
8	Know-how				Lamp Caps					
9										

Transactions-Settlements-Product Files (Basic Elements)

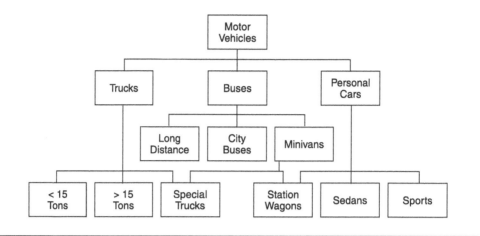

Exhibit 10.7   Supertypes, Subtypes, and Attribute Inheritance

(groups), and attribute inheritance. Classification conflicts arise when attribute inheritance lines cross one another. This happens often in industry.

Once the outlined preparatory work is complete on the classification side of DCS, a parallel identification number is allocated, associated with this classification. Such an identification number (see Chapter 10.2) is used in all transcriptions, transmissions, accesses, transfers, and search procedures. As already seen, this is the running number of the simplest linear form: the basic code <bc>. As shown in Exhibit 10.8, basic code is the metalayers of suffix and origin.

In the case in which the basic code is not remembered by the user, the alternative path is to start the search using the classification code: family, group, class — the entire process being handled through *expert systems*.[3] Recall that classification code is designed primarily to assist in classification and

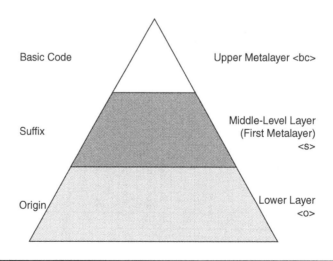

Exhibit 10.8   The Three Layers of the Identification Code: <bc>, <s>, <o>

organization — and by extension storage, update, and retrieval. The outlined parallel approach meets four objectives:

1. It permits in-depth evaluation by customizing the way the coding service is provided.
2. It fits the kind of information to be handled, including the detail to which this information will be sorted out.
3. It answers prerequisites associated with the nature and structure of computer-based retrieval operations.
4. It makes it feasible to handle different issues (and subqueries) involved in each main question posed to the database.

The kinds of questions asked by the end-user help indicate whether the organization of the indexing system should be of a general or a particular nature, which influences the procedures of retrieval and selection. If one undertakes a simulation of retrieval operations, a tentatively chosen taxonomy can offer clues on future happenings and support one tentative structure of the projected classification code over another.

Other issues of importance include the time span over which this system is projected to be valid; the possible number of items to be added and deleted, in terms of systems upkeep; and the need to ensure that this system remains as uniform and consistent with early design as possible. The availability of the necessary talent to perform the required classification functions and subsequent updating is, of course, critical.

To complete this discussion on requirements posed by real-time indexing and retrieval, a coding system must provide an able answer to data storage and seamless data search. Storage and retrieval is a communication process between the user and the database in which information is held. The interaction between information elements and their users, as well as vice versa, may be threefold:

1. Search for reference(s) by the ultimate user — whether man or machine
2. Data filtering, data analysis, and indexing, fulfilling organizational and operational requirements
3. Contribution to the wealth of the database (including updates, additions, deletions, and security controls)

In structuring and upkeeping databases, the activity described by the third number is a prerequisite for that of an organization of knowledge. A neat collection of source references, such as books, drawings, files, records, or abstracts, must be retrievable by information elements. The search for reference is, in many cases, concerned with the problem of measuring similarity and its opposite (dissimilarity). This is basic to all information retrieval systems no matter how they have been structured. The first basic characteristic of an efficient retrieval system is flexibility, as well as simplicity in design and utilization. The second is ability to use statements permitting the location of selected information elements, doing so quite readily with a minimum knowledge of the system. This is facilitated by the existence of a formal syntax that enables the retrieval operation to be automatically executed as the need arises or translated into a seamless logical sequence of actions. In this particular connection, the classification system can be seen as the semantically rich syntax of a seamless retrieval mechanism.

Because a rigorous retrieval system must be structured by means of syntactical rules and signs, the parallel code described in this chapter serves as the language. The ABCs of a good language include using a well-defined, usually finite set of characters (in this case: families, groups, classes); observing rules for combining characters with one another to form words or other expressions; and assigning a specific meaning to some of the words or expressions to serve communicating purposes (for people and machines).

Such requirements are met through the design of DCS. The steps characterizing this classification/identification procedure are simple. However, the effort necessary for implementation is substantial. By spelling out the needed criteria, order and selection become feasible. A company wishing to benefit from the implementation of DCS must pay a great deal of attention to the prerequisite organizational work. This is explained in Chapter 10.4.

10.4   A Matter-of-Fact Example of Classification and Further Definiens

The choice of both a six-digit basic (including parity) code and a six-digit taxonomical number (two decimal digits per family, group, class) has been influenced by requirements of economy, dependability, and the assurance of a short dialing system, which comes in handy today in connection with nomadic computing. A six-digit to eight-digit number is quite similar to a telephone number in most cities, a fact giving a good hint as to the possible size of an identification or classification code, as well as to the users' ability to retain either one in memory.

Take another look at the family classification matrix shown in Exhibit 10.6. Suppose one is interested in Family 44: shaped pieces. The family is divided into groups, the 100 pigeonholes. Not all of them need to be assigned immediately. It is always good to leave room for expansion. Pigeonholes of the group matrix that are being used in the classification work are assigned to specific parts.

An example is given in Exhibit 10.9. The careful reader observes that in this case, too, more than half the positions in this group matrix are kept in reserve. Each position (pigeonhole) that is filled can be further analyzed through a class matrix, which provides greater detail.

Two different examples are given in Exhibit 10.10 and Exhibit 10.11. What these examples have in common is the methodology of analysis. *If* one allocates the digits in the classification system — particularly its taxonomical part — in this way:

- KL, for family (therefore, the original matrix)
- MN, for group (a subset of the family)
- PR, for class (a subset of the group)

then one can easily see that KL is a metalayer of MN and that MN is a metalayer of PR. The existence of PR is conditioned by the MN to which it belongs, and that of MN by the KL of which it is part. That is, PR and MN have no own existence. They get meaning only within their metalayer.

With this in mind, take another look at Exhibits 10.9 through 10.11 to better understand what they represent. Exhibit 10.9 illustrates the group matrix for parts, corresponding to the KL positions in the taxonomy. Exhibits 10.10 and 10.11 provide two different examples of class matrices corresponding to MN positions. Such matrices carry forward the classification work done in the group matrix and provide a finer detail of inheritance work within a real-life environment.

Technical issues characterizing machine parts such as (primarily) shape and (secondarily) function will be classified by norm evaluation, as explained

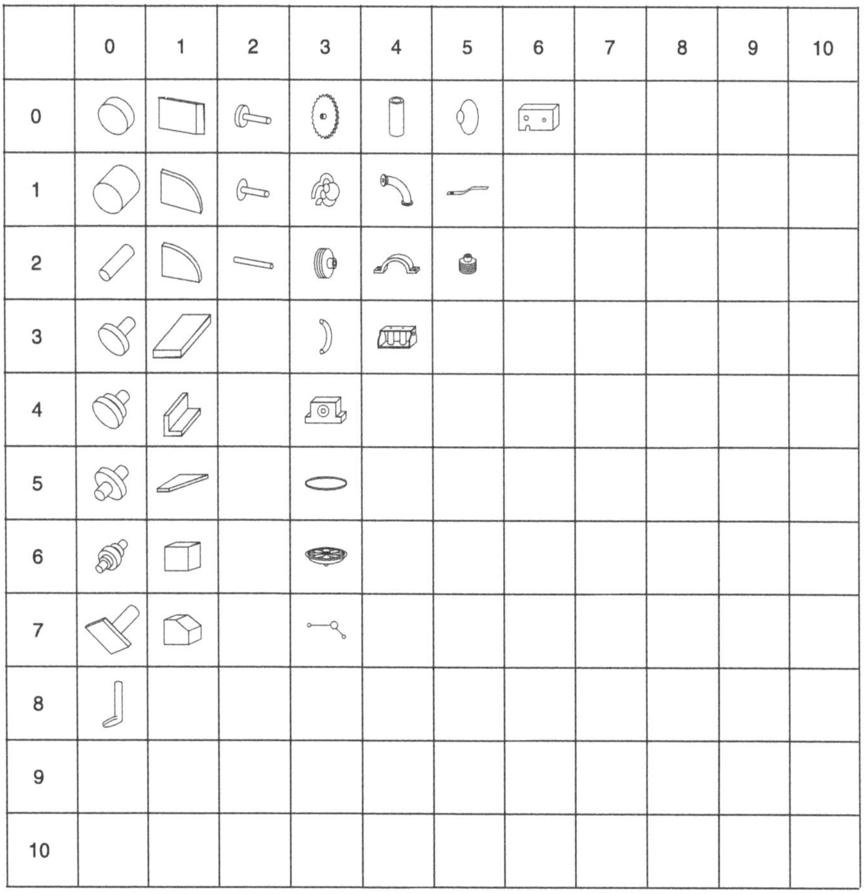

Exhibit 10.9   A Group Matrix for Parts is the Metalayer of the Class Code

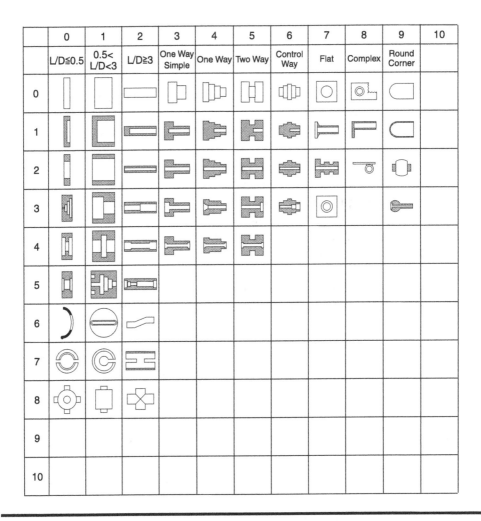

	0	1	2	3	4	5	6	7	8	9	10
	L/D≤0.5	0.5< L/D<3	L/D≧3	One Way Simple	One Way	Two Way	Control Way	Flat	Complex	Round Corner	
0											
1											
2											
3											
4											
5											
6											
7											
8											
9											
10											

Exhibit 10.10   Example of a Class Matrix Developed and Used by a Manufacturing Company

in the following paragraph. In this particular application, the choice of shape over function was deliberately done by the engineers who implemented DCS. Functional characteristics lead to further detail that is *not* taxonomical. It is expressed by the first digits of the *further definiens* — and it can be continued by bringing more further definiens into perspective. Further definiens are elements of detail that are descriptive rather than taxonomical. In an inheritance matrix, they are weak elements, specific to the class to which they apply.

Down to its fundamentals, the concept underpinning the further definiens is primarily one of flexibility in definition and of customization. Not only two different companies but also two factories in the same company do not have exactly similar classification requirements. Accounting for this fact, a global taxonomical system should be able to handle a number of exceptions without turning the classification code on its head.

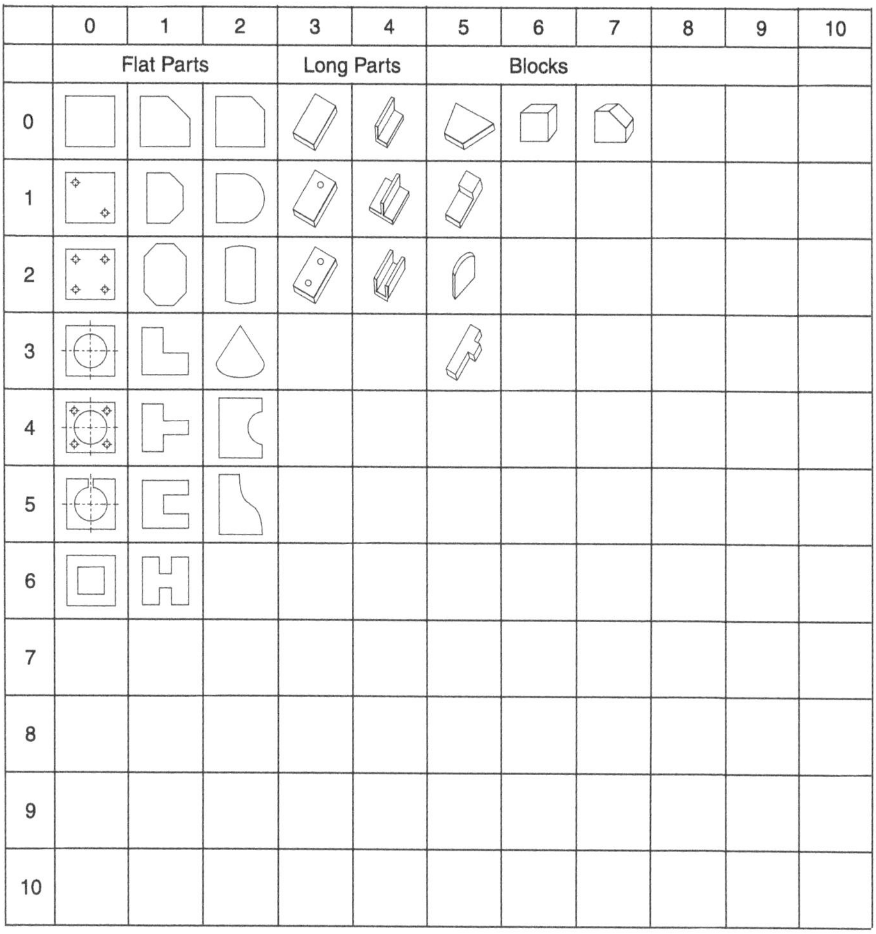

	0	1	2	3	4	5	6	7	8	9	10
	Flat Parts			Long Parts		Blocks					
0											
1											
2											
3											
4											
5											
6											
7											
8											
9											
10											

Exhibit 10.11　Another Example of a Class Matrix by the Same Manufacturing Firm

Now take a practical example. Suppose that a given manufacturing firm is faced with the problem of classifying its spare parts. After having studied the organizational prerequisites associated with this problem, the analysts establish a classification code with taxonomical structure and proceed with allocation of the first digit of further definiens. Exhibit 10.12 shows the definition of x_0 in the implementation that took place at Italcementi, a major Italian cement manufacturing company. The overall solution was:

- x_0, first digit of further definiens, is norm oriented
- x_1 identifies the part's original designer
- x_2x_3, a two-digit field, ensures that each item file corresponds with one and only one part identification number

This is by no means the only solution possible. Each company can choose its own approach on how to design further definiens. In fact, it can do so for

Exhibit 10.12   Allocation of Digits in the Classification Systems

TAXONOMICAL CODE XX.XX.XX
>   KL: Family (say, mechanical parts)
>   MN: Group, a subset of family
>   PR: Class, a subset of group

FURTHER DEFINIENS: first digit, x_0, allocated to norm evaluation
> x_0 = 0; ANSI-norm
> x_0 = 1; ISO-norm
> x_0 = 2; ISO-norm, afterward reworked by this company
> x_0 = 3; Catalog part without known norm
> x_0 = 4; Catalog part without known norm, afterward reworked
>   by this company
> x_0 = 5; This company's own old product design specifications,
>   to which cataloged parts do not correspond
> x_0 = 6; Reserved
> x_0 = 7; Reserved
> x_0 = 8; Reserved
> x_0 = 9; Reserved

each family in the matrix if this reveals itself to be necessary. For example, another company that applied DCS divided the further definiens into the following groups:

- x_0 is a one-digit decimal number that extends the classification capability of the taxonomical code without belonging to the latter. This gives some families the freedom to drop x_0 while others may need to use it.
- $x_1 x_2 x_3 x_4$ is a four-digit field of further definiens that helps to uniquely identify an item in terms of technical characteristics.

In this particular implementation, a basic code corresponds one-to-one to KL, MN, PR, $(x_0 x_1 x_2 x_3 x_4)$. Hence, the <basic code>, a running number on a first-come, first-served basis necessitates 11 classification digits: six taxonomical and five descriptive.

In yet another implementation of DCS, $x_0 x_1 x_2$ is a three-digit decimal field that identifies the company that made the original design of the machine or component. This is vital information for many parts associated with their original manufacturers. Subsequently, $x_3 x_4 x_5 x_6 x_7 x_8$ is a six-digit field acting as a box able to store and retrieve, through serial numbering, the file for each machine component or part — past the $x_0 x_1 x_2$ filter.

In practical terms, such an explanation provides considerable flexibility. This concept also applies to other further definiens (e.g., $y_0 y_1 y_2$ that are suffix oriented). As will be remembered, the suffix was added to the ID system to permit identification of nontechnical characteristics — or, more precisely, characteristics that are of a non-core technical nature; for example, in the case of lamp manufacturing, voltage and wattage of a lamp, as well as whether it is incandescent, fluorescent, or other type, are core issues. In contrast, color, such as matte or transparent, is non-core; the same is true of the brand (this vendor was handling four different brands).

Commercial characteristics (including brand name and non-core technical issues) may also need to be classified. This is done in the further definiens through the $y_0 y_1 \ldots y_n$ field(s). Order and flexibility are the keywords. The system just explained permits a flexible approach to classification and identification, while providing the possibility of bringing them together into a parallel code structure.

10.5   Coding for Organized Complexity in a Global Market

A classification and identification structure specifically designed for usage in conjunction with computer-based systems must be able to cope with the *organized complexity* that characterizes modern business and its any-to-any network connection. Organized complexity results from the existence of a large number of information elements that have a meaningful relationship between themselves, their origins, their environments, and their users.

Information elements are, as a rule, distributed unevenly within the working procedures of an industrial, commercial, or financial organization. Furthermore, operational characteristics and their change over time make the process of data management more complex. This suggests the need for a systematic arrangement of similar items into suitably selected categories that can be restructured without having to start the classification work from scratch.

As discussed in the preceding chapter sections, a coding system able to cope with demands for fully distributed storage and retrieval must allow options for the development of methods that would formalize organizational issues without ossifying them. It should also permit a flexible determination of performance criteria, including efficient search algorithms, database-wide cross-indexing, and effectiveness coupled with dependability.

Chapters 10.3 and 10.4 explained why flexibility for making alterations in system structure can be provided by dividing the classification part into *taxonomy* and *further definiens*. Taxonomical rules are unique for the entire system; more precisely, from one *family* to the next. Contrasted with the taxonomical criteria, the structuring of further definiens must consider the fact that an information system contains elements assumed to:

- ■ Have their own objective function, generally not coinciding with that of the total classification system
- ■ Present particular requirements for optimal search, preferably by a family of items (or data), with allowance for expected future activity

The solution that one chooses should therefore be one that enables a good exploitation of classification potential by family, performing the family, group, and class oriented search better than can be accomplished through generalizations. In a global context, this provides for greater individuality in a taxonomical approach within a general framework.

In the background of decisions made in structuring DCS has been a grand design that permits building the overall system step-by-step rather than trying to make everything at once, as if one wanted to have a monolithic approach. Step-by-step allows one to combine the interests of an element (family, group, class) to that of the entire system through the development of a plan leading to homogeneous solutions. Basic prerequisites include:

- A valid methodology that is properly implemented
- An understanding of the potential of classification/identification by designers and users

Success depends on management's ability to ensure consistency in the overall classification program, on the researcher's determination to test multiple assumptions with the aim of reaching efficient solutions, on the need for effectively planning for future requirements, and on the organization's propensity to evaluate many alternatives as well as to integrate diverse requirements in a coherent whole.

Based on these premises, the design of a rational and compact parallel coding system can be satisfactorily completed. The solution was made possible through the completion of a management research project on a new article identification code for two leading industrial firms: Osram in Germany and Italcementi in Italy. It has been in operation for three decades.

The idea of DCS was advanced (and implemented) after considerable study and experimentation, which permitted one to focus on both technical and marketing characteristics, promote records accuracy, improve storage and retrieval perspectives, reduce transcription errors, ensure economic data transmission, and guarantee a unique reference to articles and accounts. These design criteria are even more important today than they were in the late 1960s and early 1970s. Relatively minor upgrades are necessary to capitalize on global networks, smart materials, and expert systems.

The organizational work underpinning DCS is not limited to the classification of materials. Another look at the matrix in Exhibit 10.6 allows one to appreciate that one row is dedicated to top management information; while a second row is reserved for allocation and optimization processes connected to the sales-inventory-production (SIP) system; and the next seven rows are used for the classification of services, accounts, products, and machines. The last row is kept in reserve. The first column (rows 2 to 8 inclusive) is dedicated to labor and know-how (human resources); the second to assets, liabilities, and financial reporting; the following three columns classify raw materials and semi-manufactured products; the next three columns concern themselves with finished products; and one column is used for machinery families, while the last column is held in reserve.

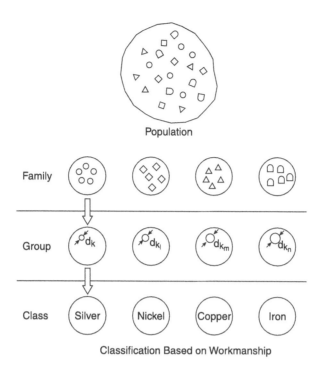

Population

| Family | | | |

Group

Class Silver Nickel Copper Iron

Classification Based on Workmanship

Exhibit 10.13 The Classification of Items in a Population According to Criteria of Homogeneity

This pattern fits practically every manufacturing company that I know, and it is well-suited for global business operations. Families 22 to 28, 32 to 39, ..., 82 to 88 classify and store data of a predominantly engineering nature. The files for each product, uniquely coded by family, are subdivided by means of groups; and as seen, greater detail in classification is ensured by means of classes.

Exhibit 10.13 illustrates the approach necessary for rigorous classification. A population is identified; it is composed of items that are first sorted into four families the analysts consider to be homogeneous. In this example, the criterion being used is shape. More detailed sorting is possible; in this case, it is based on dimension; up to 100 groups can be distinguished this way.

A still more detailed item sorting might consider the type of materials as the basis for separating goods of the same shape and dimension. This, also should be done with homogeneous lists in the background. Homogeneity and flexibility correlate. The structure of a classification system evolves as the population within a family, group, or class is sorted out in accordance with other preestablished criteria, ensuring that the objects of a classification find their proper pigeonhole. That is the goal of the preparatory work, and the more complex the environment with which one deals, the more rigorous and more ingenious the preparatory work that must be done.

Stored on smart materials, the <bc> <s> <o> code allows one to know the whereabouts of each unit. The KL.MN.PQ code makes it possible to manage the global supply chain in the most efficient way. Alternatively, taxonomy can be stored in databases and accessed when necessary.

To be successful, the implementation of DCS should begin at design level, include the factory floor and ERP chores associated with production, extend itself to warehousing for seamless inventory management, and, obviously, address marketing, sales, and service — all the way to handholding with retailers and end customers assisted by CRM. The goal must be an open system that is dynamically managed and always able to operate online in an efficient way.

Notes

1. Why *further definiens?* Why not?
2. See also D.N. Chorafas, *Computer Erfolgreich Einsetzen,* Verlag Moderne Industrie, Munich, 1970.
3. D.N. Chorafas and Heinrich Steinmann, *Expert Systems in Banking*, Macmillan, London, 1991.

Chapter 11

Practical Implementations of the DCS Solution

Information systems requirements of modern industry will not be effectively handled unless the database is properly organized and there is a rational, taxonomical way to support geographic and functional distribution of information elements. The necessity of this is highlighted by the evolving supply chain perspectives that reflect the growing number of business partnerships and the need to keep abreast of developments taking place outside one's company in the areas of engineering, marketing, and procurement.

One of the advantages of the solution outlined in Chapter 10, the parallel system for classification and identification, is its flexible code structure. As seen, DCS is based on the principle of a one-to-one correspondence between classification code and identification code. A physical item or information element is classified by taxonomy: family, group, class, and further definiens. Then it is identified. This classification acts as a filter to weed out synonyms and antonyms.

As the case studies on DCS discussed in the preceding chapter help to document, the quality of organizational effort is quite critical. Different possibilities exist for seeing this effort through a practical implementation. These do, however, have in common a fairly general principle:

- The more general a concept or a criterion, the broader its ability to accept information content — and, ironically, the less organizational effort necessary
- The more specific a concept or criterion, the smaller but more precise the information content of a given class, and the more work must be put forward to polish such a system

One after the other, the different classification systems with which I have been involved demonstrated that the process of tuning and polishing is quite important; the better designed the coding system, the faster and simpler is its upkeep and the more effective the retrieval. Also, fewer errors will sneak in. Practice suggests that it is better to put in the needed effort at the beginning, rather than chasing after (unpleasant) facts later.

Another lesson learned through experience is that, whether broad or specific criteria are used for classification purposes, it is essential that the terms defining each project and its goals are focused, reliable, and unambiguous. Inadequacies remaining in the system at the conceptual or applications level can jeopardize the entire classification effort. Different prerequisites can, however, prevail, depending on the job to be done.

Chapter 10 also brought the reader's attention to the correlation between classification and the effectiveness of inquiries made to the database. These can range, for example, from the form of an exact book title to a loosely expressed subject title, or may refer to some ambiguous date of publication. Ambiguity, and generally lack of crisp references, can be effectively handled through fuzzy engineering models as Hitachi and Nissan did so effectively in connection with auto parts identification.[1] If one has a collection of 10,000 files that one wants to order in a way that enables one to retrieve any specified document, one must select an optimal index of classification. It is usually possible to express this classification scheme in a one-to-one relation between index and document, or in one-to-many with the final choice being done by means of a secondary criterion.

As an example of secondary classification criteria, Chapter 10 introduced the concept of further definiens, explaining that although they are part of the classification code, they are not taxonomical. In the Italcementi case, for example, x_0 was assigned the mission of informing on standards followed by machine design. The case studies in this chapter build upon the principles outlined in Chapter 10.

11.1   Case Study with the Classification of Engineering Parts

Case studies on practical implementations of DCS help to explain the services that it provides. The case study in this chapter section highlights the taxonomical approach used by a leading company in the classification of spare parts. This project was promoted by the introduction of a generation of computer-aided design (CAD) machinery. What has been learned is also critical in connection with enterprise resource planning. Overall, the work was based on two premises:

1. The taxonomic organization of parts was made independent of classification of machines to which these belonged.
2. Particular attention was paid to classification of generalized parts useful to more than one machine.

The concepts underpinning these two premises are interrelated. The wisdom of the approach being chosen was documented by a preliminary study that demonstrated the importance of instituting a general reference category for spares, rather than locking oneself into the classification of machines to which these spares belong. Another premise observed in the organizational work is that group sorting (within DCS) would be accomplished along the line of employment of a given piece. This brought into perspective the different levels of usage that the pieces have.

Both the primary and the secondary criteria were studied in the course of the classification work. Exhibit 11.1 is a reminder of the process that Chapter 10 introduced. The family can be located through KL coordinates in the database matrix of DCS, the group through MN coordinates, and the class by means of PQ. Theoretically, up to one million classification possibilities exist. However, because a taxonomical system must allow for expansion, the possibilities are in reality much less. Their exact number depends on the population to which this system will be applied and on the objectives to be met.

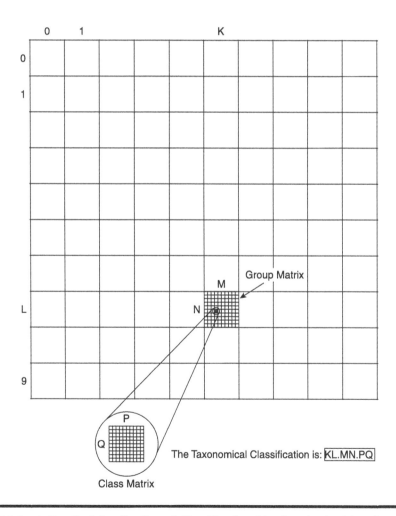

Exhibit 11.1 A Practical Application of Classification Matrices in the Manufacturing Industry

Experience suggests that less than 60 (out of 100) families are used in the original design and that, subsequently, no more than 30 to 40 of the 100 possibilities are taken in any given group and (subsequently) class. Notice, however, that expandability can be ensured by converting the classification system's radix 10 to, for example, 16. This makes more columns and rows available by increasing the size of the reference classification matrix.

It would be illogical to think that one and only one method of classification work would be used within a multinational firm, on a global scale. What is, however, advisable is to have some general classification rules to guide the hand of the analysts in their taxonomical efforts. As an example, the motor reduction gear shown in Exhibit 11.2 is classified within the DCS matrix in the family dedicated to machines to which it belongs (see Chapter 10, family 86 in Exhibit 10.4). The 10 × 10 matrix of this family might, for example, be constructed to represent:

- By column, type of electromechanical equipment
- By row, variations in reduction gear

Entry into the matrix is by column and row — in that order. Within the family, the column-and-row intersection defines the group. The two class digits may, for example, classify voltage and horsepower. This example shows the flexibility of the classification system under discussion and the ability to customize the taxonomy.

Component parts of the couple will also be classified, but in a different family. In Chapter 10, Exhibit 10.4, the family for parts is 82. One group in this family is dedicated to shells; both the shell of the motor and the reduction gear have their pigeonholes. The two, however, will be further distinguished

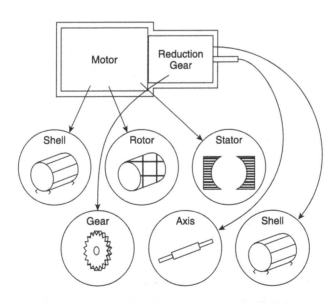

Exhibit 11.2   Classifying a Motor Reduction Gear Within the DCS System

by means of class digits. Motor shell and the reduction gear will be taxonomically distinguished from one another.

Because they are assembled parts, the rotor and stator will also fall into their own groups in family 83. Their place is a group matrix column dedicated to electrical components. The gear and the axis will be in family 82, each in its own group. The numbers of the families are only indicative, to keep up with the example provided throughout Chapter 10. It is evident that each company will develop its own classification matrix.

In the specific case study presented in this chapter, organization and classification benefited from an analysis of day-to-day utilization needs, including technical specs, production scheduling, inventory control, cost accounting, purchasing, quality inspection, and customer handholding. This number of variables suggested the choice of ways and means that avoided a complex structural solution.

Throughout the classification and identification effort, efficiency and utility were ensured by considering the eventual users of the coding system, by sampling their specific requirements expressed in the course of the last five years, and through personal interviews to update the reference to such needs. The following definitions put forward by this project help in explaining the chosen approach.

Part (P)

Elementary components — or considered as such by convention: a part of machines or other equipment, or one that becomes a part after simple adjustment or adaptation without changing its fundamental dimensions.

Part of Level "A" (PA)

This had to be identified by type and supplier. For PA, one computer-based envelope has been instituted by basic code. The focus was engineering specs. Another mini-file was created for the individual part in connection with the suffix.

The origin identified the supplier, including parts internally made by the company and its subsidiaries. Further definiens connected to the origin started with identification of the original supplier of this <bc>. Second sourcing and other alternatives were also identified. Pointers/anchors connected this reference to supplier files, cost files, just-in-time files, and quality control files in the database.

Exhibit 11.3 presents the DCS structure in this particular application. A hexadecimal ID code was used. The reader will appreciate that, except for the further definiens connected to supply chain <o>, this ID/CC diagram is not different than the one seen in Chapter 10.

Part of Level "B" (PB)

This is identified only by type. For parts B, a <bc> file is established for engineering specifications. It includes no individualized supplier sheets.

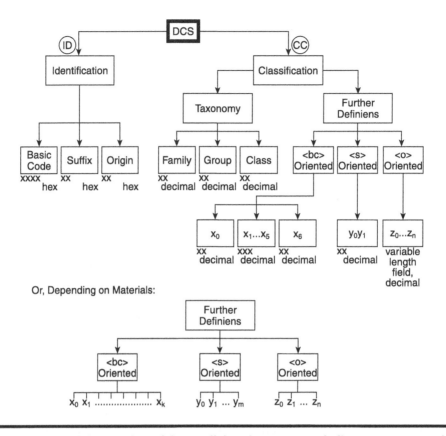

Exhibit 11.3   A Bird's-Eye View of the Parallel Code System, Including Taxonomy, Further Definiens, and Identification, As Used in the Case Study

Part of Level "C" (PC)

Semi-identified parts, classified (with only a few exceptions) up to level x_1 (as discussed below). In most cases, the x_2x_3 further definiens are not utilized in connection with PC. When complete part identification is not necessary, the values $x_2 = 9$, $x_3 = 9$ have been used.

The engineering vice president of the company on which this case study is based paid considerable attention to the cultural change of his personnel. Since until this implementation the department had kept microfiche files and these were kept in what in company jargon was known as "envelopes," he designed the schema in Exhibit 11.4 which provided for the transition between microfiche files and optical disk storage organized along the DCS methodology. Practical examples on computer-aided design (CAD) demonstrated that parts classification had to be enriched by three groups of further definiens:

$$x_0 \dots x_7, \quad \text{for <bc>}$$
$$y_0y_1, \quad \text{for <s>}$$
$$z_0 \dots z_5, \quad \text{for <o>}$$

where

x_0 = First *field* (one digit) $x_0 = 0$ to $x_0 = 8$ used for sorting, pursuing the classification of taxonomy in terms of secondary technical criterion, $x_0 = 9$ does not currently serve an information purpose

$x_1 \ldots x_5$ = Second *field* of further definiens (five decimal digits). Two cases must be distinguished:

$x_1 \ldots x_5$ = 00000 to 99998 identifies catalog(s) of the supplier(s) by referring to the supplier's list

$x_1 \ldots x_5$ = 99999; no specific information is given by x_1

$x_6 x_7$ = Identifies an envelope of basic code ("type" part), completing the classification subsystem corresponding to the <bc> in a one-to-one correspondence

$y_0 y_1$ = These digits provide cost and efficiency information associated with supplier source for this part. Such values do not influence the <basic code> but are important for selection reasons.

$z_1 \ldots z_5$ = Provide supplier information including original supplier and multi-sourcing. Also supplier's subsidiary and plant in the global supply chain.

Because this particular implementation of DCS had as a special characteristic the exchange of parts among different factories and warehouses, the study that preceded the application of the described method concluded that <o> should be polyvalent, going beyond the level of vendor information to reach the specific origin of each part at plant and country level. In other cases, a more limited perspective of origin identification is followed, where <o> only identifies the company owning the manufacturing plant.

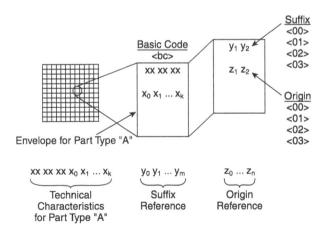

Exhibit 11.4   The Concept of a Logical Envelope in Connection with Classification/Identification

11.2   Why Do We Need Clear Text?

In the jargon used in connection with the first implementation of DCS, *clear text*[2] stood for descriptive information associated with the classification code, and therefore to item ID. This information has been designed and built along modular lines to provide descriptive identification for each classified and identified part within DCS. After study, it was decided that clear text should be composed of two sections. The first is of fixed length, 40 characters long, addressing the level of the class. In frame presentation, this text is a heading. The second is of variable length: 25 to 50 characters long. It is associated with the <bc>.

This relatively short clear text requirement was posed by two reasons, both of them basic: (1) interactive inquiry necessities and (2) economy in memory usage. These were computer-induced considerations, particularly at the output end, because the adopted solution was designed to operate in an online real-time environment.

Generally, the advantage of short, focused clear text lies in the strict discipline it imposes. Many present-day article names are illogical in content, too long in descriptive explanations, and irrational in structure; or alternatively, too short to explain what they stand for. A study we conducted prior to this implementation proved that:

- A field of 80 characters can contain the clear text of 99 percent of all pieces and materials in stock (some 200,000 of them, in this case).
- A field of 40 characters answers more than 50 percent of all requirements without undue abbreviations, while 90 percent of textual needs can be satisfied within a field of 60 characters.

To help with standardization and homogeneity, a glossary guide was developed for clear text. It carries the abridged words to be used in clear text writing (when necessary) and was made available in two tables, both handled through a data dictionary. One sorted on the abridged word basis (argument) with the complete word as a function. The other sorted on a complete word argument with the abridged word as a function. The first list was used in retrieving the clear text and for normalization reasons, the second in developing the clear text and updating it. Systems analysis ensured that, with good care, abridged words became popularized while coexisting with full words in an unambiguous one-to-one correspondence. For this reason, several basic rules have been established to guide the writing of the clear text for machines, parts, and materials. For example:

- The clear text organization should follow the taxonomical sequence of the classification.
- While standardizing the descriptive information, the clear text should be written in a way that the end user can easily comprehend.

- For clear text, as well as taxonomy and further definiens, the unit of measurement should always precede the numerical value where one value exists: V 110; or fit within the range, when a range exists: 220 V 235.
- When the information relative to x_i is absent from the clear text, but is judged to be of technical interest, it must be replaced by the sign "?". This leads to a pointer in the database where further description is found.

The use of clear text improved system performance and this was most favorably commented on by the users — and by management. The end effect was clarity, simplicity, and order, quite a contrast to the multitude of overlapping and (often) incompatible number systems and unedited descriptive texts that characterize most industrial concerns.

Such deliverables were particularly important because top management had decided to capitalize on classification/identification through radical and imaginative approaches that lead employees — from engineering to manufacturing, warehousing, and sales — out of past confusions. The experience gained from this application also taught that the design and implementation of a neat coding system can be instrumental in gaining greater efficiency and productivity. Classification interfaces exist between taxonomical reasoning and the inductive or deductive ability of managers and professionals, as Exhibit 11.5 suggests.

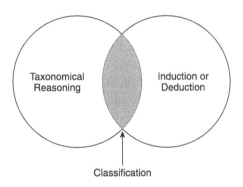

Exhibit 11.5 Classification Is at the Heart of Taxonomical Reasoning, but Also of Deduction and Induction

Ill-defined codes lead to serious errors. For example, prior to the institution of this six-digit hexadecimal numbering system with parity check, the company was using a 22-digit to 24-digit decimal number (without parity check) for end-product identification for commercial purposes. This unfortunate choice had two detrimental effects:

1. It led to many errors in transcription, given the length of the code, with the direct result of a high number of returns.
2. It did not really serve technical or commercial interests effectively because it compromised on both and had no mnemonic value.

Furthermore, this 22-digit to 24-digit code was not company standard for different products; 17 other approaches and numbering systems were used. This resulted in error rates in data transcription amounting to roughly 7 percent. With the introduction of DCS and subsequent streamlining, most error sources were weeded out and the error rate dropped below 0.5 percent.

In my professional experience, I have found that far from being an isolated example, this is a fairly general case. Even error rates of 14 percent are not unheard of. Companies overseeing networks of factories also know from their own experience that the risk of synonyms and homonyms is high. The same technical product — hence, the same specifications — may have up to ten different codes, or even more when accounting for superficial variations such as very minor differences in identical component or packaging. Many transaction and transcription errors come from these differences. In the case of DCS, packaging differences are given by <s>.

There is another identification problem to be brought to the reader's attention. The same technical product in the same package can exhibit process-oriented variations due to the machinery available in a certain factory and the skill of its workers. The existence of <o> answers this identification requirement. It permits, as well, tracing a given product for reliability (field performance) throughout its useful life and, by extension, evaluating the factory's quality of production.

The classification/identification characteristics outlined in Chapter 10 and in this chapter are very important to Internet commerce, as well as to auto-ID (see Chapters 8 and 9). A sound basis for identification will play a larger and larger role in I-commerce strategies of industrial firms, well beyond the current horizon of supporting wholesalers and retailers.

- The able use of ERP software is significantly assisted through crisp classification and identification.
- CC, ID, and clear text also serve CRM applications because they make the communication of a vendor with its customers so much more efficient.

To bring this issue a notch further, keep in mind what has been said since Chapter 1: the more sophisticated the system, the greater the extent of management responsibilities. For example, with smart tags, replenishment will be done automatically and floor intelligence will inform that "this" or "that" rack lacks an item. Because there is no personal intervention to sort out possible errors, mistakes due to identification can be very costly:

- The better founded is the organization of the classification system, the greater the dependency that can be placed on identification.

- The more reliable the auto-ID system becomes, the more can be done in capitalizing on fast flow replenishment and on supply chain and business partner relationships.

The same frame of reference is valid regarding product information and instruction automation via the Internet, including different types of automatic ordering procedures from headquarters. Rigorous organizational practices enriched with a classification methodology are prerequisites to the next important requirement: that of personalizing one's products for each consumer to keep a lock on the market and strengthen client loyalty.

11.3   How DCS Has Helped in Efficient Product Line Management

A general principle that exists with most professions is known intimately by some and ultimately by others. This is the *law of inverse cost-effectiveness*. This simply says that "what an information system loses in performance and efficiency, it gains in uncertainty, poor service, and added, unnecessary costs." I learned this principle 35 years ago at British Aircraft Corporation, the co-designer of Concorde.

Information systems can be designed in many ways, each with its own advantages and limitations. Several prerequisites must be met to make it effective for the end user. One is ensuring that transition to the new system does not bring disruptions and upheavals, while access to the database is seamless. Exhibit 11.6 illustrates the three components that come together in ensuring seamless database access by end users:

1. A streamlined information system that is architectured, integrated, competitive, and replaces old legacy software
2. A classification/identification solution, such as DCS, able to act as a pivot point of the new information technology
3. A distributed intelligent database networked any-to-any and available online at any time, in any place

The systems requirements outlined by these three components correlate and therefore, can be well-served through a common methodology. In several applications, DCS has proved to be of invaluable assistance in effective database design. The three domains shown in Exhibit 11.6 have common parts. Indeed, the intersection of these three major areas of interest provides the basis for database access by management in a user-friendly interactive manner. Seamless access to the database is effectively supported by DCS because the identification of information elements being sought is unique.

There are algorithmic and heuristic approaches at the intersection of the new information system design and the exploitation of database resources. Some 80 percent of the difficulty in using mathematics in management comes from the lack of data, and only 20 percent comes from challenges in modeling.

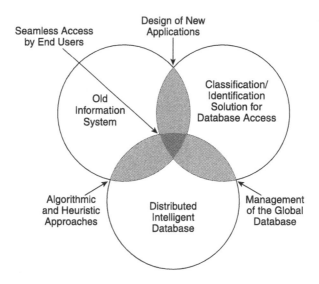

Exhibit 11.6   Seamless Database Access by Management Lies at the Intersection of Three Spheres of Interest

As systems become more sophisticated, their ability to capture, store, process, and distribute data has been significantly extended. This ability, however, is often conditioned by the efficiency of the process by which databases communicate with one another and with end users.

The significance of effective interprocess communications is even greater when one realizes the contrast in requirements between the old and new approaches to computing — the newest ones being mobile. No company can afford to start its database business from scratch to satisfy mobile computing. The ongoing solution must be kept steadily updated and able to produce results until the new structure is ready to take over and replace the old — or at least until the current solution reinvents itself in the current environment.

The design of a new classification/identification system is not the only challenge associated with a thorough renovation of a company's information technology and the way it is used to help in managing the product line in an efficient manner. Just as important is how to introduce the new system into mainstream operations without any disruptions in the supply chain. "It is," said one executive, "like changing the tires of a car while it is still running."

True to the goal that a change in product identification should not upset day-to-day operations, Osram GmbH chose a step-by-step procedure, which is outlined in Exhibit 11.7. DCS was first applied within the old information system, starting with the commercial operations — while legacy software was temporarily kept in place. Then, based on the new code system, the company's information technology processes were streamlined, new applications were added, and many of the old data processing routines were substituted. All of them capitalized on the thorough reorganization of the database, based on DCS. Eventually, the use of more sophisticated database solutions was developed to keep ahead of the curve with technology.

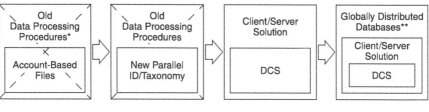

* Centralized on Mainframes
** Interconnected through a Broadband Intelligent Network

Exhibit 11.7   Phase-by-Phase Conversion from Fractioned Account-Based Files to a Client Database

Today, what I am describing finds its parallel in the implementation of advanced versions of ERP and CRM software. Increasingly, the value differentiation of ERP and CRM is in analytics. A rational classification and identification can be instrumental in building analytical applications that:

- Define a common business model for these applications
- Provide common naming, data definitions, and taxonomical rules
- Design and implement means that enforce the common business model

My suggestion is to pay particular attention to the dimensions used in CRM and ERP applications, defining attributes of analytical interest (including identification attributes) and providing a rigorous methodology for assessing data quality; also, when necessary, proceeding with reengineering (see Chapter 2).

Several lessons can be learned from the implementation of DCS to which this example makes reference. When it was fully integrated into the engineering and marketing operations, a new field of applications was undertaken, that of integrating purchasing, accounts payable, and inventories. This work was fundamental to streamlining ongoing procedures and what it involved in analysis and design can easily be seen as a forerunner of requirements posed by present-day supply chain solutions.

This was a real-life case study, and the benefits obtained from streamlining operations were not limited to what has been explained thus far. Prior to the establishment of a single frame of reference for classification and identification, which documented each product in a dependable manner, senior management had a rather hazy idea of how many distinct items constituted the company's product line. Marketing was selling some 15,000 products, but many sales people periodically expressed doubt that all these products were truly different from one another. Others doubted not only that a great many products were not truly distinct in terms of technical specifications or in regard to sales appeal, but also questioned their profitability.

The introduction of DCS and its implementation have allowed streamlining of the product line because it made feasible a unique and unambiguous product-by-product identification, and therefore a comparison. This was greeted as a major achievement by senior management. After the marketing people applied DCS with the help of the systems specialists, an analytical study established that the number of truly different products the company was selling was not 15,000 — but 7400.

This difference between the 15,000 products that management thought was in the company's business line and the 7400 that really were there is huge. The reason for this discrepancy was that the old patchwork of product identification systems had plenty of duplicates and triplicates:

- One product that was technically the same had up to 35 different identification codes.
- Conversely, up to five technically different products were found to be under the same code.

The fact that up to 35 different numbers were used to identify (and sell) the same product seems unbelievable but, in my experience, it is not unusual. Although 35 is an exception, I have often found in my practice that seven or eight different dubious IDs have been used for the same product because of plain errors, overlaps, and the fact that minor details are often supposed to constitute altogether different products.

This is a major handicap to good management of the product line. It is making business statistics plainly unreliable and leads to many product returns, which are costly and poison customer relationships. Even worse, in terms of management control, is to have five diverse products coded with the same identification number. The result is that returns are booming, adding to customer dissatisfaction, and substantially increasing handling expenditures.

The introduction of DCS corrected this awkward situation. It also helped to clarify a key subject that for years had eluded the company's accountants: how much profit or loss each product brought to the firm. Only when a unique and reliable identification system was implemented was it possible to answer this question in a factual and documented way. It was then found that, of the actual 7400 distinct products:

- 2500, mainly mass-produced items, plus a few specials made money to cover the losses of the others and leave a profit
- 850 were manufactured on-demand and therefore followed a different procedure in P&L calculation
- 370 broke even but had a good development perspective with the proper sales promotion
- 1040 broke even or lost some money but were needed to present a complete product line to the market
- 2640 lost money (some heavily); these were unnecessary to retail but had escaped attention because of misidentification

A decision was made to eliminate the 2640 products that lost money not only from the sales list (and manufacturing schedules), but also from stock.

Special discounts were offered for items that could sell at a lower price, while the remainder (and a good number, for that matter) of the condemned products were literally destroyed. An analytical study established that the carrying cost of an item on the racks over a year varied between DM 1 (U.S. $0.50) and DM 5 (U.S. $2.50), depending on the item.

11.4 Organizational Reaction to the Restructuring of Currently Prevailing Procedures

To obtain better results companywide, the organizational work described in this chapter was done by a joint group of analysts and users. From the beginning of this joint effort, project members went through engineering, manufacturing marketing through purchasing, accounts payable, and inventory control in an integrative manner. This was a job that in the past had addressed discrete islands. Each area had been handled individually.

After following the integrative approach, the analysts were amazed at how many fields the different subsystems had in common, yet they were structured in a totally different way. The needed supply chain continuity was not obvious to them during past operations because:

- The terminology used by each department and its IT subsystem was different, even if many fields came from the same source documents
- Legacy IT applications had been too deeply influenced by the punched card era and its 80-column straitjacket

For example, common information elements coded in a heterogeneous way in purchasing, accounts payable, general accounting, and inventory control included vendor references, vendor address, vendor code, part number, machine number, warehouse shipped from, plant shipped to, etc.; yet these are similar fields with lots of common references. A procedure was therefore established to weed out duplicates and inconsistencies.

To make sure where the discrepancies lay, the analysts wrote a program to compare the common fields between three subsystems: purchasing, accounts payable, and inventory control. Not surprisingly (given earlier experience), the files did not match. A number of problems were discovered in the process. The most common differences were field sizes and edit standards, followed by numbering systems, descriptive text, and keywords.

Many discrepancies also existed because of timing differences in updating cycles. But that is not all! Error correction procedures differed from one department to another, both in terms of timing and in the way corrections were made to erroneous input. Furthermore, when errors with noncritical data were detected, two out of the three departments did not bother entering the correction.

Not only procedural and conceptual but also organizational differences had to be overcome. The chosen solution was to combine the purchasing, accounts payable, and inventory control master files into a single entity to which was allocated row 2 of the family matrix (identified as SIP in Chapter 10). But the three departments reported to different senior executives in the organization, and each was jealous of its information (which it held close to its chest) — calling its resistance to integration "privacy of confidential data."

The analysts responded that integration was a way to greater efficiency. With integrated files concerning the same entities, there would be only one entry for each field, and discrepancies would be impossible. The same was true for corrections. If the vendor's address was wrong, it would need to be corrected only once and then would be consistent wherever it appeared. But which one of the three departments would have the authority to enter the corrections?

As with any other organization, there were data quality problems, timing constraints, heterogeneous sources, multiple source options for the same data (and what to do about them), as well as complexities of misaligned windows of availability. Any valid solution would require a methodology for a common approach for all feeds – and this remains valid till today with regard to enterprise resource planning, customer relationship management, six Sigma quality assurance, and many other programming products.

The more clear-eyed system analysts suggested the wisdom of achieving a single customer view as well as of obtaining distributing business intelligence that can help decision points. This further underlines the need for analytic applications — with an impact on engineering, production, and the market-place. In the case study in reference, management was divided on the wisdom of going ahead with these suggestions.

It is appropriate to note that the negative political reactions discussed herein are by no means an exception. Most companies have found that the realignment of organizational responsibilities are met with great resistance — and with frustration. Unavoidably, the board gets involved in realignment of responsibilities and in nine out of ten cases the first reaction is that, "The idea is good, but it is not immediately applicable."

Speaking from experience, when confronted with political issues that involve senior executives' careers, the board feels that the suggested restructuring calls for some organizational shifts and this would take time to resolve. For their part, the analysts react by pointing out that not only does the suggested streamlining mean order, but there is also another advantage; all the duplication of effort could be eliminated, leaving people free to carry on more creative duties.

In almost every computer shop, the duplication of effort tends to become a heavy burden, primarily because people working at intermediate manage-ment levels have friends and protectors higher up who work against any change. Much also has to do with historical reasons that add to the inertia. This is obviously absurd, but a simple reference to benefits will not ease resistance. What is needed is to talk softly and carry a big stick. That is the job of the CEO. Only a strong personality can see to it that:

- Duplication of people and machines is (finally) on its way to being eliminated.

- Each executive is able to ask for and receive online, *ad hoc* reports containing digested information from the corporate database.

In the case study under discussion, having successfully implemented an interdepartmental solution for purchasing, accounts payable, and inventory control, the analysts concentrated on expanding the application. It did not escape their attention that many of the information element fields in the three systems could also be found in the engineering master files as well as in manufacturing and marketing. The same problem also existed with other subsystems.

For example, the files on employee know-how and the payroll file had several kinds of duplicated information. Even more striking, some glaring redundancies existed relative to these files at the level of the manually maintained records that had not yet been handled by information technology. An overall strategy had to be developed and this involved several management levels.

Once again, there were organizational problems to overcome, some of them through give and take. For example, as a condition of joining the common applications base, engineering wanted to expand the vendor classification code to include a quality rating procedure. Logically, there were many good reasons for doing so, but the accounts payable people did not agree. The accounts payable department's employees were used to a credit rating code and its management was afraid that diverse evaluation procedures would be too much for the employees to digest. They were just not going to go along with it. The analysts had to explain that online interactive solutions offered the possibility of presenting every user with personalized information. They provided evidence that this could be done without having to oblige one department to use the forms of the other. They also suggested that for good order, the database administrator (DBA) must have the power to control the file structure of all user departments and make it homogeneous, while maintaining a neutral companywide standpoint. The argument was also advanced to senior management that:

- Integrated databases have become the "in thing"; they are, therefore, a competitive advantage.
- Because of this integration, forward-looking companies are more efficient than in the past.

The primary reason for discussing organizational reaction to change in the present chapter is to convey the message that even the best classification and identification study can fail if data is not seen as a companywide asset; that is, a corporate resource. This is a cultural issue. The management of change is both helped and complicated by the fact that organizations are made of people, and a person's mind does not run like clockwork. It rarely works in synergy, while just one false step can lead to controversy.

11.5   Implementing `<basic code>` in a Banking Environment

As is the case with industrial companies, the development of a coding system to serve in streamlining banking operations has often taken a twisted path. The client account number is an example of such twists. Client accounts are characterized by different codes, depending on whether reference is made to a demand deposit account (DDA, current account), savings account, foreign trade account, personal banking, or other operations. The result is that the same client relationship is represented by several incompatible numbers.

This diversity and (most often) heterogeneity in ID codes is of course irrational because it makes it difficult to have an integrated view of the client account and splits the database into discrete islands where bridges are fragile, if not outright difficult to establish. Theoretically, to remedy this situation, but practically to make it worse, the so-called "supercode" has been introduced by mainframers to link these diverse codes together. The end result is that it is often compounding the confusion.

Other things also add to the complexity of managing the customer relationship — something that no CRM software can correct single-handedly. For example, the client code (for the same entity) may vary from one branch office to another, making a client's consolidated statement a difficult operation; the same is true of other procedures followed by financial institutions that were originally designed for manual approaches but survived with computers.

This survivability of old, crumbling structures has not necessarily been accidental. Bankers often have to manually dig out a great deal of information. This data is rarely timely, is usually inconsistent from one file to another, contains errors, and often provides very little in the way of decision support. But rare is the case of end users who have revolted against this irrational situation.

Globalization, deregulation, and innovation make streamlining absolutely necessary, and DCS can find an excellent field of application among financial institutions. It permits bank-wide integration of client files with the proper identification of all accounts through `<basic code>`, `<suffix>` and `<origin>`, offering the bank a unique frame of reference:

- `<basic code>` identifies the client account on a nationwide basis, or internationally.
- `<suffix>` tells about the type of account: DDA, savings, loans, portfolio management, foreign operations, etc.
- `<origin>` is simply the branch office code or, for large corporate accounts, the central marketing service responsible for client handling.

As Exhibit 11.8 suggests, all levels of management can be served through this solution: `<bc>`, `<s>`, `<o>`. These provide the necessary and sufficient identifiers for handling all settlements involved in day-to-day operations. For loans, investments, and other functions performed by middle management,

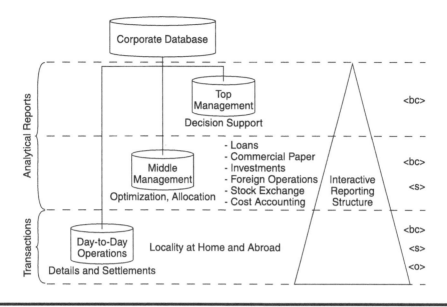

Exhibit 11.8   The Use of DCS to Organize Interactive Reporting Services for Senior Management

consolidated statements by type of account are what is primarily needed. This can be nicely expressed through <basic code> and <suffix>.

Typically, top management has particular interest not in geographical detail on every single account, but in overall account consolidation for major clients — plus the evaluation of branch office profitability (hence by <o> and critical review of lines of business by <s>). Consolidation of major clients is done by <bc>. Indeed, since the mid-1970s, tier-1 banks produce a *customer mirror* report to help judge single-client profitability.[3]

These and other examples demonstrate that DCS can constitute the pivot point for the entire structure of a bank's database, leaving the institution's human resources free to apply themselves to more analytical functions. Having solved the problem of classification and identification, system designers can address themselves to other needs on a timely basis. For example, *risk analysis:* to ensure that areas of high risk and exposure are systematically scrutinized. This, too, can be done by <bc>, <s>, and <o>.

The concept underpinning the foregoing paragraphs is that for every practical reason, supported through mathematical models, a bank's database plays a role similar to that of the electron microscope in the physical sciences. Database mining helps to enhance the capability of management to apply novel solutions to new and old problems (for example, by identifying in a documented manner problem instruments, problem operations, problem clients, and problem managers).

The method that one chooses should allow sound statistical sampling as well as statistical tests of obtained results. This has been a goal long sought by management sciences, but not very well implemented because data was not there, or it was not reliable. However, just having the data does not necessarily mean obtaining immediate results. A good deal depends on preparation, and DCS is the foundation of a sound methodological approach.

The examples considered in this chapter are abstracts from real-life applications with industrial concerns and financial institutions. As such, they help in documenting the fact that a properly designed classification and identification system assists not only in pruning and reorganizing the database, but also in making inquiry operations focus on risks and increase the organization's sensitivity to the pulse of the market.

11.6   The Effects of an Improved Organization on Accounting and Logistics

Classification is organization, and an improved organization positively influences many vital sectors in the enterprise. Chapter 12 focuses on a quantum step forward in quality assurance through Six Sigma, as a bridge between the impact a greatly improved identification system has on engineering design, manufacturing, and sales, and greater competence in quality of accounting and logistics.

Accounting, along with its rules and its procedures, has been materially affected both by the activities of regulatory agencies and by rapid technological advancements. In principle, much of the legislation and many of the rules of governmental bodies have had a beneficial influence on accounting. The same statement is valid about technology's aftermath, which has helped in improving the accuracy, precision, and timeliness of accounting statements and of logistical solutions. Such benefits, however, have been derived only by tier-1 companies, able to thoroughly understand the nature and ramifications of technological advances. It is an old axiom that the only way progress can effectively be attained is by taking advantage of new possibilities as they develop, rather than by hanging on to old connections.

To understand the sense of this last reference, return to the fundamentals, including the fact that a single structure underlies both financial accounting and management accounting, even if the form of reporting and its content may be different. The basic structure of all accounting records and financial reports consists of:

- A few elementary principles and concepts
- A set of relationships among accounting system elements
- Man-made rules and guides based on the application of principles

It is not always appreciated that the most fundamental of these principles are those regarding the *user* of accounting information who *needs to know* and *understand* the nature and limitations of data provided. The instruments to which I make reference are greatly affected by technology, but also by rules and regulations and dependability considerations that by and large are a company's own. Whether looking at a speed dial, an altimeter, an inventory level, or cash flow, to make intelligent use of information, one must understand:

- What a given figure *probably* means
- What the limitations of data obtained are
- Under what circumstances it may mean something different from the apparent signal that it gives

The typical user of accounting information and of logistics reports does not need to know how to project, structure, operate, or control the accuracy of the entire accounting system in the enterprise — or even part of it. However, that person must know to appreciate the prevailing error rate, precision, and timeliness of logistical and accounting reports.

For *if*, as mentioned in Chapter 11.2, 35 different codes pertain to the same item, and five different items have the same code, *then* for every practical purpose the value of received reports is zero point zero (0.0). As found in my 50 years of professional practice, a surprising number of companies have such high error rates in their inventory management that this 0.0 characterization of intrinsic value applies to the majority of their reports.

It is therefore evident that one of the first and most beneficial effects of a streamlined classification and identification system is the increase in accuracy that it helps to provide. It is no less vital to underline that a significant reduction in error rates will not come as a mater of course. To become a reality, it requires a concentrated effort in organization, experimentation, implementation, and testing.

This must go beyond the classification procedures thus far discussed. System analysts, logistics experts, cost accountants, and plenty of end users of accounting/logistics information must participate in this quality assurance effort. Knowledge of the meaning of an accounting or other financial instrument is in no way all the user needs to know to reach valid decisions. In addition, the user must:

- Know how to use this knowledge to solve the problems that arise during operations
- Master the art of management, which includes many matters that have little to do with the instruments themselves, but much to do with the process

For example, an important process in which accounting information is used within a business environment is that of *management planning and control*. This is the process of ensuring that there is a plan for obtaining and using resources effectively in the accomplishment of the organization's objectives — *and* that this plan is observed by all concerned.

Even the most perfect classification/identification system is a component of management planning and control, albeit an important one. Therefore, it is by no means the whole solution. To sharpen up management planning, one must tune the process of deciding what action should be taken in the future. Hence, the requirement of *prognostication*. The area covered by one plan, such as a logistics plan, may be a small segment of the enterprise or it may be its entire business. The essential characteristic of a plan is that it involves a decision about action to be taken in the future.

Planning is therefore to be distinguished from *forecasting*, the latter being an estimate of what will most likely take place — or more precisely, what will be the most likely future effect of current decisions. In logistics and in many other areas of activity, prognostication is made by means of models.[4]

Models that run in real-time are also critical for management control reasons. Management control has to do with the ongoing operations of the company; it consists of a regularly recurring sequence of interrelated activities which see to it that the right (planned) thing happens at the right time. Control activities and planning activities constitute an indivisible process in which patterns of operations interact and merge into one another.

All this is very relevant to this chapter's theme because a well-done job of classification and identification provides a streamlined infrastructure on which one can effectively build a valid accounting system, a dependable logistics solution with prognostication capabilities, and any other operations enhancing management planning and control (for example, quality assurance).

Notes

1. D.N. Chorafas and Heinrich Steinmann, *Expert Systems in Banking*, Macmillan, London, 1991.
2. Another term is *description*. However, the word *description* has been used for many diverse and incompatible purposes, while *clear text* is a new term to be applied strictly for the work to which reference is made in this chapter section.
3. D.N. Chorafas, *Commercial Banking Handbook*, Macmillan, London, 1999.
4. D.N. Chorafas, *Financial Models and Simulation*, Macmillan, London, 1995.

Chapter 12

A Sound Methodology for Enterprise Management: General Electric's Six Sigma

Originally developed by Motorola and made famous through its high-profile implementation at General Electric (GE), Six Sigma (6σ) is a program that has been successfully applied to quality assurance and cost control. Benefits derived from its implementation have been challenged by some people; facts, however, speak louder than words, and Exhibit 12.1 presents, in a nutshell, GE's savings from Six Sigma over a four-year timeframe.

To appreciate the impact of Six Sigma, recall that companies typically enjoy two kinds of *strategic advantage*. One is transitory, the result of being in the right market, with the right product(s), at the right time. This means riding a favorable tide, as long as it lasts. The other is a more fundamental strategic advantage. It comes from having in place first-class management and processes able to mobilize the organization, positioning it in a way to capitalize on business opportunities. This is the advantage that comes from smart materials, the Internet supply chain, classification and correct identification, and cost control and quality assurance through Six Sigma.

The keyword with strategic advantages is *collaboration*. Past is the time when every system designer and each user were living in an environment of their own without sharing experience. One of the major benefits derived from the Internet is that the old dream of better coordination might finally become a reality. Underpinning improved coordination is the fact that ID is unique to an individual product, and it can be so much more effective when based on an equally unique classification code.

Other necessary organizational work is associated with quality assurance and cost control. Failing to exploit this potential means that one is not working

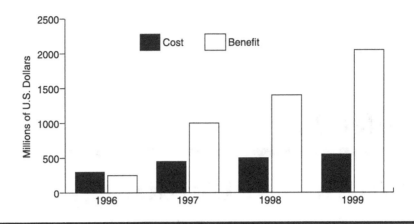

Exhibit 12.1   Costs and Benefits (in Millions of U.S. Dollars) Characterizing Six Sigma Progress at GE

for, but against the best interests of the company — giving away its competitive advantages, which will divide winners from losers in the years to come. Success in a market more competitive than ever before largely rests on steady innovation, rock-bottom costs, and high-quality products and services.

The last two — rock-bottom costs and high-quality products and services — are where Six Sigma addresses itself. One way to look at GE's consistent effort is as a disciplined process that helps company management focus on developing and delivering error-free products and services. Some people equate it with near-perfect quality, with only 3.4 defects per million opportunities for a product or transaction. Others consider Six Sigma as the best training ground for all salaried employees in high-level statistical analysis aimed to drive out both defects and unnecessary costs.

It is not that important whether the primary focus is on training in a disciplined approach to effective enterprise management, or that of cause and effect between quality assurance and cost control through advanced statistical tools. What is vital is that at a time of globalization, deregulation, and the Internet, there is in place a system of *total quality management* that can flourish, and give first-class results.

If done in a bureaucratic manner by issuing flat orders, quality control can be a hindrance. But a well-done total quality function supported by internal control has the potential to assist everyone, as well as the company as a whole. Quality assurance is very important, both in engineering and in finance. Japanese banks, for example, are masters of *quality control circles*, which were originally an American invention. Since World War II in the manufacturing industry, quality assurance has been immensely assisted by statistical quality control charts.[1] Both engineering companies and financial institutions need an infrastructure for quality results.

Down to its fundamentals, the synergy between a quality assurance policy and a cost control program is not made in a vacuum. It begins with decisions by the board on the necessity of both high quality and low cost, and is followed by a definition in depth of the methodology, tools, and standards to be used to reach such a goal. The principle is that quality of products and services should be followed up through their life cycle and checked for compliance to internal rules — while at the same time costs are swamped. This is what can be achieved through Six Sigma.

12.1   An Infrastructure for High Quality in Products and Services

Quality assurance has always been a very important issue in any industry, at any time, while swamping costs is instrumental in keeping a healthy bottom line. Today, both issues are more important than ever before because of globalization and rapidly advancing technology. Quality and costs should be subject to internal control. Tier-1 companies know from experience that they are correct in instituting an authority that sees to it that management and the rank-and-file have clear incentives and responsibilities on both issues.

Because costs and quality have much to do with one another, this mission needs to extend its reach into return on investment (ROI). The members of the board should be very interested to know that the company is doing much better than the industry average — indeed, better than its peers and its competitors. Establishing firm guidelines, doing timely supervision, and attracting new talent impacts on quality results. Speaking from personal experience, high quality is a catalyst to an attractive work environment, which adds to reputation. Motivated technical talent wants to work on high-quality projects because the work a person is doing defines his or her self-worth.

Product quality, cost containment, fast time to market, reputation, and a challenging work environment lead to improved job performance and create a virtuous cycle that increases personal satisfaction. It is no secret that successful companies are careful to populate their work groups with people who are creative, decisive, productive, and care about quality and costs. By doing so, they gain an advantage over their competitors. When he became the CEO of General Electric, Dr. John Welch recast the company in a way that mirrors what I have just described.

As manufacturers prepare to introduce the next generation of products — and in these days of rapid innovation products follow one another in quick succession — companies must not only adapt to changes in the methodology and technology, but also improve cost and quality performance. Firms that will not or cannot do so are not going to be around for long as independent entities.

The drive to swamping costs in well-managed companies has often given results that are very impressive. At GE, a customer inquiry that previously cost $80 to handle over the phone now costs just 50 cents via the Internet. With that level of savings, analysts figured that GE slashed expenses by hundreds of millions of dollars in 2000, "while pushing more than $5 billion worth of purchases through the electronic systems" it has put in place.[2]

Financial institutions can also position themselves to gain significant advantages from processes able to mobilize the organization. To bolster performance,

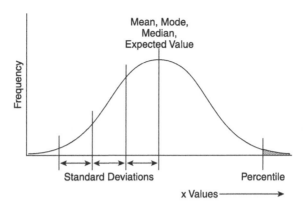

Exhibit 12.2   Normal Distribution, Mean, Mode, Median, and Standard Deviation

the Morgan Bank has implemented Six Sigma through 300 projects that are squeezing costs out of everything. Channels under scrutiny range from distributing research to selling derivatives. Thousands of managers at J.P. Morgan have attended *Black Belt* and *Green Belt* classes to learn how to slash costs while increasing sales (see Chapter 12.3). Signs posted on a board in the training center's hallway read: "Build Morgan," "Enable Morgan," "Kill Morgan." Douglas A. Warner, the Morgan Bank CEO, says these sessions helped to save $1.1 billion in 1999.[3]

What is special about Six Sigma? The standard deviation of a distribution, or sigma,[4] is a statistical term measuring how far a given process deviates from expected value. The idea behind Six Sigma is that if one can measure the number of defects in a product or process, one can systematically figure out how to eliminate them and get close to zero defects — provided one benefits from a thorough, well-structured methodology.

Within ±3 standard deviations (or 3 σ) from the mean lies 99.73 percent of the area under a normal distribution curve shown in Exhibit 12.2. The outliers are 0.27 percent, and this percentage becomes extremely small indeed outside Six Sigma. This is essentially a process of self-assessment. The standard deviations reflect status and performance of a quality program that helps to identify concrete actions, and estimate their most likely aftermath.

GE has developed and implemented an entire methodology around this statistical quality controlled concept, and it also claims that Six Sigma has changed the company's DNA — in everything it does and in every product or service it designs and markets. The basic tools underpinning GE's methodology include:

- *Statistical process control* methods that analyze data, helping to study and monitor process quality, capability, and performance
- *Other control charts* that monitor variance in a process over time and alert to unexpected variances that may cause defects
- *Process mapping* that illustrates how things get done by visualizing entire processes and their strengths and weaknesses

- A *tree diagram* that shows graphically goals broken into levels of detailed actions, encouraging creative solutions
- A *defect measurement method* that accounts for the number or frequency of defects that hit product or service quality
- *Chi-square testing* that evaluates the variance between two different samples, detecting statistical differences in case of variation
- *Experimental design* that permits one to carry out methodologically t, z, and chi-square tests regarding two populations (H_0, H_1)
- *Root cause analysis* that targets the original reason for noncompliance or nonconformance, with specifications aimed at its elimination
- The *dashboard* that maps progress toward customer satisfaction (e.g., fill rate, billing accuracy, percent defective)
- A *Pareto diagram* that exhibits relative frequency or size of events: 20 percent of the sources cause 80 percent of any problems

Pareto's law is visualized in the left side of Exhibit 12.3. Any business makes the larger part of its profits from a relatively small number of clients. The example chosen here comes from banking. In a credit institution, the top 2 percent of clients tends to bring in about the 50 percent of profits; the top 20 percent brings in the 80 percent of profits. The high-end clients, however, are always very demanding. These clients can be satisfied only by the best quality of service.

A Pareto chart might feature the reasons underlying an identified problem along the abscissa (horizontal axis of reference) and frequency or location along the ordinate (vertical axis). This visualization is complemented by the dashboard, which resembles a car's instrument panel showing chosen critical variables pertaining to the product or process under control. For example, one arrow on each dial might indicate the level of quality the customer is seeking, and the other arrow might measure how far the company is from meeting that requirement.

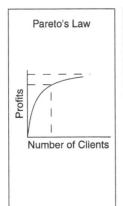
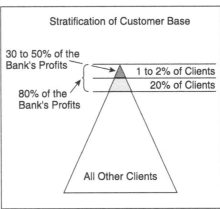

Exhibit 12.3   Pareto's Law Implies a Stratification of Clients According to Business Criteria with Emphasis on Potential Profits and Losses

GE's chairman John Welch has said that he wanted a dashboard on every customer updated weekly. While some people suggest such a goal places unrealistic demands on the workforce, I fully subscribe to the Welch guidelines. In fact, I think the dashboard should be updated at Internet time by using agents.[5] Monthly or quarterly dashboards are worse than useless — they can be misleading.

This is not the place to describe in detail the concepts behind the other nine tools in the list of ten. The reader's attention is, however, brought to the requirements posed by *experimental design* as a means of measuring, shifting, and reducing the variation in a process. This is achieved by carrying out a methodical sequence of experiments that provide verifiable results, rather than by following the classical trial-and-error approach.

12.2   Systematic Methodology Is the Best Friend of Enterprise Management

The Six Sigma procedure outlined in Chapter 12.1, along with the tools which it uses, permits one to focus on the quality, cost, and other root issues of sound management. The goal is to provide efficient help in reducing cycle time, swamping defects, and emphasizing the value of each individual contribution. The entire approach is guided by Design for Six Sigma (DFSS), a systematic methodology utilizing training tools and measurements to meet customer expectations, produce at a high-quality level, and keep costs in check.

Associated with this is a process for continued improvement known as *Define, Measure, Analyze, Improve, and Control* (DMAIC). This is a closed-loop process, characterized by GE as systematic, scientific, and fact based. It helps to eliminate unproductive steps, focus on in-process measurements, and apply the best-available technology for improvement. Through DMAIC, Six Sigma provides a vision of quality and allows people to strive for perfection. The underlying *quantitative* approach is to multiply the number of units processed by the number of potential defects per unit, which gives the *opportunities for error;* and then divide the number of actual defects by the number of these opportunities for error, and multiply the result by 10^6.

Here is an example on where this leads. Suppose that a line produces 100,000 items and each item can have up to five defects. Multiplying the number of units processed (100,000) by 5 gives 500,000. These are the opportunities for error. If there were 100 defects in this lot, then 100/500,000 = $2/10^4$. And multiplying $2/10^4$ by one million (or 10^6) obtains 200.

The outlined computational procedure produces the number of defects per million operations. A conversion table translates that number into sigma. The statistics are shown in Exhibit 12.4. Notice that the example with 200 defects per million opportunities (DPMO) is close to 5σ. It is good quality, but not as perfect as 6σ.

The reader can appreciate that the visualization of numbers helps in making them comprehensible. General Electric says that the simple Pareto bar chart

Exhibit 12.4   1 to 6 σ Defects per Million Pieces

3.4 defects per million opportunities = 6 σ
230 defects per million opportunities = 5 σ
6210 defects per million opportunities = 4 σ
66,800 defects per million opportunities = 3 σ
308,500 defects per million opportunities = 2 σ
690,000 defects per million opportunities = 1 σ

is the most widely used data display tool in Six Sigma because it identifies which problems occur with the greatest frequency or incur the highest cost. These are the *salient* problems that should be attacked first. (A *salient* problem is one to which management should bring its undivided attention as a matter of priority.)

In Six Sigma methodology, each combination of adjustments and quality correction measures becomes a system of equations that can be solved as a matrix. Experimental design allows users to efficiently test a significant number of variables — and hypotheses connected to them — in a dependable manner. These mathematical tools are at everyone's disposal, but the organization employing them must become so familiar with the method that it can take advantage of them in its daily work. Cornerstone to the implementation of Six Sigma methodology is the ability to understand and appreciate customer needs and expectations. These are defined by the customers themselves when they set basic requirements and standards, as well as target values and tolerances.

Every producer should appreciate that defects are sources of customer irritation and that they are costly to clients, manufacturers, and other service providers. Vigilance with regard to quality and costs should exist at all management and worker levels, yet it is the board's responsibility to instill an organizational culture whereby everybody looks at quality as being his or her own responsibility.

Years ago, I was working as a consultant to the chairman of a major industrial group that had the policy that the bonus of manufacturing executives was highly dependent on the results of quality audits. These were based on the pattern shown by focused statistical quality control charts. Such an approach can also serve the banking industry. For example, the policy of applying statistical quality control charts to intra-day overdrafts strengthens internal control, bringing attention to bifurcations, such as the one in Exhibit 12.5:

- In this SQC graph, up to a point in time t_1, the process is *in control.*
- Had it at this point continued under the upper control limit, it would have remained in control.
- But as it breaks it, it is *out of control* — and management must immediately take corrective action.

Different financial institutions follow different procedures on how to bring a process under control. Chase Manhattan, I am told, has established the

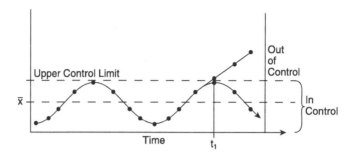

Exhibit 12.5   Applying Statistical Quality Control to Intra-Day Overdrafts or Any Other Variable

following policy. The manager of a department or project is given three chances to stretch out and then bring under control a runaway situation:

- The first time he or she gets a bad grade (Audit 4), the manager must see the vice chairman of the board.
- If the next year he or she gets an Audit 2 grade, performance is judged good; however, if the grade is Audit 3 or 4, the vice-chairman will ask for an audit follow-up.
- If in six months the situation has not been radically improved, the department or project manager is definitely out.

I would advise every company — whether a credit institution or an engineering, manufacturing, or merchandising concern — to adopt an approach that follows the general lines of this Chase Manhattan procedure. There is much to be gained if this approach emphasizes budgets, timetables, costs, *and* product quality. It should be implemented by means of both regular and major design reviews done in an agile, dynamic manner — without this process becoming a bureaucratic undertaking. And its pace should be quickened. A year is nearly an eon.

Internal control can effectively reinforce quality assurance because the goal should be one of dramatic improvements in crucial organizational performance parameters. Companies that target reduction of rework and better results in cycle time should have interactive access to quality control data of this kind. Usually, firms find difficulties in doing so because they have not taken care that such data is always available in a comprehensive form. Six Sigma is an excellent means to this end. Organization studies must define:

- Which data is needed for quality assurance and how it must be presented
- Which information collected at production floor or back-office is immediately usable in deriving a pattern
- How data collection and analysis should be done to have a reasonable degree of confidence in the results

As a matter of policy, datastreams must be exploited for maximum impact. Every process briefly stated in these paragraphs should be audited. Internal control should bring both matter-of-course quality reporting and auditing results to senior management's attention. To do so in an able manner, there must be both a methodology and tools that increase the sensitivity to what goes on in the design, production, and distribution of products and services. That is what Six Sigma helps to do.

12.3 Organizational Prerequisites to Ensure a Process Is in Control

A process that is in control provides a sense of stability and predictability. This calls for a metaprocess capable of regulating and guiding operations using quantitative data (see Chapter 7). As Exhibit 12.5 shows, variation is permitted but only within tolerances and, therefore, limits. This leads to the *critical to quality* (CTQ) concept that targets elements and practices with direct impact on perceived quality. Effective control for CTQ is provided by specialized Six Sigma practitioners, as will be seen in the following paragraphs.

To better explain the procedure put in place to assist with quality assurance, take an example contributed by Piet C. van Abeelen, vice president of Six Sigma Quality at General Electric. The reader will recall the reference to defects per million opportunities (DPMO) in the numerical example in Chapter 12.2. When Sigma levels are reported, it is assumed that there is in the background both some *long-term* and some *short-term* variation in the process under control.

Exhibit 12.6 visualizes the long-term distribution of the population, with μ as the mean and σ as the standard deviation. It also compares these parameters to short-term distribution statistics: x_1, x_2, ... x_6 for the mean and, correspondingly, s_i for standard deviations. Typically, short-term distributions represent the samples taken from a population such as the factory production line. Basically, the DPMO measurement is long term, whereas it is conventional to report a short-term Sigma Level.

Regarding this relationship between DPMO and Sigma Level (SL), there is a commonly accepted way of reporting SL that defies strict statistical definitions. The commonly accepted difference between measured long-term SL and short-term SL is 1.5σ. This is an empirically derived number.

It is conventional to measure the DPMO of a process and calculate the long-term SL to arrive at the reported short-term SL. This SL is subsequently used to calculate **z** as a *measure of* (process) *capability* (see the numerical example in Chapter 4). The **z** algorithm is:

$$\mathbf{z} = \frac{|\text{SL} - \mu|}{\sigma} \tag{12.1}$$

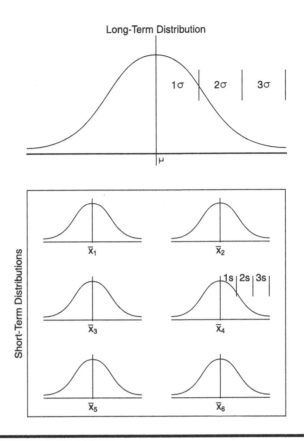

Exhibit 12.6   The Difference Between μ, x_i and σ, s_i, Respectively, for Long-Term and Short-Term Distributions

where σ is the standard deviation of the population. The **z** value is taken from cumulative normal distribution tables found in all statistical books.[6] A more familiar form of Equation (12.1) is:

$$z = \frac{|\bar{x} - \mu|}{\sigma} \qquad (12.2)$$

In Equation (12.2), μ (the mean of the population) and σ (the standard deviation of the population) are constant; and x_i is the variable of ongoing observations. The difference is that in Equation (12.1), the variable is substituted by the Sigma Level.

Technically, the Sigma Level should always be identified as either short or long term. A long-term Sigma Level of 4.5 corresponds to a short-term Sigma Level of 6 (4.5 + 1.5 Sigma Shift). Piet C. van Abeelen notes that there are many assumptions inherent in this approach, which elicits much debate; however, it is essentially a convention. It is of course wise to always check to ensure that data is normally distributed and actually measures both short-term and long-term Sigma Levels of the product or process under control.

The question obviously arises as to whether in a production floor, sales environment, or banking branch office, the people working there can implement Six Sigma and its metrics unassisted. GE answers this query by establishing organizational prerequisites. The solution is specialized personnel who can assist in implementing Six Sigma and in handholding. The CEO is the *Grand Champion* of the system. The CEO's immediate assistants and executive vice-presidents are the *Champions*.

The Champions choose projects to undergo rigorous Six Sigma discipline, ensure that each project is tied to business needs, and interview Black Belt candidates. The Grand Champion and Champions, so to speak, drive Six Sigma methodology into the culture of the firms by making it an indispensable part of their functions. The *Master Black Belts* are first and foremost teachers, who also review implementation procedures, solve problems, and mentor Black Belts.

Selection criteria for Master Black Belts are quantitative skills and the ability to teach and explain in a comprehensible manner. Master Black Belts, as well as Black Belts, are full-time positions who, among their other responsibilities, also help in developing more powerful tools. Black Belts are team leaders responsible for measuring, analyzing, improving, and controlling key processes.

These key processes typically support quality assurance not in an abstract sense, but in a measurable way that influences customer satisfaction and higher productivity. Black Belts perform mission-critical tasks and their contribution is measured in deliverables. Green Belts are similar to Black Belts but theirs is not a full-time position.

Black Belts and Green Belts are essentially employment teams. GE's operations worldwide feature some 500 Black Belts and 10,000 Green Belts. The company's global operations have 100 Champions and Master Black Belts. These make up a well-manned infrastructure of know-how which has proved to be most important because Six Sigma experts are already on hand throughout GE, when they are needed. Most importantly:

- Their presence helps in changing the company culture toward a higher level of quality conscience.
- It has set in motion an unrelenting process of continuing to swamp costs, anywhere, in any type of operation.

This system of Champions and Black Belts plays a dual role, promoting a new methodology and acting as feedback in this methodology's execution. The latter function is essentially one of measurement and constructive feedback. After quality assurance and cost control interventions are undertaken, it is critical to measure results systematically, and provide constructive feedback to facilitate continuous improvement.

Both cost control and the quality program should be handled as a steady operation rather than as a one-time shot, whose effects rapidly attenuate. Therefore, a mechanism should be put in place allowing stakeholders to supervise process improvement.

Every manager worth his or her salt knows that quality attributes and metrics for key products and processes play vital roles in establishing quality levels; benchmarking is the quantitative feedback. Therefore, it is important not only to provide guidelines for establishing quality attributes and defining their metrics, but also to ensure that such guidelines are followed by everybody in the organization.

12.4 Using Six Sigma to Analyze Manufacturing Processes and Operations in the Back-Office

Significant benefits can be derived from implementing a rigorous statistical method, in locating defects, and in breaking a customer's requirements into manageable tasks; for example, setting optimum specifications for each part of the process and accounting for how the parts interact. This lays the ground for accurate responses to customer wishes through technical specifications that are studied analytically. There is a wealth of statistical methods and tools whose benefits companies forego because they do not have the necessary know-how, and their management is afraid to take bold steps.

A good example of Six Sigma in action comes from Camco, GE's Canadian appliance subsidiary.[7] The company had tried conventional approaches to solve a problem connected to lack of rigidity in some of its cooktops, a problem that was leading to high scrap rates. Industrial engineers tried different approaches during assembly, that seemed logical, but the problem persisted. Then, using *experimental design*, engineers tested ten possible causes in various combinations. These ten causes were analyzed in 14 versions of an experiment.

Subsequently, graphical presentation allowed them to pinpoint the source of variation. The pattern was detected by hanging the parts in the oven during the enamel-baking process and analyzing the ratio of enamel on the top and underside. By tightly controlling these processes, it was possible to solve some outstanding quality issues, reduce costs, and improve yields. This is a good example of how experimental design gets people away from thinking that there is only one good method — or that 99 percent assurance is everything.

Many companies work on the false premise that their customers do not see the quality defects. They are utterly wrong on this account. Customers are not stupid. Industry leaders know that and do their utmost to increase customer satisfaction while keeping costs under control.

"Quality, as measured by our customers, could be the biggest differentiator we have going forward into the next century," according to Jeff Immelt, president and CEO of GE Medical Systems (GEMS).[8] The concept behind this statement is admirably exemplified in Exhibit 12.7, which visualizes how the concept of Six Sigma allows one to meet customer specification requirements in an able manner.

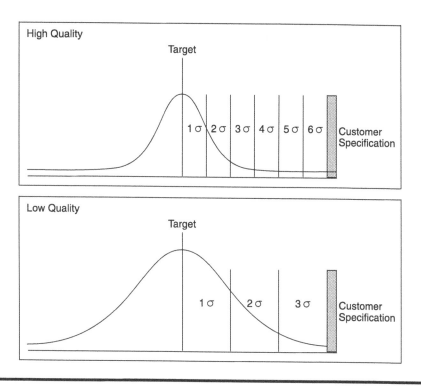

Exhibit 12.7   The Measure of Process Capability Is a Good Proxy of the Probability of Defect (By permission of General Electric.)

- The smaller the standard deviation of products from a production process, the higher the quality being assured.
- The challenge is to fit six or more standard deviations between mean value (or *target*) and customer specifications.

In the upper part of Exhibit 12.7, high quality is exemplified by 6σ. The lower part depicts the usual case of 3σ between target and customer specs. Much more than the company's reputation and its profit figures are at stake. The market is changing rapidly and it demands higher and higher product quality. The more impersonal Internet commerce becomes, the more the brand and reputation of a company will depend on the quality of its product. Ironically, this impersonal characteristic will increase with the customization of products in I-commerce, and most companies have yet to face up to this challenge.

At the same time, quality cannot be effectively controlled with due care about the bottom line. By all indications, variable cost productivity in most firms is lagging price decline and this squeezes margins. Vendors can no longer afford to be complacent. That is why this GE example is so valuable to the reader.

To turn the tide in high quality at low cost, one needs both a rigorous methodology and *metrics* — something one can measure and compute for any product, service, or process, at any time. One must also ensure that the problem does not come back again and again. This is what GEMS and the other GE divisions have done during the past five years.

The aftermath of the Six Sigma initiatives discussed above is impressive. Take GE Medical Systems' new Performix CT X-ray tube as an example. This is a process-intensive, high-technology industry with $20 million per year of scrap and rework; hence, the possibility of important savings. The chosen solution led to 100 Six Sigma projects on improving plant yield, and 200 Six Sigma projects on increasing current tube life.

One of the goals has been 0 percent dead on arrival (DOA). Reaching the objective essentially means no patient rescheduling at the hospital end. Other goals have been guaranteed tube availability and an order of magnitude reduction in *unquality cost*. Each of these aims is food for thought to practically every industry.

The sequential steps in reaching such goals are dramatized by the torrent of normal distributions in Exhibit 12.8 (from a practical Six Sigma implementation, with the permission of GE). It is not possible to go from 6.6 percent defects to 0.0 percent defects overnight. Such improvement is doable over a period of time, after:

- Identifying, qualifying, and quantifying all the factors that are critical to quality (CTQ)
- Co-involving the customers in pinpointing those aspects of product or service deemed critical from a quality perspective
- Establishing a process that permits steady quality improvements until the goal of no defects is reached

These three basic steps to Six Sigma deliverables are valid for the factory floor, the sales outlets, and the back-office. One of the back-office applications

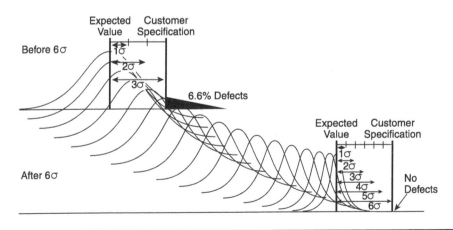

Exhibit 12.8   Three Standard Deviations Usually Fit Between Quality Control Target and Customer Specifications, but this Is Not Enough

Exhibit 12.9   Statistics in Processing Ten Invoices

(in days)
23.4
16.9
25.0
22.2
28.6
18.5
24.1
17.6
14.9
34.6
x = 22.6
s = 6.0

Note: These statistics are used as proxy of the μ and σ
parameters (see Equation 12.3).

of Six Sigma concerns invoice processing time. At GE's Ft. Myers, Florida operation, a Six Sigma project concentrated on time spent on handling invoices. Its aim has been to collect meaningful data and then use appropriate statistical measures to analyze the process. Input data came from evaluating time required to process an invoice for ten specific invoices (sample size = 10). The statistics are shown in Exhibit 12.9. The mean of this distribution is x = 22.6; the variance is s^2 = 35.8 and standard deviation is s = 6. The crucial element in connection with this distribution is customer specifications relative to the mean and the effect of s on specifications.

The ten values in Exhibit 12.9 are a sample. Samples taken over successive days suggest that the mean itself has a distribution, whose expected value indicates the *long-term capability* of the process to meet objectives. This long-term capability also has a variance. As long as the short-term capability varies in comparison to the long term, the invoice handling process has shift and drift. Typically, the short-term variation fits within the long-term distribution (as seen in Exhibit 12.6).

While the potential performance of a process over time is defined by long-term capability, actual performance is indicated by short-term statistics that represent ongoing results. The difference between long term and short term, also known as a *sigma process*, serves in exercising management control. A process is considered to be in control if it fits within longer term boundaries or tolerance limits.

These principles apply hand-in-glove to the implementation of *enterprise resource planning* and *customer relationship management*. Both ERP and CRM are processes that must be introduced and administered to obtain commendable results. They are both office processes and GE's Ft. Myers example is a good lesson on what is necessary to get the most out of these applications.

Any office process obeys the *inverse relationship* rule: as the variance decreases, process capability increases. This, in turn, swamps the probability of defect.

The probability of defect is given by defects per opportunity (DPO) (see Chapter 12.2). Using Six Sigma methodology based on statistical rules, what is the likelihood that an invoice that enters the system 35 days before it is due will get paid in time? The answer is (see Equation (12.1) and Exhibit 12.9):

$$z = \frac{|SL - \mu|}{\sigma} = \frac{35 - 33.6}{6.0} = 2.066 \qquad (12.3)$$

Looking up the **z** statistical tables, for x = 2.05s, the probability is 95.96; by extrapolation for x = 2.066, the probability is about 96.12 percent. That is, 96.12 percent will be on time and 3.88 percent will be late. The data used with this example is sample-based, but Six Sigma methodology uses x and s as proxy to μ and σ, the population parameters.

Statistics vary from one sample to another. With the GE methodology, **z** is computed through Equation (12.1) with long-term data. If one does not know the actual shift characterizing the sample, the convention is to use 1.5 Sigma shift added to the long-term **z** to get the reported short-term Sigma of the process.

While it is difficult to find a theoretical justification for this convention, in practical terms its effect is neutral, particularly in cases where the results of one period are compared to those of another. As Piet C. van Abeelen has noted, "At GE, we have placed more emphasis on comparing the Sigma Level at the start of the project with the Sigma Level at the completion of the project."

12.5   Applying Six Sigma to a Sales Environment at GE Capital

The methodology described in the preceding chapter sections impacts a whole range of business operations, whether in manufacturing, merchandising, or banking. Examples of Six Sigma applications in the financial industry are provided by GE Capital. Jack Welch is looking to GE Capital, which accounts for the larger part of General Electric revenue, to deliver at least 40 percent of Six Sigma savings in a year by driving out defects from mortgage applications, credit card transactions, leasing operations, and customer service call centers.

Customer service call centers are in the realm of CRM implementation. All companies can benefit by rethinking and emulating the policy followed by GE Capital, which has paid growing attention to the control of processes benefiting from implementation of Six Sigma. One of the better examples comes from Canada. GE Capital's Canadian subsidiary made major financial deals.

It led the syndicate providing T. Eaton with financing, after the retailer sought creditors' court protection and purchased the Marathon Realty operations from Canadian Pacific, thereby entering into the real estate market.

The definition of quality as seen by customers, therefore of targets, was based on market research. Business customers told GE Capital Canada that for them a critical quality issue was how often a salesman could answer their questions directly without having to look into the matter later on and get back to them within a certain delay. Adhering to the Six Sigma data-gathering discipline, each salesman now keeps a meticulous diary for a week, noting each time a customer asks a question and whether he or she is able to answer it immediately.

Statistics prior to Six Sigma indicated that direct, immediate answers were given only 50 percent of the time. The effort was therefore to deduce which types of questions salesmen are unprepared for, what kind of training would fill that gap, and which persons were best suited to the job of salesman — leading to best salesman personality profiles.

By implementing Six Sigma, GE Capital Mortgage identified the branch that best handles the flow of customer calls. Then, it used the model developed for that branch, which was based on Six Sigma findings, to redesign the sales process in the other branches. Says Welch:

> "Customers who once found it (the mortgage corporation) inaccessible nearly 24 percent of the time now have a 99 percent chance of speaking to a GE person on the first try; and since 40 percent of their calls result in business, the return for us is already mounting into the millions."[9]

The methodology is straightforward. Once everything in a customer-oriented process is quantified, the use of *what-if* scenarios begins: Would the newly defined sales training provide 90 percent or better direct, immediate answers? Would a more rapid paperwork processing schedule in sales handling make mail room bottlenecks irrelevant? Would adding a person in accounting give the back-office an extra hour's leeway in meeting timetables?

Experiments designed to answer these queries make use of the concepts described in the preceding chapter sections. They set a target and study the variance under different hypotheses. This permits factual and documented opinions to be used rather than using rule-of-thumb, as is the everyday case in so many companies. It also brings, to each individual's level, the sense of accountability for results and rewarding achievements.

Whether one implements a new version of ERP or CRM, salesforce upgrades, or any other project, Six Sigma methodology helps in improving the deliverables. As a result of a quality program, employees at lower levels can take additional responsibility for results of processes in which they participate. Six Sigma tools see to it that a clear system of accountability can be implemented, rewarding teams as they achieve or exceed quality goals.

The principle I have applied for 50 years in industry and finance is that employees need to be shown that the organization is committed to quality and cost control. This demonstration is best done by rewarding individual and team achievement through an incentives system. Incentives should not be limited to only one subject, such as financial rewards. People need to see the individual benefits for really improving products, services, and processes.

Rewards must be targeted, not general and abstract. GE calls x the *target*, which is essentially an expected value. Having fixed the target, it concentrates on the standard deviation. Based on the references made in the preceding chapter sections, it should be evident to the reader that the two curves in Exhibit 12.7 have the same target, but the quality of the process represented by the top distribution is significantly higher than the quality of the process mapped in the lower distribution.

Although GE did not say so, it is my opinion that the percent defective charts c and p can be nicely used in connection with the Six Sigma process and its mapping in statistically meaningful terms. Percent defective charts help a great deal in graphical presentation of the quality of an ongoing process. For example, the defects-per-unit (DPU) statistics used in the context of Six Sigma compares the total number of defects in a product to the total number of units produced. If 28 defects are present in 900 units, the total DPU would be $28/900 = 0.0311$. Based on this sample, this is also the likelihood of appearance of a single defect. A statistically valid procedure would be based on the longer term, taking the mean of the means as expected value.[10]

The defects-per-opportunity (DPO) statistics — another Six Sigma metric — are similar to DPU, except that they consider the total number of opportunities that exist for a defect to occur. If 62 defects are present in 1500 units and there are opportunities for defect in each unit, then the total DPO would be $62/1500 \times 10 = 0.00413$. This is also the likelihood of occurrence of a single defect.

A further metric is defects per million opportunities (DPMO), as discussed in Chapter 12.2. It is equal to $10^6 \times$ DPO. Therefore, *if* DPO = 0.00413, *then* DPMO = 4.13.

This approach can be used with practically any process, whether at the front-desk or in the back-office, in engineering design or in manufacturing, in sales or after-sales service, in the New Economy or in the Old Economy. Always remember, however, that while Six Sigma methodology and its statistical tools can be of major assistance, a great deal depends on the cultural change necessary to appreciate the impact of high quality and the importance of lower costs — as well as on the determination of the CEO and the board to get better and better results out of the organization.

12.6   An Internet Application Can Benefit from Advanced Statistical Tools

GE is not the only company that has shown demonstrated tangible results from implementing Six Sigma. The method is indeed valuable to all companies that pay due attention to weeding errors out of their system. If GE is a leader in this rigorous error correction process, it is because its CEO put his weight behind it and fathered it until it became the company's second nature.

As seen in consecutive chapters through practical examples, this can indeed be a very rewarding exercise. The reader will recall what was said at the beginning of this chapter on the importance of *self-assessment*, evaluating the status and performance of: a quality assurance program, A cost control program, and the synergy between the two.

I see this synergy as a major reason why Six Sigma can become a very effective way to reintroduce the notion that quality matters to the organization, as well as to identify concrete actions needed to sustain a Six Sigma program in the long term:

- Providing critical feedback to strategic planning
- Helping in setting individual and group goals, with merits and demerits associated with them

The point has also been made that the concept, method, and tools of Six Sigma can be well applied in targeting other implementation procedures such as ERP and CRM, as well as in capitalizing on the Internet online services — such as the methodology used by Alliant Food Service, which uses the Web for order-taking. What such diverse implementation goals have in common is the need to find a way to error-free operations.

Consider order entry as the reference frame. At Alliant Food Service, customer service representatives used to type phone and fax orders, a process resulting in typos and other errors. This caused, on average, three ordering mistakes per thousand cases of food shipped. Having customers order directly from Alliant's Web site, which is linked to a database of supplies, reduced errors to two per thousand cases shipped. The goal now is 0.4 errors per thousand cases.

Misordering is one of the reasons why delivery returns may become an appalling problem. Another is incomplete or incomprehensive information. Alliant's old catalogs limited descriptions of food to 19 characters. This was long and short at the same time. It was short because it made it difficult for customers to know which foods fit their needs, with the result there were 14 returns per thousand cases delivered. It was long because there is plenty of error in transcription of a 19-character field.[11]

Error rates have been significantly reduced using AlliantLink.com. Customers can get vivid details of each product, and along with it pictures. With this improvement, the numbers of goof-ups have been sharply cut to three per thousand cases shipped. The next goal is 0.3 returns per thousand cases shipped.

Out-of-stock situations provide another example of what can be obtained through a sound methodology. In the past, customers had no quick way to know when the food they ordered was out of stock. This caused, on average, 7.5 supply-shortage errors per thousand cases of food shipped. By ordering through the Internet, customers can use AlliantLink.com to check supply stocks in real-time. The result is four errors per thousand cases — half the previous rate.

What this Alliant Food Service example brings into perspective is that the Internet can make significant contributions to error reduction, and therefore quality improvements — but Six Sigma methodology and the Internet are not exclusive of one another. To the contrary, they can work in synergy, as it happens so often with different tools and methods when used effectively.

Working online on the Internet can benefit from Six Sigma because, as many perceptive people think, its methodology is an evolution of the synergy between methods study and the use of statistics. Other experts believe that the concepts underpinning Six Sigma are not so different from analysis connected to time study, which was developed at the beginning of the twentieth century by Frederick W. Taylor. The main element distinguishing one from the other is complexity. Six Sigma analyzes hundreds of permutations and combinations through experimental design, chi-square tests, and other methods. This goes well beyond work time differences to identify, in a practical sense, how to improve products or processes.

In different terms, it should not escape the reader's attention that like time study, Six Sigma gets people from all over the organization to work together on improving the end product or process — not just "this" or "that" individual piece of it. There is also a major paradigm shift that should be fully taken into account with Six Sigma as has been the case with both time study and motion study in the 1920s.

While at the beginning of the 20th century, industrial engineers were concerned with variance in productivity among individual workers, experts today suggest that processes are computer-intensive, not man-intensive. This requires rethinking statistical standards, including the fact that by and large most companies operate at roughly 2σ or 3σ. This corresponds to 308,000 and 66,800 defects per million (See Exhibit 12.4). Clearly 2σ is pitiful quality; even 4σ is nothing to crow about.

The reader should always keep in mind that each sigma increase requires an exponential reduction of defects. This takes a great deal of effort and is justified by the fact that the cost of low quality is typically 10 to 15 percent of lost revenues. According to John Welch, in GE's case this "amounts to some $7 billion to $10 billion annually, mostly in scrap, reworking of parts, and rectifying mistakes in transactions." All industries face this challenge. Whether talking about manufacturing or banking, Six Sigma should be the target under current technology — with Seven Sigma the goal later in this decade.

Let me conclude with this thought from an article by Jeffrey E. Garten in *Business Week*.[12] Key aspects of culture characterizing the new economy may be antithetical to a fundamental focus on quality. Lawrence A. Bossidy, former chairman of Honeywell International said about Six Sigma: "If a CEO doesn't speak about it all the time, then it wanes."

Chief executives, Garten suggests, are hard-pressed to sustain a continuous emphasis on quality today, because they are preoccupied with other challenges which they perceive as being more crucial to their success and survival. Among the 40 top business leaders Garten interviewed for an upcoming book, the word *quality* was not mentioned once as a major strategic challenge. Yet, in the new economy, quality is a most fundamental ingredient — which often makes the difference between failure and success in a highly competitive business.

Notes

1. See D.N. Chorafas, *Statistical Processes and Reliability Engineering*, D. Van Nostrand Co., Princeton, NJ, 1960.
2. *Business Week,* August 28, 2000.
3. *Business Week,* September 18, 2000.
4. σ^2 is the variance of a population; it is a parameter. s^2 is the variance of a sample; it is a statistic. Standard deviation is the square root of the variance.
5. D.N. Chorafas, *Agent Technology Handbook*, McGraw-Hill, New York, 1998.
6. Consequently, **z**-test tables can be used. See W.J. Dixon and F.J. Massey, Jr., *Introduction to Statistical Analysis,* McGraw-Hill, New York, 1951.
7. *Report on Business Magazine,* October 1997.
8. From an internal GE Instruction Manual, with the permission of General Electric.
9. *Report on Business Magazine,* October 1997.
10. D.N. Chorafas, *Statistical Processes and Reliability Engineering*, D. Van Nostrand Co., Princeton, NJ, 1960.
11. See also in Chapter 10 and 11 the effect of classification and correct identification on the reduction of error rates.
12. *Business Week,* December 18, 2000.

AUDITING ACCOUNTING STATEMENTS AND ENTERPRISE RESOURCE PLANNING RECORDS

Chapter 13

The Framework of Accounting, Financial Reporting, and Auditing

The art of business, suggests an old dictum, is that of making irrevocable decisions on the basis of inadequate or incomplete information. A great deal of this information is conveyed through accounting, the rules of which were established in 1494 by Luca Paciolo,[1] an Italian monk and mathematician; these rules have been continuously adapted to changing conditions and business requirements.

Change and the management of change takes many forms; one of them is adapting the rules of accounting to evolving financial, commercial, and industrial conditions. An example is the evolution of rules and regulations aimed at ensuring reliable financial reporting.[2] Another example of adaptation of accounting is the cost accounting framework, and with it the internal accounting management information system (IAMIS). Accounting is, after all, the first and foremost information network of any company.

As seen in Chapter 1, accounting underpins the entire ERP framework and the information services that it provides. Therefore, a discussion of auditing enterprise resource planning and customer relationship management will make little sense unless one first looks into the evolution of accounting during the more than five centuries since Luca Paciolo's seminal work. The present chapter offers the reader a bird's-eye view of this evolution.

Similarly, for any serious discussion on auditing the implementation of ERP, CRM, or other programming product, one should, from the beginning, clarify the term *auditing* and its role. In a nutshell, auditing is the systematic verification of books of account and other financial legal records for the purpose of determining the accuracy and integrity of accounting. Such audits can be conducted either internally by regular employees within the organization, or externally by hired professional auditors: the certified public accountants (CPAs).

While the principles of auditing are universal, this is not true of the way they are conducted. What is known as the *deliberate method* essentially means that transactions are reviewed in detail. Alternatively, with the so-called automatic method, the system of internal checks in operation that is part of internal control is relied upon to verify the accuracy of transactions. Both ways aim to ensure the integrity of accounts and records. Is there a difference between auditing and accounting? The answer is yes:

- Accounting is detailed and primarily constructive.
- Auditing is fundamentally analytical; its nature is investigation.

Accounting involves the transcription of vouchers, tracking of transactions, keeping of books, and construction of financial reports — and, in certain cases, the interpretation of those reports. Auditing starts with interpretation of reports and follows up with a critical analysis of the business under review and scrutiny. It can range from a detailed analysis of every business transaction up to a general review and survey of the business, its accounting method, the accuracy of its books, and its financial health and condition.

In this sense, accounting and auditing complement each other. They both need clear rules that are established by legislators and regulators. Such rules must be few, precise, and easy to comprehend. Neither should it escape the attention of companies and their regulators that accounting and auditing practices themselves must also become more efficient. This is accomplished through real-time bookkeeping, faster turnaround of accounting chores, less paperwork, lower error rates, better information services, an interactive visualization of results, and assistance provided to auditors by knowledge artifacts or agents.[3]

13.1   Lessons Learned from Five Centuries of Evolutionary Accounting Practice

Every civilization, ancient or modern, that had a commercial background required numerical records of some sort. There are records of commercial contracts inscribed in cuneiform characters on bricks that archeologists have excavated from the ruins of Babylon, and it is known that there were fairly elaborate accounts for farms and estates in ancient Egypt, Greece, and Rome.

In pre-Columbian North America, there was the tribute-roll of Montezuma. In a pictorial way, it gave an account of the blankets, weapons, and other wares that constituted the tribute paid by nations in meso-America. Historically, however, accounting as it is known today started with the development of commercial republics of Italy and the seminal work of Luca Paciolo in 1494 that integrated then-known accounting principles in a way similar to what

Euclid did with geometry some 18 centuries earlier. Paciolo collected, edited, and incorporated under one cover what was already known about the art of keeping accounts and explained the tools indispensable to this process, outlining the rules and procedures to be observed.

According to some estimates, the first double-entry books known to exist are those of Massari of Genoa dating from 1340 — a century and a half before Paciolo. The Massari books are in good double-entry form, which indicates that a certain system must have been in use in the Middle Ages and also suggests that the double-entry method might have antedated Paciolo by 200 years or more.

Together with double-entry accounting, the journal and ledger type of books have been significant utilitarian developments. The careful reader will, however, appreciate that while their basic concept remained relatively invariant over time, many of the tools and supports associated with them have been subject to great and sometimes rapid change — and the same is true of laws governing accounting and financial reporting.[4]

In contrast to accounting, the concept of auditing (briefly described in the introductory chapter section) is a late nineteenth century development. Auditing has been promoted by the fact that following the Industrial Revolution and the expansion of business, it became evident that it was not enough to keep accounts; one must also examine and ascertain their accuracy and dependability. The same, incidentally, is true about information provided by ERP and CRM.

Not only the daily practice of recording and auditing information, but also technology saw to it that, over time, accounting tools have changed. Indeed, technology has an impact on the very nature of accounting, on what is expected from financial reports, and on auditing. This has also been promoted by the fact that in addition to being utilitarian, accounting is descriptive. This characteristic serves well the analytical and interpretative functions of modern business.

- *Accounting, and value-added tools such as ERP, give the history of an enterprise in planning and financial terms expressed according to certain known and accepted conventions.*

In this sense, the history of the evolution of accounting is a reflection of the history of commerce and industry. By necessity, the system of signs and rules that is used must adapt itself to the needs and demands made upon it, in order to continue describing in a meaningful way everything that takes place.

- *A sound way to look at ERP and CRM is as accounting's adaptations, which take on significance when thinking about the requirements imposed by the New Economy and Internet commerce.*

To remain competitive in the first decade of the twenty-first century, companies must be able to rapidly realign not just their technology, but also their methods to changing business conditions. Accounting finds itself in the middle of this transformation. Without software such as ERP, the solutions to which the transformation in reference arrives are not necessarily tracking all data streams to their origin.

- *Homogeneity in recording and in accounts is important because, in the last analysis, basic accounting data will be used to judge the pulse of a company and of the economy.*

This statement is valid even if at the interpretative metalayer, discussed in Chapter 13.2, the rules being employed are different from one company to the next. No matter which rules are being used for inference, this process cannot function if the accounting information and statistics, on which the inference is based, are so diverse that one's understanding of the processes underpinning them might be distorted.

People well-versed in accounting procedures maintain that nothing that has to do with commerce, industry, or any other sector of the economy is impossible to describe in accounting terms of some kind. Neither is it that difficult to represent, analyze, or interpret any type of operation or transaction that has been subject to rigorously established accounting rules; and audited accounting reports offer reliable numbers to their user.

While these statements have substance, one should remember not only that accounting information is approximate, but also that many companies have to work with incomplete data. This leads to a contradiction. In mathematics, one typically does not ask a person to solve a problem without furnishing him or her all the needed information. But in solving business problems, one almost never has all of the information one would like to have to make a decision. This is as true of accounting at large as well as of specific instances such as those represented by the day-to-day use of ERP and CRM.

In nearly every case in business life, the manager can think of additional information that would be helpful *if* it were available. At the same time, there are other practical problems that need to be solved for which there are a glut of figures available. The trouble is that only a small fraction of these figures are at all relevant to the specifics of the problem at hand, and perhaps none of them is quite what is necessary to solve the present problem in a factual manner. Yet, it is inescapable that problems must be solved, business decisions must be made, and often these decisions cannot be delayed until all pertinent information is available, or it will be too late.

One has to do the best one can with accounting and other information available, and then move on to the next problem. That is how the clock of business and of the economy ticks.

It is indeed surprising how often this point is overlooked. To change this situation is nearly synonymous with changing human nature. Companies are made of people and anything the business accomplishes is the result of the actions of these people. Figures can assist executives and professionals in their daily work in various ways, but the figures as such are nothing more than marks on pieces of paper. They accomplish nothing at all by themselves.

13.2 Understanding the Role of Accounting in the Financial System

The role of accounting and financial reporting, as well as the auditing of accounting data, will be better appreciated if one thinks in terms of the decision space of an executive, manager, or other professional. Typically, in every organization this decision space is applications oriented; its main three axes of reference are those shown in Exhibit 13.1.

- Anything happening within this frame of reference must be measured; That is accounting's role.
- The economic aftermath of these decisions must be reported; that is what financial reporting is all about.
- The information contained both in the books of account and in financial reports must be reliable; that is the mission of auditing.

A person who wants to make intelligent use of accounting information, whether this comes from ERP and CRM software or any other sources, must understand what a given accounting figure *probably* means, what its limitations are, and under what circumstances it may mean something different than what seems to be apparent or even self-evident. The user of accounting information does not need to know how to design or construct an accounting system from scratch, but he or she must appreciate the reason for and meaning of numbers and the qualitative aspects underpinning these numbers.

Because the uses of accounting are so broad, knowledge of the concepts underpinning accounting reports is vital. Recall that ERP is only an instrument of information technology. Many people think its conceptual understanding is all that the user needs to know. This is necessary, but it's not enough. In

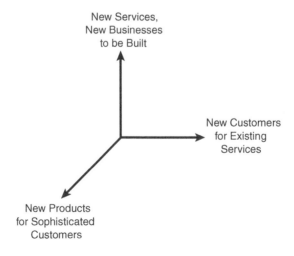

Exhibit 13.1 An Applications-Oriented Decision Space for Self-Service Banking

addition, the person using ERP or CRM information and accounting data must know:

- How to employ this knowledge to solve problems that arise in the management of the enterprise
- What the goal of the company is, with the environment defined by the industry and the market in which it operates

This is written in appreciation of the fact that there is much more to the art of management than the use of *quantitative* information that comes from classical accounting reports or ERP products. *Qualitative* information is also important, whether it relates to general accounting, cost accounting, principles underlying the construction of financial statements, evolution of the company's financial position at a given moment in time, or business performance over consecutive years.

The best way to look at qualitative information is that, above the quantitative presentation of business data, there is an *interpretative* metalayer (see Chapter 7) that can be instrumental in ensuring that resources are obtained and used effectively in the accomplishment of the organization's objectives. As Exhibit 13.2 suggests, below the quantitative accounting data there is another layer — that of the specific business infrastructure. The importance of an interpretative layer is dramatized by the fact that few, if any, business problems can be solved solely by the collection and analysis of figures. Usually, there are important questions connected to the business environment and infrastructural factors that cannot be, or have not been, reduced to numbers — yet they impact on accounting information.

The business infrastructure can change because of many reasons. Some have to do with the evolution of the line of business one is in; others with ways and means used to conduct one's business; still others, with the technology that is available, the way one approaches the market, and the manner in which the market behaves. The market that characterizes the globalized Internet economy has different characteristics from those of a static market with local appeal.

A key component of the three-layered structure presented in Exhibit 13.2, particularly of the interpretative metalayer, is *prognostication*. Its goal is less that of an estimate of what might happen in the future and much more an evaluation of future effect(s) of current decisions. This evaluation can be

| Interpretative Metalayer |
| Accounting Data |
| Business Infrastructure |

Exhibit 13.2   The Three-Layered Structure into Which Fits Accounting Information

facilitated or limited by the data one uses. In daily business practice, however, *facilitation* and *limitation* are relative, not absolute terms; they change over time because the market environment itself evolves.

Prognostication is a prerequisite to the planning function that must be performed at all levels in the organization and in all organizations. Budgeting, for example, is a systematic form of planning that uses accounting data, while the balance sheet is a means of control. Neither budgets nor balance sheets are fully objective ways of passing on data, even if many people act as if financial problems need only be presented in numerical form.

At the basis of this limited, quantitative approach is the erroneous idea that a rational decision can be made solely from knowledge of numbers. People with experience appreciate that it is wrong to forego figures, *concepts*, prognostications, deliverables, and their interaction in the solution of problems. Concepts include ideas and use rules that lead to interpretations. They may make reference to matters of precedence or jurisprudence that impact on accounting figures and, sometimes, change their meaning. While the inference one does is largely based on figures, concepts may lead to a totally different path than the one originally projected on numerical data alone.

Inference based on accounting and other financial information is vital because business people can obtain considerable insight from these statements. To do so, they need information about their own company and about their competitors, as well as about their business partners in the Internet supply chain. At the same time, there are inherent limitations in financial and accounting information — and by consequence, in ERP reports — that prevent these statements from providing answers to some of the most important questions raised about an enterprise.

The principle is that the accounts and statistics must be right. Interpretation of them is the manager's own privilege and risk. When talking about auditing the book of accounts or ERP information, what one is principally after is accuracy, precision, and documentation of the figures. This leads the auditor to question both the data and certain aspects of the process — or all of it. This questioning aims to respond to two queries:

1. Whether the accounting process functions in an effective and efficient manner
2. Whether the accounting process operates in compliance with rules and regulations

Expert auditors know that, for any practical reason, compliance with rules and regulations is, to a significant extent, a matter of interpretation. It is therefore part of the metalayer of accounting depicted in Exhibit 13.2. To the contrary, the rules and regulations themselves are part of the established business infrastructure. In this sense, at the middle layer, accounting does not prove; its mission is to announce and reveal. But the reading of accounting statements leads to *induction*, which goes beyond the simple enumeration of data.

Take as an example the accounting rules for software depreciation, which evidently apply to ERP and CRM. In March 1998, the American Institute of Certified Public Accountants (AICPA) issued Statement of Position (SOP) 98-1: "Accounting for the Costs of Computer Software Developed or Obtained for Internal Use." Its objective is to provide guidance on accounting for the costs of computer software developed or bought by entities for their own employment.

Because it introduces the concept of depreciation, the implementation of SOP 98-1 decreases costs and expenses the first fiscal year, but thereafter it increases year-over-year costs and expenses as the capitalized amounts are amortized. Because bought software such as ERP adds functionality to the existing information system, its depreciation must follow SOP 98-1. In contrast, the cost of software that does not add functionality to the present IT routines will continue being expensed as incurred.

SOP 98-1 identifies the characteristics of internal-use software, providing guidance on new *cost recognition* principles. This is significant because it changes past practices. Certain costs that were previously expensed as incurred will now have to be capitalized and amortized on a straight-line basis over three years. Accounting rules, such as those concerning depreciation, are not cast once and forever.

13.3   Why Accounting and Auditing Standards Must Adapt to the New Economy

As an opening paragraph, let me define the *New Economy*. It is the name given to those industries benefiting directly or indirectly from the latest revolution in information and communications technologies, the Internet, digitization, and software advances that alter the way people look at products and services. The requirements of these industries in terms of accounting standards significantly differ from those of the Old Economy where business was relatively slow-moving, at least when compared to today's standards.

The distinction between the Old and New Economy is important because accounting and auditing must also adapt to the new environment, work at Internet time, and use computers and models to sharpen the mind's eye. Companies in the Old Economy are still conditioned by decades-old business practices of relatively slow product innovation, unfocused inventory management, and sales and distribution that often lack marketing punch. In the Old Economy, it was enough to identify a class of items, deal in averages, and address the market at large — particularly the mass market. In the New Economy, this is an aberration. Nearly every item must be handled in a unique way because it must be personalized; and deals are increasingly concluded online.

This turns old accounting practices upside down. The trend toward personalization of goods for each consumer or business partner in the supply chain no longer permits one to measure in averages. Accounting must not only be precise but also individualized, and accounting information should

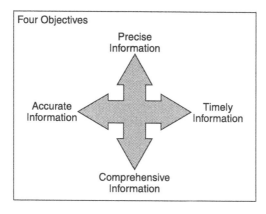

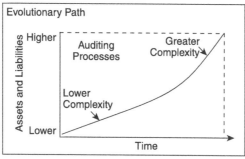

Exhibit 13.3   Auditing Should Be Rigorous Throughout the Life of the Firm and Focus on Both Objectives and Evolutionary Requirements

be handled online in real-time. This is what enterprise resource systems permit — but it is not always accomplished, let alone with diligence. Therefore, the able use of ERP and CRM systems must be audited.

The introduction to this chapter has given a bird's-eye view of what auditing is. In the modern economy, its role is steadily expanding and the process of auditing is becoming more complex as the entity's assets and liabilities (particularly the liabilities) continue to grow. Exhibit 13.3 depicts the four dimensions of the auditor's work and the fact that complexity tends to increase over time.

As the complexity of modern business grows, the task of auditing gains a much larger perspective. It goes beyond accounting books and it covers how an ERP system is used and what benefit the company gets out of it — because ERP and other programming products feed into accounting. This type of auditing follows Cicero's six evidentiary questions,[5] which are crucial to every auditor:

- *Who*, apart from the person who signed, contributed to, or was witness to this decision?
- *How* did the persons involved, alone or by committee, come to this decision?
- *Where* has the evidence been that led to the commitment being made?
- *When* was this decision originally made, and under *which* conditions?

- *What* exactly did the decision involve? Was it subsequently changed or manipulated?
- *Why* was the decision made; which precise goal was it targeted to or intended to avoid? Was there a conflict of interest?

No doubt, the answers to be given to these and similar queries are also important to the Old Economy. But the pace of the New Economy requires that such answers come fast and at a high level of accuracy. In a globalized economy, the system must work around the clock, 24 hours per day, 7 days a week. The sun never sets on the global enterprise, but at the same time the obligations and risks a company takes on also follow the sun.

Auditing of the ERP and CRM processes, as contrasted to auditing of classical accounts, must focus on precision, personalization, real-time execution, and overall effectiveness. To answer the tough information requirements implied by the foregoing sentence, the company's accounting system must be restructured — and this restructuring must also be audited.

Is the information provided by CRM, ERP, and current accounting chores enabling the company to evaluate customer relationships in the short term and in the long term? To keep distribution costs in control? To optimize inventories? To examine engineering's ability for innovation? To meet time-to-market schedules in production? The short- and long-term management information requirements are not the same, as Exhibit 13.4 suggests.

One must also position the company against the forces released by the Internet. A seminal article by Bradford Felmy in *EDPACS*[6] stated: "Choreographing an organization's entry onto the World Wide Web is essentially a project management function. All of the interests inside the enterprise must be represented. The implementation strategy must address such issues as... change control... (and) include the organization's formal policies for accessing Web sites, browsing through them, posting Web-based information, and creating and maintaining *audit trails* of the organization's Web-related data." The Internet also has other aftermaths that invite auditing's presence: the exponential growth in the number of Internet users sees to it that consumers are better and faster informed about products and prices. A company's management cannot afford to be informed about costs, prices, and moves by its competitors at a slower pace or less accurately than its clients. Business-to-business supply chains take a 10 to 15 percent cut on procurement costs, which represents billions of dollars.

Because costs matter, management accounting information should focus on minute changes in productivity. The chosen ERP and CRM solution must provide fast and accurate information enriching the company's database with the necessary elements so that subsequent datamining can bring productivity figures into perspective in a factual and documented manner. Auditing is expected to find out if this, indeed, takes place.

Not every off-the-shelf routine — ERP, CRM, or any other — has the characteristics I am suggesting. Many ERP programming products do because

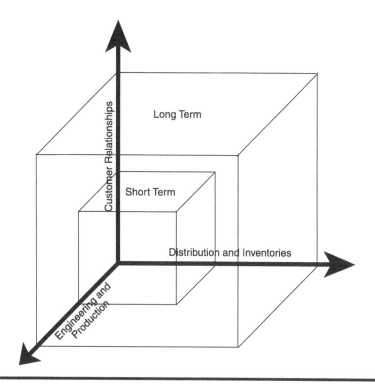

Exhibit 13.4   The Short-Term and Long-Term Information Requirements Are Quite Different in this Three-Dimensional Framework of Management Reporting

they include human resource planning, but most of the companies buying them do not exploit this facility. Auditing of the implementation and use of ERP should flush out such deficiency so that corrective action can be taken without delay.

Senior management should not be satisfied with abstract assurances such as "the implementation of new information technology has boosted productivity." This might be true in the general case, but not in every company nor in every country. What really matters is how much the company's productivity has increased. Is it more or less the quantum leap in productivity in the United States, such as 4.5 percent at end-1998 and 6.9 percent at end-1999?

The point I wish to make, which is crucial to ERP auditors, is that while many industrial and service companies have benefited greatly from the able use of information technology, just as many or even more have been laggards. These are on the sick list, and one surely does not wish to see one's own company's name written on that roster.

The accounting system should position itself to flush out danger signals connected to all matters that top management considers crucial to growth and survival. The addition of ERP software helps on the information side of this mission, but the most important element is cultural. Management should appreciate that it can no longer neglect to take advantage of the remarkable potential provided by technology and integrated advanced software solutions able to boost efficiency, cut costs, and increase market appeal.

It is as well a new mission of auditing to provide assurance that management decisions always capitalize on the fact that commercial buyers and sellers do not interact efficiently through paper-based approaches that include labor-intensive procedures. These often result in mistakes and delays. The bottom line: efficient, New Economy solutions not only improve the efficiency of transactions, but also cater to changing customer preferences and trends in most areas of operations.

13.4 Both Quantitative and Qualitative Features of Accounting and ERP Are Vital to Business

Accounting sets out to record events that have taken place, rather than to discover them. This is true even if accountants, to some extent, may have to discover facts to be able to record them. This discovery process is not concerned with the creation of data pertaining to events or transactions that have to be registered, but with the mapping into accounting books of what has taken place but might be hidden at first look.

If one looks at organizational issues, one notices (as emphasized in Chapter 13.1) that not only is accounting in direct contact with the business infrastructure, but it literally rests on it. Therefore, the accountant must have considerable knowledge of how commerce and industry operate, as well as of the laws and regulations, before attempting to audit events and financial transactions in the books. An example is the issue of *materiality;* an expense of $20,000 has no effect on General Motors, but it may have a large impact on a small family firm.

A person who is not familiar with the interpretative metalayer as explained in Chapter 13.2, may fail to recognize significant facts from non-significant, or even become confused or frustrated by reading accounting statements. As another example, a very common source of confusion, both with accounting and with ERP, is the word *cost*. There are direct costs, indirect costs, variable costs, historical costs, standard costs, differential costs, net costs, residual costs, incremental costs, marginal costs, opportunity costs, and estimated costs. Some of these terms are synonymous. Others are almost, but not quite the same. Still others are used by some people as if they were synonymous.

Therefore, accounting figures should always be discussed and interpreted in terms of the particular problem that they are intended to help solve, rather than in an abstract sense. A useful procedure to follow in approaching a specific problem is to define, as carefully as possible, the purpose for which accounting data is to be used in a given problem, and then consider how appropriate figures should be collected, assembled, processed, and presented for that specific purpose.

A different way of making this statement is that the first step in understanding accounting — and by extension of ERP and CRM — principles and figures is to gain knowledge both of the general principles on which the business world rests and the interpretive complexities associated with this

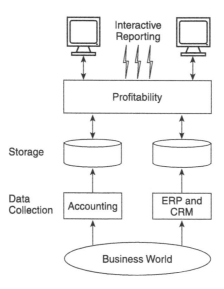

Exhibit 13.5   The Principles of Data Collection, Storage, and Interpretation Are Similar from One Company to Another, but Data Must Be Accurate, Timely, and Specific

world. As Exhibit 13.5 suggests, facts, events, and financial transactions must primarily depend for their existence upon the principles on which the world conducts its business. The data accounting collects must be specific:

- The fact that commerce booms in no way means that every company prospers.
- "This" or "that" company, or an entire sector of the economy, may suffer because of the law of unintended consequences.

Here is a practical example. Internet commerce booms, but after the late March 2000 stock market shakedown, the capitalization of business-to-business (B2B) companies has collapsed. The advent of Internet commerce led to a surge in the value of companies dedicated to B2B trades. During 1999, and the first three months of 2000, investors could not have enough of them. Then, at the end of first quarter 2000, a major correction in technology stocks turned their glamour on its head.

Accounting must capture, record, and report changes that happen both in-the-big and in-the-small. An example of big-picture change is that of March/April 2000 when the 18-percent drop in the NASDAQ Composite Index wiped $1 trillion from investors' portfolios. While that major correction was the result of an overvalued technology sector that suddenly confronted reality, the connection that exists tick-by-tick with accounting should not be missed. The current way of rather backward-looking financial statements used by business and industry does not capture the volatility in crucial assets, effects of innovative processes, or wealth effect of accumulated groundbreaking patents.

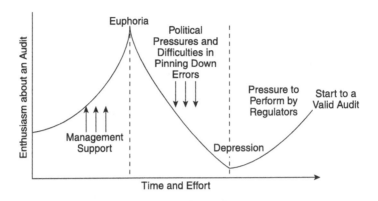

Exhibit 13.6   The Auditing of Any Major Process or Project Tends to Go Through Successive Ups and Downs

These and other assets are tracked a long way after the facts. Yet these are the assets underpinning New Economy companies. Leaving them out of current statements sees to it that investors looking for tomorrow's sources of wealth are flying blind. They are condemned to use substandard information and to suffer wild market mood swings. First-class accounting, MIS, ERP, CPM, and other software cannot cure the market's volatility, but they can provide investors with a better picture of a company's true worth.

The connection between the restructuring of accounts and financial statements to reflect strengths and weaknesses of the New Economy, and their recording through orderly accounting procedure, is evident. Auditing should not focus only on errors in accounting books and traditional financial statements. It should help in *foresight*. This will not likely happen when accountants and implementers of ERP systems take a near-sighted view of the work they should be doing, or follow a policy characterized by lukewarm analysis and too many files kept secret.

Exhibit 13.6 maps this process of successive ups and downs as I have seen them happening in the auditing of many processes and projects, particularly in IT. Given management support, the auditors start their work diligently. As difficulties in pinning down errors and malfunctions come along, and political plots mount, management support wanes and the auditors fall into a state of depression. Only pressure by regulators gets management going again, and auditing is back on track toward a valid solution.

Regulators need to grasp the technical complexities of globalization, its tools, instruments, techniques, and differences characterizing major segments. The Basle Committee on Banking Supervision has performed in the most commendable way along this line of reference, showing that it comprehends very well the broader significance of the globalized financial system — all the way to evaluating systemic risks and taking measures to avoid them.[7]

Accurate accounting records and financial reports are vital because a great deal can be learned from the analysis of differences characterizing major segments of the global market. For example, in October 1999, stock market

Exhibit 13.7   Critical Financial Statistics of Mid- to Late 1999 as Percent of GDP in the United States, Euroland, and Japan

	Reporting Period	United States	Euroland	Japan
Bank deposits	June 1999	55.2	77.8	111.7
Bank loans	June 1999	48.4	100.4	107.0
Outstanding domestic debt securities	June 1999	164.6	88.8	126.5
Value: Sum of Debt Instruments		213.0	189.2	233.5
Stock market capitalization	October 1999	163.3	71.1	137.7
Debt and equity financing		376.3	260.3	370.2

Note: Statistics selected from *ECB Monthly Bulletin,* January 2000.

capitalization in the euro countries, as a percentage of GDP, was 71.1 percent. This compared poorly with the securitized structure of the United States economy where, as a percentage of GDP, financing through the issuance of domestic securities has been 163.3 percent, dwarfing the 48.4 percent of GDP for loans by banks.

Exhibit 13.7 contrasts statistics from the United States, euroland, and Japan. This is a case where the business infrastructure is practically the same, involving commercial banking and securities (debt and equity), but the rules underpinning the economic and financial information being reported differ — and these differences help in estimating the way credit works in each major area, as well as the possible aftermath of assumed exposure.

An interesting observation, based on accounting data, is that in the United States, bank loans are about 15 percent less than the banks' intake; America is not a nation of savers. In contract, in euroland, bank loans are some 40 percent above deposits. Another interesting divergence is in the amount of stock capitalization. In this case, however, given prevailing differences in reporting rules and in calculation methods, these figures are not 100 percent comparable.

Significant are the differences that exist when one sums up debt and equity financing. The message given by the total of debt and equity is how far investors go in providing or cutting off funding to companies by, respectively, buying or declining to buy their assets and liabilities. Investors base their decisions on financial reports that must be reliable and based on international accounting standards. Because they certify the accounting information on which such reports are based, internal and external auditors play a key role in making the financial system tick.

13.5   Using Cost Accounting as a Means for Solving Managerial Problems

An auditor who is worth his or her salt will appreciate that any accounting system can be nicely designed and carefully operated, but the system is of no use to management unless it contributes to the processes of creation, reproduction, and destruction which, as seen, are constant:

- Raw material is used up.
- Machinery and tools wear out.
- Electricity is employed to power the equipment.
- Buildings need maintenance and still decay.
- Labor is consumed whether or not the deliverables are marketable.

Not only are industry's forms of creation and destruction highly specialized, but also the methods employed in the systems of reproduction and decay are never completely the same. Therefore, their input and output must be measured, *costed,* and priced — if one wants to have an opinion about whether one pays too much for what one gets.

We depend on accounting to provide a means of comparing a given position at one date with that at an earlier and a subsequent date. The same is true of days, weeks, months, and years. The surplus disclosed, after making adjustments for changes over the period between given dates, is an indication that what one takes out of the system is more than what one puts in. The revenue account shows some detail on how this surplus is made up. Production scheduling and inventory control data presented by ERP indicate, among other things, how efficiently the resources were used.

These references bring to the reader's attention the functions of *cost accounting*. The early professional accountants paid little attention to costing, but this is no longer true. The beginning of cost accounting was largely the result of the efforts of accountants employed by various enterprises to see more clearly *where* and *how* capital was used up, *whether* costs in one place were comparable to costs in another place, for the same activity, and *what* the price was that helped to recover costs and leave a profit.

The cost standards and cost accounts thus developed represented little more than the satisfaction of the early needs of management at that time — which means roughly a century ago. Financial history books suggest that the idea of coordination of cost figures with the rest of the double-entry accounting system required considerable time to take effect. This finds its parallel in the difficulties many companies encounter today in integrating ERP and CRM into their management information system.

The work done by Frederick Winslow Taylor, whose seminal article "Principles and Methods of Scientific Management" appeared in the *Journal of Accountancy* in 1911 (and later in book form) was, in essence, cost accounting. Some of the "scientific management" people were originally accountants; others were originally engineers; but all evolved into the same sort of specialist:

- A professional combination of engineer and accountant — the *industrial engineer.*
- A person intimately familiar with the problems of factory management and mass production

The epoch-making time study in the 1910s was followed by a motion study in the 1920s, and by operations research (OR) in the World War II and immediate post-war years.[8] OR has been largely based on timely identification, analysis, and optimization procedures. *Optimization* in production management and in logistics requires some type of job cost, item cost, or other process cost, and this must be done on a solid basis.

What was targeted by OR in the 1950s is neither quite the same with nor radically different from ERP's goals today. Although some of OR's tools, such as linear programming (LP), continue to be used, others have been replaced by more sophisticated solutions. In the 1950s in most industries, an immense amount of repetitive detail work was required. What was optimized in that case was the labor of stage hands. For this reason, a fairly complex procedure had to be in place to establish and maintain proper costing. Today, however, this is not a problem. The target has changed.

However, some of the aftermath from time sampling (ratio delay), Therblig analysis, time and motion studies, and the use of tables such as Method, Time, Measurement (MTM) remains. An interesting outgrowth of Taylor's work has been *standard costs,* which combined performance and productivity measurements with unit costs. Around 1917, the idea of standard costs took root and, by the middle 1920s, the movement *for* standard costs had gained considerable momentum, leading to a basic concept in logistics. Anything spent on a particular article or job was the cost of that article or job.

In the 1980s and 1990s, however, deregulation, globalization, and technology were instrumental in altering this concept. As far as present-day management accounting is concerned, it is gradually giving place to the notion that the cost to be taken as the basis for decision is what that article or job *should* cost. This is the cost that must enter into ERP, and the auditor must control that it happens that way. High overhead, low productivity, dubious quality, or other failures, as well as the results of managerial ineptitude should be charged to the P&L statement in a class — *mismanagement* — in the period in which they occur. They should not be charged to the product, nor should they be carried forward in inventory to a subsequent period.

Today, standard costs are particularly valuable for purposes of internal control, for budgeting, and for determining the probable expense associated with new products. They are one of the pillars of ERP and CRM implementation and of management accounting as a whole.

- Costing is providing a very effective link between merchandising, manufacturing, marketing, and developments in science and technology.
- Cost accounting will become even more important in the coming years as industrial processes become more complex and more innovative.

In conclusion, from general accounting to management accounting and costing, the basic principles to which reference has been made are universal in application; and if rightly understood it becomes easy to reap benefit in any system of production and distribution. The essence of the references made is one of form and purpose. As such, they integrate with the form that characterizes the evolution of business requirements and of the solutions associated with them.

13.6   Rethinking the Mission of Accounting and Its Deliverables

Whether in the New or in the Old Economy, the mission of accounting is to keep and present in an orderly fashion financial data pertaining to a company and its business. As seen through practical examples, in a dynamic, globalized market, this mission goes well beyond the general ledger, balance sheet, income statement, accounts payable, accounts receivable, outstanding loans, payrolls, cash flows, and other traditional documents. The New Economy has established its own list of *do's* and *don'ts:*

- It is *not* the mission of accounting to say if the company's price/earnings (P/E) ratio is too high (which it may be) and unsustainable, or if the firm has too much short-term debt.
- The mission of accounting is to present factual and documented figures, which will be interpreted by management to reach the aforementioned or other conclusions.

Projections and evaluations belong to the interpretive metalayer. It is part of the function of the interpretative metalayer (see Exhibit 13.2) — not of accounting *per se* — to say whether the company meet its debt payments by its projected cash flow. However, it is a mission of modern accounting to reflect the intellectual assets as well as the real-time commitments made in Internet commerce, and to provide data permitting computation of the resulting exposure. Accounting must also cover the value of the company's intellectual property. I insist on this issue because current accounting procedures do not pay enough attention to intellectual property. Yet the company's copyrights and patents can be infringed, big chunks of its intellectual property can be stolen, and the company might violate technology export controls, without any intent on its part.

While in present-day business, most of the emphasis is placed on credit risk and market risk and rightly so; legal exposure, including loss of reputation, is also present. Indeed, it is magnified by the nature of the Internet. Not only should the legal counsel thoroughly examine these risks, but the accounting system should also reflect them. This statement is equally valid for other issues connected with financial reports.[9]

If the law of the land does not foresee allowances for the types of exposure outlined in the preceding paragraphs, *then* their reporting is the responsibility of *management accounting* (see Chapter 13.5), which includes both prognostication and interpretation of all sorts of results. Here is a good way to distinguish the two functions:

1. *General accounting* must be precise, detailed, factual, documented, and abide by the laws of the land. This is the data reported to the authorities, including tax authorities, as well as in quarterly and annual statements.
2. *Management accounting* must be timely and accurate (not precise beyond the third significant digit), follow the company's bylaws, be comprehensive, provide critical analyses, and be able to visualize (through graphics) the results.

These results must be made available interactively by management accounting through database mining and special alerts — preferably in real-time. They do not need to be disclosed to third parties. They are for the company's own use and, up to a point (but only up to a point), they map the business system as one of creation and reproduction working in conjunction with processes of destruction. *Destruction* comes in the aftermath of change and decay and is unavoidable both in the business and in the physical world.

■ Nothing lasts; nothing is permanent; nothing is fixed — and a good accounting system tells that through figures.
■ Although some things in this world last longer than others, sooner or later everything perishes and ceases to exist in its present form.

In the sense just described, accounting is the metric system of variation and of volatility. By necessity, accounting figures are approximations. Even so, they are useful in recording and summarizing measurements of business facts. The careful reader will notice that, in a similar way, most data used in the physical sciences is also measurement for which scientists and engineers must acquire an understanding of the degree of approximation that is present.

The experienced reader will also appreciate that although measurements may differ widely in their degree of accuracy, each is useful for a particular purpose. Some accounting figures, such as cash on hand, may be accurate within very narrow limits; but other accounting figures, such as present value and intellectual property, may be rough.[10] This reflects the fact that a business is a complex organism that includes vastly dissimilar elements.

■ There can be no precise way of adding all these diverse elements together so as to form a complete and precise picture of the entire enterprise — a sort of a snapshot incorporating the sense of transition.
■ The problem in obtaining reasonably accurate measurements is further complicated by the fact that a rough approximation available in real-time is more useful to management than a more accurate figure published next month or next year.

All this must be known to accountants, auditors, ERP and CRM implementers, as well as to internal company users of accounting data and regulatory bodies receiving accounting reports. Indeed, one of the most important principles of accounting is the appreciation of the framework guiding its information and of the environment within which it operates. To provide data that is reliable and useful, the accountant must work both with facts and with estimates; this is precisely what an engineer does. The accuracy of any interim figure depends on the validity of these estimates and on the data feeds that one uses to prepare financial reports.

Notes

1. D.N. Chorafas, *Financial Models and Simulation*, Macmillan, London, 1995.
2. D.N. Chorafas, *Reliable Financial Reporting and Internal Control: A Global Implementation Guide*, John Wiley, New York, 2000.
3. D.N. Chorafas, *Agent Technology Handbook,* McGraw-Hill, New York, 1998.
4. D.N. Chorafas, *Reliable Financial Reporting and Internal Control: A Global Implementation Guide,* John Wiley, New York, 2000.
5. Marcus Tullius Cicero, Roman senator and orator, 106–143 B.C.
6. Bradford Felmy, *EDPACS,* July 1997, Vol. XXV, No. 1, Auerbach Publications, New York.
7. D.N. Chorafas, *The 1996 Market Risk Amendment. Understanding the Marking-to-Model and Value-at-Risk*, McGraw-Hill, Burr Ridge, IL, 1998; and D.N. Chorafas, *Risk and the New Economy*, New York Institute of Finance, New York, 2001.
8. D.N. Chorafas, *Operations Research for Industrial Management*, Reinhold Publishing, New York, 1958.
9. D.N. Chorafas, *Reliable Financial Reporting and Internal Control: A Global Implementation Guide*, John Wiley, New York, 2000.
10. D.N. Chorafas, *Managing Credit Risk*, Vol. 1: *Analyzing, Rating and Pricing the Probability of Default*, Euromoney, London, 2000.

Chapter 14

The Auditor's Independence Is Critical to the Management of All Information Systems

Auditing is one of the most rigorous tools at the service of management, and it is the cornerstone of internal control. *Internal control*[1] is the process by which the board, senior executives, and other levels of supervision want to assure themselves, insofar as possible, that what is done in their organization conforms to plans and policies — and that management control is exercised in an effective manner.

Accounting information is not only useful but also fundamental in this process of assurance that everything happens in the right place, at the right time. Without it, internal control will not be feasible. The results of internal control are used for direct supervision and as a means of motivation, communication, and medium-term appraisal.

Unless the business is a very small enterprise, its management does not personally design, manufacture, sell, and service the product. Rather, this is the responsibility of specialized units. It is management's duty to see to it that the work gets done properly, the accounts being kept are timely and correct, financial reporting is reliable, and the personnel are *motivated* to work effectively.

The enterprise resource planning (ERP) and customer relationship management (CRM) systems serve as a means of directing the company's activities for *communication* purposes. Interactive ERP reports assist in informing the members of the organization about management's plans, execution procedures, and requirements for control. CRM reports reflect on actions the organization takes by market segment, product line, and other criteria. Both ERP and CRM databases must be audited.

Interactive CRM and ERP reports can also be instrumental in *appraisal*. Periodically, management must evaluate how well employees and business units are doing their jobs. The aftermath of an appraisal of performance may be a salary increase, promotion, reassignment, corrective action of various kinds, or dismissal. Each one of these steps finds itself at the junction of three reporting systems, all of which must be audited: general accounting, ERP/CRM, and cost accounting.

The role of auditing in information technology is better appreciated if one accounts for the fact that the way one plans IT products, as well as organizes and executes IT processes, impacts upon every corner of the organization. Exhibit 14.1 illustrates the two main structural alternatives: the old, vertical way where IT is highly centralized; and the new, fully distributed IT organization. Auditing must reach every IT function, no matter where it is located.

To capably perform the work described, the auditor must be computer literate. He or she must definitely have independence of opinion. This is to the company's own advantage. Classically, organizations weed out the non-conformist elements. As a result, they respond slowly to change and fail to take corrective action. Auditor independence helps to correct this shortcoming.

- Eliminating dissent creates a group aligned behind one approach, without examining alternatives.
- Conformity and one-track minds make it difficult to predict the single best path or exercise management control.

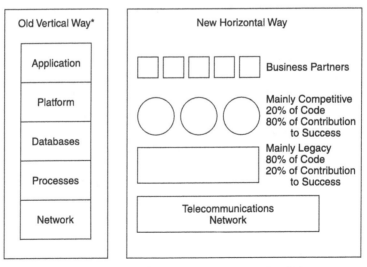

*Vertical approaches involve an immense amount of inefficiency.

Exhibit 14.1   Old and New Ways of Managing Technology Among Industrial and Financial Organizations

In contrast, an organization that tolerates dissension is able to respond to market shifts and to weed inefficiency out of its system. It can more easily change the allocation of its resources in appreciation of the fact that dissent forces a company to face constraints and produce more effective solutions.

Perfectly aligned organizations tend to reduce creativity and bend internal control. Auditor independence is one of the means to ensure that this does not happen. Independence of opinion brings with it the need to be self-sufficient as well as insensitive to praise or blame.

14.1   The Dynamics of Auditing Information Technology Products and Processes

Taken individually, each of the audits done in an enterprise assists in the short- and medium-term appraisal, but it does not present all the information that management requires in a comprehensive form. With the exception of extreme cases, an adequate basis for judging a person's or a department's performance cannot be obtained solely from information revealed by accounting records. Personal interviews are necessary to present a complete picture, and this is what the auditor should do.

The records, any records, can be manipulated. This is true not only of accounts, but also of schedules, execution plans, plan versus actual analysis, client relationship references, or entire processes covered by ERP procedures. Hence, the need to perform both regular and exceptional review activities with regard to statements by business units. Auditing must look after:

- Precision and accuracy of accounts in the books and of planning/supervisory records
- Methodology for preparation of the business unit's operational and financial statements and their proper utilization
- Consistency of application of planning and control procedures, execution policies, and financial policies

It is part and parcel of the auditor's responsibilities to perform reconciliation between business unit practices and consolidated results. This information is typically presented in the audited financial statements for the year, trimester, or any other time period subject to management control and auditing functions.

Based on the outcome of an audit, whether it concerns general accounting data, internal control processes, or ERP and CRM information, senior management can say that nothing has come to its attention that requires corrective action — or, alternatively, when the need arises, such action must be taken immediately. For example, the review procedure may reveal that financial statements have not been properly compiled, severe discrepancies exist between planned and actual activities, or sales results have been materially misstated.

These types of discrepancies are usually found through systematic verification of books of account, vouchers, other financial and legal records, as well as plans, executions, and their reports. As discussed in Chapter 13, auditing is the job being done for the purpose of determining the accuracy and integrity of any type of document or process under inspection. The auditing of ERP accounts, for example, aims to ensure that they show the true condition and result of operations. Auditing is certifying to the statements rendered by ERP reporting procedures; or, alternatively, it is bringing discrepancies to senior management's attention.

The reader will recall from Chapter 13 that auditing must address accuracy, precision, and other characteristics that help to ensure the reliability of information used by management. Whether talking about ERP, CRM, decision support system (DSS), or MIS, there is reference to communications-intense functions, as Exhibit 14.2 suggests. These impact greatly on the way one steers a company toward a successful course — provided the information used is reliable.

Audits can be conducted externally by certified public accountants when the work concerns general accounting, or by specialized consultants in the case of ERP, CRM, and other IT operations (see also Chapter 15). In ERP's case, the company's own employees could do the audit, but consultants are independent professionals and hence better able to convince that the accuracy and integrity of ERP records were determined without political pressures — indeed, that ERP programming products were properly used in the first place.

Generally, certified reports submitted by auditors and special reports by consultants serve as the basis for determining sound condition or flushing out discrepancies and prevailing negative trends. Public accountant reports are

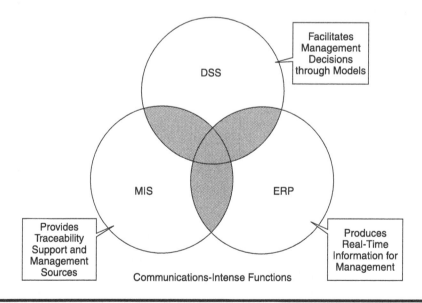

Exhibit 14.2 The Definitions of MIS, ERP, and DSS Overlap, but There Is Also a Difference Between Them

used by banks for extension of credit, and by regulators in determining action in bankruptcy and insolvency. They also assist in providing information to stockholders, bondholders, and other stakeholders, determining action in fraud cases, and helping as documentation in preparation of tax returns.

The objectives sought by a consultant who specializes in the auditing of information technology are, of course, different. If the mission is to audit the implementation of ERP and generally the management of the company's ERP operations, the consultant will look after:

- The level of technology being used and associated know-how
- The way this application fits with other software
- Whether there have been changes in bought software resulting in implementation problems
- If there is appropriate guarding against poor methods, employee carelessness, and inadequate records

The results of this auditing are a safeguard for senior management because careful examination of prevailing conditions and of records ensures the dependability of the information infrastructure of the firm. Subsequently, the interpretation of these records will lead to a critical analysis of the way the company conducts its business. Auditing can reach all the way from a general overview of methods and procedures to a detailed examination of every book.

The review and survey of business operations and their accounts present the background plan for the specific and painstaking examination of what is found to be weak points. This is of invaluable assistance to managers who cannot hope to have all of the various phases of operations at their fingertips at all times. Senior executives rely on their assistants to advise them and to consult with them in a great many matters of daily operation, but they also want to have the disinterested opinion of outsiders able to check on ERP, CRM, and other IT problem areas, and to provide sound advice, comment, and analyses to their client.

In practically every company, the progress of business in general has contributed to the development of auditing ongoing IT practices, although the greatest impetus has come from companies with decentralized operations managed by delegating authority. The board and CEO of these companies are faced with an acute need for reports that allow them to determine *if* policies and procedures are being observed by middle and lower management; *if* the state of the company's IT is ahead or behind that of its competitors; and *if* the interests of the firm are adequately protected in terms of IT support.

Companies that depend a great deal on IT to keep ahead of competition have used ERP auditing as an investigating agency and for making special surveys. This has the effect of looking more closely at weak spots and of assigning more precise responsibilities. It has also provided senior management with a feedback channel whose input is a little bolder and a little more controversial than what they usually hear through the hierarchical line of command.

14.2   Using What Has Been Learned from Managerial Auditing of ERP and CRM

One of the factors that has contributed a great deal to the development of technology auditing is that the rapid advances in computers, communications, and software accentuated the need to swamp costs. Product innovation is the motor of the New Economy; but if management is not watching every dollar like a hawk, the company will run straight into treasury problems. This is likely because in most businesses today, normal and routine operations are administered by remote control, including reports, statistics, and directives.

These have, to a significant extent, replaced personal observations, evaluations, and instructions. To give added assurance that received reports are accurate, delegated duties are faithfully performed, directives are properly interpreted and executed, and matters requiring consideration are promptly brought to attention, management finds it necessary to maintain an active inspection and analysis service.

The auditor should by no means be restricted to certain definite routines or denied full access to all the records. Neither should the auditor limit fundamental activities to the detection and prevention of fraud or errors. This is the old concept of auditing, which prevailed until the late 1970s and viewed internal control almost entirely as a fraud protection agency. Since the early 1980s, however, companies have recognized the potential value of auditing for rendering *constructive services* of a much broader nature.

Over the years, practitioners (and writers) have adopted various strategies in an endeavor to distinguish between the more restricted and the broader type of auditing procedures. The title that best describes current practice, and the one that appears to predominate in technology operations, is *managerial auditing*, indicating an activity utilized as an aid to management rather than as a clerical function.

The requirements posed by managerial auditing see to it that *technology auditing* is in full evolution. The process underpinning it can be expressed both as a systematic companywide effort and as a largely custom-made project such as ERP, patterned and molded to satisfy the particular needs of a project or of top management. In both cases, technology auditing should remain an independent appraisal activity within the organization, a basis for protective and constructive services to management.

The best way of looking at technology auditing is as a type of control that functions by measuring and evaluating the effectiveness of other types of supervision. As such, it deals with a great many issues because technology has infiltrated all aspects of operations and it is, by excellence, cross-departmental. The aim of addressing operating processes in an investigative sense is to assist management in achieving the most efficient administration of the company's technology investments, and pointing out existing deficiencies that call for appropriate corrective action.

The auditing of technology is by no means a new practice. Electronic data processing (EDP) audits have been performed for several decades but they have usually been of a rather elementary type or they have focused on a limited number of rather serious defects. This is still necessary, but it is not enough for CRM and ERP audits.

Like managerial audits, CRM and ERP audits must go well beyond the nuts and bolts, and cover the *dynamics* of IT as a system. Also, they must be executed without any conflict of interest. Conflicts of interest do not exist in the nuts and bolts, but are common in the dynamics — when, for example, the same external auditors who do them, usually certified public accountants (CPAs), are also the company's consultants in IT.

In fact, the Securities and Exchange Commission (SEC) is very well aware of the contradiction described in the preceding paragraph, and in September 2000 it launched a campaign to change the state of affairs by splitting the auditing and consulting functions of the five major firms of certified public accountants: PricewaterhouseCoopers, Ernst & Young, KPMG, Arthur Andersen, and Deloitte & Touche.

The SEC's action is discussed in Chapter 14.4; but before going there, one should look into what a sound procedure implies in terms of ERP auditing. The earlier approach was limited to the left three boxes in Exhibit 14.3. Internally, it was typically performed by one or two systems experts attached to the audit department; however, in my experience, their mission — and even their experience — was too limited.

Sometimes, these people were put there more because the director of EDP did not want them in the EDP department than because the board and senior management had *really* decided to audit the IT function. It is not surprising, therefore, that these EDP auditors were refused access to vital technology functions and their report, when they made one, was put on the back burner.

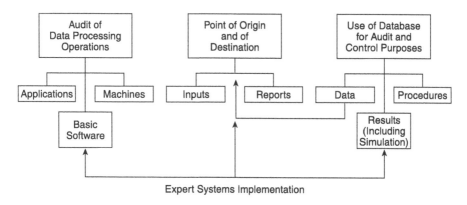

Exhibit 14.3   The IT Audit Function Has Grown Over the Years and Continues to Expand

In parallel with this, there has been a confusion about the mission that EDP auditors were given. Many companies, particularly financial institutions, had a large control department whose function was to weed out errors in the EDP input (and there were a great many) and to distribute computer outputs to their recipients. One of the big banks for which I was consultant to the board had some 500 people working in this department and hunting data input errors. This unwarranted employment could be eliminated through real-time data collection at origin, but the EDP culture was batch and it would not easily change; in addition, this loafing was protected higher up the organizational ladder.

Of course, there existed some exceptions. In another institution with which I was associated, it was possible to implement real-time data collection with the result of an 80-percent personnel reduction in this pseudo-control activity, and further shrinkage in personnel a year down the line. Some of the savings in manpower were put in IT auditing, and this led to the uncovering of a variety of inefficiencies and outright frauds.

For example, one of the programmers working for many years for this credit institution had written a small routine that rounded up the cents in client accounts and credited them to another account conveniently opened by his wife in her maiden name. Every time, for every client, the swindle was cents, but there were millions of accounts closed every month, and this had gone undetected for years.

By gaining experience in the ways and means of detecting sophisticated fraud and by developing a method to flush out other types of planned or accidental errors and deviations, it was possible to put in place a well-rounded IT auditing operation. This was enriched with database mining made available to all auditors for their daily work. Spreadsheets and simulators permitted the auditor to experiment on the aftermath of his or her findings. Within a few years, the auditing solution was enriched with expert systems searching for weak points in databased elements, documents, and procedures: from expense accounts, to documentation for loans and IT procurement practices.

This real-life example is important in this discussion on auditing ERP and CRM. In more than one way, it outlines the type of solution one should be seeking. In my experience, it is unwise to limit this solution to the ERP function, even if this is possible. The auditing of ERP should be looked at from a dual perspective: (1) IT auditing's contribution to keeping a company ahead of the curve in a technological sense, and (2) that of limited liability — a concept that dates back to the beginning of the modern corporation in the mid-nineteenth century and has been instrumental in getting the process of auditing under way.

14.3   How Can One Capitalize on the Concept of Limited Liability?

The concept of limited liability might provide a useful parallel to each business unit's responsibility in terms of technological leadership and associated auditing of IT. If one looks back in corporate history, one sees that only by the mid-nineteenth century a distinction began to be made between *capital* and *revenue* of a limited liability firm. This was necessary for the purpose of determining what was distributable as dividends. It was left to the British Companies Act of 1862 to establish the first legal recognition of the principle of freedom of incorporation, which redefined the notion of limited liability and provided direct accountability to shareholders.

The British Companies Act of 1862 also required that all associations of more than 20 persons must be *registered*. The organization of the Institute of Chartered Accountants in England and Wales, in 1880, was largely the result of requirements that developed under the Act of 1862 and its subsequent amendments. These amendments provided for better focus on the notion of *personal accountability*.

One can try to apply this notion to the implementation and follow-up on performance of bought software, taking ERP as an example. Chapter 1 outlined the functional applications areas of ERP and, as the reader will recall, these range from general accounting responsibilities to production planning and quality assurance (manufacturing) and human resources management (personnel).

A global organization will have many pyramids with ERP and CRM type information. A going concern, however, is *one entity* and the distinct pyramids must integrate together, as shown in Exhibit 14.4. Each of the departments cited in Exhibit 14.4 — marketing, manufacturing, procurement, and personnel (among others) — has a liability if the programming products perform less well than expected. This is a type of limited liability to that department because as a profit center, it will be penalized if computers and software performance are substandard. But at the same time, it is a broader, companywide liability that can hurt the bottom line and can snowball from one department to the next.

Something similar to this effect of underperformance was felt in the mid-nineteenth century with limited financial liability. As a result, the British Companies Act of 1862 led to provisions covering *audits* and the *role of auditors*. For the first time in the history of business, it was specified that at least once every year the accounts of the company should be examined and the correctness of the balance sheet ascertained by auditors.

The first auditors were to be appointed by directors, and subsequent auditors were to be elected by shareholders. After the Act of 1862 not only did auditing become a breakthrough in the prudential and rigorous internal control of an incorporated company, but it also helped to formalize the functions of corporate finance by establishing a means to ascertain whether accounting and financial reporting procedures were or were not dependable.

This is what I consider the missing act in IT auditing, as exists in the majority of cases. The old EDP stop/go inspection procedures continue to dominate. As a rule, members of the board do not feel co-involved in selecting IT auditors or in commissioning an IT audit under the board's authority. Although companies that have asked me to do an IT audit did so at the board's chairman or vice-chairman level, these were exceptions rather than the industry rule.

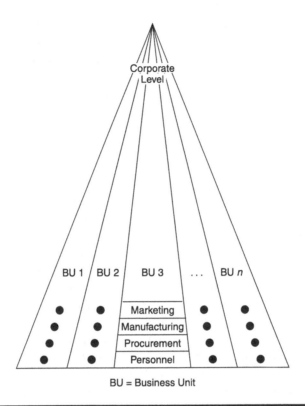

Exhibit 14.4   Each Independent Business Unit Uses ERP and CRM Software for Its Own Purposes but the Results Must Integrate at the Corporate Level

What is more, many line managers and some board members get very nervous if the IT audit reveals ineptitude and major discrepancies. In contrast, they behave in a totally different way with regard to bad financial news because this is an issue whose twists they can understand. Many senior executives do appreciate that, fundamentally, corporate finance serves two important functions:

1. To provide the basis for continued operation
2. To provide a means of assessing the funds necessary to handle the business

But being computer illiterate, they fail to see that the message conveyed by either or both of these functions fully applies to IT. In accounting and finance, part and parcel of both functions is to provide the additional capital to cover the costs of operations, estimating income and cash flow, and generally synchronizing the many factors that comprise a going business.

The board appreciates that this financial responsibility must be audited. However, IT has not yet reached that level of comprehension and appreciation of the board and its members. Yet, the modern, globalized enterprise that works at Internet time is in essence *information in motion*. High technology

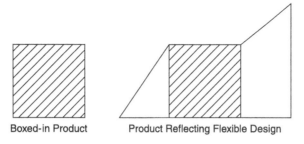

Boxed-in Product   Product Reflecting Flexible Design

Exhibit 14.5 The Design of ERP Auditing Should Reflect the Principle of Flexibility, which Today Characterizes Advanced Engineering Projects

is just as important to its well-being as financial staying power. Therefore, technology audits must be steady and performed by a qualified independent person or entity. Such audits should provide the basis for continuing operations of each business unit — and on a corporate basis.

A different way of making this statement is that under no condition should IT audits be boxed into one function, whether it be ERP, CRM, general accounting, or anything else. They should be cross-functional, cross-department, and cross-area of operations, along the concept of greater flexibility shown on the right-hand side of Exhibit 14.5. This, incidentally, is what is targeted today in engineering when one strives for a truly flexible design that can be adapted to the different markets of the company's operations.

Do not forget that IT audits should serve as the means of assessing the level of sophistication of the technology used to run the business. IT audits should look into deliverables and their timetables, evaluate the quality of IT personnel, propose training and other remedies when necessary, and be shielded from the political pressures that invariably exist in every organization.

Regular and rigorous auditing of accounting books and of IT is so important because accounting and the corporate database, in which accounts and statistics reside, stand in the interface between financial reporting and internal control. In the popular concept of corporate finance, stocks and bonds are instruments with which funds are raised. This is true, but it also raises some crucial queries:

- What is the scope of management's responsibility for other people's money?
- Is it possible to realize sufficient earnings to preserve assets and cover the ever-recurring capital needs?

The point has repeatedly been made that accounting, as such, does not answer these and similar queries. What it does is that it provides information that helps in documenting the answers that are given. The answers themselves must observe the rules that public responsibilities of corporate financial management are of a twofold nature: direct and indirect. Both apply equally well to information technology; *direct* responsibilities are readily defined, although not always easily put into practice. Hence the call for the exercise of prudence and care is required to operate on a sound, reliable basis. This does not mean avoidance of reasonable and inevitable risks of business operation, but there should be evidence that exposure is kept within limits, that management is in charge, and that ethical standards are observed.

Indirect responsibilities are more general in character as well as being more difficult to define. For example, to what extent does corporate management have responsibility for the economy? For the community or communities in which the company's main facilities are located? For monopolistic conditions? For employment and unemployment? For inflation? For innovation? For the promotion of arts and sciences? And, most importantly, for conditions that allow the private enterprise system to continue to exist? The audit of accounts tends to target both types of responsibility. In contrast, ERP audits are closely linked to the direct type of managerial accountability.

14.4   Why the Functions of Auditing and of IT Consulting Must Be Separated

Since the beginning of the profession of chartered accountants, or certified public accountants, to which reference was made in Chapter 14.3, the guiding theme has been independent public oversight. This notion of *independence* on behalf of auditors should dominate all audits — internal and external —whether they regard accounting books and financial records or the implementation of technology. In financial markets, independent audits allow investors to rely on overseers to protect their interests.

It is the responsibility of senior management of the auditing firm to ensure that there is no conflict of interest. This can sometimes happen. A 1998 probe at PricewaterhouseCooper's Tampa (Florida) office found that employees were buying stock in companies they audited, violating a basic standard of independence. When the report came out in January 2000, it documented 8000 violations, with half of the firm's partners having conflicts.[2] In information technology, independent audits *allow* senior management to take an uncompromised look at IT, including MIS, ERP, CRM, and other applications.

But are audits made by CPAs independent, when the CPA also acts as consultant to the company on IT — indeed takes an active role in shaping the company's technology policies and applications? This conflict of interest is what Arthur Levitt, Jr., chairman of the Securities and Exchange Commission, targeted with his September 2000 action to sever the ties between the CPAs consulting arm and its parent company.

According to news published by the financial press, Levitt is determined to halt a wave of auditing failures that have cost investors $88 billion in the 1993 to 2000 timeframe. Levitt wants to institute measures that put an end in what he sees as a conflict of interest between accountants' duties as auditors and the profits they earn as consultants to the same clients. This conflict is refuted by the Big Six CPA firms, opposed in varying degrees to the SEC's drive.

Exhibit 14.6   Lost Market Capitalization by Companies After Being Audited by CPAs

Company	Debacle in $ Billions
Cendant	11.3
MicroStrategy	10.4
McKenon HBOC	7.9
Columbia-HCA	3.8
Oxford Healthcare	3.4
Sunbeam	1.2
Green Tree	1.1
Waste Management	0.9
RiteAid	0.8

Source: Business Week, September 25, 2000.

What Arthur Levitt says about consulting at large by CPA companies is even more pronounced in connection with IT projects, which are the fastest growing sector of the advisory business. With consulting at large now contributing 51 percent of their revenues, and growing three times as fast as their basic auditing functions, the CPA companies are dead-set against slamming the door on future business opportunities such as the SEC wants.

The SEC's thesis regarding conflicts of interest is unassailable. In terms of financial aftermath, it is backed by statistics on differences in market capitalization because of a job done in a not-so-diligent way. A sample is shown in Exhibit 14.6. There is also the fact that, during the last few years, companies have been restating their audited annual financial reports at an accelerating pace: 104 in 1997, 118 in 1998, and 142 in 1999.

Down to basics, these corrections reflect anything from revised accounting rules to discovery of outright fraud. The SEC is developing evidence in at least two cases: Waste Management's $3.54 billion writedown of 1992–1997 profits; and a $55.8 million earnings restatement at high-flying software developer MicroStrategy. The accountants' consulting work and their financial ties to clients compromised their audits.

Although there are no similar numbers in the public domain regarding losses suffered by companies because of conflict of interest by CPAs in their dual function of auditing financial records and IT consulting, my own professional experience is littered with the aftermath of such conflicts. They range from pushing a certain brand of hardware into the client company's EDP shop, to advising top management on buying "this" or "that" software package — even sending the chief executive a contract to sign with clauses protecting the vendor rather than the customer. Whenever I came across such violations of professional duty, I did my best to contain the damage. Invariably, however, this becomes a political fight because there is, on the balance, personal prestige involved — if not deeper conflicts.

An interesting fact from the past is that when in the 1960s Price Waterhouse and other CPAs developed EDP consulting services, they did so to help clients who needed assistance in managing their computer-based systems and procedures — and also to improve their applications base in a way that was independent of the vendor's advice. Things changed when this line of business boomed, particularly so in the 1990s. In the early 1990s, the Big Six CPAs earned about 30 percent of revenue from different lines of management consulting, including IT. By 1999, they earned 51 percent of their income from IT-related services, while auditing services dropped from 45 to 30 percent of revenue.

There have been reasons for this boom. The fixing of Year 2000 (Y2K) problems is believed to be one of these reasons. Another more important factor is Internet-based systems for supply chain management, customer handholding, and enterprise resource planning, as well as the transition from mainframe-based legacy software to client/server oriented applications.

Most of these IT projects came roughly at the same time, and this had direct impact on the reliability of the resulting implementations. The fact that systems skill is in short supply further emphasizes the importance of IT auditing by truly independent agents. ERP auditing has been at the eye of the storm because the Year 2000 bug has had much to do with ERP business, such as production planning and the control of inventories.

Today, troubles associated with Y2K problems are a thing of the past, but issues connected to large, mainframe-based internal management information systems, which were for many years the accounting firms' specialty, are still present. Only the better-managed companies have truly moved to client/server solutions. They did so in the early 1990s and thereafter used Internet software and put their business on the Web.

CPAs do understand that conflicts between two different lines of business that oppose one another in integrity terms can lead to trouble. Therefore, they have, to varying degrees, tried to do something about distancing themselves from their consulting activities.

- In 1996, Arthur Andersen separated itself from Andersen Consulting. But almost immediately thereafter, the parent company developed a new consulting function under its wings, therefore keeping alive the potential for conflicts of interest.
- In December 1998, KPMG spun off its consulting arm but retained a 51 percent share. The SEC felt KPMG had kept too much equity of the spin-off, rather than divesting itself of this asset. Analysts on Wall Street suggest that KPMG plans an initial public offering of stock for a majority of its consulting business.
- In May 2000, Ernst & Young sold its consulting arm for $11 billion, effectively getting out of advisory services.
- In September 2000, PricewaterhouseCoopers notified the SEC that it was negotiating to sell its consultancy to Hewlett-Packard in a deal that could net $18 billion.

Everything taken into account, CPAs do not really want to be closed out of the consulting line of business. Rather, like Arthur Andersen, they want to rebuild consulting practices or even enter into joint ventures. Arthur Andersen, for example, has a joint venture with IBM to help companies install IBM's Internet commerce software. This hardly fits in with independent auditing services and therefore the discussion on what might and might not constitute potential conflict of interest is sure to rage for some time.

14.5 Auditor Independence Requirements Promoted by the Federal Reserve and the Securities and Exchange Commission

During the 1990s, both the Federal Reserve and the Securities and Exchange Commission became increasingly vocal regarding the need to improve the quality of financial reporting. They have also underlined the need for a company's directors to play a greater role in supervising the preparation of the company's financial statements. This has been concretized in the Fed's case through the promotion of COSO financial reporting standards.[3] The Treadway Commission, which set the principle reflected in COSO and implemented by the Federal Reserve Banks and major credit institutions, has been concerned with the fact that during the 1970s and 1980s there was a gradual but noticeable erosion in the quality of financial reporting. This is manipulated by earnings reports that reflect the desires of management rather than underlying financial performance, and the motivation to satisfy Wall Street expectations that may be overriding reliable, even common-sense, business practices.

The Treadway Commission's criticism focused primarily on practices by various companies of earnings management to satisfy analysts' forecasts, particularly the use of broad charges to smooth out earnings in later periods. These types of *creative accounting* practices could have been — and should have been — detected and deterred by the company's board of directors and, in particular, by the company's Audit Committee.

As a result of these concerns about the adequacy of oversight of the audit process by independent directors, in September 1998 the New York Stock Exchange (NYSE) and the National Association of Securities Dealers (NASD) established the Blue Ribbon Committee on Improving the Effectiveness of Corporate Audit Committees. This committee's goal has been to address ways and means for reliable corporate financial reporting. In February 1999, this Blue Ribbon Committee released a report containing recommendations aimed at strengthening the status and independence of Audit Committees, and promoting mechanisms for accountability among the Audit Committee, the company's independent auditor, and senior management.

Following the report of the Blue Ribbon Committee, the SEC adopted new rules designed to improve disclosure relating to the functioning of Audit Committees and to enhance the reliability and credibility of financial statements.

In the aftermath of these rules, a public company is required to include a report of its Audit Committee in its proxy statement stating, among other things, whether the committee:

- Reviewed and discussed the audited financial statements with management
- Received certain disclosures from and discussed various matters with the independent auditor
- Recommended to the board that the audited financial statement be included in the company's annual report

The SEC rules also require that public companies disclose in their proxy statements whether their Board of Directors has adopted a written charter for the Audit Committee, attach a copy of such charter to their proxy statements once every three years, and disclose each year whether the members of the Audit Committee are *independent* for purposes of rules applicable to a self-regulatory organization.

Subsequently, in July 2000, the SEC proposed amendments to modernize its rule governing auditor independence, making fundamental changes to existing regulations. The first rule reduces the number of employees of audit firms, and members of their families, whose investments in or other financial relationships with an audit client would compromise the independence of the audit firm.

The second rule is to specify certain financial relationships between the audit client and the audit firm, or the audit partners and employees who work on the audit or are in a position to influence its outcome. Particularly targeted are relationships that would preclude the auditor from being independent — which, as seen on repeated occasions, is crucial — all the way from auditing accounting books to auditing the implementation of technology.

The third rule identifies certain non-audit services that, if provided to an audit client, would compromise the auditor's independence. These services include rendering or supporting expert opinions in legal, administrative, or regulatory filings or proceedings. Not included in this exclusion list are services advising clients on internal controls, risk management, and technology — which, in my judgment, is regrettable.

The SEC rules also require that a public company's independent auditor review the financial information included in the company's quarterly reports prior to the filing of such reports. In doing so, the independent auditor must follow professional standards and procedures for conducting such reviews as established by generally accepted auditing standards.

I bring these auditor independence requirements by the Feds and the SEC into perspective because they characterize very well what must be done to ensure independence of opinion by IT auditors. During our meeting in London in September 2000, a senior financial analyst suggested that not only has a rigorous and regular technology audit become indispensable to the modern enterprise, but it also must achieve what Lady Margaret Thatcher's government never lacked: a sense that whatever tactical adjustments might be necessary, it knew where it was going.

Rigorous auditing of ERP, CRM, and other computer applications is, in the final analysis, a matter of self-interest. No company can face the toughening competition of the Internet supply chain without first-class information technology. But neither can a company afford to spend huge amounts of money on IT each year without a clear sense of direction — or without internal controls and audits able to ascertain if the technology being used is ahead of the curve, the personnel is well-trained, the deliverables are in place and on time, new projects are coming on stream, and return on investment is at a high standard.

Notes

1. D.N. Chorafas, *Implementing and Auditing the Internal Control System,* Macmillan, London, 2001.
2. *Business Week,* September 25, 2000.
3. D.N. Chorafas, *Reliable Financial Reporting and Internal Control: A Global Implementation Guide,* John Wiley, New York, 2000.

Chapter 15

The Ongoing Change in Information Technology's Auditing Practices

It is no secret that since the early 1980s with the advent of personal computers, local area networks, client/servers, disk farms, expert systems, agents, real-time simulation, off-the-shelf enterprise resource planning, and other forms of advanced software, information technology has undergone a radical change. Equally profound, as documented in Chapters 13 and 14, has been the evolution in auditing policies and practices with regard to IT. Even leaving for a moment aside the question of auditor independence, the joint effect of change is that:

- Auditors are getting a growing number of request to perform a thorough investigation of the status of IT in a given company.
- Sometimes, the new demands exceed the confines of auditors' past training and exposure, and they do not feel sufficiently proficient to do them.

Therefore, before looking into specific issues connected with ERP auditing practices (presented in Chapter 16), this chapter concentrates on the task of bringing to the reader's attention specific problems posed in auditing IT — and how auditors have managed to go from "here" to "there" in their investigative work.

Speaking from personal experience, my first advice to IT auditors would be to know the strategy and core functions of the company for which they are working. Core functions are those essential to the engineering, manufacturing, and marketing of products, as well as in the provision of services. They include design, production, inventory management, sales, delivery, and quality control of what a company offers to the market.

It is only obvious that core functions vary from one sector of the economy to the next and from one company to another within the same sector. Take a credit institution as an example. In commercial banking, core functions are accepting customer deposits, making loans to customers, proceeding with credit and actuarial assessments, managing the bank's own investments, underwriting financial issues, developing and managing new products, and trading in securities. Information technology (IT) solutions should help all of these channels in an able manner, both individually and in the aggregate. Therefore, the implementation of IT should be rigorously audited to determine whether this has been done in the best way possible.

One of the core functions of some — but not all — credit institutions is to provide custodial services and to ensure trustee functions. Virtually all banks today are engaging in derivative financial instruments for hedging and for speculation, aimed at developing and sustaining fee services, and are capitalizing on the globalization of financial markets. IT's role is most crucial in all these channels, and effectiveness, efficiency, and return-on-investment of IT should all be audited.

When I perform an IT audit, I start with the premise that the IT applications the company undertakes are not necessarily an outstanding success in costeffectiveness. The independent audit should therefore say what must be done in using IT to make the functions more efficient; swamp costs in all channels, including overhead; increase stockholder value; managing risk by instrument, desk, trader, counterparty, and globally; and generally be equipped with the best that IT can provide. Issues such as top-notch information technology and effective real-time risk management are core for *all* companies, and they are in constant evolution. An independent audit might look at policy in IT at large, and the quality of its implementation. Or it might be specific, focusing, for example, on project management, return on investment, organization and structure of databases, database mining, software development and purchasing, the Internet connection, or security and privacy connected to computers, databases and networks.

15.1   A Model for Auditing the Implementation of IT on a Global Scale

The introduction to this chapter pressed the point that in addition to being a good technician, the auditor should know the strategy of the bank and its core functions. On the technical side, the auditor must be able to take a detailed inventory of current applications asking, at each step, a number of critical questions:

■ Do the applications under investigation fit the company's strategy?
■ Can the current hardware and basic software support this strategy?
■ How can the current applications be restructured to improve performance?

For example, *if* the mission of the auditor is to take an inventory of ongoing IT projects and critically analyze them, *then* pertinent questions include: Are the existing platforms able to effectively support current applications? Can they take over the new applications that enhance or succeed the current ones? Which project should be given priority? Which should be restructured? Which should be killed? In my personal experience, part and parcel of the IT audit is to offer documented evidence on:

- Reconstructing current applications
- Evaluating new systems design
- Bridging the chasm that may exist between applications development and infrastructure
- Targeting solutions that bring significant competitive advantages
- Providing factual evidence about the quality and performance of IT personnel

Because the reason for investing big money in IT is to serve both management information requirements and day-to-day operations in an able manner, the IT auditor should make it part of his or her mission to ascertain that technology investments are always commensurate with the importance of the function being served. As Exhibit 15.1 suggests, this is not currently the case. Hence, there is plenty of scope in auditing IT from a money allocation angle and a return on investment viewpoint.

The IT auditor should always keep in perspective that over the last 30 years, computer power has increased by 35,000 times, and communications channel capacity has increased by 40,000 times. A good question to ask in an IT audit is how much of this power has been allocated to top management functions? Also, what kinds of structural changes have taken place in the company during the last three years? Did the company profit in a significant way from technology's advances and from IT investments?

Furthermore, with the Internet and the trend toward globalization, an IT auditor who is diligent in his or her work will search to ascertain whether IT

Exhibit 15.1 Technology Investments Should Always Be Commensurate with the Importance of the Function, and the Same Is True of the Tools

management has developed a sound model for global operations — which respects and supports the strategy established by the board. This is one of the jobs I am doing. In my experience, a model for global management should incorporate:

- *Topology of the markets* in which the company operates
- *Currencies* in which the products are sold and materials/labor are bought
- *Customer profiles* based on the business done; these must be served by knowledge-assisted artifacts[1]

For example, in finance there is a need for at least three customer profiles: treasurers, institutional investors, and high net-worth individuals. These profiles change from one area of operations to the next. Therefore, they should be customized according to local cultures, business opportunities, and customer drives. In today's highly competitive business environment, average approaches are counterproductive.

The right way to implement CRM is not just a matter of running the programs on the computer. It is to grasp the possibility to improve, by an order of magnitude, marketing performance and compare it to marketing costs. Today, most sales programs fail to measure the potential value of a customer; companies typically look only at past transactions, failing to appropriately consider future business prospects.

Business experience teaches that what someone spends today is not always a good predictor of what he or she will spend tomorrow, as life situations and spending habits change. Is the CRM implementation the information technologists have put in place significantly increasing the focus of marketing? If no, why not? If yes, how are the deliverables comparing to what IT has promised? To what it offered prior to CRM?

The CRM example in Exhibit 15.2 stresses the importance of value-added modules that help to enrich a given solution. It is the mission of IT managers and of their project manager(s) to make this value differentiation. After

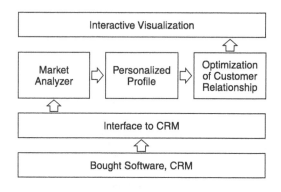

Exhibit 15.2   Value-Added Modules Over Bought Software Help to Significantly Increase the Deliverables

implementation, it becomes the duty of the auditor to investigate if this indeed has been done in an able manner, and report accordingly.

Another duty of the IT auditor is to examine how well bought software has integrated with the existing information technology environment of the company: How efficient are the interfaces that were provided? How well is the data flow managed? How strong are the analytics? A key asset of a good IT solution is its ability to manage workflow. While many processes in an organization are reasonably standardized, others are not because they are presenting their own specific requirements.

Purchase order authorization is an example where many people may have to sign off a form. Is the ERP solution the company has chosen streamlining this process? Reducing the time lag? Ensuring that the right people see requests at the right time? Providing the information to deal with them promptly? A good way to demonstrate workflow capabilities is to determine if the software speeds up applications processing and provides greater accuracy in response to customer requests.

Gaining the advantages of speed and accuracy is a major "plus" because it is making our businesses more competitive; however, many companies using CRM and ERP programming products do not take advantage of this "plus." Has the IT department capitalized on all competitive features of the software the firm bought and implemented?

Another channel for investigation into IT by means of a focused audit is whether the technology the company uses integrates unstructured information from multiple sources in multiple formats. This should include text, graphics, pictures, and voice, and present to the user a visualization that is easy to comprehend, access, and interact with.

As an example of flexible interaction, a replication feature of the software can ensure that the same version of information is available across different servers in the organization. In this way, all end users are accessing and employing homogeneous information elements, although each end user capitalizes on a personalized format. Such features are at the heart of a sound information management program.

It is inevitable that a model targeting the auditing of information technology and its implementation in a company will take the most careful look at IT management and ask, Is it up to the challenge? The model will also examine whether there is strong project management in place, which can be ascertained in every aspect of ongoing projects, and whether there is a clear structure of command and control. Accountabilities must be properly outlined, and there must be in place real-time information technology that serves the business in the most able manner.

15.2 The IT Auditor's Obligation Is to Bring to Top Management's Attention What Is Being Done the Wrong Way

Perhaps no phrase can better describe the obsolete and ineffective mentality, coming from the 1960s but still commanding a large followership, than the one I hear quite often: "All applications can be done with the existing type of equipment and our traditional basic software." If the same statement was made 30, 20, and 10 years ago, a company would still have been a very happy user of punched-card machines. And if the same concept prevailed in transportation, people would still have been traveling by horse and carriage.

Top management decisions are necessary to break out of this vicious cycle of EDP. The problem is that board members and senior managers in a large number of companies remain computer illiterate. This being the case, they do not understand that they are in a hole, even if IT auditors tell them so with plenty of evidence on hand. Yet, as the Law of Holes aptly advises: "When you are in one, stop digging" (attributed to Dennis Healey, former Chancellor of the Exchequer in the United Kingdom).

The statistics shown in Exhibit 15.3 come from an IT audit I did in late 1997 at the request of the board of a well-known financial institution. This audit concerned five different channels, one of them being payments services. Classically, payments has been manual-intense, but it is only reasonable to expect that after more than four decades of spending money on computers, it would have been at long-last automated. It did not happen that way.

- More and more equipment and rather classical applications software put into payments services every year only absorbed the yearly increase in millions of transactions.
- In contrast, the hard core of manual operations was a very tough nut to crack, primarily because the director of IT and his immediate assistants resisted the introduction of new technology such as expert systems and agents.

This resistance has been most regrettable in terms of end results. This is not the only instance in which the majority of IT professionals, and most particularly IT managers, fail to appreciate that the language that people use forms their minds and shapes their thoughts. If one uses obsolete tools and

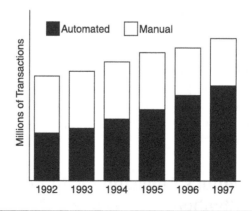

Exhibit 15.3   Even Among the Larger Banks, the Level of Automation in Payment Services Is Slow

programming languages — which is the case today with a big chunk of business and industry — the company is losing twice:

- It is being damaged *vis-à-vis* its competition by falling behind in its technological infrastructure.
- It is paying an inordinate cost for software that it develops with old, ineffectual, used-up computer tools.

If the IT auditor wants the company for which he or she works to overtake its opponents, then this entity must be much better equipped than it currently is. In other words, the company should take full advantage of high technology rather than following the beaten path. This requires a steadily upgraded infrastructure that involves:

- Enterprise architecture
- Intelligent networks
- Internet supply chain
- Smart materials applications
- Expert systems and agents
- Enterprise resource planning
- Customer relationship management
- Distributed deductive databases
- Seamless database access and datamining

Ease of use of the company's technology is another crucial issue to be audited. From the Internet to wireless networks and optical systems, there are innovations everywhere that should be examined for cost-effectiveness. IT auditors must be on the lookout not only for the most technically advanced solutions, but also for man–machine interfaces that often spell doom for new technologies.

As the global economy takes on speed, more questions have to be answered if the IT auditor cares to ask them: What data is available to the IT auditor? How dependable is it? Is it updated in real-time? How can the IT auditor access it? How can the IT auditor get *meaning* out of it?

The IT auditor should also be aware that, to a significant degree, there is correlation between organizational solutions and the way in which information technology is implemented and used. Exhibit 15.4 makes this point. There is a day-and-night difference between the information requirements of the two-dimensional organization of the 1920s defined by Alfred Sloan and the twenty-first century's federated entities and virtual corporations made possible by the Internet. Closely connected to this is the fact that the purpose of valid information technology solutions is threefold:

1. To offer and continue delivering competitive advantages
2. To provide sophisticated support to managers and professionals in real-time

3. To stimulate thoughts for new, more far-reaching value-added services to clients

The IT auditor should appreciate that a first-class solution is the one that can achieve all three goals admirably. This cannot be said of the large majority of current approaches characterized by low technology. Most companies suffer from technology despite vast IT outlays and, in many cases, because of them. They often do nothing more than throw money at the problem. When this happens, the source of the trouble is with the members of the board of directors, chief executives and senior managers, ossified policies and procedures, or IT practices followed over many years independently of the company's strategic plans.

These are the issues the IT auditor must have the courage to say wherever and whenever to whoever is in charge. Throwing money at the problem will not solve the current and coming challenges, and it may make matters worse by giving false hope that a better solution is around the corner because it bought ERP, CRM, or some other programming product that is *en vogue*.

In terms of priorities, immediately next to top management orders regarding the direction to be given to IT investments, comes the skill and know-how of the information technologists themselves. Are they able to design and support multidisciplinary interfaces to visualization and visibilization requirements? Can they manage heterogeneous databases? Do they understand the notion of metadata? Are they improving upon current approaches through the use of emerging technologies?

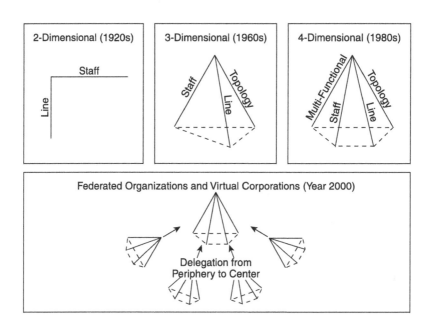

Exhibit 15.4   Seventy Years of Evolution in the Dimensions of Industrial Organization and Structure

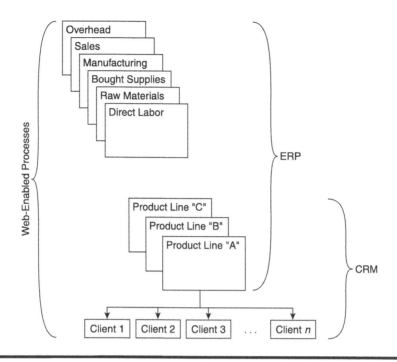

Exhibit 15.5   Establishing and Optimizing the Cost Allocation Procedure

Part of the IT auditor's challenge is to comprehend both the end user's and the technical viewpoints, and reflect both of them in his or her findings. It is also necessary to appreciate the impact of different solutions being contemplated in terms of costs and effectiveness. As Exhibit 15.5 suggests, the implementation of ERP, CRM, and Web-enabled processes, and their steady upgrade (see Chapter 7), is a good opportunity to rethink and optimize cost allocation.

Chapter 13 emphasized that cost control is a steady preoccupation of modern industry. No company can escape from a steady, careful, continuous watch over costs and survive. Eventually, unnecessary costs in the ERP and CRM implementation, as well as in other domains, will find their way to the client, resulting in damage to the company's relationship and in lost clients and lost income.

No less important from an IT audit viewpoint is the fact that the company may have in its database a wealth of information, which it is not necessarily using in the best possible way. What is "best" at a given state-of-the-art the IT auditor can learn by visiting business partners in the supply chain and competitor firms, and even by investigating advanced applications in unrelated industries.

Retailers, for example, are using their customer base to sell financial products such as life insurance, market funds, and pension funds. Is the CRM solution that the information technologists have chosen able to provide such services? Insurance companies also come into the banking market, opening up deposit facilities. There is a proliferation of services in the financial industry, to take just one example, and plenty of opportunities for banks but also for non-bank banks to get ahead of the competition. It is up to the IT auditor to determine if the company gets a real competitive advantage from its invest-ments in IT.

15.3   IT Auditing Must Be Done at Different Levels of Management Control

Because internal auditing is a tool of management, any organizational level can make use of it, even if regular annual audits are made for the board and exceptional audits are usually commissioned by the CEO. The possibility to ask for audits, particularly IT audits, up and down the organization leads to the notion that there may be different types of auditing reports customized by reporting level, such as:

- Company proprietary
- Senior management
- Departmental supervision
- Technical and security issues

If classes of auditing activity and associated reports are being distinguished, they should be related to the level of management addressed, properly accounting for area of operations, scope of duties, and resulting responsibil-ities. All these factors can vary according to the auditing mission.

Company proprietary internal auditing is the highest level at which the internal auditor acts as a direct representative of the proprietor of the business — the shareholders and the board. Basically, the chief auditor is appointed by and reports to the Audit Committee. As such, the chief auditor is completely independent of all other management personnel.

If an internal audit function is created by charter, through bylaw provisions, or by action of the board of directors, the internal auditor generally assumes the rank of a corporate officer. At the proprietary level, the auditor's scope of activities is generally very broad. If the audit targets IT, then the study is concerned with the effectiveness of information technology and its impact on strategic plans, as well as on operating, managerial, and professional activities.

Internal auditing made to serve senior management is a more common level. In this case, the auditor is a representative of one or more executives. As such, he or she may report to one of the executive vice-presidents, a particular senior-level committee, or other management authority of similar status.

As a general rule, the higher the reporting level of the auditor, the greater the range of *protective* services the auditor is expected to provide. As a rule, investigative services rendered by a modern internal auditor to top manage-ment cover a wider range than those performed by his or her predecessors. Within reasonable limits, it is the auditor's responsibility to protect management against such matters as:

- Violation of policies
- Deviations from procedures
- Non-reliable financial reporting
- Exposure taken with financial instruments
- Increasingly sophisticated fraud
- Waste and different hazards
- Inadequate internal controls
- Noncompliance to regulation

In many cases, the auditor works primarily for and under the direction of the person or entity commissioning the study, and must fulfill the requirements of the mission assigned. At the same time, the auditor must report findings to the Audit Committee of the board. The scope of activity is usually defined by this dual aspect of responsibility.

In terms of departmental-level assignments, the auditor should always determine whether or not the system of internal checks contributes significantly to the prevention of fraud, elimination of errors, and flushing out of other mishappenings, as well as whether the finding of audits are followed by corrective action.

As a practical example, in January 1999, the audit department of a major credit institution received the mission to study, in conjunction with an independent consultant, how well IT attributed time and money to the solution of the company's Y2K problem — and how this compares with industry standards, if any. Exhibit 15.6 shows the averages in the financial industry established by this study. The audit found that the company in reference had spent more time on code correction, but not enough on testing. Corrective action was immediately taken to redress this situation.

This example brings to the reader's attention the fact that departmental internal auditing has a more limited perspective in control activities. As another example, an internal auditor whose mission was to study the implementation

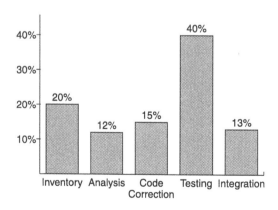

Exhibit 15.6   Percent of Time Typically Allocated by Companies to Each Phase of Year 2000 Problem

of ERP saw the scope of his work limited to the investigation of databases and written records rather than to the broader activities connected with enterprise resources planning.

The reason for this constrained view lies in the fact that the audit had been authorized by the Executive Vice-President/Finance, but the area where the field work had to be done was under the Executive Vice-President/Manufacturing. The boss of manufacturing was opposed to the ERP audit, and the executive committee avoided reaching a decision — leaving it up to the two EVPs to resolve their differences.

This procrastination can happen at any time, anywhere. However, the way to bet is that it will not take place if the auditing request has been made by the executive committee. In this case, the auditor would probably be granted authority to operate on a much broader basis. In my experience, the auditing department frequently gets more specific assignments such as:

- IT overhead
- Programmer productivity
- Maintenance cost
- Disbursements
- Accounts payable
- E-mail problems

rather than broader scope audits that are cross-departmental. Because the nature and extent of an audit can vary significantly from one exercise to the other, it is always wise to distinguish between those activities that address the whole of a big chunk of the IT function and others that merely deal with part of the system or constitute an internal check.

EDPACS provides a good example of the role played by auditors in connection with e-mail and Web access.[2] In the background is the fact that some Web site users appear to waste most of the workday browsing Web materials whose subjects are not related to their job. There is no lack of *recreational browsers* used at the expense of the firm.

A simple way for the auditor to identify the possible undetected occurrence of such situations, *EDPACS* suggests, is to use an ASCII editor to view the user's browser cache. This capitalizes on the fact that the browser usually stores the HTML code, including both the addresses and the graphics of the last 300 or so sites that have been accessed.

Another simple IT audit approach is to produce a complete list of all of the URLs that have been accessed in a sample of days within the past month. Sampling inspection can be quite revealing, and the auditor can focus on the pattern of some of the users once there is evidence that company rules have been discarded, or are not followed in a persistent manner.

These internal checks are a control activity designed to function as an integral part of the company's operating system. Their technology orientation often contrasts with the classical internal audit, which is the type of control created to function around routines and procedures intended to stamp out fraud. Both types of *investigations* should definitely be performed by inde-pendent-minded auditors.

Finally, the classification of errors is an important organizational activity associated with all types of auditing. The *intentional* error of principle, omission, or commission may arise from deliberate planning, usually carried out by a dishonest employee. The *unintentional* error of principle, omission, or commission is simply a mistake that comes from carelessness or lack of sufficient know-how on how to work with the system. Both intentional and unintentional errors lead to incorrect technical application of accounting or incorrect IT application. Typically, the two kinds of errors result in wrongly kept accounts and records; this has repercussions in many operational areas.

An error of *omission* is the failure to make an accounting ERP, CRM, or other type of entry, which biases the content of the book of accounts, production plans, inventory controls, and financial statements. An error of *commission* is usually the result of carelessness or deliberation, but which also leads to incorrect accounts and statements. For these reasons, the findings of auditing must be followed immediately by corrective action and the appli-cation of demerits. Failure to do so sends throughout the organization the perverse message that tricky business has its rewards.

15.4   A Practical Auditing Example of Supply Chain Relationships

As supply chain applications move on and grow in importance, companies are confronted with some critical choices. Where in the supply chain does the organization really belong? If a company moves too abruptly in some new direction, what becomes of its business partners? Other queries are of a technical nature and have to do with tools, models, and forecasts.

Software that prognosticates and mediates supply and demand could both help and hurt traditional supply chain relationships. Hence, there is plenty of scope in auditing the aftermath. Many Internet-enabled companies, for exam-ple, let their clients as well as brokers buy and sell large lots of excess inventory in online auctions. This eliminates the need for traditional parts brokers, but it also creates new intermediaries whose behavior patterns have not yet been established.

Some retailers are now pitting shipping companies against each other in auction-style bids, describing how many loads they have going out, along with weight, volume, and destination. Carriers are monitoring that and bidding in real-time. Before starting in this line of business, one should know whether the thus-far obtained results are written in black or red ink.

A growing number of perceptive people believe that because of the complexity of modern business, there is a need for audit in all domains mentioned in the preceding paragraphs. While rendering protective Internet-based services remains an important phase of an audit department's function, it is advisable to establish internal rules about themes and events making it appropriate to call in internal auditors — particularly those with responsibility in IT services. The auditor possesses no authority to issue orders or directives; the auditor only inspects, examines, appraises, and recommends. However, the extent and quality of constructive contributions by IT auditors enhances the value of an audit to senior management.

For example, the auditor analyzes events in the Internet supply chain and compares their aftermath with that of classical similar operations. A factual and documented report raises many issues that should receive management's attention on how an Internet supply chain works — when enriched, for example, with smart materials. These are issues that senior management may not be able to analyze unassisted.

At the same time, although the auditor is expected to report on issues that are believed worthy of the consideration of management, he or she should be careful not to diminish the responsibility of other agencies that are adequately reporting. To perform well this balancing act, auditors should be well-informed on business functions, including those on the Internet, their objectives, and their mechanics.

The problem is that such mechanics may go deep in terms of needed skills. An example is applets, the Java programs that can be loaded automatically onto personal computers or other devices and run at the push of a button. Potentially, applets can do almost anything, including nasty things. For example, they might introduce viruses into the computer system into which they are inserted, doing so in a vicious way. A Java applet is able to reproduce itself and send itself back out over the network from which it arrived. The creation and deployment of network-based computer viruses with Java is a real possibility and should be audited.

The process of attaining proficiency in this work has been sometimes likened to the process of erecting a building. It begins with the laying of a strong substructure of adequate technical training to provide support for the superstructure into which will accumulate subsequent experience. Being a professional person, the auditor must undergo a training of proportions adequate to the requirements of the control activity with which he or she has been (or will be) entrusted. For example, in connection with supply chain audits, training must be adequate in Internet-based technical breadth and scope, including the handling of business partnerships. Just as necessary is hand-on experience in the implementation of ERP and CRM systems.

The more emphasis that is placed by industry on Internet commerce, the more auditing the design and operation of supply chains gains in importance. I have seen many cases where overconfidence leads to major mistakes in supply chain solutions. The culture of the auditor should be that of questioning the obvious.

Confident of its market hold on mainframers, IBM showed no sensitivity to customer wishes and drives at the dawn of the personal computer era. Therefore, it lost the opportunity to control the supply chain of the emerging PC market of the 1980s and eventually its suppliers became its biggest business threat. As examples:

- Microsoft gained control of the operating system on which 90 percent of the world's PC depend.
- Intel's chip architecture came to dominate the PC industry. Compaq, Dell, and Gateway turned IBM into a PC marketing laggard.

This is a useful lesson for auditors of strategic plans and product plans. Dell's success has shown that who controls distribution can lead to swift gain in the balance of power in the supply chain. Wal-Mart is another example. Dell and Wal-Mart amassed the marketing clout that determined their suppliers' pricing, promotions, packaging, and expediting schedules.

Supply chain auditing might have informed IBM's top management way ahead of the loss of market leadership. The board and CEO should appreciate that what makes supply chains tick changes over time. Today's computer companies, even the most glamorous vendors, may not hold their position in the future for other reasons than those that contributed to IBM's demise in the late 1980s.

Any shop with prices higher than Internet prices is bound to lose. Store prices are higher than prices on the Internet because they need to justify investments in real estate and buildings. Costs matter. Wal-Mart, for example, could be highly vulnerable to Internet-based competitors who can undersell it by 20 percent from electronic storefronts.

The auditor of a firm's marketing strategy and pricing structure must recognize that the winner will be whoever is adding the most value in terms of engineering design, marketing insight, distribution channels, and technical innovation — doing all that at rapid pace and at low cost.

The supply chain auditor must also appreciate that the shift in paradigm may see to it that an otherwise sound plan turns on its head. For example, the auto industry's new emphasis on value/content through electronics can lead to a motor vehicle market in which built-in electronics become more important than steel in cars. All told, the Internet supply chain brought to the foreground five top factors that determine a company's clout: (1) content, (2) lean production, (3) high quality, (4) low cost, and (5) fast timetables.

The auditor should appreciate that continued success is dependent on the company's ability to compress cost and time. The search for this sort of solution describes the necessary intricate network of the supply chain, along with value-added CRM and ERP software supporting direct sales and build-to-order models.

All auditors should recognize that in the New Economy, faster clockspeed works in the company's favor. One has to be ahead of the industry in the transition to the next generation of technology, which plays into the margin equation. But at the same time, there is nothing more expensive than carrying old component inventory. In PCs, for example, this devalues at 1 or 2 percent a month. Inventory turnover must be very carefully audited.

These are vital references to supply chain auditing. Indeed, experts suggest that the way companies succeed is by combining marketing information, suppliers' relationships, and third-party sales and service to produce the right product at the right price. One of the key lessons learned during the last few years is that performance and producibility requirements cannot be designed independently. Neither can products, processes, and supply chains be optimized independently. They require cross-functional teams. The auditor should fully appreciate this fact.

15.5 The Role Auditors Can Play in Internet Decisions, Product Reviews, and Time-to-Market

Let me start with a company's active presence on the Internet and the role auditors should play in ensuring that such a major decision has in the background a lot of homework that led to factual and documented decisions. Because the entry fee for Internet presence is steadily rising, a company's I-commerce orientation should not be part of a trend in joining the bandwagon, but a deliberate choice. This is all the more important because what most companies care about today is to do something with the Internet — practically anything — while those already present are thinking of creating an Internet spinoff or making an IPO.

Just prior to the late March 2000 NASDAQ crash, I happened to meet on separate occasions with three CEOs who were contemplating making an Internet spinoff to be followed by an IPO. When asked what they would put in it, they had no precise answer, other than this was a question for their assistants. One of them added that he thought his firm would look dumb if it did nothing.

These are indeed very unbusinesslike ways of doing business, and I think there is plenty of scope in calling in an independent auditor before losing face and money in empty-shell Internet spinoffs. This is written with full understanding that CEOs today are under investor pressure to put on the Internet a piece of their product line — or at least to establish a supply chain.

Events that followed NASDAQ's crash at the end of the first quarter of 2000 demonstrated that the urge to drive up market value through some kind of quick action can be a dangerous game. While Internet commerce and its associated business drive are one of the New Economy's motors, the crust of the cake should not be confused with its substance. The company would win through a "me too" policy.

An independent auditor's mission in this connection is to ascertain whether the CEO and senior management are confusing doing something, anything, about the Internet with the real work of transforming the company. Such an audit should keep in perspective that, as Abraham Lincoln aptly said, one can fool some of the people all the time or all the people some of the time, but not all the people all the time.

If increasing stockmarket capitalization is the domain in which an independent auditor's expertise is wanted, *then* he or she should focus on product reviews and sales reviews. "In our bank," a senior executive of a credit institution said to me during a meeting in New York, "we hold regular product review meetings in which participate representatives from finance, the legal counsel, (market) risk management, credit risk, information technology, and taxation." The mission of such product review meetings is to:

- Establish whether the new product or service makes sense
- Evaluate the exposure this new product entails, both under normal conditions and under stress
- Analyze the profile of the investor(s) to which this product would appeal, including the risk profile

In my experience, risk profiling proves to be invaluable when financial products are priced. Therefore, some institutions have also established a broker review process that tackles both broker profitability (hence commissions) and client profitability in the sense of market value associated with projected trades.

An independent auditor's contribution is important because brokers may have conflicts of interest in estimating volatility, as happened with NatWest Markets in March 1997. Therefore, the independent auditor should carefully review assumptions and hypothesis — including in the examination the information technology that the institution has available to support, promote, and control the new product.

Another IT-related domain in which there is plenty of opportunity for improvement through focused audits is timetables for deliverables. Long delays are often associated with software projects. Other products also suffer from management's inability to control timetables. When Ross Perot was a member of General Motors board, he once said: "We win a war in four years; why does it take five years to design a car?"

Independent audits can also make a contribution to the quality of software. The top responsibility for sophisticated, high-quality software resides with the originating software developers. They must take the lead in implementing good control techniques, ensuring that software continues to meet required specifications and is free from errors. But an independent auditor who specializes in software development and testing challenges the obvious and contributes a fresh look.

No matter how wise, IT management is not well placed to evaluate software quality and delivery timetables because it is directly involved in both counts, and there may be conflicts of interest. Therefore, the contribution of an independent auditor should be sought, with the aim to obtain a knowledgeable opinion free of political pressures. This can save a significant amount of money in the longer run.

One of the best examples of money going down the drain in IT is the Westpac-IBM fiasco of 1984 to 1991 (Westpac was, at the time, Australia's second largest bank). In seven years a rumored half billion dollars was spent, and finally this king-size project was killed because there were no deliverables and it was going nowhere. An independent audit worth its salt should have followed both the management views and technical views of the Westpac project known as "Core System for the 1990s" (CS-90).

The management view had been that the CS-90 project did not sell itself to senior management; it did not address executive-level requirements; and the promised deliverables offered no added value. Beyond this, the project overran its budget many times, and project management had lost control of both costs and timetables.

The technical view was that a split project management (between Westpac and IBM) made matters worse than they might have been. CS-90 was too mainframe based; the project used either obsolete or unready development tools; and CS-90 rested on unsettled software: repository, information warehouse, system application architecture (SAA), OS/2.

Audits of information technology should be done well before spectacular failures like the Westpac-IBM fiasco spark controversy, ending in loss of prestige and major financial woes. Throughout this long stretch of time, nothing was allowed to change, except by way of decay, in a project that found itself years too late and hundreds of millions of dollars short. CS-90 had become a hit-and-miss affair until Westpac's board finally decided to do away with it.

Notes

1. D.N. Chorafas and Heinrich Steinmann, *Expert Systems in Banking*, Macmillan, London, 1991.
2. *EDPACS*, July 1997, Vol. XXV, No. 1.

Chapter 16

Auditing Enterprise Resource Planning Software and Its Implementation

The successful implementation of enterprise resource planning (ERP) software is inseparable from the usage of a companywide, streamlined accounting system. This is why so much emphasis is placed on accounting and on the auditing of a company's books in the preceding chapters of Section III. The synergy between ERP and accounting can be seen from different perspectives:

- Both systems act as measurements, thereby as aids in better management through dependable metrics.
- Both are a means of communication, conveying the facts of business to all levels of management.
- Both provide the tools for planning and controlling the distribution of the fruits of production.

The contribution of ERP to the success of the company that implements it lies in the making of intelligent measurements of events occurring in the conduct of the company's business and its financial significance. Auditing of ERP must ensure that the study, analysis, and interpretation of these measurements, and the utilization of accounting data in the exercise of informed judgments, indeed follow the board's policies and rules.

Whether discussing bread-and-butter ERP implementation or ERP's transition into a Web-enabled application, the auditor must appreciate that no business is conducted in a vacuum. Therefore, one of the requirements is the auditor's adequate understanding of internal and external relationships affecting ERP. This is essential to the recommendations made to management. Both internal and external relationships will guide the auditor's hand in evaluating the contribution of ERP software in such matters as maintenance of inventories in the face of changing price levels, ways and means in seeking lower costs through better methods for planning and scheduling, and optimized distribution plans through better use of the Internet supply chain.

Each measurement that leads to a management decision to fine-tune or change a course of action in the interest of greater efficiency contributes to profitability. The collective weight of all such decisions helps in optimizing the use of human resources and of capital.

People with experience in ERP auditing further suggest that companies are well-advised to use ERP information in improving their system of incentives. In the background of this concept lies the fact that, to a considerable extent, the secret of achieving the best possible balance in the production, warehousing, and distribution of goods is a matter of incentives. Economic rewards must in some way be related to the personal initiative, individual effort, and risk being taken.

Compensation irrespective of achievement which is factual and documented can be deadly because output is bound to fall to the level of the worst-performing worker. Both human labor and capital must have the promise and prospect of commensurate returns as an inducement for taking risks. Management, too, must have a reward, in proportion to achievements, for its capacity of successful generalship. The auditing of ERP will be deficient without due attention to human resources and to incentives.

16.1 Case Study in Auditing a New Implementation of Enterprise Resource Planning

ABC[1] is a manufacturing company. Its management did lots of homework in preparing itself for an ERP solution that was projected to liberate it from old data processing and its slow-moving, error-prone, batch legacy programs. The first major application chosen in connection with the implementation of ERP software was procurement. Management divided the company's entire purchasing process into the following discrete but interconnected activities:

- Updating bills of materials
- Controlling inventory levels
- Deciding on items to be ordered, and levels
- Negotiating with suppliers
- Issuing purchase orders
- Controlling deliveries, etc.

Particular attention was paid to real-time updating of the corporate database, with emphasis on all files accessed and handled by the new ERP software. This was followed by an audit which established that while each of the new applications was well done, in a general sense the system put in place was incomplete. The original project had foreseen that practically all files from engineering design to manufacturing, warehousing, and sales had to be updated in real-time. This, however, could not be achieved because most of the legacy routines being retained worked batch, and file management could not handle real-time updates. The auditors also noted in their report that they had not been asked to examine the ERP project prior to its implementation, in which case such deficiency might have become apparent. Another issue that struck them during the audit was that ERP project management consisted primarily of old hands who had not undergone a rigorous training for cultural change.

Real-time update was a new experience for project management, which prior to the audit had taken care to divide its engineering, manufacturing, marketing, and finance activities into smaller functions without paying particular attention to interleaving batch and real-time functions. The hypothesis was made that such division saw to it that the system was in control and it was not necessary to restructure and update all corporate files at once. The audit disproved this assumption.

The mapping of the company's manufacturing activities into a block diagram of homogeneous functions is shown in Exhibit 16.1. A matrix approach was taken so that the functions described by this chart became standard throughout ABC's global operations, wherever there were manufacturing facilities. This was a good initiative. The production database was organized along this frame of reference and functions could be accessed horizontally, cross-border, and vertically in an integrative manner. However, file management was wanting, leading to frictions between IT and user departments. The ERP

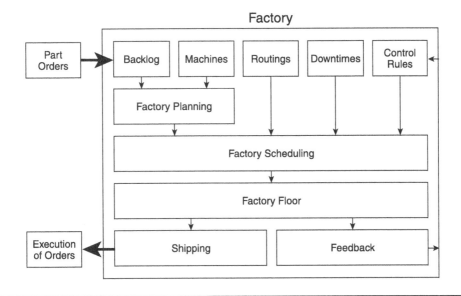

Exhibit 16.1   Mapping Manufacturing Activity into a Block Diagram of Homogenous Functions

audit also demonstrated that the implementation timetable was too long. To get its organization ready for the new system, ABC spent three years rethinking its business — from product and market strategy to global engineering design, to reallocation of manufacturing capacity, and to restructuring of warehousing in five major countries of operation.

The company's board and CEO did not like the results of the ERP audit. The CEO thought that the deliverables were influenced by a latent personal hostility between the people in charge of auditing and IT. The decision was therefore made to ask for a new audit by an outside consultant.

The first mission given to the consultant was limited to the strategic viewpoint: how well the ERP solution serves corporate strategy. To this the consultant answered that ERP implementation indeed serves the company's business strategy — and this is a major improvement over the former parochial data processing services ABC had been using for three decades.

The consultant's audit, however, cautioned on the double need for database restructuring and cultural change at all levels of management, which he characterized as the top benefits the company can get from the implementation of ERP. In a confidential letter addressed to the board and the CEO, the independent consultant said that the gap which resulted in batch versus real-time database update was the weakest link in IT support of the entire enterprise.

The independent audit also brought senior management's attention to the fact that even though there was a diversity of IT platforms used by the company and a certain laxity in reliability assurance, ERP implementation was reasonably good. The consultant pressed the point that it is only reasonable that a globally operating enterprise should expect as a maximum a mean time between failures (MTBF) of three months, and a mean time to repair (MTTR) no greater than one hour.

Exhibit 16.2 shows availability of transaction processing systems as a percent of downtime. At the time of the independent audit, ABC's availability was 99 percent, which is quite poor. The study suggested an immediate upgrade to 99.9 percent, which under current technology is perfectly doable. This would have meant a system downtime of less than an hour per month for enhancing all applications that performed online — such as the ERP system.

The independent auditor also stated in his conclusion that within a year, as a maximum, the goal should be four 9s, which amounts to 99.99 percent.

Exhibit 16.2   Reliability and Availability for Transaction Processing Systems

Downtime	Availability	Evaluation
1 hour/day	95.8%	Very Bad
1 hour/week	99.41%	
1 hour/month	99.86%	Doable
1 hour/year	99.9886%	
1 hour/20 years	99.9994%	Tough

This would have required major system upgrades, well beyond those necessary for a real-time database update required for a state-of-the-art ERP implementation. This is a good example of how an ERP audit helps to uncover system weaknesses that at first sight might seem unrelated to ERP; yet failure to attack head-on such weak points ends by compromising overall system performance.

The independent auditor did not fail to bring to management's attention the fact that lower than 99.9 percent system reliability has a negative aftermath on productivity because of resulting interruptions. Quality, cost, and yield correlate and impact management control. In a highly competitive market economy, the consultant said, quality and yield expectations steadily rise, leading to the need for implementing tighter management control.

Subsequent to this external audit, the ABC company did a new internal study, which found that improvements in quality, cost, and yield indeed make or break the benefits derived (and to be derived) from ERP — because they impact all the way up and down the supply chain. Suppliers cannot be asked to deliver goods ready for use at a specific quality level if the ABC company itself is lax on the quality of its product and timetables.

The consequence of these audits has been that both cost and quality came under senior management's spotlight. The board appreciated that conventional thinking that cost is not the driving factor in the company's own operations, as well as in selection of suppliers, has become an anachronism. ABC not only revised its own plans based on ERP input, but also informed its suppliers about the unacceptability of cost escalations due to labor inefficiencies, poor quality assurance, and multiple reworking of design faults.

The CEO of ABC called the CEOs of its leading suppliers to inform them that these mishappenings might have been tolerated in the past by manufacturers in their desire to bring product to market at a faster pace, but they would no longer be acceptable; neither would they be a necessary consequence of innovation or just-in-time delivery. If anything, they would be anathema to well-managed companies, and ABC wanted each supplier to understand these facts.

16.2   Reorganizing and Auditing the Infrastructural Services to Improve Overall Performance

While the audits to which Chapter 16.1 made reference were going on, ABC decided to purchase and implement CRM software. This time, auditing was involved at the original project level and the examination that followed the first phase of this study suggested the assignment of a senior systems specialist as Web executive (not to be confused with CWO functions discussed in Chapter 1). The Web executive's mission was to oversee information solutions based on internet technology and to solve problems resulting from supply chain relationships connected with CRM.

Eventually, this process evolved into managing the *extrastructure* (see Chapter 1). As he gained experience and his job gained momentum, the Web executive was also asked to manage ABC's procurement program, working closely with suppliers to get them online. This led to a dual responsibility: Internet sales and the Internet supply chain, with the result of taking on *de facto* Chief Web Officer (CWO) duties.

However, the database problems resulting from the real-time/batch split persisted. Therefore, the management of ABC decided to appoint one of the company's most capable professionals to audit and subsequently handle the *infrastructure*. This work was primarily organizational, aimed at exploring where the bottlenecks and weak links were with respect to developing distributed real-time applications.

ABC's organization (Orga) team was also asked to focus on lead-time and on possible solutions related to tools and technology, in the context of applications that either accompanied the ERP and CRM software or were scheduled for implementation thereafter. The organizational work capitalized on statistics available from ongoing applications (including some subsets of ERP) to understand the pattern of data handling. Five activities retained the team's attention: gather, reconcile, process, store, and analyze information. Because of low technology characterizing ABC's database, *analyze* was the junior partner among the five, as shown in Exhibit 16.3. The Orga team found that while management thought about 70 percent of installed computer power was devoted to data analysis, this was an ill-served function.

The executive in charge of the Orga team did not limit himself to discussions with internal IT and the information technologists of its main business partners at headquarters. He conducted a survey in ten different ABC decentralized business units, asking them to identify what they believed were the outstanding problems within the context of getting a new infrastructure up and running.

The independent auditor who reviewed this organizational study was impressed by the accuracy of the results. What particularly attracted his

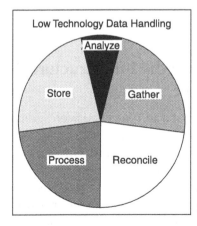
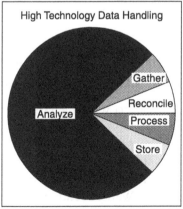

Exhibit 16.3   The Need to Increase the Depth and Breadth of Analysis Without Increasing Costs Is Served by High Technology

attention was an input/output analysis that served to determine generic sequencing in data handling, emphasized data analysis, and examined whether it was performed correctly within the firm; or, when not so, where were the shortcomings.

A thorough organizational study was undertaken by ABC using the introduction of ERP and CRM as an opportunity to revamp the infrastructure, and also including functional unit integration and product-level data analysis resulting from the test of information flows. As the obtained responses were critically analyzed, the infrastructure was reviewed for possible organizational enhancements and technical improvements.

In the past, IT audits had suggested the need for methods of quantitatively judging infrastructural changes. They had also pointed out the need for models that would help to faciltate reliability measurements and upgrades in systems reliability. The Orga executive agreed with the auditors' view that model-based testing should be used when measuring uninterrupted EPR functionality. He also pointed out that a much higher reliability of IT technology than the one currently at ABC would lead to productivity improvements, and a higher product and process quality level.

Another organizational study examined end-user data requirements to establish product-specific pass/fail criteria. For example, does the data reflect in detail the ongoing daily work? The planning requirements? The expected outputs defined through scheduling? A bird's-eye view of what has been considered in the examination procedure is shown in Exhibit 16.4.

Other organizational issues of a more managerial nature were harder nuts to crack because they involved egos. The ABC company had for many years

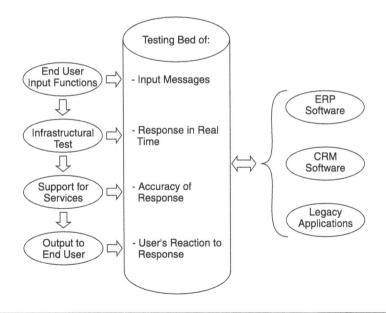

Exhibit 16.4   Analysis of Dataflows for an ERP Implementation, with End-User Functionality in Mind

a first-class cost accounting department and a standard cost system able to track down deviations between planned and actual cost for each product and process. The cost accountants have been working for the treasury with some ties to industrial engineering.

When a satisfactory data flow started coming from ERP, the cost accountants took it upon themselves to analyze this data, presenting the outcome as an audit of production efficiency. The production people objected to this cost analysis, pointing out that it was too mathematical and that, in manufacturing efficiency, not everything is a game of signs and rules.

"In mathematics, and in most of the physical sciences," said the EVP Manufacturing, "there are definitions that are valid under a wide variety of circumstances. In the case with most accounting and production control definitions, their wording depends on different environments, situations, and standards." In an executive committee meeting, the EVP Manufacturing further stressed the point that in a number of practical cases, different figures may superficially resemble one another and may even be called by the same name — but in reality, they reflect different events.

For his part, the EVP Finance made the point that the auditors must appreciate that some accounting figures, such as amount of cash on hand, may be accurate within very narrow limits; while others are tentative, awaiting further confirmation or requiring appropriate tests of their dependability. "The problem of obtaining truly accurate measurements," said the EVP Finance "is further complicated by the validity of some of the inputs we receive."

The CEO objected to this proposed narrowing of scope of the auditors' work to the inputs, by pointing out that the accounting horizon has significantly broadened and so has the nature and range of its functions. Auditing is no longer primarily concerned with ascertaining past financial conditions, but it targets, as well, forecasting conditions that facilitate or inhibit the protection of assets. "No lesser authority than the SEC promotes this concept," the CEO said.

Because a great deal of results are essentially dependent on personal judgment, the CEO insisted that in a modern enterprise the auditing of accounting information, and of data streams from large-scope applications like ERP, must be appraised from the standpoint of steady and rigorous management control. That is where it finds its usefulness. In a complex society and in a dynamic market, management control concepts and objectives must constantly be reexamined in light of changing conditions: discarding principles that have become obsolete or redefining them so that they have greater current applicability.

16.3   Challenges Associated with ERP and CRM Software Reviews and Audits

Complete and current documentation always plays a crucial role in auditing the application or the programming product itself. Block diagrams, structure charts, lines of code, data flows, data declarations, procedural calls, the programmer's notes and flags — in short detailed notes, including specifications, which are regularly upkept must be available. Without them, it is not possible to do a first-class job.

This is rarely the case with in-house programming developments, but there is no excuse for getting anything other than complete and accurate documentation with off-the-shelf programming products. This statement is evidently valid in connection with ERP, CRM, and any other routine — except for the fact that client companies are not so careful with bought software and do not demand the quality documentation to which they are entitled.

It is therefore necessary that auditing takes a close look at bought software and the completeness of its documentation. With ERP programming products, particular attention must be paid to how well their inputs and outputs integrate with legacy routines that will be retained in the new applications environment, at least for some time. Most existing auditing and review methods tend to focus on possible defects that would lead to incorrect output. No single method is perfect in doing this job, just as no single method suffers from all the limitations that are likely to happen. This statement is not limited to bugs. While error detection is important, correctness is not the only desirable characteristic of new software. The systems concept underpinning its development, flexibility, portability, reusability, and maintainability are other factors with which an audit should be concerned.

Is the bought CRM software integrating into the company's current environment without having to massage the code? Is it contributing to the creation of an intelligent front-office? Which way is provided for closing the loop between CRM business intelligence and existing front-office applications? Between CRM and ERP? Between CRM and accounting?

The real sense of these last queries is that companies with experience in CRM implementation increasingly speak of the need to close the loop between marketing automation and other important applications. They find it rewarding to use customer intelligence to promote horizontal integration, campaign management, and marketplace response with production planning, logistics, and accounting. Their synergy affects critical factors such as:

- *Efficiency:* getting things done better, without having to constantly change the frame of reference
- *Coordination:* grouping people with complementary skills to collaborate on a project, no matter where they are located
- *Competency:* making sure that staff have the information and the skills necessary to get and keep ahead of the competition
- *Responsiveness:* ensuring that the organization can react fast, accessing information and skills without loss of time.

The reason I emphasize the need for auditing these CRM functionalities and their synergy with other modules is that a software product might have no errors, but its usability can be drastically reduced if it is not integrated in a flexible and adaptable manner. When this happens, it will not provide added value.

Auditing should stress the efficiency of technological solutions, the value differentiation they offer, and their future adaptability. These are characteristics sufficiently complex that their determination cannot be ensured by an inspection that limits itself to visible errors or fraud. Being at the top of productized applications:

- ERP and CRM software stands at the interface between commodity programming products and proprietary applications; as an intermediate layer as shown in Exhibit 16.5.
- The input to ERP and CRM applications must fulfill the requirements of both the open architectural environment and the company's own proprietary routines. This should be done not only at present, but also in the future as the environment changes.

One of the most consistent problems with software reviews that I have found in my practice is that the product is usually examined from too narrow an angle, or it is expected that quality characteristics of all types will be flushed out through a few tests. When this is the case, it is no wonder that some spectacular failures are taking place with programming products.

Detailed tests are, of course, time-consuming, and there is no assurance that a 100-percent inspection of the code will make the programming product confess its weaknesses; however, there is no other way than rigorous testing — at least as far as I know. A good method for ERP and CRM auditing and testing is random input generation.

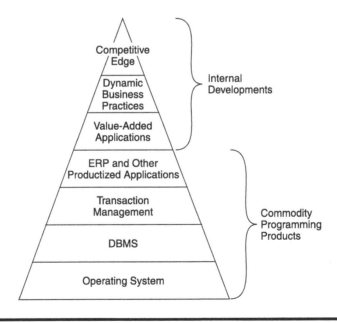

Exhibit 16.5   ERP and CRM Stand at the Interface Between the Open Architecture and Proprietary IT Supports

- Expert systems acting as test runners simulate inputs (including mouse-clicks) connected to the application under test.
- Other test runners call application programming interface (API) functions, using random parameters for that purpose.

The concept is to keep the ERP software under test applying one input after the other, both by simulating end-user interactivity and by experimenting with inputs from, and outputs to, other online applications in the company's environment. The result will be more valuable in subsequent hands-on testing, where human elements execute test cases interactively against the software that is about to be bought or has indeed been purchased but not yet implemented.

Hands-on testing is necessary both to add flavor to the functions of the simulator and to correct the latter's downside; applying random inputs makes it difficult to control their sequencing, which may lead to gaps in test coverage. A hands-on approach implements a desired test sequence, one consisting entirely of actions that are representative of real-life implementation of the ERP or CRM system placed under stress.

Auditors will be able to develop a first-class model for both automated and hands-on testing if they are careful in making explicit the domain definition, enumerating the system inputs and outputs, and generating test cases capable of traversing the model. They should do so only after obtaining a good understanding (not just an impression) of the system's functionality and its design characteristics. In fact, for each input they encounter, analysts doing the test should answer three queries key to describing system behavior:

1. What are the specific design and performance characteristics?
2. At which level of processing cycle must that input be available?
3. What happens after the input is applied and processed by the system?

This should be done not in an abstract sense independent of time, but in connection with a realistic clock window connected to real-life performance. A well-done ERP audit will also look into the contractual clauses of the bought software and the company's ability to take over maintenance should the vendor fail. Vendor failure is the Achilles heel of a programming product.

The way that I handle this issue is to contractually require the vendor to deposit the source code with a public notary, a contractual clause being that this becomes the company's property if the vendor is bankrupt, asks for creditor protection under Chapter 11, or is otherwise unable to perform the maintenance of ERP or CRM routines purchased and implemented.

This is by no means a call to do in-house maintenance. In most organizations today, maintenance of existing code occupies far too large a portion of the development group's time and skills, while product quality is static or worsening despite the increased maintenance load — and quite often because of it. For this reason, one of the advantages of any bought software — one that I will not forgo under any condition — is that the vendor does the maintenance. However, there should be a clause to assure continuous upkeep in case of vendor failure.

Do not forget that since its beginning, the software industry has always been in the midst of a crisis. With the exception of some brilliant ideas which are a person's brand new thing, like the spreadsheet, software development and maintenance require too many specialists making projects expensive and difficult to manage. This is particularly evident with in-house developments whose timetable is often slowed dramatically because of:

- The complexity in delivering the baseline functionality expected by users
- The lack of high performance tools to easily create interoperating custom-made solutions
- The fact that maintenance of existing applications software absorbs the lion's share of available human resources

Over and above this comes the fact that for nearly two decades the classical computer vendors could not create radically new designs because of conflict of interest between serving their clients in a more efficient manner and safeguarding their installed income base. Proof is that ERP software has come from third parties, usually start-up, and not from the big, established computer vendors. The latter still produce software that does not adequately address business problems and should not have been developed in the first place.

16.4 Looking After the Sophistication of ERP and CRM Applications

Any ERP application worth its salt is characterized by the parallel goal of increased productivity on behalf of its users and improved integration with the existing computer-based environment. This has led tier-1 organizations to the development of a strategy that allows them to effectively master the process of change, both in regard to human capital and in computer-based support.

Similar to regular design reviews, ERP and CRM audits are supposed to enforce consistency and help ensure that when proceeding with upgrades in implementation, one is on firm ground. Top-tier companies also appreciate that the value of software comes not only from its intrinsic characteristics and the way it responds to current and projected requirements, but also from time-to-delivery to the end user.

Time-to-delivery of sophisticated software features and functions must definitely be audited. This is slowly becoming an accepted principle. The CIOs who used to sit in the audience of some of my seminars and laugh when they heard other organizations state that they had rules that systems projects should never go ahead if they would require more than six months to delivery and more than six people on the same project are no longer laughing.

These CIOs now realize that many originally worthwhile projects lost a great deal of their value as delays and high costs set in. True enough, in old EDP, a great many projects required a multiple of their original estimate in terms of dollars and elapsed time. But this is a counterproductive practice condemned by well-managed companies.

Today, even 6-by-6 projects (six people working over six months) are too big and too slow. Since the early 1990s, competitive companies have been delivering at least prototypes and products that can be implemented at the pilot level in a short timeframe. The need for software time-to-delivery criteria is no longer a debatable issue, and it is not uncommon to have projects that take two people over two months, or even over two weeks.

Auditors should pay attention to time-to-delivery of ERP functionality. They should become well-informed on how much effort by computer specialists goes down the drain because the analysts' and programmers' time is lost for trivia. Even with off-the-shelf software, precious time and money is wasted in slow motion by:

- Poorly managed projects
- Monolithic type applications

Whether it is ERP, CRM, or any other programming product, the implementation should be modular, along the schema presented in Exhibit 16.6. It is now necessary that an ERP package is used end-to-end. Its different subsystems can be phased in and start giving results — thus contributing to return-on-investment — before the whole functionality is supported.

It is the auditor's job to flush out implementation delays and other forms of waste. "In our company, there is a cultural fear to have large projects that slip," suggested a senior IT executive. "We have shorter and shorter milestone criteria." The self-imposed rapid deadlines for these subsystems have allowed this organization to:

- Get the benefit early in the implementation cycle
- Do mid-course corrections, as needed, seamlessly to the users
- Follow-up on obtained results with new developments

Along the same line, the ERP auditor should ascertain if all of the company's business lines benefit from the project, know how far advanced it is, and feel free to react to any slippages. IT auditing should be controlling every software project and the quality of its results, both from a technical standpoint and from that of end-user satisfaction.

Industrial history is littered with examples in which delays in deliverables have killed a service or product. In 1997, Sun Microsystems dropped Hot.Java because browsers by then were free and it did not make business sense to continue investing money in its development. Hot.Java had missed its window of market opportunity, and its expenses had to be written off.

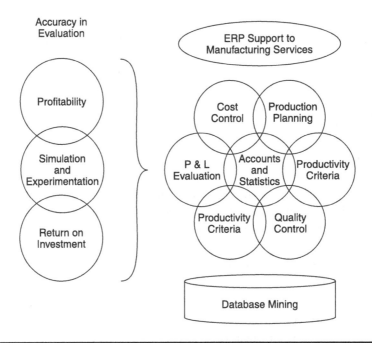

Exhibit 16.6   Information Provided by ERP Can Be Instrumental in Accurate Evaluation of Performance, Given the Proper Infrastructure

The greatest success stories in IT are those of products that came quickly into service, when the market was vibrant and competitors were still behind the curve. In the late 1980s as expert systems came online, both Marks & Spencer and American Express used them to assist clerks who authorize credit-card charges. This permitted both companies to move ahead of competitors by featuring:

- Faster transaction processing than other retailers (in the M&S case) and credit-card companies (in the AmEx case)
- The ability to cut in half the number of authorized charges that turned bad, which was a credit risk breakthrough[2]

Results were obtained by fast but ingenious implementation and by linking the expert system into the company's mainstream IT operations. This type of *quick response* application requires a tip-top team, an open architecture, and the wisdom to proceed in a modular manner. This permits customization at the end-user end without having to manipulate mammoth software that acts as a foreign body within the existing information processing environment.

Another example from the same timeframe explains how properly managed technology facilitates the end-user's job. Together with Nissan, Hitachi developed an expert system that permits a garage mechanic to do a *fuzzy inquiry* or a *quick inquiry* — his choice. Both functions are incorporated into the artifact so that an inexperienced person can readily retrieve part numbers for an auto repair job.

Fuzzy inquiry means that the information with which one starts is scanty. The exact part number is retrievable by simply entering a few items regarding the car model (for example, classification code employed on the automobile inspection certificate, model/type marked on the model number plate, or general designation such as body style). *Quick inquiry* works faster but requires exact input. It addresses nearly one million information elements that can be rapidly retrieved in a priority manner.

I bring these applications into perspective because they fit nicely into the realm of ERP implementation. It is part of the value-added applications layer depicted in Exhibit 16.5. The ERP audit should always address the question of whether or not the company has been able to value differentiate bought software through ingenious add-ons. Artifacts such as the Hitachi-Nissan expert system help to increase the population of users by combining runtime efficiency and choice of user-friendliness.

Ease-of-use is enhanced through explanations interactively available; end-user interaction facilities should avoid too many specifics in the programming environment that are alien to the end-user. Fuzzy inquiry, for example, is an inference mechanism, part of what I call the *human window* — an efficient end-user interface that must be incorporated beginning with the prototype level.

Expert systems may be a development of the mid- to late-1980s, but they brought along some novel ideas that have struck a chord at the end-user's end. One of them, the Dipmeter Advisor, had 42 percent of its code devoted to the human window. This interface was one of the best graphical presentations available at the time, and proved most valuable in gaining user acceptance for the entire computer program.

Auditors of ERP systems should retain the following notion from this discussion: flexible, knowledge-enriched man-machine interfaces extend the software's portability and improve its attractiveness to end users. Advanced graphics is another value differentiation. A critical question to an audit should be: Is the ERP or CRM programming product being examined and tasted at the top of its class in terms of human interfaces?

16.5   Both Return on Investment and Software Reliability Should Be Audited

It is proper for auditors to remember that, for many of them, the basic training is in accounting. While the examples discussed in Chapter 15 and in this chapter, are to a large degree, technical in nature, the fact remains that *return on investment* (ROI), a financial criterion, should always be present in any audit. At the bottomline, the test of any solution is: Does it pay?

How much should the ROI on technology be? There is no unique rule or exclusive answer. In my opinion, and that of a number of companies with which I have kept a close connection, ROI in technology should be 22 percent or better. This is not easy, but it is doable. To be achieved, it requires proper planning and targeting, well-chosen projects, first-class people, and fast time-to-delivery schedules.

ROI can be greatly assisted through the choice and use of high technology. Low technology is waste of money; it does not have any return on investment. ERP auditing should always keep this in perspective. Flat earth implementation of both ERP and CRM is quite common — but it is not rewarding.

ROI criteria see to it that a new applications project should be subject to a financial threshold for approval. Nothing is independent of money and of the quality of applied skill. IT directors and all implementers should not only establish a thoroughly studied budget for a new software project, but also incorporate the notions of risk and return. As every trader and every investor knows, risk and return correlate. Control is achieved by considering the risk and cost involved in a technology and what one gets out of it in commercial and financial terms.

If the ERP project is on the borderline between positive and negative return, the screening has to be much finer. Emphasis must be placed during auditing on changes in design able to significantly increase the value of deliverables. In fact, it is a sound practice that every IT proposal be scrutinized in that way because much depends on how well that proposal has been studied.

Particularly focused must be the evaluation in terms of financial performance, which the auditors should follow up on several occasions. ERP projects are in no way immune to this procedure, and there should also be a method to apply demerits. If an ERP project is outside company standards, for example, the auditors may have to ask for more money to audit it because they need to train people more rigorously to follow up on the deficient project.

Experience with auditing IT projects tells me that effective software policies can only then be established, and followed, if one changes the way one thinks about and implements software projects. This means moving away from the current labor-intensive activity in which each application is hand-crafted from individual requirements, and adopting a technology-intensive approach in which more is invested in the development of high-quality reusable components. Together with emphasis on quality and reusability come other issues, including:

- Projected software life cycle
- The role played by prototyping in assisting both end users and software engineers
- The way projects are managed and controlled
- The technology being used and the way it is being used

Software reliability is an entity unto itself, but at the same time it is a composite of the factors outlined in the above four bullets. Reliability is not ability; it is the probability that a component, machine, or system will not fail under specified operational and environmental conditions over a given period of time.

It is important that an ERP audit examines software reliability. Such estimates are made by building probability models using data collected during operations enriched by stress testing. Stress tests typically aim to measure outliers, by and large connected to two types of events:

1. Success instances in which the software correctly processes input under stress conditions
2. Failure events in which the programming product exhibits out-of-specifications behavior

Examples of failure events include errors in computation, mishandled database access, errors in teleprocessing, or outright premature termination of a computing sequence. One of the challenges facing both the ERP auditor and the systems specialists is to find a solution wherein successes and failure events are represented not only implicitly, in function of some definition of *time*, but also by predefined class of likely errors. Complex systems consist of many components, and end-to-end reliability is a function of the reliability of each of these components.[3]

Exhibit 16.7 dramatizes how fast system reliability drops as the number of component parts of a hardware system increases. Companies that have been able to individually identify whose reliability should be tested, and follow up on them, have developed interesting models for stress testing. Some of these have found their way into ROI calculations because each interruption in processing diminishes the level of expected returns. Analytical software reliability evaluations tend to be more rewarding with bought software, such as ERP, because such programs are better structured and input/output points are easier to identify.

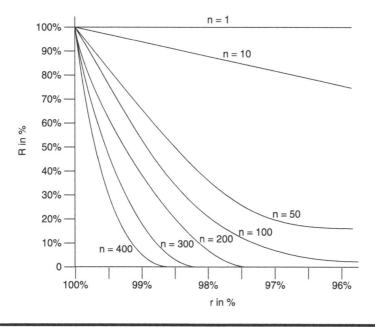

Exhibit 16.7   System Reliability as a Function of the Average Reliability of the Components and the Number of Components

Stress treatment can deliver valuable analytical results when the assumed distribution governing failure events has empirical support and when stress testing procedures cover much of the application's functionality. Without empirical data and the resources to perform substantial testing, it is not possible to reach valid conclusions about software success and failure events.

One of the methods being used in connection with software reliability studies is that of state transitions represented through a Markov chain. The rationale is that *if* one has the outcome of a series of tests and maintains counts of state transitions, *then* one can develop a pattern of software behavior. This provides a record for test coverage and could lead to an evaluation of dependability.

ERP and CRM applications offer themselves to this approach. Available experimental results tend to indicate that the use of transition probabilities may alleviate the need for *a priori* assumptions that do not explicitly incorporate software behavior into their logic. Also, recent advances in automating the generation of states and state transitions tend to make the modeling process practical even for larger systems.

The further-out aim of software reliability estimates is to detect patterns in the way failure events occur and use them to predict future failure events. This can lead to maintenance procedures that improve software quality. It also has an impact on ROI and should be part of auditing ERP and CRM software.

Notes

1. The facts behind this case study are real-life, although the scenario in this chapter section is based on the experience not of one but of two different companies. Therefore, I chose the fictitious name ABC.
2. D.N. Chorafas and Heinrich Steinmann, *Expert Systems in Banking*, Macmillan, London, 1991.
3. D.N. Chorafas, *Statistical Processes and Reliability Engineering*, D. Van Nostrand Co., Princeton, NJ, 1960.

Chapter 17

Auditing the Outsourcing of a Company's Information Technology Services

Outsourcing is one of those terms that mean several things at the same time. From a cost perspective, the goal is to use outside suppliers to reduce expenditures and improve corporate efficiency. This is supposed to enable management to focus on core activities and improve profitability. Such an outcome can be expected if, and only if, everything goes well with the outsourcing contract.

From the viewpoint of deliverables, outsourcing means using outside suppliers to capitalize on available skill, extend the reach of a certain process, or take non-core activities out of the mainstream of one's attention. Whether it is done to reduce costs or improve efficiency, acquire skills, or for some other reason, outsourcing emerged as a much talked-about management strategy in the late 1990s and beyond.

As a strategy, outsourcing is or can be applied to virtually every facet of a company's operations. It includes areas such as information technology, logistics, staffing, direct marketing, technical consulting, healthcare, factoring, invoice processing, fleet vehicle management, business rental services, and teleservices.

Companies tend to rely more and more on outsourcing, but the results are mixed. The outsourcing of a service does not release a company from its responsibilities. In regulated industries, the supervisors keep a watchful eye (see Chapter 17.3). There are also areas where outsourcing can be an unmitigated disaster (see Chapter 17.5).

- Some outsourcing contracts are badly mismanaged.
- Outsourcing will not work for cutting-edge products whose specifications demand high quality.

Therefore, the outsourcing strategy itself and, very obviously, the outsourcing contracts, projects, and other agreements should be audited on a regular basis. It is by no means enough to look at employment numbers and crow about "the company having fewer employees than those of a decade ago for higher turnover," or "that the ratio of market cap to book value has soared." Rather, one must must audit the deliverables, paying full attention to accuracy, quality, timing, and cost; and take the proverbial long, hard look at the legal aspects of outsourcing, including a contract's aftermath.

In the *Christoffer v. Poseidon* case in the United States, a writer was engaged to rewrite stories based on Homer's *Odyssey*. Was the writer merely paid to do the work, or was he also paid for the copyright on what he wrote? The boards of some companies say: "Develop a world-case R&D outfit? Forget it! We would be better off scrapping internal R&D and just buying up hot tech start-ups or outsourcing our research." Olivetti followed that policy in the early 1990s and (for all practical purposes) this company is no longer on the corporate map.

There is less risk in outsourcing the more trivial day-to-day activities that are down the corporate ladder — such as janitorial services. The challenge comes in manufacturing or product designs that depend on focus and first-class skills. Sure enough, they take up a great deal of a company's resources, but at the same time they are also the core business of the company.

The pros say that with the Internet in place, there now exists a mechanism to find and do business with the most efficient provider of a company's core services. This allows a company to consume less of the resources that are in short supply these days and cut the outlay of big money. However, it is not as simple as that because at the same time the company may be cutting down its hopes for the future.

Experience thus far available with outsourcing in different walks of business life tends to challenge prevailing assumptions concerning the wonders of outsourcing. This experience refocuses attention on competitiveness and forces management to reconsider the best way to perform work that needs to be done. Outsourcing has certain advantages, but it may also be one of the most difficult processes to manage — and quite costly to reverse the problems it may cause. Therefore, it requires steady vigilance and a company's auditing must be given a very clear mission to reach into and control the outsourcing business partner's operations.

17.1 Auditing Is a "Must," with Both Good News and Bad News from Outsourcing

Management considering outsourcing is well-advised to ask itself some basic questions: What are we going to outsource? Why are we outsourcing? How are we going to be in charge of this process? What is the projected cost/benefit? How are we going to get the most from an outsourcing arrangement? An even more important query is: Which are the core activities that we do *not* want to outsource?

Under no condition should there be a "we too" attitude: "Others do it, so we too must outsource." True enough, as shown in Exhibit 17.1, the trend in outsourcing has been on the increase in the 1995 to 2000 timeframe. Some projections for the coming years say that such a trend will continue, but this does not mean that *we* have to outsource just because other companies are doing so.

The statistics in Exhibit 17.1 are from the United States. By and large, until recently, outsourcing services were mostly an American phenomenon. Big service deals, such as the $2.4 billion contract IBM signed with Cable & Wireless in September 1998, have been instrumental in opening up the outsourcing market in Europe. By year 2001 there is a rumored backlog of service contracts that would smooth the bumps in market demand for outsourcing services in the coming years.

Thus far, success stories in outsourcing also come from the United States. Cisco Systems owns only two of the 34 plants that manufacture its products. This process has been highly automated. Roughly 85 percent of the orders come into the company without ever being touched by human hands, and 52 percent of them are fulfilled without a Cisco employee being involved.

"To my customers, it looks like one big virtual plant where my suppliers and inventory systems are directly tied into an ecosystem," says Cisco's CEO. "That will be the norm in the future. Everything will be completely connected, both within a company and between companies. The people who get that will have a huge competitive advantage."[1] Yet very few companies are so well-organized. Many look at outsourcing as a way to relegate responsibilities rather than to be super-efficient.

As should be expected, technology companies are more prone to and more able in outsourcing than others. IT is one of lines put on the block. Hewlett-

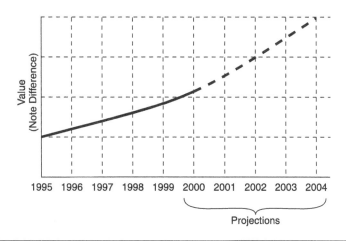

Exhibit 17.1 Outsourcing Grows in Value but this Does Not Imply that One Must Follow the Herd

Packard believes that many companies will outsource their computer operations to telephone companies, Internet service providers (ISPs), or computer makers. HP is even thinking of cutting deals, forgoing up-front payment in exchange for a share of future revenues — a source of reverse outsourcing.

In a way, buying off-the-shelf ERP software is a way of outsourcing the analysis and programming effort that would have to be put into developing such functionality at home. This makes sense. It is better to buy off-the-shelf software than reinvent the wheel by developing ERP in-house. Buying packages, however, is a totally different proposition than outsourcing the company's own IT responsibilities. The programming product is there, available to be thoroughly examined and tested. Even then, as Chapter 16 has advised, auditing should play a key role in ERP software, from purchasing to implementation.

In principle, IT is a core line of business in any modern enterprise. Therefore, it should not be outsourced totally. Citibank reached this conclusion after a long, rigorous study. Other credit institutions took the opposite direction, and at least some of them came to regret it. Chapter 17.5 discusses Morgan Bank's *Pinnacle* project, the goal of which was to hand day-to-day computer support to an outsourcer, but it seems to have turned sour.

Disasters can happen at any time, anywhere, even if the people promoting IT outsourcing say that computer service companies offer less variable, more predictable results than in-house IT solutions. If everything was so positive, the regulators would not have been that careful in laying down precise rules on senior management responsibility and outsourcing accountability (see Chapter 17.3).

If IT is at all outsourced, it should be limited to operations belonging to the structured information environment characterized by the old EDP chores. The difference between a structured and an unstructured information environment is briefly explained in Exhibit 17.2. The unstructured information environment, which includes client handholding and innovation, is this company's cutting edge. It should be never contracted to outsiders. The structured environment is typically served by old technology:

- Services provided by a structured information environment are much more tangible and measurable than those of an unstructured one.
- This permits a company's auditing to exercise its powers at the outsourcer company's risk, and come up with a finding that allows immediate corrective action.

Auditing the outsourcing contract for IT is the subject of this chapter, but IT is by no means the only service that can be outsourced. All other tasks should also be audited (for example, direct marketing services, fleet vehicle management, healthcare processing, business rental services, and teleservice).

IT is not the area where outsourcing important business activities started. To my knowledge, that honor goes to a variety of labor-intensive services such as temporary employment, executive recruitment, permanent placements, outplacement services, skills training, and consulting. There is, however, a huge

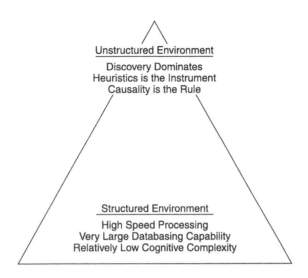

Exhibit 17.2   A Structured Information Environment Can Be Effectively Audited, Leading to Corrective Action

difference between consulting and massive forms of outsourcing. Consulting projects must be focused, capitalize on difficult-to-find skills, gain from the view of independent professional(s), and be *limited* in time. IT outsourcing is characterized by the opposite decision factors: they run on an unlimited time basis, ask for no independent viewpoints, use rather common skills, and usually lack focus.

Human resources contracts fall somewhere in between. Dynamic economic and social trends that developed in the 1990s transformed the temporary staffing sector. Such things as a need for flexibility in the workforce and the drive for cost containment have enabled companies to shift fixed salary costs to variable costs and avoid some of the training expenses. The use of temporary workers from the labor pool's unemployment roster of the past few years has also been a contributing factor.

In a way, outsourcing staffing requirements and outsourcing IT correlate. Technology is both proliferating and changing rapidly, thereby creating a huge demand for skilled personnel. Also, the knowledge gap between technology advances and actual implementation has resulted in growing market demand for IT skills. There is, however, a major difference between temporarily getting IT workers and wholesale outsourcing of IT operations.

If for strategic, cost control, or other reasons, the board decides to do outsourcing, then outsourcing can be done selectively, always keeping the audit function as pivot to any solution. For example, companies often turn to systems integrators:

- For expertise in large-scale systems engineering
- To implement an open systems architecture
- To introduce advanced technologies for which there is no internal skill

In other cases, outsourcing complements in-house capabilities, essentially constituting a technology transfer. Auditing should then carefully examine *if* the outsourcing contract is limited in time and in-house personnel are properly trained during technology transfer.

However, to get the most from any selective outsourcing deal, management must do plenty of homework prior to awarding a contract. There should be a thorough *needs evaluation* that includes a comprehensive description of what is to be potentially outsourced, an estimate of the resources required to perform the work in-house after the contract's end, and a careful analysis of available outsourcing solutions — with pluses, minuses, benefits, and costs.

17.2   Beware of Credit Risk and Operational Risk with Outsourcing Contracts

Some people say: "Outsourcing might work if it allows executives to concentrate on primary goals, if skilled staff are not available, or if our business requires major investment in new technology." These are three excuses whose aftermath would be seen some years down the line — when it is too late to redress a bad situation.

It is unmanagerial to work only on the basis of potentially positive *ifs*. Management should always consider outsourcing that may not work *if* cost savings are projected lightly; *if* relinquishing control is too risky; *if* services to be obtained are poorly defined or understood; *if* the outsourcer sells his services as a sideline; and, most importantly, *if* the contract assumes considerable *credit risk*.

Credit risk exists with any contract, not only when a bank lends money. The outsourcer, the company's counterparty, may fail. This will leave a gaping hole in the company's IT operations, and lead to scrambling to put together again an IT department on a moment's notice.

Fire brigade approaches are not a sign of good management. Therefore, *if* after a thorough examination of pros and cons, the company decides to go for an outsourcing contract, *then* the lawyers should be called in to elaborate *a priori* the clauses that will apply in case of outsourcer's failure — including provisions for the transfer of:

- Responsibilities associated with the outsourcing contract
- Personnel who will come under the company's wings
- Source programs of applications software
- Computers, communications gear, and software that should be transferred to permit the company's IT to restart

To a very significant extent, this resembles what was discussed in Chapter 6 about elaborating contractual clauses for bought software — but at the same time it is broader and deeper because it has associated with it so much more operational risk[2] than the single purchase of off-the-shelf programming products (more about this later).

Only lightweight management would forget about outsourcing exposure because of credit risk. Everything else may be positive about an outsourcing contract (which is not so often the case), but one day the outsourcer asks for protection from creditors under Chapter 11, or goes right out of business. In my opinion, the evaluation of credit risk taken with the outsourcer is a core activity for any company's management.

Outsourcing is not only a matter of technology and know-how, but also — indeed, even more so — of *trust*. Trust can be defined as confidence in the successful continuation of a relationship and positive expectations about the other party's motives as well as behavior. Trust and virtue correlate. Virtue was defined by Socrates as knowledge that cannot be taught. The virtue of the company's counterparty gives the company confidence that counterparty behavior will respond to company expectations and honor company goodwill.

People participating in the research that led to this book have suggested that they experienced great difficulty in developing trust in outsourcing projects when this requires the cooperation of third parties in tough, high-stress situations. To appreciate this statement, one should keep in mind that there are two types of firms going for IT outsourcing contracts:

1. Large firms that tend to be insensitive to client requests, particularly those of smaller clients
2. Small firms that are much more sensitive, but do not have the financial backing, and, therefore, the credit risk is much higher

Part of the problem in managing internal IT and then outsourcing IT is that each organization — client and vendor — is an independent entity and evidently pursues its own goals and financial policies. This impacts both credit risk and operational risk — starting with the lack of complete project control in an end-to-end sense.

Operational risk is a complex issue into which integrates a significant number of fairly disparate factors. These range from management risk connected with corporate governance due to lower quality of management; to information technology risk, organizational risk, transactions risk, payments and settlements risk, and many others. Operational risk is the danger of losses sparked by failures in operational processes and systems that support them. This type of risk exists with all business activities and is an intrinsic element of industrial processes, internal procedures, and technical infrastructure.

Few companies appreciate that outsourcing their IT operations significantly increases *their* operational risk. The irony is that they eventually add to this exposure through ill-studied contracts that lead to friction. Friction results in distrust, and distrust hurts performance. The next step is finger-pointing as each firm focuses on its own interests and seeks to explain how the counterparty failed in "this" or "that" part of the project.

Operational risk embedded in counterparty relations is diminished when mutual trust leads participants to work closer together rather than seek ways to deflect blame. Quite often, intercompany relationships involve a psychological contract that acts as a metalayer to the formal, written contract. This psychological contract consists of unwritten and largely unspoken expectations held by the counterparties about each other's obligations, prerogatives, and contributions.

To a large extent, it is up to the service providers to figure out what their customers want and how to give it to them effectively and economically. To become appropriately informed, they should ask plenty of questions and listen to the answers. Both parties in IT outsourcing should appreciate that there is a lot riding on the outcome, particularly when outsourcers and other service providers start to live up to their clients' expectations, and outsourcing companies are well prepared, and therefore able to help them to do just that.

Auditing should always seek out and verify compliance with the written contract, but there is little auditing can do in relation to the psychological contract, other than saying that the chemistry between the two parties does not work. Auditing should also take a careful look at the volatility in credit risk associated with the outsourcer, which the opening paragraphs of this chapter section addressed. Assistance in this mission may come from both the company's credit department and from independent agencies such as Standard & Poor's, Moody's Investors Service, Fitch IBCA, and others.[3]

The reference to the contribution of independent rating agencies should be seen from the angle of the credit risk that the company assumes when it enters into an outsourcing contract. The principle is that a common, well-understood, and believable indicator of exposure adds transparency to any credit risk measurement profile.

In a way, the use ratings by an independent agency represent a degree of outsourcing the credit risk analysis. In principle, it is more efficient for one credible agency to rate companies than for each market participant to conduct its own research. This is a good example of outsourcing because it saves money for all involved, and it provides a level ground for the evaluation of credit risk. There are also constraints. In the financial industry, for example:

- Rating process can be so much more effective if each investor understands each credit risk within the context of his own portfolio of exposures and risk tolerances.
- At the same time, outsourcing credit risk analysis duties can only be accomplished up to a certain extent through rating. It would not cover quality of work in IT outsourcing.

In connection with IT outsourcing, auditing should accomplish the jobs outlined by both bullets. Timeliness of processing, quality of work, security of data, confidentiality of reports, and other characteristics weigh heavily on how well or how poorly the outsourcer performs its duties and fulfills its contractual clauses.

17.3 The Regulators Have Established Guidelines for Accountability in IT Outsourcing

The audit department is well-advised to follow rulings, directives, and guidelines established by regulators for accountability in IT outsourcing. Even if these address primarily financial institutions, they contain sound advice that can guide the hand of the IT auditor in an effective manner. An example is recent guidance by the Federal Reserve about the outsourcing of information and transaction processing.

In March 2000, the Fed issued a supervisory letter (SR-00-4) to the attention of bank management. Its theme was risks associated with outsourcing of critical information and transaction processing activities, as well as the risks that might result. To face such exposures, banks are expected to implement controls over outsourced IT that are equivalent to those that would be implemented if the activity were conducted in-house.

The Fed says that a bank should show sufficient due diligence to satisfy itself of a service provider's "competence and stability, both financially and operationally, to provide the expected services and meet any commitments." This due diligence identifies the duties of auditing in connection with both inter-wall and outsourced information technology. Essentially what the Federal Reserve is saying is that the same diligence in IT auditing should be extended all the way to the activities being subcontracted to the outsourcer. The Fed also provides guidance on numerous outsourcing controls, including:

- Issues that should be addressed in contracts made with third-party providers of outsourced services (see Chapter 17.2).
- Maintenance of access to critical information by the contracting of a credit institution and its authorized agents
- Contingency business, including resumption planning for outsourced functions should anything happen to the contracting firm or its systems

The Federal Reserve has also elaborated on the controls needed in connection with outsourced arrangements by banks with service providers located outside the United States. But I would particularly like to stress the attention of a company's auditors to the implications of the third bullet. Outsourcing does not mean relegating IT to somebody else. A company retains full responsibility for it, and contingency planning is a "must."

It could as well happen that the company itself becomes the outsourcer. For this case, too, there exist regulations. In late June 2000, the Office of the Controller of the Currency (OCC) issued an Interpretive Letter (No. 888) declaring that, under the excess capacity doctrine, it is permissible for a bank to offer its electronic storage and retrieval system to external clients for financial and *nonfinancial* activities. This Interpretive Letter first declares that federal banking law permits credit institutions to provide electronic imaging services under a variety of circumstances, including:

- Financial and nonfinancial document handling for banks and other financial institutions
- Good-faith excess capacity made available to nonfinancial entities for data and document processing services

Regarding excess capacity, the OCC says that it has been already applied with respect to a variety of resources, including real estate, electronic facilities, and other resources acquired in connection with acquisitions of companies engaged in various activities. The OCC Interpretive Letter also states that good-faith excess capacity can arise for several reasons, among them:

- Because of the characteristics of the market, available facilities may exceed the bank's current and projected needs.
- The equipment that is presently installed and must be paid for might have capacity beyond what is necessary to meet peak period demand.

As is to be expected, and as auditors should always do, the OCC also focuses on the risks faced by each bank that outsources IT functions. A case in point is a bank outsourcing its internal audit skills to the firm that performs the bank's external audit. This is not unheard of. On July 27, 2000, the *American Banker* reported that an OCC survey of national banks in the Northeast revealed that "one third outsource their internal audit function, and half of those use the same firm for the external audit."

The problem is one of putting in place the right safeguards. When a bank selects one firm to provide both internal and external audit services, the arrangement creates an inherent conflict and eliminates the normal checks and balances that can be expected to operate where the internal and external audit functions are performed independently. Therefore, the OCC cautions bank boards of directors that:

- Outsourcing the internal audit function in no way relieves the board of directors and CEO of their responsibility.
- Establishing, maintaining, and operating effective and independent audit programs is a matter of their personal accountability.

This means that in the regulators' opinion, outsourcing — particularly the outsourcing of internal audit functions — obliges the institution to have an internal officer of unquestioned stature, competence, and integrity supervising the work of the outsourced internal audit. He or she must report directly to the board of directors or the Audit Committee. Evidently, a similar principle must apply with outsourcing IT.

American regulators have special concerns about internal audit outsourcing arrangements at smaller community banks. At smaller companies, neither the bank nor the outside auditors have the staff or resources to implement the protective procedures recommended by the federal bank regulatory agencies. The maintenance of independence can be even more important in banks that lack the resources to manage their internal audit effectively. In a similar manner, the maintenance of IT skills internal to the company is not a matter that is negotiable.

It must be noted that European central banks are also just as diligent in bringing to management's attention the risks involved in outsourcing, as well as the fact that responsibility and accountability rest squarely with the board and senior management of the company doing the outsourcing. Regulators will not accept reckless approaches. This is exemplified well by the basic principles for outsourcing and outskilling of the German Federal Banking Supervision Office.

The German regulators have made all credit institutions under their jurisdiction aware of the fact that any agreement with a third party necessarily involves opening up policies and procedures; therefore, it must be explicitly approved by the board of directors and senior management of the outsourcing company. Clauses in any agreement must specify standards for working with the vendor, and means for their observance as well as their auditing.

This auditing should take place, and outsourcing evaluations should be done, on an ongoing basis. Not only should there be a written contract, but this must also include detail on conditions and controls. In all matters involving IT outsourcing, confidentiality and security of information must be the cornerstone of any outsourcing decision.

- *Auditing rights*, say the German regulators, must be spelled out to enable the bank to conduct a meaningful analysis of third-party performance.
- The outsourcing contract should specify that both the credit institution and the supervisory authorities must have access to all third-party working papers, reports, and databases.

Each one of these references may need to be audited at any time, at the discretion of the outsourcing company or of the regulators.

Assets must not be commingled because of outsourcing. If they are, ownership of each asset should be fully identified. Furthermore, the bank's internal control system must be extended to all outsourced functions.

The German Federal Banking Supervisory Office also instructs the institutions under its control that to counteract operational risk, the bank's senior management should maintain, at all times, overall responsibility for all factors affecting the proper execution of operations. Among other issues, cost supervision is very important because costs increase with time — subverting the original conditions of the contract. A similar point is made about security. These matters are brought to the reader's attention because their applicability goes well beyond credit institutions — to practically cover all companies.

17.4   Controlling the Conditions that Induce Management Toward an Outsourcing Decision

In many of the research meetings that led to this book, it was suggested by the counterparties that one of the key reasons that makes management decide in favor of outsourcing is that "this" or "that" competitor firm offers its clients greater speed, flexibility, or expertise than in-house IT; and to match it, one needs outsourcing. In other cases, outsourcing may be the only alternative for creating a new product or service, because of:

- The cost involved, and hence the bottom line
- Available technical expertise ready to be tapped
- A way to escape organizational conflicts, so relevant in mergers and acquisitions

Consider these two arguments. First, the matching of competitors' speed, flexibility, or skill through outsourcing is a fake. This is what a company should be doing by significantly upgrading its own resources. If it cannot achieve that through internal drive and expertise, it cannot buy it in the marketplace either.

There may be more substance, however, with regard to the message conveyed by the three bullets, although there are also perils. In late 1997, Novartis, the Swiss pharmaceutical company formed from the merger of Ciba and Sandoz, reorganized its corporate IT because the merger revealed a number of areas in which IT services were being duplicated.

In the course of this restructuring, Novartis chose outsourcing, embarking on an outsourcing joint-venture with IBM and a new IT company currently owned 70 percent by IBM and 30 percent by Novartis. Under the terms of this seven-year contract, this company will eventually be transferred 100 percent to IBM. This means that by 2004, Novartis will find itself without internal IT, or will have to duplicate its functions.

The irony of this outsourcing "solution" has been that it did not necessarily reduce employment at Novartis. Instead, the 220 staff members originally employed by Ciba and Sandoz were to be based at Novartis' Basle headquarters, taking on responsibility for corporate applications development, networking, data center, and IT support. At the same time, outside of corporate headquarters, responsibility for IT services at the company's business units in over 100 countries remained in local hands. In other words, the duplication of IT costs and functions started on day 1. This is as good an example as one can find of pure mismanagement.

This is one example out of many that demolishes the argument that many companies outsource IT and other resources to get to market quickly, while at the same time they hope to reduce costs and benefit from flexibility. Companies often make the wrong assumption that they will be able to scale back as they please. It does not work that way because:

- They retain most — if not all — of their original IT staff, adding to costs through the new contract.
- The outsourcing contract they sign does not provide clauses about the hoped-for flexibility.

Another argument heard these days is that the Web would work its miracle when it comes to IT outsourcing. This, too, is smoke and mirrors by the unable who is being asked by the unwilling to do the unnecessary. Auditing must be very careful not to fall into the trap of such euphoric thinking that the Internet is the miracle solution to everything.

True enough, as seen in Chapter 3, Web-based activities are causing some companies to take a fresh look at their outsourcing needs, including technology transfer and exit procedures. This, however, should not be confused with relegation of management's responsibilities.

Telecommunications is another example where lots of homework is required prior to outsourcing. In a traditional deal between a corporation and a telecommunications outsourcer, the corporation entrusts the entire telecom services, or a segment of its business, to a third party. This is sometimes done on a global basis. But benefits will not come automatically. There are many prerequisites to be met.

The keyword to a successful telecommunications outsourcing deal, and one that makes more sense than in data processing, is preparation. Top management should focus on IT management's ability to define the telecommunications mission in concrete, no-nonsense terms — as well as its ability to put the vendor's offering in the context of the company's interests and the kind of alternatives the market offers.

This study should be carefully audited. As a rule, the formality and discipline required to prepare a Request for Information (see also Chapter 6) yields a comprehensive and fairly accurate description of the services sought. It also provides the basis on which to judge the ability to direct and supervise outsourcing suppliers from a single well-written set of technical, financial, and managerial requirements.

The quality of the Request for Information, and subsequently of the Request for Offers, should be audited both for conformance to company policies — and regulators directives — and from a technical viewpoint, including security, back-up, and disaster recovery. Quite similarly, in evaluating the vendor's responses, there are both general and special aspects to check and to audit.

- A properly prepared proposal should describe the outsourcer's management methods in depth, to understand *if* the provider masters the functions that it sells.
- References should be given to past success on similar projects; and these must be quantifiable, backed up with names of clients who can verify the statements made.

As explained in detail in Chapter 6, professional credentials are critical. Therefore, such references should give a sense of whether the outsourcer can adequately deal with complexity, control costs, assume the risks, respond to deadlines, and observe established standards. The outsourcers' proposals should provide a detailed plan for migrating to their service offering and another plan for migrating back again to the company, if necessary.

Should there be a transfer of property — even one contemplated some time in the future — the technical proposal should identify tangible and intangible property to be transferred, including hardware, software, licenses, leases, goodwill, and — very obviously — existing workforce. It must as well spell out terms and conditions for acceptance of the outsourced solution and its deliverables.

The audit of the contract should concentrate on terms and conditions for canceling or modifying outsourced IT services, including contingencies for the outsourcing client. Contractual clauses should spell out the milestone(s) and termination date(s), if any. Because no contract lasts forever, an outsourcing negotiation should look at a deal throughout its life cycle, such as five to seven years and pay attention to the question of how to exit the deal by way of organized, acceptable practices.

The audit should appreciate that if it is difficult to establish the clauses regarding guarantees and deliverables in a rational manner, it is even more difficult to get people to focus on the divorce. As a result, too much is left open to post-completion, or better times. Too often, management wants to get over the IT outsourcing negotiations and says, "Let's sign the deal and work out the details later." The audit should sanction such arguments.

A well-written outsourcing contract would be most careful to define the authority of each party to assign, supervise, and remove personnel from the IT program, set and observe precise performance guarantees, and write down guidelines on the use of proprietary information. Part and parcel of the same reference is definition of ownership rights where new joint developments are contemplated.

In conclusion, no two outsourcing deals are alike, but the best have service-level agreements and change control procedures. They incorporate — even demand — built-in penalties, either financial or in the form of additional services, should service levels go awry. Companies now see the need for an exit strategy at the time of initial negotiations — and must prepare for it.

Experience with outsourcing deals that went sour, such as the examples in Chapter 17.5, suggests that guidelines should be put in place for services and metrics, including how measurements are carried out, and the terms of the deal should be reexamined on a regular basis. Open-eyed companies also want access to information on the quality of services being managed for them, often through monitoring or diagnostic tools implemented as part of the contract.

17.5 Case Studies of IT Outsourcing that Has Turned Sour

These days, more and more companies are outsourcing their information systems. They do so because they do not understand that information technology is part of their *core business* and that outsourcing can have a negative strategic impact, in addition to the other operational risks they are taking. KPMG did a study on outsourcing involving 123 large companies. What it found was that:

- 40 percent of the dissatisfied companies indicated that they are too dependant on their supplier.
- 37 percent indicated that they lack influence over service levels that they receive.
- 35 percent complained that they have no control over their supplier.

Many companies are determined to ensure that, the second time round, they will get a better deal. As a trend, however, companies are getting increasingly disenchanted with the results of outsourcing. A growing number of reports indicate that roughly three out of four firms have serious concerns about the whole outsourcing process, or at least some aspects of it.

In my experience, wholesale outskilling and outsourcing projects lead nowhere. The General Bank of Luxembourg signed a contract with Andersen Consulting for 50 systems experts to work for three years. A long time after this timeframe elapsed, the project was still going. This is the usual case with most companies — not a once-in-a-lifetime affair.

Bankgesellschaft Berlin has been employing 90 expatriates in-house to revamp its risk management system. By a strange twist, all attention seems to have focused on IT, not on internal controls. What has escaped management's attention is that when the internal controls system is poor, no IT outskilling would fill the gap. The restructuring of internal controls and of IT should go hand-in-hand. However, if there is a priority to be given, then this should go to internal control.

A valuable addition to these two examples, which comes from the banking industry, is the case of a consortium set up to serve a major airline, two hotel chains, and a car-rental business with the best that IT can offer. The *Confirm* project is one of the better-known failures in outsourcing. Here are the facts. In the mid-1980s, the *Intrico Consortium* was formed by American Airlines Information Services (AMRIS), Hilton Hotels, Marriott Hotels, and Budget Rent-a-Car.

The goal was to develop, use, and market the most advanced reservation system. Known as *Confirm*, this project:

- Was cancelled five years down the line after a number of lawsuits
- Featured millions of dollars in overruns
- Led to bitter accusations among the senior executives involved in this disaster

Confirm's original goals became unattainable as hundreds of people working for so many years lost sight of what was wanted. Something similar in terms of high costs and low results characterized IT outsourcing by Cable and Wireless Communications (CWC). In early September 1998, it was announced that CWC would pay $3 billion to IBM Global Services to solve incompatibility problems between its customer management systems then used in CWC's IT infrastructure. IBM Global Services was to take responsibility for:

- 750 millions instructions per second of mainframe capacity
- 7.4 terabytes of information to be made available to the system
- 15,600 desktops and 370 midrange computers and servers

Under the ten-year contract, IBM was supposed to do away with the various legacy billing systems then in operation. They were to be replaced by IBM's own Integrated Customer Management Systems (ICMS) software. This was supposed to enable CWC to provide customers with a single bill for multiple telephone lines and cable TV services. It did not quite happen that way.

In early 1998, IBM installed ICMS in the networks formerly owned by Nynex. As part of the deal, CWC was transferring 1000 staff members to the IBM Global Services unit, but it retained ownership and operation of its customer databases. CWC expected to recoup its costs over the ten years in wage bills, overheads, and through greater efficiencies. This, however, would prove difficult because IBM planned to hire 400 additional staff members, in addition to the 1000 personnel transferred from CWC.

A similar story with additions to personnel rather than trimming characterized J.P. Morgan's outsourcing. In mid-1996, J.P. Morgan signed a seven-year contract with a consortium known as the Pinnacle Alliance. The goal was to handle day-to-day computer support. This contract, which was worth $2 billion, put together some of the rivals in IT: Computer Sciences Corporation (CSC), Andersen Consulting, AT&T, and Bell Atlantic.

The Pinnacle Alliance established its own offices within the Morgan Bank to manage four major data centers (in New York, London, Paris, and at the Delaware headquarters), as well as other core IT systems. CSC has been the lead supplier, managing about 80 percent of the Pinnacle business, and was directly responsible to Morgan and the other Pinnacle members.

- Critics have been questioning whether this outsourcing strategy can work, pointing out that it is not really cost-effective.
- In J.P. Morgan's case, within a year and a half of Pinnacle's start, the bank added people — it did not slim down.

According to reports, one third of Morgan's IT-related staff, amounting to more than 900 extra people, have been added to the bank's payroll in less than a year and a half since the time Pinnacle was set up — May 1996 to October 1997.[4] Most of the new recruits were employed to run new computer development projects started after the IT transfer or support critical systems the Morgan Bank considered too vital to outsource.

The pros say that, no matter the expense, outsourcing liberated the bank to get down to its strategic goal of putting technology experts physically closer to the traders who create the bank's revenue. But to the critics, the split between new developments and established operations, between competitive systems and legacy programs, has taken its toll.

IT outsourcing can also be costly in terms of assets, as the case of Banca di Roma documents. Originally, outsourcing companies asked for payment in hard currency for their services when they took over a project. But this has changed. With a 1997 outsourcing contract, EDS took equity in the Italian bank as down payment. Such is a different sort of compensation:

- EDS was given 2 percent of the equity in Banca di Roma for the bargain price of 160 billion lire ($91 million).
- The outsourcing contract for managing the bank's IT resources has been projected to last ten years.

This contract is said to be worth between 2.3 and 3 trillion lire ($1.4 billion to $1.7 billion) in the long run, but experts think it will eventually cost much more than that. It is the largest of its kind thus far signed in Europe, although this honor may not last long because there are also other organizations that are moving in the same direction. In fact, some are selling to third parties all of their in-house IT business.

In 1997, Banco Ambrosiano Veneto, a major bank in northern Italy, sold off its IT operations in a bid to slash administrative costs. The stated goal was cost reduction at an estimated level of $200 million over the next ten years.[5] Even if this materializes — which is not at all sure — $200 million is a drop in the bucket for a major bank and in no way justifies losing control of its IT. Based on false hypotheses, the board decided that information technology lies outside the bank's core activity — a patently incorrect statement, and decreed that outsourcing would lead to significant savings from improved efficiency (??) — incorrectly interpreted as being the trivial sum of $20 million per year, at best.

How wrong senior management can be is further shown by the fact that this deal did not come cheap. Banco Ambrosiano Veneto would have to pay out over $600 million during the ten-year period to Germany's Systemhaus, the IT services division of Daimler Benz. This is part of the cost of running the bank's divested IT operations, although the credit institution retained its co-involvement in applications development, evidently at an added cost.

Financial institutions that have a better sense of return on investment and profitability have come to exactly the opposite conclusion. Citibank also thought at one time about outsourcing its legacy programs. This took a two years study; but in May 1997, two days before signing, the bank wisely pulled out following a revolt by its business managers and for return on investment reasons.

As the disasters in IT outsourcing discussed in this chapter section document, auditors should always be eager to study the many failures that have occurred with IT outsourcing to provide themselves with experience on what can go wrong. Each case study gives a useful message on outsourcing pitfalls. I would not go as far as to say, as some critics do, that the only thing that has been consistent with the results of outsourcing is their inconsistency. However, IT outsourcing is a concept that needs a breath of fresh air and a sharp pencil. A rigorous audit can provide at least some clarity on the do's and don'ts.

Notes

1. *Business Week,* August 28, 2000.
2. D.N. Chorafas, *Managing Operational Risk. Risk Reduction Strategies for Investment Banks and Commercial Banks*, Euromoney, London, 2001.
3. D.N. Chorafas, *Managing Credit Risk*, Vol. 1: *Analyzing, Rating and Pricing the Probability of Default*, Euromoney, London, 2000.
4. *Information Strategy,* October 1997.
5. *Information Strategy,* July/August 1997.

Chapter 18

Case Studies in Auditing Financial Statements and ERP Reports

Case studies are the best way to examine the scope, extent, and character of auditing practice. They allow one to consider some of the problems that auditing may encounter, and make it possible to illustrate constructive practices, possibly counterproductive practices, factors entering the auditor's line of reasoning, ways followed in outlining findings, and means used in forming conclusions.

First and foremost, the successful auditor is independent of political pressures, is alert to the possibility of unfavorable work conditions, and knows that he or she can come across unexpected findings even if these may seem improbable. An auditor must consider all possibilities and develop sufficient evidence to prove that errors, omissions, fraud, major discrepancies, lack of compliance, and other events do or do not exist. The auditor must be careful about accepting plausible instead of factual explanations and must document evidence and question the obvious and take the time to turn all stones, even those neatly placed, to see what they hide.

The experience embedded in past cases is so important because the size and complexities of modern companies provide ample opportunities for errors, and sometimes for malpractice. In this sense, case histories are a good means for illustrating the character of internal audit practices, outlining some of the problems that can be found along the way.

Because so much depends on the auditor's alertness and ability to detect all deviations from norms and flush them out, even if they may have a plausible reason, the auditor must have access to all documents connected to the audit. Special attention must be paid to events lying in the gray area between legality and illegality, usually exemplified through some kind of dubious instances. In principle, the successful auditor is:

- A constant student of human nature, which is inseparable from the execution of daily work and assignments pertaining to control operations
- A person who has learned to review and appraise business activities in light of corporation interests, with the goal of safeguarding the assets of the shareholders

In terms of specific auditing projects, Chapter 15 presented the auditing of IT operations; Chapter 16 focused on auditing enterprise resource planning and customer relationship management systems; and Chapter 17 dealt with auditing the outsourcing of a company's IT services. The present chapter begins with the principles of analyzing and auditing financial statements and ERP reports.

The auditing of financial statements is followed by small case studies, each focused on a specific topic (for example, the implementation of CRM software, adequate but obsolete controls applied in an ineffective way, the aftermath of inadequate internal controls, and defective inventory management and subsequent corrective action). What so often surprises me in industry is that corrective action by senior management is a path that sparks controversy within and outside the firm.

18.1   Analyzing and Auditing Contents of Financial Statements and ERP Reports

The two principal financial statements are the balance sheet, which reports the financial position of a company at a given moment in time, and the income statement (or profit and loss [P&L] statement), which summarizes its performance over a given period of time. Both the company's own management and other stakeholders can obtain from these statements useful information about the going business. There are, however, inherent limitations in information contained in these financial statements. These limitations prevent financial statements from providing the answers to all ongoing issues. Even some of the most important questions raised about an ongoing business may not be addressed.

This reference to limitations of financial statements is important in the context of this book because it applies hand-in-glove to ERP reports. ERP reports can be seen as assimilated financial statements. Information-wise, they find themselves in the catchment area of the balance sheet and of the income statement. Therefore, analyzing and auditing them is an important function contributing to the reliability of their content.

To appreciate the sense of the reference made in the preceding paragraph, recall that the principles and conduct of business have advanced over time, resulting in a growing array of financial operations. These operations have become more involved, and this has ramifications. Errors embedded in statements being produced can devastate a company. The possibilities of fraud also increase. Therefore, the preceding chapters emphasized the point that audits must cover a far wider scope than they formerly did. It is also necessary that auditors:

- Keep pace with the evolution of the operations, including products, markets, and technology
- Contribute in leading the business to a state of reliable financial reporting[1] and dependable documentation

Dependable documentation is a basic reason why audits must be executed in connection with ERP information and associated reports. The role of the auditor goes beyond the detection of errors and fraud, as seen in the case studies presented in this chapter. Furthermore, in the past the auditor made many surprise visits so that employees would be caught if they were in arrears in their work or did sloppy work, guilty of mistakes that they had not taken time to locate, or involved in fraud and had not had time to cover such dishonest transactions.

Presently, however, in the majority of cases, the auditor's visit is a carefully planned arrangement. Auditing by surprise is done online, interactively by accessing the databases. In contrast, the broad business service and the analytical nature of the job the auditor does when visiting one of the company's sites make preliminary arrangements necessary so that the auditor's work will be more rigorous, performed in the minimum of time commensurate with good practice.

Within the general area of his or her duties, whether addressing the broader context of financial statements or ERP and CRM reports and procedures contributing to them, the auditor must follow a comprehensive code of accounting principles. These should be kept current by intensive research. The auditor must be able to make a realistic definition of truth in accounting — including technical matters — aimed at producing representations that are trustworthy for the purposes intended and able to give an accurate appreciation of facts.

Supplementing this body of principles that should guide the auditor's hand is the achievement of standards, terminology, and methods of presentation. This is a company challenge, rather than one befalling each individual auditor alone. There must also be adequately defined requirements for disclosure aimed at ensuring accounting truth and technical truth.

Auditing functions, including ERP auditing, will be so much more effective if there is comparability and uniformity of rules throughout the organization, as well as uniform methods of presentation in financial statements and ERP or CRM reports. This is an organizational duty, to be ensured by senior management.

Only through the achievement of these operational characteristics can the auditing of ERP reports and statements build confidence among the people using the findings and trying to tune-up the system. The effort to make the company's reporting structure more reliable as a whole is not a part-time job; indeed, it is the core of auditing.

Within this broad framework, it is also to be expected that auditing and other internal control systems and procedures will continue to be refined. For example, cost accounting needs its subordinate body of concepts and principles (see Chapter 13). In an end-to-end ERP environment, distribution costs must be given the same consideration that manufacturing costs get. Both are critical to financial planning and both give input to financial reports. The principle guiding this implementation of a subordinate body of concepts to good governance must be uniform and should be applied in all corners of the company — not just in one location — in an effective manner.

By "all corners" I mean throughout the network or R&D laboratories, factories, sales outlets, and all other locations through which the company operates. An end-to-end solution can lead to an increased understanding of the details of business activity. In turn, this permits auditors to state with greater assurance whether or not financial statements and ERP reports are fairly presented and conform to generally accepted principles — consistent with those followed in the preceding month, quarter, semester, or year.

Audits must pinpoint exceptions with a high level of assurance. Human errors may exist in all corners of operations and of inspection. There are many transactions that two equally well-informed and well-intentioned auditors might treat differently, and this fact prohibits anyone from stating that the final statements are precisely accurate. Therefore, in making their examination, auditors should not rely only on a detailed rechecking of the journalizing and posting of each transaction. Rather, they must satisfy themselves that the accounting and every other reporting system they audit is designed to ensure that data is processed properly — and that it can be handled analytically by all authorized persons. In other words, they must affirm the existence and effectiveness of both the internal control system and the methodology being used. This is the theme of the first, second, and third case study.

18.2   Case Study: A CRM Application that Left Much to Be Desired

At the origin of this case study was a request by the marketing department to audit the recent implementation of CRM which, according to the marketing czar, had failed to meet most of its objectives. The primary goal of the application under investigation was a CRM-based collaborative processing aimed at:

- Managing and distributing business intelligence to those who need it for improved performance or for their sales quotas
- Integrating this business intelligence with unstructured information elements to make available a pattern of market behavior

Supported by the newly installed CRM software, collaborative processing was supposed to give users a single Web interface from which to gain access to all CRM business information allowing them to publish information, subscribe to and receive multiple types of data streams based on time or business events, discuss and share customer intelligence with others inside the organization, and distribute this information to business managers via technologies such as the Web, groupware, and office systems.

This was the primary goal, but the results being obtained did not provide for what was planned. When the tests were made, the chosen CRM Information Portal was theoretically able to help organize, find, access, understand, publish, and subscribe to business information, but the practical output of the application fell far short of this goal.

IT had exercised its discretion in choosing this CRM programming product. The marketing department had set the objectives, but was only slightly involved in the Request for Offers, the system tests, and the final choice. This junior role had already produced some friction between marketing and IT. Marketing executives, however, had seen the results of the tests and judged them to be rather satisfactory.

After the CRM implementation, the obtained output fell short of objectives, and marketing put the blame on the IT department. It said that IT had not taken the necessary precautions to ensure that CRM business intelligence results were appropriately combined with unstructured information such as office data, web streams, live feeds, and presentations.

Neither was the distribution of CRM business information as timely as was promised — or should have been. According to marketing, CRM was no more than 20 percent successful. Other woes included wanting support or pervasive devices like WAP phones, PDAs, organizers, and browsers. Everything pointed to less-than-expected performance by the CRM Information Portal. This, marketing said, reduced business efficiency because it made it difficult to deliver information in an integrative way, with personalization, featuring *publish and subscribe,* and permitting automatic delivery.

Alerting was one of the missing features. Marketing said that what it got out of CRM implementation was some *déjà vu* supports for customer lists, sales statistics, and customer chat on the Web site. IT answered that the promised CRM functionality was embedded in the programming product, but all company departments had to collaborate to bring it to the fore. Instead, they kept their information close to their chest.

The audit found that while the portal could act as a single user interface to many existing applications, the original specs for business intelligence tools and analytic features were not fulfilled. Nor was it easy to extend CRM's collaborative processing to business partners because customers and suppliers themselves were not ready for this kind of pass-through implementation.

In a private chat with the CEO, the chief auditor suggested that some of the promised wonders of CRM were, in the auditor's judgment, hype. In addition, the programming product that was chosen did not respond to requirements established by market research that preceded the CRM's choice. The market research had brought in evidence that customers prefer sites that:

- Are easy to navigate
- Can be personalized
- Offer efficient online service
- Enable users to contribute and compare opinions

The chief auditor further stated that the company had too many legacy IT applications that were not ready to provide support for such services, even if the bought software might have ensured such services under ideal conditions. Also, in the chief auditor's opinion, there was evidence by marketing that customers coming online were intolerant of glitches and poor customer service.

Where the company failed the most, in the chief auditor's mind, was in getting itself ready for advanced Internet services of which CRM was supposed to be a part. To meet customer demands, the auditor said, the company would have to think more like a retailer, adding that not only manufacturing companies but banks too have learned this. For example, their lead bank said that a third of customers opening an online bank account over the course of a year closed it again, citing as reasons complicated navigation and unsatisfactory customer service.

As for collaborative processing — which is supposed to allow customers to subscribe to receive information about products and services and to make use of interactive supports in order to transact business — the CRM package did not deliver as promised. This made it difficult for the company to fulfill its promise to provide more personal customer service. The CEO asked the chief auditor to prepare a written report with his findings and submit it to the Audit Committee.

In terms of obtained substandard results, the auditor's final report criticized the vendor, CRM package, IT department, and the other company departments for less-than-expected contributions. The vendor had promised a collaborative infrastructure that capitalized on its unique experiences and technology in information management. This was not delivered. In terms of the company's own internal control accomplishing what was promised in terms of required integration of people, places, and things, this too left much to be desired.

- *The people* were the product planners, salesmen, and customers who by working online should have been able to receive interactive supports.
- *The places* were both physical and virtual, where people needed to come together to collaborate — whether brick-and-mortar or the Web.
- *The things* were what people created: physical products and data they capture, store, classify, analyze, and share.

The auditor's report suggested that the company's internal control had an important role to play in improving performance in all three bullets, alerting management to dysfunction before things reach a breaking point — and without having to wait for the next audit. However, a different inspection had shown that the company's internal control system was rather obsolete and unable to work at Internet time. Therefore, the audit suggested that top management must see to it that internal control is being tuned to work like a clock.

18.3 Case Study: Obsolete Controls Applied in an Ineffective Way

An internal auditor was making a systematic review of procedures and controls relating to inventory management. No mishappening had come to his attention since his last examination, at which time controls and checkpoints were considered to be reasonably adequate to protect the company's manufacturing and sales activities, as well as stakeholder interests.

However, because of the likelihood that there had developed a difference between currently implemented controls and their expected effectiveness, the auditor inspected various routines, such as inventory accumulation, its classification, segregation, costing, weighing, shipments, etc. The auditor saw this as one more check done because of good professional conscience.

Company procedures provided that a logistics employee would inspect shipments, observe the loading of trucks, ensure that inventory and billing records were updated, and perform some added chores. The auditor already knew that company procedures, which detailed what was to be done, were established during World War II years and were not updated to reflect the use of computers and, more recently, supply chain operations.

It was precisely the much heralded Web site of his company that led the auditor to question the continuing use of procedures that were old and, to the auditor's thinking, not as effective as in the past. The auditor felt that while these procedures might have been good for the decade of the 1940s, they simply did not reflect the major changes that took place during the ensuing 60 years and most particularly the Internet supply chain. Another issue that bothered the auditor was that, until recently, the company had failed to train its examiners how to use the computer as their mind's eye, to help in their findings, and how to control whether written procedures corresponded with the systems in place.

The auditor in question was approaching retirement and was the last member of the auditing department to learn how to use a computer; he became computer literate between the last inspection and the current one. Given this newly acquired background, which this auditor wanted to apply before retirement, he could perceive some significant difference between the formerly effective but totally manual method that still characterized big parts of inventory management and the online solution that was introduced in sections of the inventory chain, but still lacked procedural standards.

Using his newly found computer literacy in the best manner he could and his procedural experience from past audits, the auditor did a number of checks to establish if there was appropriate linkage between the new and old parts of inventory management. Once discrepancies came to his attention during the course of his inspection and observation of ongoing routines, he recognized the existing exposure and the risks his company took in inventory management.

The auditor saw the identified gaps in inventory control as being his responsibility, and he correctly judged that the best course was to analyze the possibilities involved in online updates of inventories where error tracking was procedurally absent. Having identified a couple of the weak links, he brought this matter to the attention of the director of auditing. The latter reported the case to the CEO.

The CEO called the CIO into his office and asked him about the gaps. The CIO said he was aware of discrepancies between old and new inventory control modules, but this required lots of programming and at the time there was not enough manpower. Nevertheless, he planned to do it, suggesting that instead of bothering with systems issues, the auditor should concentrate on possible fraud because of the gaps.

This was the mission given to the auditor: look after accounting fraud and forget the technology side. With this, the auditor's job was refocused. Nothing of a suspicious natured occurred on the first day. However, on the second day, the auditor observed an employee altering database information without original documents. When asked about the vouchers, the employee answered that he had them already classified.

The auditor did not like the employee's answer and therefore asked for, and received, authorization to look into the entire input operation concerning bills, shipping orders, and inventories. What he found was that the old directives on how to update the books were discarded because of direct computer input, but neither the organization in general nor IT in particular had bothered to put in place new systems and procedures.

This example illustrates how seemingly obsolete controls can become totally ineffective or put altogether on the back burner — without ever being replaced by new ones. It also illustrates how important it is for the auditor to inspect the application of controls and the way they are working, being alert to possible weak links or an outright breakdown of the internal control system.

Just as important is the message that the auditor was absolutely correct in bringing to senior management's attention the IT failure and organizational shortcomings. However, his findings were snowed under and put aside because the CEO was both computer illiterate and a weak executive; the CEO accepted at face value the CIO's argument that "he could not close the gaps now" because of personnel shortages, and his assurance that what had to be done would be done at some unidentified date in the future when programmers became available.

It is because of such conditions that internal auditing should be vigilant, both in an accounting and in a technological sense. Both are essential to the maintenance of effective management controls. This case study should also be seen within the perspective of ERP and CRM implementation.

It is not common today to find computer-illiterate auditors, but it is often the case that ERP- and CRM-illiterate auditors control the systems and procedures connected to either or both packages. This leads these auditors to being insensitive to failures that might be deadly because the company's operations have radically changed and now support an Internet supply chain, but the necessary revamping of systems and procedures has not taken place — and may still be some years in the future.

18.4   Case Study: The Aftermath of Inadequate Internal Controls

A newly hired internal auditor, just out of college, was reviewing the control over shipments. His mission was to evaluate the adequacy and effectiveness of existing procedures. Current company procedures required that all invoices, shippers, and gate passes be pre-numbered by the printer. This ID would be pivotal to their usage, storage, processing, and eventual retrieval.

For accounting purposes, numerical sequence had to be followed for all forms used: shippers had to be traced to billings, and billings had to be checked against what was recorded. Under existing procedures, gate passes were prepared in duplicate. The original was collected by the plant guard at the exit gate; the duplicate remained with the issuing department. There were also some exceptions. A new sequence accounting was made when a department head requested a new book of gate passes. When this happened, the agent was required to surrender the previous book containing the duplicate copies. The auditor felt that this exception procedure might create a loophole, but said nothing, waiting to find some evidence. He also saw another major problem: the *time lag*. What I just mentioned in terms of internal control took place several weeks or months subsequent to the issuance of a new book. Many things could take place in this slippage of time — from errors to fraud.

As the auditor noted, gate passes taken up by the guard at plant exit were not forwarded to the accounting department for checking against billings, nor for approval as non-billable items. The latter included a variety of goods, such as loaned equipment, employees' personal property, non-salvable material given to employees, etc.

The auditor perceived the possibility of unauthorized removal of company property by bypassing regular shipping and billing procedures. Therefore, he decided to test some of the gate passes collected by the exit guards against billings and other accounting documents. To do so, he selected the current month's gate passes accumulated in the plant protection office, took a sample, and performed a test. Here in a nutshell are the statistics:

- 90 percent of passes examined had customer billings and therefore complied to current procedures.
- 7 percent of passes related to non-billable items, covering removal of employees' personal property and loan of equipment.
- The remaining 3 percent of gate passes, however, could not be identified with any accounting record.

Therefore, the statistics could not be reconciled.

This company had been using expensive mainframes since the early 1960s. Software was typically developed in-house. Some of the programs had been rewritten a couple of times during the elapsed 40 years, but the majority of these routines were 20 and 30 years old or more. As the young auditor found out, nobody had bothered to change procedures, updating and streamlining them to fit the information processing environment as it evolved over time, with major patches attached to the old programs.

A year before the auditing in reference, the company had acquired an ERP suite. The information technologists were still working on it to introduce it to this factory. The young auditor learned that the board (composed of a majority of computer illiterates) had decided to retain not only the creaky mainframes but also the obsolete procedures, amending if necessary the bought software. This was decided at the suggestion of the CIO, who was an old-hand with the mainframes. The younger IT analysts and programmers objected to this decision, but they were told to keep their mouths shut.

The young auditor was also told that a couple of the younger analysts and programmers in the ERP workgroup had suggested that all factory operations should be brought into the new system. The factory manager, however, vetoed that and ordered them to concentrate on the introduction and use of ERP for production planning and inventory control activities. The CIO agreed with the factory manager.

By all evidence over the years of his tenure, the factory manager was unaware of the fraud going on at his factory's gate. Passes taken into the sample and taken by the young auditor were made out to "Bearer" instead of showing the name(s) of the person(s) using them. These passes authorized the removal of company property but did not indicate the nature thereof or the volume — or other information requiring the removal.

A further investigation into this matter involved 12 full months of vouchers, and their examination made it evident that something more than inadequate control was the cause. One of the thus-far trusted middle-level managers had convinced a shipping clerk to join in an arrangement to remove goods from the plant on a gate pass, while omitting preparation of the usual shipper from which billings originated.

These findings disclosed not only the inadequacy of internal controls, but also the fact that company property had been removed without authorization over a considerable period of time; yet nobody had taken corrective action. It was therefore necessary not only to strengthen the system of internal controls but also to alter the accounting procedures so that this loophole was closed.

Confronted with this evidence, the factory manager said that he was stunned because he trusted his people. He authorized the accounting change, but still objected to the extension of ERP functionality gate-to-gate. The company's vice-president of manufacturing supported the factory manager. Two years down the line, when the ERP implementation failed, the company said the fault was the vendor's; his wares did not respond to the user organization's specifications.

18.5   Case Study: Defective Inventory Management and Corrective Action

According to ongoing procedures, the annual inventory of the First Manufacturing Company, which has typically included both overages and shortages, was considered by management to be (in most cases) satisfactorily accounted for. But there were exceptions. For example, reconciliation between the physical inventory and book figures was not always smooth. Indeed, sometimes the two deviated by a considerable difference, but the board typically decided to write off the missing assets.

To provide documentation for the write-offs, the accounting records were checked and a new physical inventory was taken. While some minor corrections were made as a result of the second inventory, big shortages in physical inventory remained. The CEO then proposed to the board that these had to be written off because there was no way to recover the lost material.

Confronted with this situation, a new vice president of finance demanded an *ad hoc* audit — and a rigorous one for that matter. The internal auditor's first move was to review the mathematics of the physical inventory, including charges and relieves to the book inventory for the past 12 months. He examined the basis for costing the shipping material and went through the procedure of computing the monthly credit to book accounts.

This audit went deeper than all those that preceded it, and it revealed that the cost of shipping material for each type of goods had been determined many years ago, but it was inadequate under present conditions. This inadequacy remained even if different values were reconfirmed periodically to detect any changes that might happen. Book inventories were relieved and shipping expense was charged at years-old standard cost (see Chapter 13), on the basis of products shipped. The auditor's review of the accounting procedures did not disclose other major gaps that might justify the shortage. But the failure in reference did stimulate his thinking, a critical factor in the solution of investigative-type problems.

The auditor visited the receiving department to study its routines and observe the physical handling of incoming material, and then went to the packaging department, where various sized boxes were made, and reviewed specifications, bills of material, and the accounting for material transferred to packaging and shipping. Next, the auditor visited the shipping department for the purpose of observing packaging and shipping routines.

One thing that attracted the auditor's attention during the examination of the shipping department was the occasional putting aside of a defective or damaged box. These boxes were sent to the salvage department. Because of professional conscience, the auditor paid a visit to the salvage department. There, the auditor learned that several non-usable boxes were received each day and a high percentage of those non-usable boxes were disposed of as scrap.

No figures were available as to the volume of boxes scrapped, but the salvage foreman did a quick estimate of aggregate value at standard cost. Following through on this lead, the auditor found that the shipping department had not reported on boxes scrapped; and the salvage value realized had been credited to scrap sales in full, but no credit had been given to the book inventory accounts for material scrapped.

Correctly guessing that the real cause for the shortage was physical conditions rather than bookkeeping, the auditor adopted the strategy of a patient observer. He carefully reviewed the physical movement of all shipping material from time of receipt to the dispatching of the product, repeated his tours of observations, and finally came to the core of the matter: for years there has been in this company a well-orchestrated misuse of property.

When informed about these findings, the vice president of finance took action. Contrary to the weak character of the CEO in the case study in Chapter 18.4, the vice president of finance was not a person to accept a half-baked solution and live with it. He asked for an extraordinary executive committee meeting and insisted that the person in charge of the company's organization and information technology (O&IT) department be fired.

The new boss of O&IT was no old-school mainframer; he chose some of the department's best people and gave them the mission not only to solve this problem but to restructure the entire chain of inventory management. A classification study was done along the lines explained in Chapters 10 and 11. Mathematical models were developed to help in the management of inventories; and a new, rigorous procedural solution was developed to track all goods from input, to in-process status, and output — including scrap.

In inventory control terms, this led to a significant reduction in errors because the analytical approach that has been applied permitted much better item identification. The fairly impressive error reduction results obtained in two warehouses "A" and "B" against a third warehouse "C," which was kept under the old method for control reasons, are shown in Exhibit 18.1. The difference in error rates with the new method is striking. Savings in the first year exceeded by a large margin the cost of implementation.

Once the classification and identification problem was solved, the next step was the development and use of mathematical models to assist in effective inventory management. Item-by-item, inventory excesses and shortages were tracked as deviations. The decision was made to follow up at the 99-percent level of confidence — hence, $\alpha = 0.01$.

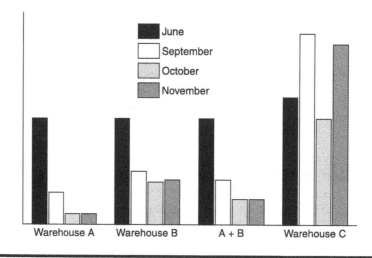

Exhibit 18.1   A Thorough Classification and Item Identification Help in Hunting Down the Error Sources and Improving the System's Accuracy

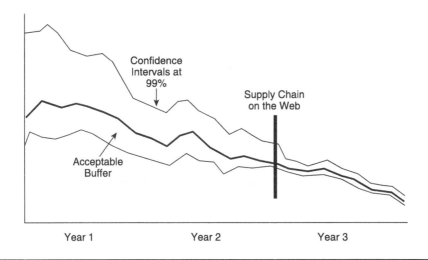

Exhibit 18.2   Trend Line Confidence Intervals in Inventory Management and the Temporarily Acceptable Buffer

The system was developed as a prototype in three months, underwent a three-month field test to determine its strengths and weaknesses, was improved during the following month, and took two more months to implement at the larger factories and warehouses that represented more than three quarters of company business.

The next major goal of this project was that of stabilizing the system and bringing outages and surpluses under control. This did not take place quickly because it required a significant amount of organizational work. With the board's approval, the implementers decided to assign a money tag to inventory over the "zero surplus/zero outage" line. It was agreed that:

- This buffer over the optimal was accepted only temporarily, until model risk and learning effects were overcome.
- The success of inventory management operation was to be judged by the steady reduction of surplus/outage over a period of three years.

Exhibit 18.2 shows the trend line of the buffer and confidence intervals. Above the buffer is unwanted excess inventory. Under the buffer is out-of-stock conditions. The two statistics were brought together to characterize the distribution of inventory control results, the effort made to swamp the differences, and the trend line. Over nearly two years, both overstocking and out-of-stock steadily decreased at the 99-percent level of confidence. The trend line of the buffer also headed south. But the real breakthrough happened when the company established a supply chain on the Web. This made it possible to show some very interesting results during the third year.

*   *   *

The careful reader should not have missed the fact that this case study includes no reference to ERP. This is deliberate. While during the last couple of years, ERP software has been used, senior management is convinced that 80 percent or more of the success factors behind what has been achieved are related to the thorough organizational work that changed the company's culture, its systems, and its procedures. The contribution of bought software was part of the other 20 percent.

18.6   Case Study: Economies Realized Through Focused Internal Auditing

The firm that is the focus of this case study, the Second Manufacturing Company, is a global firm that derived about half its income in its country of origin and the other half abroad. During an examination of accounts payable at a foreign subsidiary, the auditor observed that the same material was quoted at two different price levels. The difference was not trivial; if the lower price was "A," the higher price was "3A," and depended on the way this material was delivered.

The auditor also observed that the large majority of purchases were made by the company on a "3A" cost basis, which was puzzling. He could find no justification for this significant discrepancy in prices. Nothing was written in the record, nor had anybody at headquarters alerted him to it, although this was the first time he had done such an audit in the foreign subsidiary.

The auditor thought that this major cost difference should have been known at headquarters. Apparently, however, it was not. Otherwise, he would have been informed about the need to pay particular attention to such deviation. As a result of such uncertainty, the auditor decided that it would be wise to be better informed about this case before calling his boss in the home country.

While discussing this particular issue of a very significant price discrepancy with the purchasing manager of the foreign subsidiary, the auditor heard that it was not always possible to take advantage of the lower quoted price. The given reason was that the subsidiary lacked sufficient storage space to handle purchases of large lots at "A" cost; hence, it had to pay a premium.

Reviewing the purchases for the past two years, the auditor discovered that they averaged about 40 tons per month, or 500 tons on an annual basis. Applying the differential in price, he calculated that major savings would result if adequate storage facilities were indeed available. This led to a meeting with the general manager (GM) of the foreign subsidiary, who was asked why headquarters was not informed of this fact. The GM answered that this was a local problem, and he had already planned to solve it locally.

The GM said that he did not need the big boys from the parent company looking over his shoulder. Armed with this statement, the auditor called his boss at headquarters and asked for authorization to enlarge the scope of his study at the foreign subsidiary. He also explained that this triple cost might

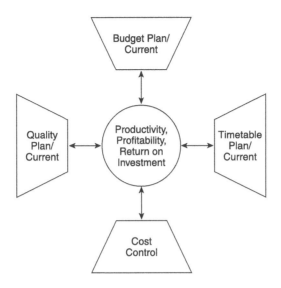

Exhibit 18.3   ERP Can Serve to Integrate into One System Controls that Were Once Used Dispersed and Stand-Alone

be the tip of an iceberg. Somehow, from the discussion held thus far, the auditor got the impression that this foreign subsidiary was not following the parent company's policies and directives on a number of other issues as well.

For example, the auditor pointed out that in his judgment the needed internal controls were dispersed and substandard. They were not integrated into a system similar to that at headquarters and at other foreign subsidiaries that he had audited. Specifically, after the implementation of ERP software, this company had the integrative schema shown in Exhibit 18.3 for plan versus current evaluation of budgets, outgoing quality, costs, and timetables.

At headquarters, the director of auditing discussed this issue with the chief financial officer and the CIO. It was decided to extend the mission of the auditor only after he got to the heart of the matter with the problem he had already identified. This would have killed two birds with one well-placed stone; it would have tested the conceptual and analytical ability of the auditor to unearth costs in an opaque environment and documented the sincerity, or lack of it, of the foreign subsidiary's GM — a local national.

The auditor proceeded as instructed. His study on availability of space and on cost data for added storage facilities sufficient to handle larger lots revealed that — given the significant price differential — new storage costs would be recovered in less than two years. The company owned enough land for warehouse expansion.

Armed with these findings, the auditor reported to headquarters that the foreign subsidiary had the necessary land adjacent to railroad siding on which to erect the required storage facilities. He also presented details of estimated building costs and of a rapid depreciation timetable capitalizing on the huge price differential currently paid by the purchasing manager.

Convinced of these findings, headquarters approved the erection of the recommended storage facilities, provided that the foreign subsidiary's GM was in agreement. The latter objected to this solution, pointing out that if the storage problem were solved, it would mean renegotiating the contract with the main supplier with a significant reduction in the price. This would have soured relations with the president of the supplier company, who happened to be the son of the president of the local banana republic.

This issue went to the board and because it was political, the board decided to have another test case prior to reaching a decision. The next example of discrepancies the auditor found was that of freight charges. His audit documented that there was room for quite significant savings by clearing up issues, consistently overlooked by the local management, in terms of shipping expenses.

At the base of these savings connected with freight charges was the fact that the local railroad company required a minimum weight established for a car. This had to be paid for, even in cases when the car as loaded did not reach the fixed minimum. Because of the physical character of the material being shipped, the probability was high that loaded cars might not meet this minimum weight although they were completely full.

The management of the foreign subsidiary never bothered to look into this matter. In the auditor's opinion, what made a better solution possible was the fact that by rearranging the contents to take full advantage of available space, the minimum requirement could be attained, thereby saving the freight penalty. In fact, as the auditor noticed, shipments from suppliers (and to customers) were often received (made) with less than the minimum carload weight. In contrast, other shipments were overweight; hence, more money had to be paid to the local railroad company.

When contacted by the auditor and the purchasing manager, these suppliers explained that because of the physical characteristics of their products, it was difficult to load cars to minimum weight. Further investigation, however, showed beyond doubt that more efficient loading could be arranged, with contents stacked in the car so as to permit additional loading.

Once again, the GM intervened, ordering his purchasing manager not to involve himself in this case concerning freight costs. However, the GM could not order the auditor to stay out of it. The auditor informed headquarters about a number of cases that had come to his immediate attention, demonstrating the feasibility of rearrangement of loading to obtain minimum carload weight.

For example, the auditor learned that a saving in freight costs was frequently possible in other local firms he had visited by improving the scheduling and purchasing routines, as well as by consolidating shipments. In fact, a couple of companies had recommended to evaluate alternative delivery routines, such as air express, parcel post, trucks, railway express, and freight cars, to optimize costs.

It so happened that this auditor had learned cost optimization at college. His professor had taught him that a good way to analyze transportation costs for optimization reasons was to begin the study by paying attention to the higher cost shipments because that is where, in all likelihood, the savings will lie. This required:

- Reviewing a representative number of freight price lists
- Receiving comprehensive explanations about cost differences
- Getting convinced of the real reason for rush shipments

As the auditor had learned in college, a frequent "real reason" was the lack of adequate control in purchasing, production, and distribution. His professor had further pressed the point that supply chain patterns must also be examined. Certain suppliers are making daily shipments in small lots, with a resulting high freight cost because of conflicts of interest.

The auditor did not fail to report his findings to headquarters, and along with them his recommendations. He also pointed out that to properly evaluate alternative lower cost possibilities, it would be advisable to examine different tariffs, analyze the cost incurred, determine the total tonnage transported, and, using quoted tariff rates, simulate the cost structure under different alternative hypotheses. He had also learned that in this country there was also plenty of room for negotiating tariffs, but that the subsidiary was not taking advantage of this possibility.

The CEO understood the point that the information in reference was helpful in building up optimized costs schedules, but he still asked the auditor to conduct a third study. This focused on salaries, particularly among the senior employees.

The CEO's reason for delaying his decision was to test once more the sincerity of the GM — in connection with nepotism in the banana republic. Once he was convinced that incompetence or worse was the real cause of the high costs and that the GM could not be relied upon, he flew to the foreign subsidiary himself and fired the GM on the spot.

Notes

1. D.N. Chorafas, *Reliable Financial Reporting and Internal Control: A Global Implementation Guide,* John Wiley, New York, 2000.

Chapter 19

Qualification of Auditors and Implementation of Auditing Standards

The qualification of auditors, establishment of auditing standards, and implementation of these standards are three highly related issues that impact on one another. Auditing standards should not be confused with auditing procedures. The latter relate to acts to be performed, while the former deal with objectives to be attained in the employment of auditing procedures being undertaken and measures of the quality of the performance of auditing, its investigations, and its deliverables.

One of the issues to which auditing standards pay increasing attention is the auditor's professional qualifications, including training, experience, and judgment. Judgment must be steadily exercised in the conduct of an examination, in questioning the obvious, and in reporting the findings in a comprehensive way.

To be qualified as an auditor, a person must not only know the rules, appreciate the standards, and master the auditing tools, but must also have and maintain a high degree of independence, as so often underlined in this book. The auditor should possess personal and technical attributes such as those described in the case studies in Chapter 18, including a thorough knowledge of the operation of modern accounting and technical practices and a penetrating mind coupled with knowledge of the business organization for which he or she works.

On several occasions, the point has been made that the detection of fraud is only one of the auditor's responsibilities. In the modern enterprise, other responsibilities include advice as to the form of business organization, incorporation procedure, engineering and manufacturing issues, Internet supply chain practices, and purchasing and sales procedures. The auditor's work will be half-baked without this knowledge of the company, its people, and its products, as well as what makes the company's people tick.

Training in business law is another must. This not only means the laws of the land where the auditor works, but also more subtle laws of trade concerning purchases, sales, contracts, negotiable instruments, bankruptcy, and insolvency. There is a very subtle difference between legal practices and those paralegal.

In addition, many of these laws are interwoven with accounting practice. The same is true of taxation, and training in taxation is another must. To save money for his client, the auditor must have a thorough knowledge of all taxes affecting the company and their deals. Taxation is also an ever-increasing source of work for the certified public accountant (CPA).

Just as important is knowledge of cost accounting (see Chapter 13). Sometimes, product pricing leads to disastrous operating results. Mastery of budget preparation and control is also necessary. The audited company budgets and their observance or overrun provide valuable information from a management control viewpoint.

The careful reader will appreciate that too many things are expected from the auditor, and the same person cannot be an expert in all of them. Therefore, according to prevailing opinion among professionals, the days of the audit generalist are over. As we have seen in chapter after chapter in Section III, it is impossible to adequately audit today's technology-driven companies without specialists. Globalization and the Internet add to the requirements of an investigation that must be increasingly analytical.

19.1   Challenges Faced by Auditors, Needed Know-How, and Possible Loss of Independence

One can start with CPAs as an example of challenges faced by the auditing profession. If historical evidence is any guide, then it could be said that, in the United States, auditors have faced the likelihood of conflicts of interest ever since 1933 when Congress decided that public companies, not the government, would pay for audits.

In 1997, to improve a system that was wanting in checks and balances, the Securities and Exchange Commission (SEC) established the Independence Standards Board (ISB) with the mission to shape the auditing profession's rules. The SEC originally wanted an ISB dominated by investors and academics, but when the board was launched, accountants held most of the seats.

In year 2000, the SEC brought into perspective the need to further improve public oversight of accountants and auditors with the further-reaching goal of sending the audit profession back to its roots as vigorous guardians of investor interests. There is logic in this argument because when the public loses confidence in the markets, or when the reliability of the findings and the numbers is questioned, the whole system that makes up a free economy is jeopardized.

Nobody would probably dispute this issue if it were not for the fact that to keep their professional skills in top shape, auditing firms feel they should be deeply engaged in consulting. The regulators, however, think that consulting compromises an auditor's independence. Hence, more or less, the SEC has been proposing a ban that the auditing firms say could cripple their business in consulting and, therefore, their ability to attract top-notch people.

The CPA companies suggest that the less qualified their intake at the bottom of their organizational pyramid, the fewer master auditors they will have at the top. Therefore, they will not be able to face their clients' increasingly polyglot audit requirements. The conflict boils down to a challenge that has the power to shape auditing's future.

Among themselves, the case studies in Chapter 18 have underlined the polyglot nature of contributions expected from the auditor, which help to define the quality of his or her work as well as the close link of the work to internal control practices.[1] Through practical examples, this chapter will document that another prerequisite in terms of skills is a thorough knowledge of finance.

- The auditor is constantly dealing with accounting books, and therefore with money and the use of money
- Because of this, to be most efficient, the auditor must become well versed in all phases of finance and understand derivative financial instruments.

Technology is also a big challenge. The top CPA companies advance the argument that consulting on information systems and Internet commerce puts them on the cutting edge of modern business. From that leadership position, they can start to measure items that are the cornerstone of management control, such as customer-service quality and the internal control system.

As seen through practical examples in Chapter 18, these items are not on balance sheets, although they are considered to be crucial to a company's survival. Auditors also need to develop a method of appraising continuous financial statements that provide real-time information instead of the classical delayed historical snapshots characteristic of current filings.

Nobody argues against the idea that the auditor must be computer literate. The question is if this entails a loss of his independence because of consulting assignments, and if the ability to read virtual financial statements warrants it. Either way, the auditor must have a complete mastery of how to use high technology, from datamining to modeling in connection with auditing procedures. In practice, the auditor must be fully conversant with new technological developments. Through training and experience, he must develop the faculty of analyzing every situation that develops in a business. Otherwise, the most important phase of auditing — its analytical phase — is lost.

Equally important is the constructive ability of putting dispersed items together into a comprehensive picture. This is even more important when the auditor acts as an examiner both of accounting books and procedures and of more general managerial issues. These duties were explained in Chapter 18. They should be performed in a way to ensure that the auditor constructs proposals so that they aid the client in taking corrective action.

The characteristics briefly described in the foregoing paragraphs infer that while there are many people who practice as auditors, some do not meet the academic and professional requirements imposed by modern business. Therefore, a heavy duty rests on supervisory bodies passing upon applications for CPA registration to screen out those without valid professional justification to that claim.

The question is often raised of how the young person just entering into an auditing career as junior assistant can measure up to the requirements of background and experience for professional competence. The answer is not only formal training, but also proper supervision and review of his or her deliverables. A key role in on-the-job training is played by the nature and extent of supervision and review of accomplished work by experienced supervisors.

- Senior auditors charged with the responsibility of selecting qualified people must exercise sharp judgment in their review of the work done by junior auditors.
- Experience being definitely a matter of greater exposure, supervisory review must accept variance in auditing practice as long as the deliverables meet reporting standards.

The opinion expressed by the professional auditor upon completion of his work, and the report being submitted, is a mirror of his or her professional skills and integrity. The crystallization of this opinion is influenced by both generic and specific skills. For example, several considerations should be borne in mind in connection with ERP auditing so that there is no misunderstanding of analytics in addressing important functions.

Seen from this perspective, the examination made by the auditor is not necessarily to be regarded as a process of routine verification; it is not uncommon for the auditor to carry out sophisticated controls, each being an important phase of the examination of accounts. The notion of confidence intervals, discussed in Chapter 18, is increasingly integrated into reports of a financial nature.

In showing exceptional skills, the auditor aims to ensure him- or herself and his or her company of the wisdom of professional reliance on analytics, and therefore upon the system of factual and documented records and representations to senior management. As old hands in the auditing profession appreciate, this and ethical values are what professional conduct is all about.

19.2 The Difference Between Internal Auditors and Certified Public Accountants

Chapter 19.1 addressed the qualifications of both internal and external auditors and the characteristics of their work. Internal auditing and external audit complement each another. The role of internal audit is very important, but it is no substitute for audit by a certified public accountant — and vice versa.

Internal auditors and CPAs render a distinctive type of service that cannot fully be performed by the other party. In terms of skill and type of work, the two fields of auditing have much in common, but their objectives are different, even if to a large degree they are complementary. Over and above the mission of the classical auditing of books and certification of accounts, internal auditors would examine the dependability of enterprise resource planning as well as customer relationship management and other applications. This examination typically focuses on records, procedures, databases, and other systems components — all the way to internal control. Recall from Chapter 18 the key role played by internal control in the proper functioning of systems and procedures.

The most important mission of external auditors is the audit of accounting books and financial statements, although during the last four years, regulators increasingly demand that they certify the proper functioning of internal controls.

When they work diligently, both internal and external auditors can detect errors, fraud, and mismanagement. The internal auditor can do so just as effectively in an arranged visit as in a surprise visit, provided he does his homework prior to the hands-on inspection through database mining (see Chaper 19.3). For the external auditor, this will typically be an arranged visit.

The concept behind the statement made in the preceding paragraph is that technology enables the internal auditor to perform the *discovery* part of the work online through datamining, prior to the interviews he will conduct during the visit. Working interactively through computers is not only an efficiency tool, but has become necessary as the purpose of audits has expanded. The ABCs of this broader perspective of an auditor's responsibilities are outlined in Exhibit 19.1.

A strong internal auditing department with a proper level of competence and independence is a valuable agency, not only to management but also to the CPAs and the regulators themselves. The scope of the CPA's examination and the amount of detail work that he or she may consider necessary will depend on the evaluation of results obtained by internal audit functions. In principle, *if* the CPA has complete confidence in the company's internal audit activity and is satisfied that internal audit has fully discharged its responsibilities, *then* he or she can curtail the extent of his or her detailed work to a substantial degree. This is possible because the external auditor will be using the results obtained through the internal audits in the report. The CPA's work is obviously helped by the knowledge and experience of internal auditing, provided that this department has a significant degree of independence.

As seen, the independence of internal auditors is better assured when the department reports directly to the Audit Committee of the board. At the same time, for reasons of the external auditors' independence of opinion, the Audit Committee should review and disclose all relationships with their auditing firm, proving to shareholders and regulators that consulting work does not compromise audit independence. The Audit Committee must make sure that both internal and external auditors observe generally accepted auditing standards.

Exhibit 19.1   The ABCs of Modern-Day Purposes of Auditing

A. Determine and report on financial condition and earnings of a business for:
   1. shareholders
   2. the board
   3. senior management
   4. bankers
   5. prospective investors
   6. fiduciaries
   7. supervisors
   8. tax authorities

B. To detect fraud and errors of:
   1. principle
   2. omission
   3. commission
      whether this is intentional or unintentional, by insiders or outsiders, due to humans or machines, defective internal controls, substandard information technology, or other reasons.

C. Study and analyze the technical and procedural solution followed by IT, unearth sources and causes of malfunctioning:
   1. estimate the damage being created
   2. study the responsibilities for it, and
   3. suggest needed corrective measures
      This should be done for all applications, new and old, in-house developments and bought software, central and distributed processing — in short, everything concerning computers, communications, and databases.

This still allows the auditors to carefully exercise informed judgment as qualified professionals, although safeguards are in place because of the fallibility of human judgment.

As seen in Chapter 19.1, because the auditor is exposed to the risk of poor judgment and might be sued for that, he or she, whether internal or external, should be knowledgeable about the law. Part and parcel of legal competence is the ability to ensure independence of mental attitude and approach. Both ethics and professional bodies guard against the presumption of loss of independence.

Let me stress the sense of the word *presumption* because intrinsic independence is synonymous with mental integrity, and its possession is a matter of personal virtue. Over many years, lawyers have developed the expression of *presumptions of law,* or inferences, that are sometimes conclusive — but more frequently they are not.

Insofar as such presumptions have been enacted as stipulations in the profession's code of ethics, they have the force of professional law for the auditor. Without excluding the bearing of other rules, the following five are at the top of the list in connection with the internal and external auditor's independence:

1. Financial interest in a client's business
2. False or misleading statements, intentional or not
3. Contingent fees, including consulting
4. Commissions and brokerage fees
5. Part-time occupations incompatible with control activities

In the last analysis, independence means honest disinterest on the part of the auditor in the discovery process, as well as formulation and expression of opinion. An auditor's report must be a reflection of unbiased judgment and objective consideration of facts as determinants of that opinion. It is written to inform the persons and entities receiving it; it is not written to please the reader.

Sometimes, loss of the auditor's independence may be due to conditions usually considered to be of an unusual nature. In cases of collusion, conditions of an unusual nature may subsequently indicate error in judgment or manipulations leading to undependable findings — reflecting biased opinion or unreliable data. The auditor may not be a valuer or appraiser of goods or properties, or an expert in materials or commodities. It is, however, part of the auditor's work to learn from expressing an opinion, because professionally he or she is concerned with a thorough evaluation and disclosure of fair value.

Specifically in connection with ERP applications and the content of reports, the auditor must be versatile with planning premises, control procedures, supply chain arrangements, and market values. The auditor should be able to do, on his or her own, marking-to-market — or, alternatively, evaluate such estimates whether or not they are reasonable and documented under current conditions.

The audit of CRM will consider, among other issues, application personalization, effectiveness of client information, sales analyses, product promotions, follow-ups on quotas, and improvements in client handholding. The auditor cannot possibly express a learned opinion on these issues if he or she does not know their deeper meaning and the exact reasons why they are important to the company. The same reference is valid for evaluating competitor performance and auditing CRM information channels.

When undertaking anything in the nature of passing judgment on valuations of others, whether this includes prices of products, inventory valuations, or effects of volatility, the auditor who is not versatile in marking-to-market is stepping outside the rules guiding professional accountants as such. He or she must therefore be competent in finance to take such steps.

Similarly, auditing ERP and CRM records implies not the attitude of a prosecutor, but a judicial impartiality that recognizes an obligation on the auditor's part for fair presentation of facts. He or she owes this impartiality not only to management and shareholders, but also to the creditors of the business, the authorities, and those who may otherwise have a right to rely on the auditor's report.

19.3   Resident Internal Auditors, Traveling Internal Auditors, and Services Provided by Datamining

When considering duties and responsibilities of internal auditors, it is helpful to recognize two alternatives: (1) the resident internal auditor and (2) the traveling internal auditor. This distinction is not trivial because their authority, duties, and responsibilities vary from one company to the next. Likewise, their work programs, procedures, and methods of reporting are likely to be somewhat different.

Several companies with distributed operations have been known to employ traveling internal auditors to periodically contact and control the activities by decentralized business units (see also the case study in Chapter 18.6). Such contacts are usually made on a semester or yearly basis, which in my opinion is not at all satisfactory. Usually, the frequency of visits will vary according to the needs of a particular firm and of its outlets.

Other companies elect to place a resident internal auditor at each location, who would ordinarily report to the director of auditing located at the main office of the company. Even when subsidiary operations are highly decentralized and operate under a local management, the resident auditor would depend on promotion and salary from his boss at headquarters — and not from the local manager.

Whether resident or traveling, the internal auditor ordinarily has no administrative or directing authority. However, some companies confer upon their traveling auditors varying degrees of authority to initiate corrective action with respect to clerical errors, documented fraud, and certain other exceptions. In some cases, the authority granted is more extensive and includes managerial prerogatives.

Should there really be today a differentiation between resident and traveling auditors, when database mining offers the possibility to do very valuable investigations online, no matter where the business unit undergoing audit is located? This is by no means an academic query. Here in a nutshell is what can be done through datamining in auditing terms.

First, consider the challenge of datamining and what such a procedure involves. Database mining is by no means just a matter of *accessing* information elements. The tough part lies in data search, selection, and consolidation because many databases are characterized by a mix of legacy and competitive solutions, with the result that there is heterogeneity, unreliability, and a relative inaccuracy.

All three are relevant to a large chunk of stored information elements, although the situation is better in accounting than in other domains because of legal consequences.

Another challenge associated with datamining is evaluation procedures for market parameters, pricing formulas, and other vital factors.

This is bad news for auditing ERP, CRM, and other applications files and reports. The good news is that the online auditor today has at his disposal a golden horde of tools for database mining. Statistical analysis tools are not just histograms and pie charts; datamining increasingly uses pattern recognition, identification of outlayers, data interpolation and extrapolation, and data reduction techniques.

Toolkits readily available include random number generators, correlation and regression analysis, confidence intervals, chi-square test, *t*-test, experimental design, and data filtering (parametric, polynomial, relational, Boolean).

This impressive array of tools is an important reference because, as seen on several occasions, the auditor's work increasingly goes beyond classical work relating to accounting books, balance sheets, and income statements. The way to bet is that tomorrow's auditors will increasingly be using:

■ Monte Carlo simulation
■ Fractals and chaos theory
■ Strange attractors
■ Fuzzy engineering
■ Genetic algorithms[2]

The more these tools become sophisticated and the databases become richer, the more the auditor working online to examine events and patterns in databases (like any other professional) would have the means to press his or her viewpoint, asking: What is available to me? How dependable is it? How can I access it in a seamless manner? How can I get meaning from it?

For years, company databases have been recognized as a corporate resource. Now they are beginning to be exploited in that way. However, it should be appreciated that for managerial and for professional purposes, the able exploitation of database contents calls for a first-class online mechanism and easy-to-use human interfaces. Auditors who are able to put the database under stress and oblige it to confess its secrets do so through *inverse functions,* which when properly used allow large question and answer tables to be built, and *inductive inference,* which calls for fast patterns with algorithms able to compact tables into decision rules.

The able exploitation of databases can present significant advantages both in analysis and in management communication. As president of Chase Manhattan, Dr. David Rockefeller was in direct contact with an estimated 15,000 senior people worldwide. Many called during the day for a follow-up on discussions. In this, Rockefeller was assisted through direct access to his database. It is a matter of business efficiency to be able to press a button and bring up all information on the calling party. Online access to the senior executive's database guarantees a personal approach to business transactions.

A similar statement is valid for the auditor but, as already seen, the latter also has more analytical interest that requires digging deeper into the database. Therefore, the auditor must be assisted by both a methodology and a machine-executable formal language accepting concept expressions. In the early 1990s, this procedure was called an *idea database.*[3]

The exploitation of an idea database requires pattern matching, an inheritance mechanism, list processing, and recursive observations. These permit interactive, in-depth database mining, extracting from storage significant information; focusing on accounts, financial reports, ERP outputs, customers, markets, and products; and helping in fine-tuning the auditor's findings. The difference between old auditing chores and those made feasible through high technology is like night and day.

19.4   Consistency, Materiality, Conservatism, and Separation of Duties

Online database mining significantly helps the auditing mission, but there is also a great deal of legwork to be done by the auditors. In addition to the examination of the adequacy of internal control and of the methodology of the accounting system, auditors must test, in a meaningful way, how well internal controls and record-keeping systems are working.

For example, it is part of the auditor's mission to verify the existence of assets inventoried and recorded by ERP, such as physical inventory; confirm the accuracy of accounts receivable; control errors and fraud in accounts payable; check bank balances, etc.; and also to make sure that important or non-routine transactions are recorded in conformity with generally accepted accounting principles — and therefore comply with rules and regulations.

The auditor should be aware of the fact there is a natural human tendency to think only about part of the consequences of a decision to overlook some less-common but equally important elements that are sometimes embedded in documents. For example, although a growing cash balance superficially looks good, this is only half the story. It makes a considerable difference whether credits offsetting debits reflect income from profitable operations or from emergency bank loans.

No audit is worth its salt if it does not pay due attention to the datastream behind stored information elements. In any audit of accounting books and ERP/CRM records, the end result is important — but not only the end result. Transactions must also be mined and scrutinized. Underpinning the reference to a well-rounded examination is the concept of *balancing*. Three balancing techniques are outstanding and each is served through database mining:

1. Fundamental debit-credit structure, the pillar of double-entry accounting
2. Parent-subsidiary relationship, in which the total of subsidiary terms must always equal a control total
3. Sum-up technique, in which the sum of cash and paid bills must always equal a predetermined total

By providing a check on arithmetic accuracy, these approaches lessen the risk of loss through dishonesty or pure error, as well as the chance that some part of a transaction will be overlooked. The sheer mass of work to be done sees to it that accounting sometimes has problems of omission; that is why the auditor should be doubly careful.

The principles to which the previous paragraphs make reference are valid throughout the duties the auditor performs. It matters little if the information elements being studied come from enterprise resource planning and customer resource management applications or classical accounting routines. A sound auditing methodology will always reflect four distinct but interrelated concepts: (1) consistency, (2) materiality, (3) conservatism, and (4) separation of duties.

Consider first an example on *consistency*. When a company takes a cash discount in paying bills to its vendors, this discount can be treated as revenue or as a reduction in purchase price, while cash discounts not taken can be treated as an expense. The consistency convention requires that once management has decided on one of these methods, it will treat all subsequent events of the same character in the same fashion. Tax authorities are very touchy about consistency of accounts.

The company's own management should also want consistency. If a company makes frequent changes in the way it handles a given class of events in its accounting records, comparison of its quantitative figures for one period with those of another period will be difficult, if not outright impossible. Or, alternatively, it will require reconstruction of accounts on one homogeneous basis.

- Consistency implies that changes in the method of keeping accounts are made neither frequently nor lightly. This has been always true of financial matters; today, it is just as valid for enterprise resource planning and customer relationship management information.

Information elements pertaining to ERP, CRM, and any other application should be absolutely homogeneous and consistent throughout the organization, regardless of whether one is using programming products from different suppliers, or, for example, the ERP implementation is made in different factories and in different countries.

- The lack of consistency in ERP information simply means the impossibility of mining the databases online, interactively, or substantially greater information handling expenses.
- The wealth of datamining tools and methods outlined in Chapter 19.3 is significantly reduced in importance if several heterogeneous environments prevail; yet companies are not careful about this issue.

An auditor should include in his or her opinion the statement that database access was seamless and the figures were prepared in conformity with generally accepted accounting principles; that these principles were applied on a consistent basis; and that heterogeneity in data resources was kept to a minimum. If there were changes in practice, these must be spelled out in the auditor's opinion.

Materiality has both a practical and a legal meaning. There is a doctrine *de minimis non curat lex*, which means that the court will not consider trivial matters. Similarly, accountants, ERP/CRM implementers, and auditors should not attempt to record a great many events that are so insignificant that the expense of recording them is not justified by the usefulness of results.

- What is recorded must have material importance.
- This material importance should be judged in the context of every application.

Expert auditors nevertheless appreciate that while theoretically this rule is perfect, there may be practical problems. There is no general agreement as to the exact line separating material events from immaterial events. The decision depends on judgment and common sense, which leaves much to be desired in terms of accuracy of records. It is therefore important that a company defines what is material and what is not.

Both for general accounting and for ERP/CRM information, the principle of *conservatism* dictates that when one has a reasonable choice, he or she should show the lower of two asset values for a given item; or, record an event in such a way that the owner's equity is lower than it would be otherwise. In practical implementation terms, this principle says anticipate no profit, and provide for all possible losses.

ERP records should be conservative. For example, inventories held for sale, supplies, etc. are normally reported not at their cost, which is what one would expect in accordance with the cost concept, but rather at the lower of their cost *or* their current replacement value. Marking-to-market is an alternative if:

- There is a market for the goods in question, which is not always the case.
- The marking-to-market principle is consistently implemented for all inventoried goods.

The law of the land should essentially be observed, but in many cases the law itself is in full evolution, and in other cases it is unclear. Regulatory authorities do their best to improve the clarity of their rules. For derivative financial instruments, Financial Accounting Standards Statement 131 requires that *if* management's intent is to hold them to maturity, *then* they must be marked-to-market. Hence, replacement value becomes the overriding concern.

The concept of *separation of duties* is also extremely important to any and every company — and to its auditors. No one person should be responsible for recording all aspects of a transaction, nor should the custodian of assets (whether storekeeper or cashier) be permitted to do the accounting for assets. The principle is that one person's work is a check on another person's doings. This does not eliminate the possibility that two people will steal through collusion, but the likelihood of dishonesty is reduced.

In accounting, double-checking is assisted by the *voucher system*. Every incoming bill is inserted into a voucher that contains spaces permitting authorized people to signify their approval of the appropriateness of charges — and therefore of the accounting entries being made. There should always be in place a system of checks and balances but with direct entry to computers, the company's protective armory presents some gaps.

In conclusion, whether it be accounting information or ERP/CRM records, the test of a corporate system lies in the results being produced and in their timeliness, accuracy, and dependability. These results must be judged from the standpoint of the company and its management as a whole, and not just from any one department or group of interested parties.

Because the uses to which a corporate information system is put and the controls to which it is subject change from time to time, all parts of the data intake, storage, production, and delivery machinery must be adapted, in a dependable manner, to meet such changes as they occur. Short of this, mining financial information, inventory control data, production planning documents, client accounts, billing, sales statistics, and other ERP/CRM records — or for that matter auditing them — would be a hazardous affair.

19.5   The Types and Nature of Reports Submitted by Internal Auditors

Prior to concluding this chapter, some thought should be given to the ways and means used by an auditor to make his or her findings known. The type of report rendered by internal auditors varies according to the level of control being practiced, goals of management, purpose served, and level of reporting. The more common types of reports include oral, by questionnaire, letter, memorandum, and formal.

With the exception of a highlights presentation to be followed by letter or memorandum, *oral* reports do not constitute a satisfactory method of reporting the outcome of an audit because they do not provide a record of findings and opinions of the auditor. Oral reports may however serve as a preliminary to a formal report to be issued on a survey or investigation. Their principal use is to:

- Make known matters of an urgent nature that require immediate consideration
- Supplement some other form of report through person-to-person presentation

The *questionnaire* type of auditing report consists of a series of pertinent questions, usually arranged by audit feature. This makes sense when such questions are simple and can be answered by *yes* or *no* — or by the insertion of check marks to indicate the audit action — plus some brief comments. Questionnaires are useful in ERP and CRM reporting as they serve a dual purpose; they are a program of audit coverage and a type of summary report that records findings.

Sometimes, questionnaires can be quite detailed to ensure coverage of all pertinent matters. Their principal advantage lies in uniformity of coverage while permitting the use of less-skilled examiners with the assurance that at least the recorded list of objectives will be met. The downside of questionnaires is that they lead to a stereotyped form of auditing, stifle initiative and constructive thinking, and tend to turn auditing into a routine job.

I personally advise against written questionnaires and checkmarks. It is better to use the *letter report,* generally considered to be a higher level than the *memorandum.* This is not necessarily the correct assumption because the letter report is rather informal and generally rendered in multiple copies to various interested parties. Usually, it is brief and therefore does not cover some important issues, and it might even leave gaps because of items that are not recorded. However, it is better than checkmarks on a questionnaire.

If a letter report is used, then the original copy is given to the auditor's reporting authority and other copies to authorized persons interested in the findings. Because of aforementioned reasons, use of a letter report should be confined largely to the field of feature auditing, in which short and frequent reports are submitted. Letter reports are also employed:

- To supplement the formal written report, in which case they play a constructive role
- As an interim report, covering matters requiring prompt consideration by management

A *memorandum* is more structured than a letter report. The memorandum is generally used in those instances where an internal auditor works in close association with his or her immediate superior or executes a project requested by a higher-up authority. In such cases, the auditor's superior would clear those matters that pertain to his or her area of responsibility and pass on to other management levels whatever information is necessary.

A memorandum form of report serves well the purposes of ERP and CRM investigations. This approach is common when the auditor is working primarily for the benefit of a departmental level superior. It is usually rendered on inter-organization stationary or on specially designed forms.

In general, the *formal report* is used by the professional internal auditor, developed from a carefully edited draft copy and bound in an appropriate cover. Its physical characteristics are similar to the reports issued by the public accountant, but the contents are more detailed and may be less structured than those presented by external auditors. The formal report is preferred over the more informal letter or memorandum whenever it serves company executives other than the auditor's immediate superior. Properly prepared, the formal report adds a degree of confidence in, and respect for, the auditor's ability and documentation of his or her findings.

In terms of established procedures, it is desirable — and in most companies it is the usual practice — to send all reports through the medium of correspondence so that a permanent record of the action taken can be provided. In such cases, the auditor should receive copies of all correspondence exchanged between the report follow-up executive and other officials of the company. The auditor is then in a position to know:

- What type of action has been taken
- How matters of exception have been handled
- What items may need further consideration at the time of the next audit

Regardless of the form of reporting the audit's findings, sufficient and competent evidential matter must be included. This is obtained through inspection, observation, inquiries, and confirmations, and it affords a reasonable basis of opinion regarding the financial statements or ERP/CRM information elements under examination.

The auditor's report will definitely state whether financial statements, ERP and CRM records, and any other audited information have been presented in accordance with generally accepted principles. Such principles are established through years of practice in business and industry and should be consistently observed in an audit. For example, there should be concrete evidence — not hearsay; and informative disclosures in statements and records should be regarded as reasonably adequate. If this is not the case, it should be explicitly stated as such in the audit report.

Finally, as I never tire of repeating, auditors should not diminish the quality of their work because of friendship, management pressures, political plots, various forms of secrecy or lack of transparency, or their own kind hearts. Instead, auditors should heed the advice of an Athenian senator in Shakespeare's *Timon of Athens*: "Nothing emboldens sin so much as mercy."

Notes

1. D.N. Chorafas, *Implementing and Auditing the Internal Control System,* Macmillan, London, 2001.
2. D.N. Chorafas, *Rocket Scientists in Banking,* Lafferty Publications, London and Dublin, 1995.
3. D.N. Chorafas and H. Steinmann, *Supercomputers,* McGraw-Hill, New York, 1990.

INDEX

Index